The Unholy Land
The Struggle for Virtue and Unity in America

By
Daniel B. Rundquist

Published by
NEW PLYMOUTH PRESS, LLC
HICKORY, NORTH CAROLINA

Copyright © 2025 by Daniel B. Rundquist
All Rights Reserved, including the right of reproduction in whole or part in any form.

No original part of this publication may be copied, reprinted, reproduced, electronically or digitally stored, disseminated, or transmitted in any other form, format, or by any other means including but not limited to photocopying, scanning, recording, writing or printing without the express written permission of the publisher.

Where the NIV Bible is quoted, THE HOLY BIBLE, NEW INTERNATIONAL VERSION®, NIV® Copyright © 1973, 1978, 1984, 2011 by Biblica, Inc.™ Used by permission. All rights reserved worldwide.

Front Cover: Design by the author, photo by Benjamin Miller
Back Cover: Photography by Alyssa Minton

January 2, 2025

Revised 8/1/2025

Ebook Edition
ISBN-13: 978-0-9862967-7-2
Paperback
ISBN-13: 978-0-9862967-9-6
Hardcover
ISBN: 979-8-9854038-6-2

REL108000   RELIGION / Christian Church / General

This text contains personal perspectives, ideas, discussion, theories, conjecture, conclusions, and opinions regarding history, historical figures, religion, and American culture and politics. The people, places, descriptions, events and all other material contained herein are not intended to accurately reflect the actual lives, events, statements, performance, thoughts, intentions, or actions of any entity, group, organization, institution, agency, company, church, club, person or persons, living, dead, or rumored to be dead. Some names may have been changed to protect the identity of the innocent.

Commentary on *The Unholy Land* from pre-publication readers:

"A bit of a harrowing spiritual journey for the author...a timely and poignant commentary on the state of our faith in America."

"A tremendous undertaking executed with clarity, courage, and fortitude. The ending was just as surprising to me as the preface."

"The work that was poured into this book is astonishing. I could hardly lay it down."

"Well researched, captivating in details, and presented in a conversational style that welcomes the reader."

"It's an important work that ought to give us pause as Christians for self-reflection. What exactly are we doing and why are we doing it?"

"Having read Mr. Rundquist's book, I found that going back to my own church on Sunday left me with more questions about my faith than answers."

Preceding title in this series

Tears for Byzantium
The Entropic Course of American Exceptionalism
By Daniel B. Rundquist

New Plymouth Press, LLC
December 1, 2017

ISBN-13 978-0-9862967-5-8

For Sharon

In Memory of the Reverend Don Sieh

What did you start in the waters at Nokomis, sir?
I do now understand that it will end far from
there, but in a place perhaps more familiar to us both.

The Unholy Land

Table of Contents

Foreword	9
Preface	11
Acknowledgments	25
1. For Want of Virtue and Unity	28
2. Disorderly Conduct	41
3. Virtue and Unity	74
4. One Nation Under Gods	92
5. The Christianity of the Byzantine East	101
6. The Christianity of the Roman West	125
7. The Modern Christian Church in America	158
8. Customizing Christianity	204
9. The New Religion of the Left	234
10. Whose Christianity is it Anyway?	254
11. Separating Church and State	280
12. Christianity in Action	296
13. Restoration of American Virtue and Unity	305
14. Epilogue	363
Final Notes	370
Chronology	371
Bibliography and Additional Materials	407
Endnotes & citations	416

Foreword

Something is wrong in the United States of America. We can all feel it, bubbling just under the surface. But, like a 'check engine light', just because we know *something* is wrong doesn't mean we know *what* is wrong.

Is it illegal immigration? Heavy-handed government regulations? A broken education system? Or is it income inequality? Systemic racism? Out-of-control free markets?

Your answers will largely depend on where you fall on the political spectrum. And plenty of talking heads – on the Right and Left – will gladly confirm whatever you already think and offer up a quick and easy diagnosis. But what if all the surface problems are merely symptoms of a deeper disease? What if we're trying to cure our cultural cancer by popping a couple of ibuprofens?

In the following pages, Daniel Rundquist cuts through the weeds and get to the center of what's ailing our republic. And when he pulls back the curtain, the diagnosis is remarkably simple: We've lost our goodness. As the French diplomat, Alexis de Tocqueville once warned, "...if America ever ceases to be good, she will cease to be great." And that is exactly what's happening. We've lost our goodness, or virtue. Until we reclaim it, we will continue wandering in the cultural and political wilderness we find ourselves in. But that's not even the worst of it. Without virtue, we'll never live up to the most basic definition of our name: the *United* States of America.

Without virtue, division, identity politics, and polarization will rule the day. And so, these two powerful forces, virtue and unity, will either stand or fall together. We can make all the laws in the world. We can attempt to reform our education system. We can debate until we're all red in the face. But until we've learned virtue again, none of it will make a difference.

Dan moves beyond a mere diagnosis of our cultural situation. He recognizes that, historically, the Christian Church has had the responsibility to step up and be the guardian of virtue in any culture where it's gained prominence. Unfortunately, many denominations and churches have failed to take that responsibility seriously. At times, they've even made things worse.

This is not an easy story to read for those of us who are committed to the Church; especially not for someone like me – a pastor of a non-denominational Christian congregation. And yet, it's important for us to remember how our forebears have often let down the standard.

At times, we've lost sight of the true mission of the church. We've gotten distracted with seeking after 'relevance' and spectacle. We've caved to the social media culture of the day, exalting diamond-studded celebrity preachers instead of the meek and lowly Jesus.

Instead of being salt to an increasingly rancid culture, the American church has lost its savor. And, as Jesus said, it's in danger of being "good for nothing, but to be cast out, and crushed under men's feet" (Matthew 5:13).

America will only regain her virtue when Christian denominations and individual congregations determine to return to the simplicity of the gospel. We must eschew comfort, artificial 'relevance', and cheap grace. We need to rethink worship, recognizing its sacramental character and deep symbolism. We need to return to a Christianity that's centered on the local congregation rather than the latest NYC-based celebrity pastor. We need to move beyond merely "asking Jesus into our hearts" to living in the fullness of our calling as men and women made in the image of God. In other words, we need to become more Orthodox.

By doing this, we may be able to reclaim our role as guardians of virtue rather than mimics who parrot the latest cultural fad. It is my hope and prayer that the American Church will begin moving in this direction.

In the Epilogue, Dan writes about his first steps into Eastern Orthodoxy. While I'm not Orthodox myself, I've come to recognize that they have a tremendous amount to teach us Western Christians – even if we never convert. But we need to open our ears and be willing to listen to voices that aren't exactly like ours.

I'm so thankful that I've had the opportunity to get to know Dan over the past year or so. He's challenged me to rethink some things I've taken for granted. He's reminded me of the dangers inherent in a 'sola scriptura' world where "everyone believes what is right in his own eyes." And he's been a good friend.

Though we certainly don't agree on everything (who does?), he has caused me to reflect more deeply on the problems plaguing our nation and how we might address them. I hope and pray that in these pages, he'll do the same for you.

C. C. I. Fenn
6/9/2020

Preface

2016, A nation in jeopardy

I understand now why people drink. I'm referring to the hard core drinkers. Even with all the various challenges I have faced in my life, it finally took the "Christian church" to drive me to my first drink. Others may have a multitude of reasons to be sure. They may well be depressed after a survey of the American landscape of the 21st century—certainly my least favorite century. Oh, how I do so despise the 21st century! But for me it was Christianity.

There are plenty of factors that may contribute to substance abuse in the general population. The heavy burdens of life, the unrealistic expectations of others; the losses and disappointments throughout the course of life today can wear on even the most hardened people. There is a nowhere person can go to avoid their own tragedy and so substance abuse becomes for them the only escape on Earth short of death, and too often overconsumption is also the cause of it.

If that were not enough, consider how obvious it is that the world at large is simply a broken place. America is today a culturally and economically bankrupt nation, in spite of the headlines you may read that seem to advertise the opposite; perhaps in better shape than most other nations, but it's still broken. No matter how much we hope for it or work towards it, the American Dream is simply out of reach for millions of Americans, and the wealthiest nation on Earth can no longer live up to the expectations of its own citizens or of the world.

No one even talks about the American Dream anymore; it has become clear that America has been cheated out of its own bright future by its controlling political classes which are comprised of the globalists. This is the new world of the Forgotten Man and is a result of greed, corruption, and the successful execution of the Saul Alinsky plan for converting a capitalist society into a totalitarian Socialist one.[1] These plans were laid bare in America in 2016 by a new president who doesn't fit the "go along, get along" political mold of his predecessors. Some believe that President Trump is their savior. I believe that he is a mere speed bump on the road that leads to a national annihilation.

For the American liberal Leftists, any heavy drinking is likely due to their deep hatred of an American president and his opposing party, followed by a subsequent depression, and utter mental derangement over losing the election to a populist republican president in 2016 and again in 2024. For average American Christians, any overindulgence is likely something else. Both groups have responses that have impacted American Christianity.

We like to label this drinking as "alcoholism" out of convenience, and then want to try to treat it as if it is a disease like diabetes or cancer, but I'm not entirely sold on that approach. Any addiction is a symptom of a problem, not a cause of itself. In order to correct it, we must get to the root of the problem and properly address it. Perhaps the source for this alcoholism is that deep down, people have lost all hope in their lives and they have concluded that it is better if they can numb their way past their days one drink at a time. Absent of hope, they have resolved that it is the best they might do for the remainder of their time.

I have lived in the American "Bible Belt," for decades and I see a storm that has been quietly brewing here. Or perhaps it is better described as a slow freeze, with a gradual chilling of true Christian faith. When I discuss this among the local Christians, it has become fashionable for them to simply excuse it, calling it, "the falling away." We have Christian churches on every other street corner here in the Bible Belt, but does that help? Beneath the thin veneer of our American churches lies the tempest of ignorance and confusion. None of them can seem to deliver on anything they preach—unless the results are nothing more than emotionalism and other warm "feelings." These churches say that they are all about "the Bible," but disagree with each other as to what it means. They all love their personalized "Jesus," but where can we discover the genuine peace, glory, and power of the Christian faith?

The absolute final respite of peace and hope that a person might turn to; that last bastion of peace, preserve of truth, beacon of light and righteousness remaining on Earth for all mankind should be the Church that bears the name of Christ. Today, however, this is no longer the case—and now, as I have explored and learned how it has been managed over the centuries, I'm not totally certain that it ever really was for America. Christianity, it has been said, is the greatest story ever told, but looking around; it doesn't seem to be able to live up to that venerable billing these days.

Does Christ call us to operate an endless series of opposing churches in His name where often shallow minded simpletons are expected to meet each other every week in complete ignorance? Is there no room for understanding that is beyond the local mantra of the members' own opinions and beliefs? Is no thought to be given to the understanding or consideration of early church writings and their applications to help accurately deliver the message of the Gospels? What about (dare I ask) debate on a theological point? The Japanese have an old adage, "The nail that sticks out gets hammered down," and so it is with these church institutions. I have been the nail more often than I care to recall.

Without a doubt there is a grand conspiracy at work to destroy Christianity. That's not a theory, an idea, a concept, or some paranoia borne from my personal experience. It's not a new plan, either. At some venues it is overt, in others it is subverted and secret, In America, it is often clothed in a sheep-like attitude of "welcoming friendship and inclusion." Nearly all of these incremental steps towards destruction have been incredibly successful in the United States and are likely operating in a church near you today.

In a broader world view, if one were to create a list of all the ills that the world has suffered by those claiming to represent Jesus Christ or His interests they would indeed fill entire volumes. The same could be said for followers of other religions. Religion is broken, and in particular, the universal concept of Christianity is false—and untold millions of people have been abused across the centuries in the name of it. Is this not a valid enough reason for us to discard Christianity today?

I must reluctantly admit that my own experience with Christianity has been very discouraging and at times was ultimately abusive; mentally, physically, and emotionally. In fact I had just been tossed out of another church, "made unwelcome" I suppose, in June, 2015 when I first began to compose the present work. It is difficult to imagine another institution more twisted and maligned by mankind over centuries as that of "Christianity."

The late Evangelist Billy Graham explained why all this is so:

"We do not fail to enjoy the fruit of the Spirit because we live in a sea of corruption; we fail to do so because the sea of corruption is in us.[2]"

In addition to the attempt to unravel this subject for myself and in so doing address my personal distress, it is also my aim to do so for many; for my family, friends and my fellow citizens. My compassion for them prevents me from merely addressing a problem only to keep the results to myself; the clues and answers squirrelled away in my forgotten journals spattered with ink, so that friends should continue in confusion and darkness. The risk in publishing these findings and opinions are clear as any writer knows; heated criticism and potential for intolerance of persons with opposing views. I have no choice but to accept that risk.

This composition has indeed been more difficult for me to complete than even I had expected. If I had elected not to tackle the present subject, I might well instead have been engaged in the attempt to resolve some other grand mystery, such as the origins of the universe or quantum physics rather than to explain Christianity's role in American society. However, upon completion of the present work, I am now nearly convinced that tackling the former subjects might have been preferable. Moreover, I have also come to understand why many writers so often elect to live a rather reclusive life. Composition such as this is a solitary task that demands a steep toll on the writer in every way—physically, mentally, emotionally and spiritually.

It is perhaps unfortunate that it is impossible for me to divorce myself from the content of this work. Because of this, I wish to state up front that I do not want to give readers the impression that I am promoting membership in any specific American Christian churches. I am absolutely not. In fact I'll say right here that you should not join a church as a result of reading this work. Why? Because there is often a great chasm between the message and teachings of Jesus Christ, and the theology and doctrine found in American Christian churches today, which I will soon illustrate.

At the time of this composition, I was not a church member anywhere and had not been for some time. It was my choice to stay away, mostly for the want of not knowing where to go anymore. The general trends for American church membership show that I am certainly not alone. But I had my reasons, and they were serious and substantial.

American Exceptionalism in Jeopardy

If such a comprehensive list of cultural ills were made, one could not help but to notice that the entire history of civilization is punctuated by the domination of mankind by rulers, tyrants, emperors, kings, warlords, and despots. Mankind's historical lot in life is to be subjugated by a small and powerful group which sets themselves above the rest. Time and again we see the results across history—war, bloodshed, poverty, strife, economic turmoil, and perhaps the worst of all effects (I would argue), wasted human potential.

On July 4th, 1776 this long standing cycle of history was broken by a new nation with a new idea—a political experiment. The people of the thirteen colonies in North America had decided that subjugation by an absentee king far across the ocean was no longer suitable or acceptable to govern them. They believed that they could do better. So it was that they embarked to discover the answer to the question, "can man govern himself?" The United States of America at once became an exceptional experiment. It was to become, and still is, the exception to the historical pattern of subjugation of men on earth.

Thomas Jefferson (among many others) was a key figure in both forming and explaining this new concept to the world with statements like,

"Under the law of nature, all men are born free, every one comes into the world with a right to his own person, which includes the liberty of moving and using it at his own will. This is what is called personal liberty, and is given him by the author of nature, because [it is] necessary for his own sustenance.[3]"

The American Founders and Framers did all they could to create a just representative republic in America that was durable yet flexible. Most of all, the Constitution and Bill of Rights sought to maintain a polite distance from government intrusion into the lives of its citizens, and define the individual rights of the people in such a way as to prevent this new government from eliminating their rights. They understood that the nature of all government entities is to expand and seek to eventually subjugate its citizens.

At the conclusion of writing the last page of *Tears for Byzantium*, I was left with so many more discussion points in my own notes that were simply beyond the scope of the first book. I also found that I had amassed a rather large personal library in the process. The volumes containing the world's history of the Greeks, Romans, America, their maps, art, and archaeology, or at least a more than a usual portion of it were now at my fingertips.

However, I hope that as a non-scholar, non-theologian, my investigation might be less susceptible to the influences of the modern academic groupthink or "go along to get along" processes that seem to run the nation as well as organized religion these days. Initially, it is apparent that the politicians and scholastics have been in charge of Christianity's course for far too long.

There are important lessons that we should have learned from Rome, Constantinople and many other empires, kingdoms, and governments. Base human nature, however, does not seem to change across the centuries and now we find that many of the same things that impacted the Greeks, Romans, and Byzantines are indeed many of the same things that plague all attempts to civilize a people; waste, fraud, abuse of office, greed, graft, corruption, lust for power, nepotism, cronyism, envy, despotism, tyranny, neglect, betrayal of the electorate, and a host of other things which have contributed to the decline and destruction of nations past. The discovery and understanding of history makes it clear to me that America has some very hard times ahead.

Because Christianity is an ancient faith, it is naturally enveloped by and intertwined with many historical world events. As I did in the previous volume, I will keep an eye toward the ancient Christian East which predates all modern western "developments" of the faith after 1056. Perhaps our Byzantine predecessors might help us navigate a solution either by their example of their successes or their failures.

Now it is important that I pause here for just a moment. Historical events stripped of their context can seem to be incredibly insensitive and brutal to us today. While history holds the reports of the terrible and seemingly damning events, it is fair to temper these facts and events with sensibility. Specifically, that sensibility arrives in the understanding that your humble author must recognize that judging the ages-old actions and activities of the Roman Catholic Church by today's morals, laws, standards, culture, and expectations is an extension of something called *presentism*; interpreting past phenomena in terms of current beliefs and knowledge. It is rather important to remember that most everything in the world has changed since the time of these events. Attempts to condemn Roman Catholic leadership today based on past decisions, actions, and world events solely through the relatively sanitized lens of our 21st century American culture are intellectually dishonest. Neither is it fair to cast aspersion upon today's Roman Catholics because of it.

Discovering the truth in any of it requires a process akin to peeling an onion—taking the subject today and peeling back the layers one at a time. But as we peel away these layers we discover that the answers are often progressively more difficult to accept from our Western perspective, and can shake the foundations of "what we know."

What I have come to understand is something that would seem quite obvious to the older generations—that America's path to sanity will be determined by the very same things that the ancient Romans relied upon to found their Republic; and also that which our own Founders had relied upon to charter our new nation: virtue and unity.

The focus of this work

Indeed America really only has two problems; the lack of both virtue and unity. I believe that the root cause of ninety percent of all America's issues come down to the absence or mismanagement of these. Solve these two things and America could be well on the way to restoration. But doing so in a 21st century Age of Information and a culture of no-strings, instant gratification is indeed a huge ask for Americans. Our survival as a society, however, will rely upon it. The entire text here focuses on the roots of these key questions: What are unity and virtue? Did America ever possess these things? Who in the American culture were the "keepers" of these, responsible for training each new generation? What happened to them? How do we get them back?

In the absence of virtue and unity, one can expect the massive void in society which is soon filled with the usual machinations of evil. This ultimately manifests in a violent, foundering culture (if it is to be called such a thing) permeated with things like violent crime, injustice, greed, prejudice, racism, corruption, dishonesty, cowardice, ignorance, incompetence, selfishness, carelessness, hopelessness and even civil war. In these conditions, it is easier for a nation of people to become submissive to an authoritarian central government (out of desperation) than it is for the people of a free republic to govern themselves and to maintain their own liberty. I believe that this is the grand strategy of the Leftists in America, and I am certainly not the only one to propose that notion. There are many commentators and pundits who agree with that statement.

Without virtue and unity, the representative Republic of America cannot survive for very long. These are the common binders of all our citizens. Those not bound by a common sense of virtue and unity are often outcasts—they are the criminals who prey upon the weak, the poor, and the aged. They are corrupt on many levels. It is for this reason governments are instituted to separate these from the larger society, to bring them to justice and punish them. Only today, they are being used as a tool by the Left to "undo" the American Republic. These malcontents are excused, encouraged, promoted, and often celebrated in popular Leftist culture. Sadly, small and powerful groups of nefarious people have been using Christ to push some political or personal agenda ever since His time. One has to ask, where is the Church?

For the rest of us, it is virtue and unity that binds us citizens together in a cohesive bond transcending individual opinions, cultures, languages, race and religion into what we once called the American Melting Pot. Ideally, virtues are applied to create just laws, and it is virtue again used to execute them fairly and justly adjudicate disputes and challenges in the court of law—the "Rule of Law" is supreme in America, not the rule of men. Without virtues there is soon a general collapse of the system—which, as I have previously demonstrated in my earlier work[4], has been the object of those opposed to the American Experiment almost from the start.

It could be effectively argued that true Christianity has greatly contributed to the ultimate improvement of the human condition over the centuries[5], punctuated by long periods of tragedy caused by those falsely claiming the banner of "Christian." It could be equally argued by many that Christianity and religion in general, have deprived humanity from a track of positive development, and both arguments seem to have merit depending upon the place in history being discussed. This, however, is not the defining point of Christianity in America today.

The Unholy Land

While rarely executed in a perfect way, as mankind is flawed, the message of Christ's love and His hope for mankind conveyed by the Gospels has ultimately been a positive one across the ages. The general message of Christ is carried on by imperfect people— everyone from politically charged Popes with funny hats in Europe to snake handling sects somewhere in the remote hills of the American landscape.

The reality is that Christians cannot control who claims to carry the message of the Gospel, although the Roman Catholic Church has tried for centuries to do just that. There seems to be no "perfect" Christian churches on this planet and so it is precious time spent in vain if you are searching for that one absolutely flawless place to worship. Instead of perfection in a church, should we be looking for something else? This is also what I often hear from American Christians. But how could this be true? Christ left us a Church that He established, not a Bible book to be worshipped. How could His Church not be reflection of His image?

While I might fill pages, surely even chapters describing the merits of one Christian denomination against another that's not my aim. Given my lack of formal training in the subject it might well prove to be a baseless and bias effort. I don't seek to drive the readers to one particular place in Christianity, but rather to discover genuine Christian faithfulness should I be fortunate to find it. I don't presently know where that is, nor have I any clue as to where it might eventually be found. Even if I am able to do so with this work, the reader must of course still seek and discern answers for themselves. With this in mind, we will see how this brief investigation unfolds.

Mr. Thom S. Rainer, the president and CEO of Lifeway Christian Resources is convinced that nearly 100,000 American churches are in decline or are in danger of closing their doors today.[6] Why are the American Christian churches foundering and failing today? Is it realistic to explore the notion that not only has the church failed to maintain virtue and unity in American society, but that the church has caused people to see a dead faith from their seat in the pews where there should instead be hope, truth, and love? There have been many writers and pundits before me who have postulated exactly that. We may well discover that modern churches, too, are suffering from the same lack of virtue and unity that befalls the nation. Without some perpetual source of virtue and unity to renew each generation, America (and her churches) will soon become just another chapter in world history.

The Composition

With the completion of the first volume in this series, I sought to awaken readers to the notion that much of what is happening to America today is not a new phenomenon on the globe. In fact many of the events of today are clear echoes of the Byzantine past. If, as a nation of responsible citizens we can again seek to educate ourselves to learn the outcomes of the past, we might find a roadmap to our own future and avoid repeating mistakes along the way.

This new work began in a somewhat different way. When I first sat down to begin this present piece, my original aim was not so much to attempt to offer more insight to solve America's civic problems. After decades of being personally kicked around and pushed out by so many churches and their church people, I rather sought to attempt to resolve my own problems with churches. It became apparent that what I uncovered and learned in this process is not just about what has happened to me, but also that which is affecting our nation. While it may be taken on its own, I intend for it to be taken in order, after *Tears for Byzantium*.

It would take a lot more than just a few shelves of good books to properly address in depth the roots of American problems, and I absolutely understood this. I don't believe that any one writer or thinker could achieve such a task even if he had a lifetime to dedicate to the project. As an American and a Christian, I am by definition an "insider" living in the environment which is the subject of the piece.

It is admittedly difficult to be apologetic and at the same time objective as a Christian while composing this work. I will attempt to set aside my hopeful beliefs that modern Christianity is benevolent in the name of objective indifference, but I already know that I will likely fail in that ambition. I will always maintain the hope of benevolent Christianity that I was taught from my childhood, even though every church I have been a part of in the past has more or less rejected me.

This work was certainly a challenge for a layman to piece together, but also one filled with not a small degree of personal anxiety; facing the stark realization of how unlikely it was for me to join any church, anywhere, ever again. This is not because of writing this book, but rather because I didn't believe in churches anymore. It was like discovering that the long term relationship with a close friend was really one-sided.

As a Christian, how would you feel if you suddenly understood that nearly all of what you see going on at church was not Christianity? But not having any belief in "churches" anymore is a seductive comfort. It means that I am taking control of my own faith, and not Christ. Perhaps this is also as problematic for me as it is for other Christians.

I would ask the kind reader for one thing only; to make the honest attempt to step outside "yourself" for the brief time needed to read the entire work. Set aside, albeit temporarily, your own bias, your own dogmas, and what you know is right. For American Christians, some of what follows in the text may be quite uncomfortable to learn and process if you have never been exposed to it. I know that it has been for me.

I believe that most American Christians genuinely seek the truth of Christ and are not psychopathic subversives purposely attempting to derail the faith. I do hope that the reader would make the attempt to be objective rather than discounting the content out of hand if it does not initially match their own views or is "offensive" in the obnoxious and often dishonest thin-skinned modern day sense. For any who are unable to set aside their own beliefs in this fashion, I apologize in advance if the work raises a flurry of annoyance, alarm, hatred, disbelief—or proves to be just plain wrong. I would prefer a debate or constructive conversation about your concerns instead of summary judgment based upon your biases.

Rather than get bogged down in the weeds of so much theological detail and doctrine[a], I think it's a better use of effort, time and space to work within my scope to address the Christian landscape in America on the whole as much as it is possible, and then illustrate only salient details. As a result, while we will also submerse ourselves into a whirlwind review of the history of the Christian Church in order to gather some context. We will not explore too many of the deeper questions of varying theologies. Christ is not in question here, only mankind's role in in shaping, (mis)managing, and applying what "Christianity" has been across the ages, and is today.

---

[a] There are, of course, differences between "liturgical" and "non-liturgical" protestant traditions. That stated, note here that throughout the text I will refer to "Protestant" or some variant of the word with the broadest definition of:

Noun
1. Any Western Christian who is not an adherent of a Catholic, Anglican, or Eastern Church.

The Unholy Land

Many writers and others have weighed in on the present subject across all history, that I felt I would be remiss not to include as many of them into the conversation as seemed proper. It is for this reason I have included a rather large number of quotes as input from a broad collection of sources who have offered opinions on the subject matter over time.

Some readers will doubtless criticize this practice and accuse the writer of merely "filling pages," but I can assure you that this is not the case. I thought this to be important both for me as research and for the reader to hear opinions other than my own.

As a result of this general philosophy the reader will note that I have included quotes and observations from a broad panel of humanity spanning the entire history of Christianity, including: nine authors/novelists, eight presidents, four each philosophers and saints, three each metropolitans, statesmen, CEO's, professors, two each writers, monks, theologians, historians, pastors, one each French Aristocrat, Evangelist, Native American Indian Chief, army general, British writer, psychologist, French nurse, Jewish convert to Christianity, archaeologist, archbishop, abolitionist, pope, comedian, emperor, pundit, activist, satirist, Abbott, Supreme Court Justice, poet…and a certain selfless stepson and humble carpenter from Galilee.

Something else I'm guilty of in this text is what is known as "scripture proofing"; the practice of using individual Biblical references to support an opinion. Every popular Protestant pundit seems to do this anyway as a matter of procedure. As I said, I am guilty of it as well but in the interest of full disclosure, you at least know about it upfront. Am I right, am I wrong? You must examine the material and decide. If I am wrong, it's not the first time that's happened.

---

2. An adherent of any of those Christian bodies that separated from the Church of Rome during the Reformation, or of any group descended from them.

Adjective
1. Belonging or pertaining to Protestants or their religion.

This is to quell any potential confusion over use of that rather unwieldy term as it is being applied here.

The Unholy Land

I am a firm proponent of learning history and an adherent to context. As a result, I believe that some level of both historical and conceptual context should be provided. For this reason, I have included some brief snapshots of world chronology at the end of the text[7]. I cannot stress strongly enough the need for Americans to learn world history, if not through a school, then on their own. It is more fitting to have included it here than in my prior work as Christianity has without question affected and shaped world history.

I will proceed with a brief and basic discussion of how Christianity evolved. This material is not a history lesson, but rather presented to illustrate the cultural, personal, and psychological obstacles mankind has placed on itself that are now barriers between us and Christ. The practice of modern popular Christianity in America as it turns out, is very much its own worst enemy.

Unfortunately, I am not dispassionate enough to divorce myself from the present work. It is therefore also my story. Please understand that I approach this work with the humility of an ordinary broken man, and the resulting work intended for peers to discover rather than for critics, scholars or theologians to critique. I would not wish any reader to leave the piece with the notion that your humble author thinks himself in any way something he is not. Nor do I pretend that I know the right way about anything. My aim instead is to motivate my fellow Americans and Christians to take care to learn history—both of our nation and our faith—with an open mind. To encourage these to take an honest, yet potentially uncomfortable look at what we have become, and to focus on discovering the genuine faith.

I consider myself a student of everything, and an expert in nothing; merely reporting what I have seen, learned, and understood while using that experience to further thoughts on the restoration of our nation. For any reader who might mistakenly believe that I have all the answers you can skip on over to the last chapter (Epilogue) and save your time, for therein is written in some 700 words the entirety of what I know for certain.

We can only deal with the historical facts as they are, in as much context as such a brief work may provide, and in my case, small doses. This is because the information does not come to us without a price. There is an occupational hazard for both the writer and the inquisitive reader; one cannot simply "unlearn" something uncovered from annals of history. It can be a stressor to learn so many things that are uncomfortable to know about a matter held so close by so many.

The Unholy Land

Following the introductory chapters, I take the reader on a rather brief tour of history and the events of each of a few major branches of Christianity in turn, chronologically, and in length and depth roughly equivalent to their population of Christians; the largest distribution of which is Roman Catholic, second is a few various predominant sects of Protestantism, and third is the Eastern Orthodox Church.

Please bear in mind throughout that the work is not intended to represent scholarly or comprehensive coverage of these subjects. The work here is admittedly unfinished and forever in progress so long as humans breathe. Any labors by a layman on this particular subject are doomed to be inadequate from the start as the learning and conversation continues; even artists say that art is never completed, it is only abandoned. Neither did I begin this work because I thought it would bring me fame, wealth, joy, peace or happiness—in fact the process for the composition of this work has proven to have delivered precisely the opposite.

Dear reader, understand that this text is not delivered to you out prejudice, hatred, malice, or avarice of one religious group or another. Rather one born of an all too personal frustration, grief, isolation, despair, and sorrow for the state of the practice and direction of the Christian faith, and the affect that has had on me as well as the American fabric. So it is with regret and remorse, I offer what may seem to amount to a rebuke to many of our Christian churches, but it is rather a lament delivered in hoping that such a text might lead to some degree of discovery of genuine Christianity and ultimately a potential for a course correction of our nation.

At times, this Christian message of the Gospels has contributed to the honest desire to bring virtue, unity, and hope to an otherwise uncivilized and dark world. At other times, the Message is deliberately twisted by men, misconstrued and abused by all manner of malcontents for any variety of malfeasance, from false justifications for war and taxation to slavery and murder. But the good work of genuine Christians is never perfect, never complete, and never more needed than it is today.

-DBR

Acknowledgements

In chronological order, special thanks to:

Mr. Jim G. Teachey

Mr. John Maierhoffer

Dr. Dan Greene, Senior Pastor at Christian Fellowship Chapel, Granite Falls, NC.

Pastor Mack Jarvis, First Baptist Church, Hudson, NC.

Mr. Dru Schneeberger, Mr. William McNeill, Mr. Arnold Wilson

The faithful of Archangel Gabriel Orthodox Church, Hickory, NC.

Mr. Phillip Felts

V. Rev. Father Paul Schellbach and Fr. Christopher Foley

Pastor Casey Fenn, Rock Chapel Church, Granite Falls, NC.

Ms. Sarah Hodgins, beta reader and pitcher of religious curve balls.

Mr. Joseph T. Sermarini, Forum Ancient Coins, Wilmington, NC, for free use of their photography.

Mrs. Alyssa Minton, portrait photography.

V. Rev. Father Alexander Logunov and V. Rev. Father Mark Mancuso

The faithful at the parish in the Name of the Icon of the Reigning Mother of God in Charlotte, North Carolina

The faithful of St. Timothy the Apostle Orthodox Church, Hickory, NC.

Mr.& Mrs. Chris VanAllsburg

> *"Midway along the journey of our life*
> *I woke to find myself in a dark wood,*
> *for I had wandered off from the straight path.*
>
> *How hard it is to tell what it was like,*
> *this wood of wilderness, savage and stubborn*
> *(the thought of it brings back all my old fears),*
>
> *a bitter place! Death could scarce be bitterer.*
> *But if I would show the good that came of it*
> *I must talk about things other than the good."*
>
> ~ Dante Alighieri, 1314

It would be wrong for me to stay silent on the knowledge of such matters.[8]

1

For Want of Virtue and Unity

"Agreements the Indian makes with the government are like the agreement a buffalo makes with the hunter after it has been pierced by many arrows. All it can do is lie down and give in."
Chief Ouray, c. 1868

"The only good Indians I ever saw were dead."
Philip Henry Sheridan, 1869
U.S. Army General

The root problems with the lack of virtue and unity in North America began long before the founding of the United States of America. For centuries prior to 1776, the Europeans and others had been arriving on the continent, exploring, and settling in North America. This required a steep learning curve of adaptation and innovations that many of the colonists failed to master. On the other hand, the Native American Indian Nations had already developed successful life strategies and changed relatively little of their own culture. They preferred to live as they had—continuing to choose their own modes and methods of life instead of adopting the cultures of the arriving Europeans who were ill-prepared for frontier life. Their differences with the Europeans did not end with lifestyle and culture; their religion was not centered on the Christian Bible or the God of Christianity as it was for most people of Europe.

Contrary to what might be considered and accepted as the popular view today, the American government was not promoting a course of war against the Nations from our Founding. In fact, in his first annual message to the people—the State of the Union Address—, President Thomas Jefferson stated the following on December 8, 1801:

"Among our Indian neighbors also a spirit of peace and friendship generally prevails, and I am happy to inform you that the continued efforts to introduce among them the implements and the practice of husbandry and the household arts have not been without success; that they are becoming more and more sensible of the superiority of this dependence for clothing and subsistence over the precarious resources of hunting and fishing, and already we are able to announce that instead of that constant diminution of their numbers produced by their wars and their wants, some of them begin to experience an increase of population.[9]"

Either President Jefferson is lying, or somewhere between December, 1801 and January, 1865, America lost something very dear to her that has proven difficult to replace— those old friends, virtue and unity. It should not be a surprise for anyone to learn that the catalyst for the shift in values during this span of years was in fact greed. The railroad boom started just three years after Thomas Jefferson's death in 1829, and the expansion of rail across the nation fueled much of the motivation for controlling Indian lands and removing the Indians and their claim to the land by any means possible.

By the 19th Century, the dramatic culture clash between an industrialized "Christian" nation and the "pagan" Native American Nations was troubling for both parties but in dramatically different ways. The U.S. government had decided that they must, and would, conquer the North American continent at all costs. Not content to attempt to coexist with the Native American Nations, subjugation became the order of the day as the post-civil war American government pursued a deliberate course of extermination of the Native Peoples. It remains the single most shameful period of American history that I can recall[b] and a national disgrace which has never been properly addressed.

---

[b] Some might consider the period of slavery as the most egregious, however, that practice predated the formation of the United States. The United States government, once formed, took positive measures and eventually ENDED the practice rather than starting it. By contrast, in dealing with the Native American Nations, the United States Government sought the eradication of the entire race by military force.

For the Native American Nations, it was not so much that they were poor negotiators of the many "treaties" offered to them by the American government, (although they were never formally educated to do so, which should be considered an unfair disadvantage,) but at the time here was an essentially a pre-industrial style culture negotiating with a European style, educated, and militarily powerful Industrial Age culture. It was never an even handed negotiation, nor was it ever a fair fight, and a fight that did not even need to happen.

The Native American Nations for the most part, I believe, might have preferred to make a lasting peace with their new neighbors once they understood the full capability of their adversary; they were never going to attempt mounting a major assault to invade Denver or San Francisco, for example. They had not the ability, the resources, nor the organization for any effective major military-style offensive anywhere.

The American government ultimately wanted and demanded unfettered control and ownership of all the land and, in the case of many areas like California and Colorado, the gold, coal, oil, and other resources that lay within it. There was also a firm belief at the time that the "uncultured" Indians had no place in the 19th Century. They were often manipulated by the American government and used to fight against their own people as a strategy of their total elimination—the age old "divide and conquer" technique similar to that employed by the ancient Romans.

Chief Noah Sealth, better known as Chief Seattle, was a key figure relatively late in the discourse. In his poignant and tragic 1854 oration he clearly illustrates the wide cultural disconnects from the Native Americans' perspective, worthy of our time here to pause and examine it:

"... Big Chief at Washington sends us greetings of friendship and goodwill. This is kind of him for we know he has little need of our friendship in return. His people are many. They are like the grass that covers vast prairies. My people are few. They resemble the scattering trees of a storm-swept plain. The great - and, I presume - good, White Chief sends us word that he wishes to buy our land but is willing to allow us enough to live comfortably. This indeed appears just, even generous, for the Red Man no longer has rights that he need respect, and the offer may be wise, also, as we are no longer in need of an extensive country.

The Unholy Land

"There was a time when our people covered the land as the waves of a wind-ruffled sea cover its shell-paved floor, but that time long since passed away with the greatness of tribes that are now but a mournful memory. I will not dwell on, nor mourn over, our untimely decay, nor reproach my paleface brothers with hastening it, as we too may have been somewhat to blame.

"Youth is impulsive. When our young men grow angry at some real or imaginary wrong, and disfigure their faces with black paint, it denotes that their hearts are black, and that they are often cruel and relentless, and our old men and old women are unable to restrain them. Thus it has ever been. Thus it was when the white man began to push our forefathers ever westward. But let us hope that the hostilities between us may never return. We would have everything to lose and nothing to gain. Revenge by young men is considered gain, even at the cost of their own lives, but old men who stay at home in times of war, and mothers who have sons to lose, know better.

"Our good father in Washington - for I presume he is now our father as well as yours, since King George has moved his boundaries further north - our great and good father, I say, sends us word that if we do as he desires he will protect us. His brave warriors will be to us a bristling wall of strength, and his wonderful ships of war will fill our harbors, so that our ancient enemies...will cease to frighten our women, children and old men. Then in reality he will be our father and we his children. But can that ever be? Your God is not our God! Your God loves your people and hates mine! He folds his strong protecting arms lovingly about the paleface and leads him by the hand as a father leads an infant son. But, He has forsaken His Red children, if they really are His.

"Our God, the Great Spirit, seems also to have forsaken us. Your God makes your people wax stronger every day. Soon they will fill all the land. Our people are ebbing away like a rapidly receding tide that will never return. The white man's God cannot love our people or He would protect them. They seem to be orphans who can look nowhere for help. How then can we be brothers? How can your God become our God and renew our prosperity and awaken in us dreams of returning greatness? If we have a common Heavenly Father He must be partial, for He came to His paleface children. We never saw Him. He gave you laws but had no word for His red children whose teeming multitudes once filled this vast continent as stars fill the firmament. No; we are two distinct races with separate origins and separate destinies. There is little in common between us.

"...Your religion was written upon tablets of stone by the iron finger of your God so that you could not forget. The Red Man could never comprehend or remember it. Our religion is the traditions of our ancestors - the dreams of our old men, given them in solemn hours of the night by the Great Spirit; and the visions of our sachems, and is written in the hearts of our people...Day and night cannot dwell

The Unholy Land

together. The Red Man has ever fled the approach of the White Man, as the morning mist flees before the morning sun. However, your proposition seems fair and I think that my people will accept it and will retire to the reservation you offer them. Then we will dwell apart in peace, for the words of the Great White Chief seem to be the words of nature speaking to my people out of dense darkness.

"It matters little where we pass the remnant of our days. They will not be many. The Indian's night promises to be dark. Not a single star of hope hovers above his horizon. Sad-voiced winds moan in the distance. Grim fate seems to be on the Red Man's trail, and wherever he will hear the approaching footsteps of his fell destroyer and prepare stolidly to meet his doom, as does the wounded doe that hears the approaching footsteps of the hunter.

"A few more moons, a few more winters, and not one of the descendants of the mighty hosts that once moved over this broad land or lived in happy homes, protected by the Great Spirit, will remain to mourn over the graves of a people once more powerful and hopeful than yours. But why should I mourn at the untimely fate of my people? Tribe follows tribe, and nation follows nation, like the waves of the sea. It is the order of nature, and regret is useless. Your time of decay may be distant, but it will surely come, for even the White Man whose God walked and talked with him as friend to friend, cannot be exempt from the common destiny. We may be brothers after all. We will see...

"...The White Man will never be alone....Let him be just, and deal kindly with my people, for the dead are not powerless. Dead, did I say? There is no death, only a change of worlds." [10]

To summarize Chief Seattle's key points:

1. The white man has no need for the friendship of the red man, and there is little in common.
2. Seattle assumes (hopefully, but knowingly errant) that the white people in the U.S. government is benevolent.
3. He recognizes that they are outnumbered by the whites and have little hope of survival.
4. He acknowledges that the whites are getting stronger while his own people are getting ever weaker.
5. He feels that the white man's God and the red man's God are not the same entity. He feels abandoned by the white man's God and their own.
6. He acknowledges that their young men often act in vengeance with violence and the elders are not able to restrain their actions.
7. At the conclusion of the agreement, he expects to be protected by the government against their traditional enemies.

8. He concludes that the white race and the Indians cannot share in the new American culture.
9. He is willing to accept the government's offer, which seems to be mostly out of capitulation than anything else.
10. He still hopes that the whites will deal with his people justly.

Why did it happen this way? A telling key is this: of Chief Seattle's observations, I would offer that #5 above could be a most important take away point. Everything else is largely circumstantial. How can there be two Gods, one for the "white man," another for the "red man?" The Reverend Billy Graham wrote:

"Christianity is not a white man's religion and don't let anybody ever tell you that it's white or black. Christ belongs to all people; He belongs to the whole world.[11]"

Fast-forward to the loathsome 21st Century where through our media, academia and revisionist history we are now being brainwashed into believing that all white people today are inherently evil and the plight of the Indians and other non-whites all around the globe is only further proof of that. But that is simply not the case. Race (or color if you happen to prefer) does not cause people to be either inherently good or evil and any assertion to that effect is absolutely absurd. While the actions of the American government against the Native American Nations in the 19th century absolutely cannot be justified, I think that the true cause can certainly be discovered, understood, and defined at its root. It is an issue with the content of character, not of skin color.

One of the key issues separating these Native American Nations and the American government was a result of differences between their basic outlooks of the natural world. The Americans settlers were culturally divided by their view that saw the land as a resource they could use to drive the advancement of their independence, influence, economy, expansion and wealth--ultimately raising their standard of living. They brought with them new concepts of law, private property rights, and rules of commerce. The Native Nations had lived for centuries without any need for these modern inventions, and generally saw the Earth as a source for life, not a resource to be plundered for profit. They saw no point in seeking to change their standard of living to match that of the Europeans.

"By 1870, the number of miles of rail tracks in the United States had grown to around 50,000 and was increasing by about 6,000 miles (or 12%) per year. About 10% of America's non-farm labor was devoted to expanding the rail network, about half of the production of the nation's metal industry contributed to the related construction boom, and nearly all the business on Wall Street revolved around railroad finance."[12]

To achieve this goal, the Native American Nations were often provoked to violence by the American government, and when they acted—whether in self-defense or offensively, both government and the media quickly vilified these actions in order to strike fear into the western settlers and the public at large. The Native American Nations were vilified. Fear would drive the public to support the effort to destroy the Native American Nations at all costs.

It was not long before the motivations of the American government at the time became primarily driven by greed, and to a slightly lesser degree, ego. It clearly had the means to execute whatever strategy it might choose in order to eradicate the Indian Nations—open pitched battles, forced starvation of isolated tribe settlements during the winter months, subversive tactics to pitch one tribe against another, and so on.

American military commanders took full advantage of the disorganization and fractural nature of tribal relations to promote division and to defeat them tribe by tribe, negotiating a treaty with this one, and pushing suspicion on another to keeping them fighting each other. Then government officials would violate or ignore the terms of their treaties in most cases.

When these treaties required the Indians to move from X to Y area, and the Government was to provide food and supplies for them to get through the winter—often the supplies deliberately did not arrive, and the tribe starved to death. This process continued until the Indians ultimately saw themselves as outnumbered, weakened, and without any hope remaining...finally defeated.

The Unholy Land

For the American government, its complete lack of virtue created a large void which they eagerly filled with policies of unprecedented greed and brutality resulting in nothing short of a program of murder and ethnic genocide. In an effort to solve the "Indian Problem" and remove the Native American Nations from their lands east of the Mississippi, President Andrew Jackson forced the relocation of 100,000 Native Americans when he signed the Indian Removal Act into law on May 28, 1830.[13] This event became known as the Trail of Tears. These tribes were to be sent to live in government designated areas west of the Mississippi River.

Virtue and greed cannot coexist in the hearts of men. The entire episode might have been avoided completely if virtue had instead been the order of the day and the extermination of another race of people had been recognized as the evil it is. In no way do the actions of the American government reflect the notion of being "a Christian nation" as has been claimed by the American brand from the start.

On the side of the Native American Nations, the situation was hopeless. While they certainly lacked savvy negotiation skills and a strong position to negotiate from, they also lacked some other key strategic elements that might have saved them, or at least strengthened their hand to settle treaties more in their favor and to enforce them. They simply lacked any power from which to negotiate. They lacked numbers of warriors, military technology, organization and discipline, unity and fortitude.

The confrontation with the American government found them ill prepared to cohesively defend their land, people, and culture. Eventually, as their numbers dwindled and they were forced to capitulate in the face of the brutality of the American government; the survivors were shipped off to small parcels to eke out their remaining years in defeat and disgrace.

For the Native American Nations lacking unity, there could be no hope whatsoever for an effective defense against a powerful common enemy. Unity might have enabled them to resolve or set aside all their internal tribal differences, tribal politics, real or imagined claims against each other, and "old school" type spats for the greater purpose of unifying the Nations to deal with the common threat of the encroaching American government. Once unified, they might have organized themselves to present a strong front to deal with the threats.

The Unholy Land

In the absence of unity, a society eventually discovers that common goals (such as diplomacy or defense in this case) can never be effectively achieved. In the end, the Native American Nations needed unity to secure their own support across their many different tribes. It could have provided them a better, stronger negotiating position. But this did not happen.

The American government checked its virtue at the door and pushed ahead to prosecute nothing less than a slaughter of Native Americans in an "ends justifies the means" sort of way. In the absence of virtue as a societal basis, laws are soon passed for the aggrandizement of some Americans at the expense of the rights of others and their very lives.

The end result was the inability to avoid the inexcusable and tragic outcome that was to become, in my opinion, the worst national tragedy America has ever suffered, worse than our Civil War. The reason I put it to the top of that list is because the men who fought the Civil War went to fight with honor and as a cause of country (right or wrong), and they faced soldiers who were roughly equally equipped and trained for 19th century warfare. The battle plans (if we wish to call them that) against the Native American Nations on the other hand, was a war without honor, without just cause—it was extermination.

More than a hundred years later, America now struggles culturally almost everywhere you want to look. Today we lived with "the war on terror" for two decades. What a perfectly stupid phrase this is, carefully concocted, no doubt by cowardly American politicians to tiptoe around identifying America's actual enemies. Is it even possible to have a war against a *thing*? Are we still fighting the "war on poverty" declared by President Johnson in 1964 or the "war on drugs" declared by President Nixon in 1971? One might as well declare that America is fighting the "war on sadness", or the "war on aggressiveness", or the war on _____(fill in the blank with your own random term).

The Unholy Land

"We the people" might easily conclude that there is a "war on common sense" in our nation. The very creation and use of this phrase (The war on ____") illustrates the absence of the two things I have been explaining all along in this work so far, virtue and unity. For if our politicians had any virtue, and the American people their unity, then possessing the courage to properly identify an actual enemy of the United States would not be difficult; we might avoid use of the phrase to justify every political motivation that comes along. Uncontrollable deficit spending and ever increasing public debt would never be permitted. Waste, fraud, and abuse at all levels of government would nearly evaporate. Political greed and graft would cease. It is simply too much to hope for.

Virtue and unity affect everything…one could make an organized list looking like this:

- **Lack of Virtue**, contributing to:
    - Ignorance of the rule of law, contributing to:
        - Injustice; poor or inconsistent application of the law
            - Social unrest
        - Unethical or no standards at all, contributing to:
            - Misrepresentation of the law to the public
            - Incompetent elected officials at all levels
            - The rise of dishonest politicians instead of statesmen
                - Poor, shortsighted, or unjust domestic public policies contributing to:
                    - Political unrest
                    - Civil war
                - Weak international policy, contributing to:
                    - War
                    - Trade deficits
                    - Graft and corruption
                    - Public debt
                    - Corruption
            - Self-aggrandizement
    - Greed, contributing to but not 100% causal of:
        - Corporate greed
        - Political graft and corruption; nepotism and criminal activity among the elected officials
        - Poverty, contributing to:
            - Reduction in the general standard of living
            - Abortion

- - -
        - Creates systematic infanticide to control the population of poor people without regard to human life
        - Crime, contributing to:
          - Creation of cyclical and serial criminals
          - Strain on the judicial and penal systems
        - Encourages "hopelessness" which contributes to
          - Homelessness
          - Lack of education
          - Hunger
          - Substance abuse and addiction
          - Crime (see above)
          - Poor personal life choices unconcerned with outcomes
            - Intergenerational poverty cycle
      - Economic failures
        - Elimination of the "American Dream" while it is replaced with a new, ever-changing, lower standard, ultimately arriving at wretchedness
        - Dependence upon government for education
          - Reduces free thought, speech, and new ideas
          - Controls outcomes for students
          - "Public opinion" replaces factual realities
        - Dependence upon government for subsistence
          - Surrendering of individual rights and liberty to the government due to circumstances
- **Lack of Unity**, contributing to:
  - Selfishness & ego
  - Racism (affecting all races)
  - Needless divisions along other cultural lines (useful to politicians), contributing to
    - Civil unrest
      - Rioting/looting
        - Strains the law enforcement capacity and training
    - Hatred between Americans ("Us versus Them" mentality)
    - Legal issues/lawsuits
    - Distrust between neighbors instead of friendships being forged.

- Uninformed misunderstandings and assumptions, generating confusion
- Inability of the American people to hold government accountable in a unified manner
    - Government achieves its goal of defeating the people
        - Individual rights are extinguished
            - The Bill of Rights is erased in the culture, in practice, and in memory
            - Taxation and regulation can be levied without fear of political redress
        - Government can establish an unbridled dictatorship

In the 1830's French aristocrat, diplomat, political scientist, and historian, Alexis de Tocqueville, became exasperated by the problems he saw in America and the world at the time. Although written nearly two hundred years ago, his observations of America at his time are still the headlines of today:

"Has every other century been like this one? Has man always confronted, as he does today, a world in which nothing makes sense? In which virtue is without genius and genius without honor? In which the love of order is indistinguishable from the lust of tyrants? In which the sacred cult of liberty is confounded with contempt for the law? In which conscience casts but an ambiguous light on the actions of men? In which nothing any longer seems forbidden or allowed, honest or shameful, true or false? Am I to believe that the Creator made man only to allow him to flounder endlessly in a sea of intellectual misery? I do not think so." [14]

There are today so many things America must do to restore our culture, and we cannot be certain that Americans are even up to the task. Many have already arrived at the level of wretchedness and hopelessness the political elites have worked so hard to create.

In a recent LendEDU survey of 1,238 employed Americans, it was discovered that 35% of respondents would permanently trade their right to vote in all elections for a mere 10% immediate raise in wage. 113 people in that same group indicated that they "would give up their child's or future child's right to vote in all elections for life" to get the 10% raise.[15] This is indeed a simply pathetic state of affairs to discover such civic poverty in the values of the people whose ancestors once built our great nation.

The Unholy Land

The restoration of virtue and unity transcend modern political idealism. I will demonstrate that the absence of these is indeed at the core of the decline in the United States. All the other items that I will mention after all have their roots in these two sets of standards.

2

Disorderly Conduct

"In Christianity neither morality nor religion comes into contact with reality at any point.¹⁶"

Friedrich Nietzsche
(1844 – 1900)

Most conscious adults realize that religion is broken and by now you are wondering what sort of myopic writer begins a book by stating the obvious in a saturated genre that already has enough volumes to fill a hundred libraries. It's a fair question, and thank you for asking. My favorite historical figure is President Thomas Jefferson. Even this prolific thinker would never dare to engage in a polemic book on this topic, advising:

"I write nothing for publication, and last of all things should it be on the subject of religion. On the dogmas of religion as distinguished from moral principles, all mankind, from the beginning of the world to this day, have been quarrelling, fighting, burning and torturing one another, for abstractions unintelligible to themselves and to all others, and absolutely beyond the comprehension of the human mind. Were I to enter on that arena, I should only add an unit to the number of Bedlamites.¹⁷"

Without completion of the first page of my text, the project is already doomed to fail in any effort to bring any enlightenment to the subject at all—and I should be considered a "Bedlamite" by my own American hero. This is neither helpful nor encouraging to ponder. To me, it sounds like Jefferson saying, "*You are on your own, here, buddy.*"

If Jefferson would not dare to bother with any of it, why would I attempt it? Why engage it all and risk the heartache, headaches, and the endless hours of work for the mere reward of criticism and public scorn? Who will bother reading it other than the critics? It's because I often see potential in people that they don't see themselves, in this case, my fellow Americans.

Another answer is because I have to. It would be impossible for me to have surveyed the landscape of my religious pursuits, having failed so spectacularly, and not make any attempt to examine why in an effort to get to the root of the issue. Oddly, only recently I discovered that the answer of this bizarre need comes from The Myers & Briggs Foundation. If Myers & Briggs are to be believed, then as an INTJ personality, I must fix things—I am hard-wired to make every attempt to improve processes and solve problems, more or less. I am compelled by an inner desire that never goes away and cannot be turned off. A description of folks with the INTJ personality type reads, in part:

"They have an inner world rich with endless possibilities. When combined with their Thinking-Judging (TJ) preferences, this gives them the drive to constantly improve everything. They are the strategists – the "better idea" people – of the typological world. Everything has room for improvement – words, plans, designs, ideas, even people. In the INTJ's eyes, even the best can be made better...Their capacity for intellectual and conceptual clarity gives INTJs the vision and the will to see things through to completion...Their tendency is to improve just about anything, even things that are working well. They'll want to fix it even if it isn't broken...As natural conceptualizers, INTJs are the perfect think-tank specialists – intrigued by the future, stimulated with a rich imagination, and supported by their willingness to be accountable. They are often looked to for solutions to complex problems.[18]"

The Unholy Land

I must agree that this does seem to be a startlingly accurate assessment of me. Because of this, I am always trying to make sense of the world around me, especially when it seems to make absolutely no sense whatsoever, as in the case of modern American Christianity—one of the most complex issues of all time. As a result, I have spent countless hours feverishly researching and hunting down the causes and attempting to find a solution. It is far more effort than should be expected from any lay person and one that has unfortunately taken a personal toll. It had to be done, and I believe that I have indeed answered many of the questions brought on by the problems that I set out to resolve, even if my immediate conclusion coincides with the observation of none other than Pontius Pilate, when he asked, "what is truth?"

In the 21st Century, Christianity finds itself on the ebb of a culture that again wants to forsake the message of the Gospels. The self-centered Western culture in particular has been slipping away from Christ's teachings for the last hundred years or even longer. To be sure, there is no shortage of critics, skeptics, and victims of those claiming to represent Christianity. The history of the practice of the faith provides plenty of ammunition against itself for anyone who wishes to use it.

This latest decline (let's say 20th century and forward) has been fueled not entirely by atheists or Agnostics, but instead by a broader group of liberal political elites and their willing accomplices in government, academia, and the media at all levels which has contributed to the miseducation, indifference and apathy of the masses.

Fundamentalist Christians, too, are guilty as well of twisting the Gospels and Christianity into new and bizarre manifestations of the faith, in order to fulfill their own personal, financial, or political ambitions. The result is something not Christian in nature or practice.

It is a mess to be sure and it is these issues that are the focus of the resulting work laid before you.

Even as a lifelong Christian, I have become a wholly reluctant but fervent critic of what passes for modern Christianity in so many places in America. The practice of the Faith has been often polluted and diverted away from its proper focus and genuine purpose with the advent of self-serving televangelists, country-club style suburban denominational and "independent" churches preaching all joy, love, and happiness, or alternately, hellfire and brimstone.

The Unholy Land

Then we have the "super-churches" where the pastor's message is merely piped into other local churches on Sundays on video because he is too big of a superstar to be seen in person by all his followers. *His* followers...not necessarily followers of Christ. It is almost as if precious little has changed since the first century when Christianity was in its infancy and anyone could claim it and create a new and strange doctrine around it. This continues today. **All of this serves to weaken our nation now.**

I have come to understand American churches differently today than I ever have before, and it's not good. After I was pushed away by people at the last church, I now ask myself what is the point in even going to church? I truly dislike what I have witnessed at most churches these days and who could blame me? From the time I was quite young and growing up, to as recently as a few years ago, I can hardly find a Christian church that (as a member, not a visitor) did not present me with some corrosive issue, tumultuous problem, unnecessary clash, or terminal turmoil—all "man-made" crises, not Christian or even Biblical issues.

I have been going to churches for decades. Now I must accept the quite uncomfortable uncertainty of the distinct possibility that I am simply neither any kind of Protestant nor am I a Roman Catholic. How was it possible for me to arrive at this desolate personal spiritual landscape over two years of self-imposed exile? Perhaps I'm not the only person with this problem.

This is a simple "tin-foil hat theory" for consideration:

[put on your tin-foil hat now...]

Americans have been put into a forced economic and cultural decline for the past sixty years, orchestrated by the oligarchs of the Leftist elite political class. They use constant monetary inflation and fraudulent trade agreements to undermine the American citizen's financial security, their ability to create lasting wealth with their labor, and achieve their personal potential to create and maintain intergenerational wealth. This in turn, forces a slow but absolute process of decline causing more and more otherwise productive citizens into a spiral of intergenerational poverty.

The Unholy Land

Like a giant vacuum cleaner, banks and corporate entities continue to suck up as much profit off the people as they possibly can, while returning to them pennies for their pay in proportion. Whatever people have left as disposable income after taxes, interest, inflation and mandatory insurance is simply not enough to create any lasting wealth of their own and in most cases just enough to get by month-to-month for the remainder of their lives.

The poverty causes the newly made poor to desperately search for answers, for hope, and there is our government—ready to answer with a few paltry handouts, funded by the taxes of those who still think working will get them ahead in life. Never is it quite enough to get out of poverty, but enough to nearly live comfortably relative to the poor in the rest of the world. This causes the intended effect of more dependence on government, and creates a mechanism to centralize all power to the political class—its true aim all along.

Americans are then left to wonder what happened to the "American Dream." While American politicians are perpetually promising that they are the source of "reform" and some far-off "future prosperity" in order to garner votes, the citizens are left to shift for themselves as best they can in an ever-declining, ever-expanding socialist state, complete with uncontrollable public debt and planned currency inflation.

Politicians who run our government then seize the political opportunity to promote class warfare promising to continue to wage a "war on poverty," with more and higher unconstitutional welfare entitlements, more stipends for college students, direct payments to illegal aliens, and by raising the minimum wage, which in itself is merely inflationary.

The proof that Americans are being played here can be discovered in the lack of any real positive results of these nefarious plans. In fact, every time government "solves" a problem they created, the results are even worse. All such programs have only resulted in higher taxes, more debt, and increasing inflation. Bear in mind that no nation in the world has ever spent or taxed itself into prosperity, which is the only plan our government has executed--tax and spend.

All this contributes to an ever-shrinking middle class –the "Forgotten Man," while the ranks of the poorer serfdom class continue to swell in the "wealthiest nation in the world." It is a nation with policies and regulations designed to cause exactly this. It is not at all accidental.

America is continually flooded with outside influences; namely infiltrated by masses of people not at all allegiant to America, its constitutional government, our laws, or our traditional cultural norms. Many of these are very hostile to the West. These are fed, housed, educated, and treated with medical services all paid for by the American taxpayer, who is constantly being bled dry of his earnings and his savings. These masses, when they do work, will accept below market wages, artificially forcing natural wages down. Some are promoted into public offices at every level and immediately begin the process of changing the regulations of the United States to crush the traditional American culture of liberty and the rule of law; instead forming policies that mirror their home nation, feed their own greed, and facilitate the Leftist agenda for America.

The abused American citizens look for hope. They search for meaning. They look to the church, but find nothing different; no holiness, little to hold on to and not much meaning. They may turn to drugs and alcohol to soothe them in their struggle. With it comes substance abuse and addiction—where again, government sets itself up as profiteer from the sale of alcohol, tobacco, and prescription pain killers and then presents the solution for addiction with programs and penal incarcerations. This, my dear reader, is the new "American Dream" of the elite political class—an America that is jobless, penniless, and bonded as servants to a political elite class; hopeless without their "help."

[remove tin-foil hat now]

Whether we can lend any credence to this "tin foil hat theory" or not, there is a significant body of clear evidence and data, both current and historical to support it or portions of it.[c]

What about the church? America has long been considered a "Christian nation." Today, 75% of Americans identify themselves as "Christians."[19] If that is so, then it would stand to reason that the charge for the maintenance of two key Christian social principles,

---

[c] I documented many of these concerns in Tears for Byzantium, Pub. 2017 New Plymouth Press, LLC

Unity and **Virtue** among the people should rest with American Christian churches. Not only that, but if we are a Christian nation, what about all the rest of the tenants of the faith?

A recent **Lifeway Research** study shows that the vast majority of self-identified Christians in the United States hold to beliefs that are not at all Christian and are in fact, heresies.[20] There is evidence that those self-proclaimed Christians surveyed are totally theologically incompetent:

"A full 60 percent agreed that "everyone eventually goes to heaven," but half of those surveyed also checked the box saying that "only those who believe in Jesus will be saved." So either these folks are saying everyone will eventually believe in Jesus, or they hired a monkey to take the survey for them."[21]

What we have witnessed across the past century and especially in the latter half of the 20th century is largely the abdication of this responsibility by Christians as a whole and a subsequent "falling away" of church followers. This falling away is reflected in the devolution of the practice of the faith, American culture, our elected officials, our laws, our economies, in our style of dress, our food, our music, our media, our attitudes, our values, our lack of business ethics, and the depreciation in the quality and depth of our personal relationships. How do American Christians stop acting as hypocrites and heretics? We will soon examine this as well.

Somewhat parallel to the United States stands the timeline of the Byzantine Empire, which was the largest and longest surviving Christian Empire on the planet (May 11th, 330 AD - May 29, 1453) It was finally crushed with the invasion of the Ottoman Turks. The Byzantines unfortunately also failed to maintain virtue and unity among their people. Why?

Are these two examples of falling away from the values which are supported by Christianity related? Perhaps these answers might not so difficult to discover. This has almost always been the case to a greater or lesser degree throughout the ages, certainly in the west and not only in America; The 16th Century Roman Catholic church was seen as departing from Christian values which became a primary catalyst for the Protestant Reformation. Today, these matters are just as problematic today for the post-Reformation Christians as they ever were.

Church attendance is on the decline in the United States has been trending that way for decades. When asked in a recent survey, "Worshiping alone or with one's family is a valid replacement for regularly attending church," 58% of American respondents agreed.[22] These see little or no value in attending church. Why?

Perhaps participation is more stable today than in years past, but not increasing either. In fact, when asked in 2016, Americans continued to believe that religion is really not as influential as it once was. In a survey that year, 72% of the respondents indicated that religion is losing its influence on American life[23]. That report also concludes, in part:

"The most significant trend in Americans' religiosity in recent decades has been the growing shift away from formal or official religion. About one in five U.S. adults (21%) don't have a formal religious identity. This represents a major change from the late 1940s and 1950s when only 2% to 3% of Americans did not report a formal religious identity... The increase in those claiming no religious identity began in the 1970s, with the percentage crossing the 10% threshold in 1990 and climbing into the teens in the 2000s.[24]"

To explain these trends one can delve deep into the ongoing study of Secularization Theory which is essentially an unending debate regarding how and why patterns of religion within a society either rise or fall over time. For a simpler and more direct explanation, the late Evangelist Rev. Billy Graham had his own opinions on the matter:

"The Christian faith has become a cheap faith because we too often live as if it has no value. We complain when the preacher runs over a few minutes on the Sunday sermon and consider it a great inconvenience to return to services once or twice more in the same week. No wonder so much of the world does not consider our faith relevant when we are not even willing to give of our time, much less our freedom or lives, for what we say we believe in.[25]"

Larger still looms the fact that both liberals and conservatives have used Christ to inject their own politics into the public square, as a propaganda tool for whichever political cause they may champion. It is the same technique that had been used by the Roman Catholic Church for centuries prior, and the ancient paganists prior to that. Americans though do have the choice not to tolerate it, and the proof that is "the dog just won't eat the dogfood" anymore—church attendance and memberships are not improving or are actually in decline.

In a recent article for *The Gospel Coalition*, writer Joe Carter lists the changing numbers of Protestant church membership in America starting from roughly 1950's/60's to 2012/13. Here is what he shows us[26]:

Christian Church (Disciples of Christ), decline of 67 percent.

Reformed Church in America, decline of 62 percent.

United Church of Christ (Congregationalist), decline of 52 percent.

Episcopal Church, decline of 49 percent.

Presbyterian Church (U.S.A.) (PCUSA), decline of 47 percent.

United Methodist Church (UMC), decline of 33 percent.

Evangelical Lutheran Church in America (ELCA), decline of 27 percent.

Lutheran Church-Missouri Synod, decline of 20 percent.

American Baptist Churches, decline of 2 percent.

Church of God in Christ, increase of 1,194 percent.

Presbyterian Church in America, increase of 790 percent.

Evangelical Free Church of America, increase of 749 percent.

Assemblies of God, increase of 430 percent.

African Methodist Episcopal Church, increase of 114 percent.

Southern Baptist Convention, increase of 46 percent.

What we see is a picture of many denominational churches in decline—but others increasing at a rather rapid pace. What is causing this shift? Mr. Carter proposed that "The mainline churches are finding that as they move further away from Biblical Christianity, the closer they get to their inevitable demise."[27] It would appear that he is correct. People who truly seek the genuine Christ and His Gospel cannot be fooled but for so long, and many of the denominations that are turning themselves into mere extensions of a political party are paying the price—a road to unpopularity and (one can hope) their eventual self-extinction. *Go woke, go broke*, the adage is true.

Other potentially contributing factors

Ask a conservative American about this trend and you might hear that an underlying cause is the deliberate invasion of America by millions of both legal and illegal aliens over the past decade or more has caused a forced dilution of many American values and has injected concern and fear across many in the Christian community.

Predominate religions and cultures in the geographies of origin for these millions of immigrants and illegal aliens are not necessarily friendly to or compatible with Christianity nor congruent with the traditional American culture. At the same time that Christian churches and their communities began to suffer from the "falling away" they were witnessing a massive influx of unfriendly foreigners facilitated by the American government's nonexistent immigration policy. These foreigners bring with them their own culture, standards, and religions which can and do begin to influence entire American communities.

Religious sentiment behind these trends might be summed up by people like Katelyn Beaty, editor at large for *Christianity Today* who stated, in part,

"In contemporary conversation about how Christians should relate to their [non-Christian] neighbors, there is a great mourning and coming to terms with how we have a new responsibility for living out the faith, differently than we did 50 or 60 years ago....Many white Christian communities are struggling, and probably reacting on some level of fear that the institutions and faith communities that have enjoyed promise and privilege and power in Western society are losing them.[28]*"*

The patronizing tone of this article seems to imply that "white" American Christians have "had their time" and now just need to "suck it up" and accept whatever anti-Christian sentiments the invading aliens have in store for our American communities—"sit down and shut up." As if Christ Himself is a pacifist, too.

Couple these events with the anti-Christian Obama and Biden Administrations who for years installed legislation and policies which are hostile to religious liberty and targeted at American Christians. This agenda has now been documented to have been supported and executed by their willing accomplices in media, academia, medicine, and so on.[29] It is little wonder why Christianity is taking it on the chin in the United States.

As far as church decline in America goes, these are the macro trends which are still evolving. And while it might seem fitting and convenient to try to pin much of the blame for the decline onto "illegal aliens who are invading our culture," there is a lot of something else going on here with many different factors to look at.

It could be that many Americans are actually now discovering that their own churches are becoming "politically aware" and that these churches are today supporting views, politicians, parties, and public policies that are quite contrary to the doctrine and dogma of the genuine Church and the Word of God. But what is the genuine Church? I have no idea how to answer that so early in this work, but we are going to investigate this question over the next few chapters until perhaps I can, or until they stop selling me Port.

Not content with the research of others, I surveyed a few people to gain some insight at the ground level. There were not enough respondents to form a valid scientific sample group and that was not the point. I was looking for personal experiences.

One such respondent of my survey was raised Roman Catholic, but as an adult is now he is Agnostic. I asked him why he abandoned Roman Catholicism as an adult:

"There was the pedophilia in my church. 3 of the 5 priests were pedophiles and some of the nuns knew about this and didn't do anything about it. I myself wasn't a victim of the pedophile priests but I knew kids who were. What also bothered me was the idea that I kept hearing from my catholic school teachers that Catholicism was the one true faith and that if you weren't a catholic you were doomed to hell or at best limbo...I couldn't believe what my teachers told me: that my friends who were not catholic were doomed. After high school I started reading about other religions and other philosophies, and found that there were things I like about them...God seemed too complex to me to be subsumed under the one religious brand. What also bothered me was the brutality of some of the teachers at my

Catholic schools. If you said something out of line or laughed when you weren't supposed to, too often you were physically punished, made to kneel on your hands, or stand in a corner holding a stack of books on your outstretched hands. I once saw a nun put a kid's head out the window and bring the window down on his neck." [30]

But this respondent did not give up on finding his peace. When asked about his present beliefs he wrote:

"My present belief is a diverse, multi-faceted, open faith. I study the Jewish faith and Catholicism and Buddhism, and existentialism and on and on. For me what's important is trying to understand life and make it better for everyone."

The vast majority of the remainder of respondents generally indicated that church was simply unnecessary for Christians. That somehow their "personal relationship" with Christ was really the only matter of importance. Church is seen as "imperfect," "optional" and viewed as something entirely separate from the notion of Christ or Salvation. This modern view got me wondering if the Christians of the First Century up to the Sixteenth Century would agree with that sentiment. Of course if the "church" experiences these people had were similar to mine or the Agnostic respondent to my survey; then of course there would be no reason for anyone attempting to be a Christian to attend one of these "churches."

Because of my own experience, I might suppose that the American Christian churches are failing due to their own ignorance, incompetence, and mismanagement. Mismanagement of budgets, time, resources, and relationships in many cases to be sure, but mostly the mismanagement of their service in their communities. They all take pride in their own invented dogma and doctrine; there is mismanagement of their message, and their own organizational structures. Leadership is terribly lacking today and in its vacuum, age-old pride and ego often fill the void and are now widely tolerated within church structures—used by people who are unqualified but believe that they "mean well," or worse, just there to make money.

We shouldn't at all be surprised by this. America invented the "self-esteem" movement in the 1990's where an enormous amount of focus was placed upon building the self-esteem of children beyond the rational. "Everybody gets a trophy because you are all winners!" This cultural program created children who came to understand that regardless of their level of education, knowledge or skill that the world is centered upon themselves—what they think, what they believe, what they want. As adults, Christianity can now be both an ornament they display as part of their chosen identity and a project they will control and manage according to their own opinions, demands, wants, and beliefs--and that is not genuine Christianity.

It is true for a whole lot of folks that they seek to be a part of something larger than themselves in their communities, and what better way for these "self-esteemers" to maintain or improve their own image of self-worth but to engage in a cause, an adventure, a movement---whatever it may be. For those who have no actual cause to promote or support, modern religion often affords them that opportunity. In the real world, a person might not have any skills whatsoever or even be a criminal, but in western religion he can often become whatever he wants to be.

It does not matter if you cannot balance your own checkbook, you can still be elected to serve as the church treasurer. It does not matter that you never even heard of Robert's Rule of Order, you can be the chair of the Deacon Board. Maybe you are a person who has the worst marriage—you can teach a couples' Bible study. A pedophile might help with the church youth[31]. If you're a "transgender" person then the Anglican Church hopes to hire you for their priesthood.[32]

American Christian churches become a modern "Fantasy Island" where, for a short time you can become another person and feel like an important part of something larger than yourself. For Christians, there of course can be no higher calling for a person of faith than to serve Christ. And so begins the disastrous train of well-meaning but unqualified, potentially inadequate, untrained, unstudied, ineffective, ignorant, and often plainly incompetent people attempting to help—but in reality running churches completely amok and into the ground. But, they say, good intentions always trump results especially when the churches rely upon volunteers. What are churches expected to do? Toss out everyone who isn't perfect?

The Unholy Land

Individual and petty church politics comes into play and always has at every church, I am told. We can only imagine the heavy-duty dosage of politics affecting the Vatican for many centuries now. But local churches of all stripes suffer from the effects of church politics. This is not of Christ but comes instead to us by the undefeatable pride and ego of mankind in his endless desire to attempt to manage God, His church, and his fellow man.

What happens today when people turn to religion, specifically to Christianity to find meaning and hope? Well, let me tell you, modern Christianity in America is a fickle mistress. I'm not going to share the following so that you can feel sorry for me. Please don't. I accept it as a valuable learning experience about Bible-thumping "believers." It did take me forty years to understand why all of this happened.

Growing up we changed churches a lot. I counted seven different churches we were members of in succession by the time I was fifteen, including a Swedish Covenant church and a long train of Evangelical/charismatic style ones. I knew then that we had left some of these churches under duress due to whatever circumstances had developed for my parents.

In adulthood, I can add five more churches with at least eight or ten more "visited" in between, covering most of the major protestant denominations. (We never visited a Roman Catholic or Eastern Orthodox Church.) Those were simply not considered. The biggest problem with these "churches" is that they were all "dead ends," as they never delivered on the "promises" they preached or arrived at anything that approached what they claimed to be about, personally or corporately as a church. These places all seemed to be comprised in a similar way; there were about eighty percent of their members who formed a "core group" and about twenty percent of the rest who generally drifted in for a year or two and then moved on to the next church. In adulthood, I always intended to be in the former group, but no matter my efforts, I ended up in the latter group.

Growing up, my Mom always tried to get me into summer Bible camps hoping to make sure I had some kind of Christian based anchor, and I can't blame her for that. About 1980, I was sent to some camp in Minnesota that seemed to have its own private lake. My camp counselor might have been a good guy; he was pretty young, too. You would expect that they would teach us kids all kinds of guy stuff like starting a campfire, carving a cross out of a twig, shooting a bow and

The Unholy Land

arrow, and playing horseshoes or something, but no. My counselor spent the week teaching us all how to tie a proper hanging noose from a length of rope. In retrospect, he probably needed treatment for depression or something.

When I add up all the singing, the bible study, and the preaching that went on at that camp I can't say that any of it left a lasting impression on me nor did it really help to develop a genuine Christian life habit. Decades later, I don't remember any songs or scriptures we might have learned that week, but I still know how to tie a proper noose.

When I was in the 9th grade, I lived in a single parent home. My Mom and I were part of yet another independent Evangelical style church. Money was always tight and we never seemed to have the resources we needed most of the time. There was a private Christian K-12 school there operated by this church and my mother, clearly understanding the rot and decay of the Minneapolis Public School System was able to get me into this little private school on a hardship waiver. It was promoted in every way as a "faith-based" school, but I was probably the financially poorest student there. I was put into an environment of upper middle class kids and had no idea that I was poor and attending for free--but the others sure did. It soon was made apparent to me and I was always by myself. I tried to make a few friends but kids are kids.

The curriculum was certainly much better than the public schools, although I had nine hours of "study hall" at school every week. There were mandatory Bible classes as any other class, like Sunday School all week long. I was able to keep up with my grades but certainly not destined to become a Rhodes Scholar. Classes began at 7:00am and the day ended at 3:30pm. After that it was a 1.5 hour ride home on the school bus. I lived the furthest away so I was the first on in the morning and the last to be dropped off. It was always a long day.

Within a few short months, I was soon forced out of that school—not because my grades were lacking, or because I was a troublemaker...or maybe I was. It was because my hair was an inch or more over my shirt collar— too long and deemed by the administration as "un-Christ like." That seemed ironic considering that every image of Christ seen anywhere in the world shows the Lord with really long hair. But by this time it had become obvious that my hair was truly not the issue; I was absolutely an odd duck and instead of anyone approaching me with anything resembling "Christ-like compassion," I was instead managed out of the school under a pretense of a dress code violation.

Realizing what was truly happening and why I was being sent away, it was the first time in my life that I ever took up for myself a bit. On my last day, I went to turn in my books to the various teachers. My math teacher had a class in session and I snuck in quietly and laid my textbook on his desk. He turned from the chalkboard and addressed me in front of his class, pointing at me and saying, "You know something Mr. Rundquist, you're never going to be President!" I stopped and turned to face him and replied, "Maybe not. But when I'm your age I won't be teaching 9th grade math." Satisfied with my answer, I left and walked home.

About that time, an Evangelical-style "Reverend" named Kyle befriended my mother at our church and quickly worked his way into our lives. I know what immediately comes to mind, and no, there wasn't any of that going on that I knew about. He wanted to "help" us. Kyle spent more time over at our house after work than he did at his home. Obviously his home life was lacking; we never once saw or met his wife. Perhaps if he had spent more time with his wife he would have gotten along better with her. I think this played out in his behavior.

This certain Reverend Kyle went to our church although he was not the pastor. He was always talking about God and he absolutely knew the words of the Bible cover to cover; well-intentioned, but his application of the scriptures was often misguided. He would bring us a bag or two of groceries now and then to keep us fed and I'm pretty sure he would leave us some little bit of cash on occasion as well. I know that he was well-intentioned. Kyle, however, saw himself as crusader of sorts, injecting himself into our lives to try in his own way to fill that void of a single parent family. He wanted to fix what he saw was going wrong with our lives while providing his version of a role model for me and my older brother. We became his active project. My brother and I would have none of it. As a teenager of fourteen, I despised Kyle. My older brother had no time for this nonsense and wisely stayed away—he soon moved out and was busy doing productive things with his life, like working full-time at a garage.

The Unholy Land

We saw Kyle all the time. All day on Sunday at church, then throughout the week here, there, at home—he was everywhere. I noticed that Kyle was always careful to deal with me away from my mother. I was forever getting lectured and scolded for who knows what by Kyle. He would always conclude by saying, "Be nice to your Momma; your Momma loves you." Hey, thanks for that revelation, Captain Obvious, —I wouldn't have figured that out without you.

Over the time we suffered him, Kyle inflicted us with his life stories. Through these stories, I gathered that Kyle had grown up on a farm sometime during the 1850's. He milked cows and goats, and probably sheep and horses, too—he milked them all to hear him talk. He wrestled bears and coyotes on the open plains. On his family farm at the age of ten, he dug ditches and wells with his bare hands while blindfolded at night in the rain; built barns, fixed tractors, invented the modern water tower and God only knows what else according to him. He went to school barefoot in the snow uphill in the dark while being chased by packs of wolves. He was a big, tough guy in his 40's now, whose rugged independence would have shamed Davie Crockett.

But Kyle thought that if he did it, everyone else should do it the same way; he was on a mission. Kyle was a man of the Bible and he knew that book cover to cover and could quote any passage of it, as if it were his own words. He liked to throw scripture around whenever he saw an opportunity for it. Because of his own beliefs in the Bible, he carried himself in a pious manner wherever he went. He felt that I needed a kind of Bible-thumping male mentor to make a real man out of me—he set himself up as part father, part pastor. He wanted to toughen me up. I was just not ready to take any pointers from a guy I absolutely hated—because he was certainly no father to me.

I recall once that the roof was leaking on our very old house. It was a two story house with the very high ceilings on both floors and a full attic so that roof was much higher up than on a typical two story house. Kyle was serious when he yelled at me for days for not just climbing up there by myself to fix the roof. After all, he had put a whole new roof on a barn by himself during a tornado when he was eight wearing only a loincloth while being accosted by wild bees.

The Unholy Land

But this was the twentieth century. We don't make teenage city boys who know nothing about roofing risk their lives on top of a nearly three story high building for the sake of a few shingles. We call a handyman or a roofer. Or better yet, it seemed that Kyle should put on his own tool belt, go fix it himself or shut his hole. I might have helped him if he had asked me to (I promise it would have been an unfortunate accident if he had slipped and fallen...). My making that suggestion would have been considered "disrespectful" and I was afraid it might get my teeth knocked in by the guy. Kyle shook his head, lamenting the situation and said I was just plain lazy. He never did fix the roof as far as I can remember; I think that my brother eventually had to come over and do it.

In his mind, Kyle created bizarre and dramatic constructs out of my normal teenage activity. I think it was so he could denounce whatever I was doing and inject imaginary drama into everyday situation—with laughable results. It was like having William Shatner following me around and verbally narrating the play by play of my life.

My favorite example of this was when I went fishing. When I was in my teens, I lived to go fishing. It was the top activity in my life. Nearly every day of summer vacation, rain or shine, I was out fishing somewhere. We lived a mile or so away from the Mississippi River and were even closer to a local tributary, Minnehaha Creek. The point at which these two bodies of water converge is the place I spent most of my time. This particular summer I was quite proud to have caught over two hundred fish.

One beautiful Sunday evening my friend Steve and I were at the point, out in our chest waders, standing on the very front edge of the sand bar, always perilously close to being washed out into the river while enjoying the fight of the smallmouth as usual. It was nearly dusk at the time and some other anglers on the shore had started a driftwood fire so they had some light. There were maybe six or eight of them, and they never bothered us.

I sort of liked the inaccessibility of fishing at this point where the creek met the river. Our parents would generally not come out there due to the distance and the rugged terrain, as you had to go down some three hundred feet on foot and hike a quarter mile through the woods at Minnehaha Park to get there. That was a bit imposing for aged knees. But on this particular evening, here came Kyle, with my poor dear mother in tow. It was a shock to see that he had found us and that he had dragged my Mom all the way down to the river's edge.

The Unholy Land

Apparently, it was not enough that I went to church with Mom and Kyle that morning. Kyle believed I should have been at church in the evening also. But I didn't take orders from him. I did mention to him many times that he was not my Dad. But let's not confuse his issues with mere facts. Here was Kyle, standing on the shoreline some hundred feet away from us in his Sunday best, his polished leather shoes sinking into the wet sandy shoreline. He outstretched his arms like Charlton Heston portraying Moses about to part the Red Sea, and began his long series of overly-dramatic pleas in a distinctly loud, clear voice;

"Danny!" No one outside my family ever called me Danny but him. "Please come back to your Momma!" His booming voice echoed across the river valley in that strange, almost accented tone of his.

Steve knew who he was only because we had talked about him. We looked at each other and smiled, ignored him, and continued to fish.

"Danny, your Momma loves you! Why do this to your Momma?" Kyle again pleaded loudly.

Steve and I continued to ignore him. We wanted the other anglers on the shore to think he had the wrong fellows. They were all looking at Kyle like he was crazy. He was acting the part for sure.

"Danny, please come home. Don't run away like this! Don't do it. You have so much to live for! Don't do this to your Momma. Your Momma loves you!" Kyle continued. And he kept repeating these phrases over and over, calling out louder and louder.

No one was running away from home. Maybe other teens somewhere in town were out partying, drinking or into drugs that summer night, but WE WERE FISHING AT THE RIVER. It's all we ever did, all summer long. Mom always knew she could find me there. This was as normal a teenage activity as any parent could hope for in the late twentieth century and Kyle made it sound like me and Steve were suicidal homosexual runaway heroin addicts camped out at a flop house and prepared to join a traveling circus the next morning. I said Kyle was no father to me—a Dad might have brought his own fishing pole and joined us boys for a while.

The Unholy Land

This was unfolding like a bad scene from a poorly rehearsed high school play. Steve and I had to turn our backs to him because we were laughing so hard we were crying and had to continue to pretend we didn't know him. Kyle continued to repeat these same exhortations over and over for nearly half an hour before they finally left in the dark. We made for home about an hour or so later when I figured Kyle had left our house; when I arrived, my Mom wasn't even angry.

Even though I could never be as industrious as my brother, I was not a lazy kid contrary to Kyle's belief. Having survived Kyle in 1982, I spent a part of the summer of 1983 stranded in Aspen, Colorado on some hair-brained quasi-religious summer work camp. I was roped into this by the perhaps well-intentioned but yet again, maligned, Kyle. The idea was that "summer work" was available there and some adult uber- Christian organizer named Bob rented rooms at an empty ski chalet (a glorified motel at the base of the mountain) at a very cheap summer rate. He then put four guys to each room, charged us each maybe $80 a week for rent and we were supposed to be able to clear some cash while spending the summer in Aspen, as the jobs in Aspen generally paid higher wages than the same jobs at home. He said most of the boys would come home with two to three thousand dollars saved up. It all sounded good and of course Kyle would have me out of the way for six or eight weeks.

I did not fly to Aspen. We could not afford the airfare. Instead, I tagged along with some of the other suckers—I mean participants, who were taking a private van. About half of the other guys were college age and already had jobs lined up from the previous year. I would have to go and find work on my own once in Aspen. I remember that we were required to attend the Pentecostal style church on Sundays and Wednesdays but most of the rest of the time we were free to come and go as long as we left our rooms before eight in the morning (they did a room check to make sure that we were not sleeping in) and had work in town. There was an evening curfew; we had to be back in our rooms by 10pm. Initially, we all took the city bus everywhere we had to go, but as the weeks wore on, I'd ride my bike that I brought with because that was free.

I tried to find work washing dishes or laundry at one of the larger hotel restaurants in town but the hotel manager would not hire me—even though he was looking for someone to work in the dish room. His reason surprised me.

The Unholy Land

"You're one of those boys from the Christian camp over at the Highlands, right?" He asked.

"Yes, that's right." I acknowledged. What--was it that obvious? It's not like I had a t-shirt that said "I'm one of those Christian camp boys."

The 1983 boy's group in front of the Aspen Highlands, the author on the right.

"Yeah, well we corrupted the last couple of guys from your group that worked here before," and all his help within earshot laughed. "I can't hire you. The camp director was pretty upset. I'm sorry."

I didn't know it was legal to pass a guy over for a job because he is a Christian. But I had no time to make a Federal case about it.

I had visited nearly every retail store in the town twice looking for work and was in Aspen for three weeks before I found a job. It was difficult to find work as a fifteen year old. Everybody knew that legally you had to be sixteen for work. Everybody, that was, but me...and Kyle. As a result I was less than truthful on more than a few applications as my rent tab was piling up, while my very small amount of cash was nearly gone because I had to eat. I was finally hired to clean animal cages and aquariums at the pet shop for a few hours a week. To supplement this, I took day work at Ballet West as a set up stagehand at $6.85 per hour for a couple of days while they set up shop.

Finally, after weeks of looking, I found some regular work as a part-time busboy for $4.50 per hour at a pretentious little coffee and croissant shop called *Pour La France*. While I was glad to have some work, it was clear that I did not fit in here with the whole wealthy Aspen crowd at all. The customers were aloof and snobby. But I worked hard and gave all I had to this work and was satisfied with it.

Because the food in Aspen was too expensive for me to eat out and I was nearly flat broke, I resorted to eating scraps from the plates in the bus pans and taking home stale food from the trash at the end of the night. I didn't think of it as garbage, but rather sustenance. What they were throwing away was certainly better food than I could afford.

The Unholy Land

Cheap thrills: We took an afternoon and scaled the Aspen Highlands in 1983; Author is the weirdo crouched on left.

After about eight weeks in Aspen it was time to go home. While I paid what I could on the cumulative rent bill, about 25% of it, the camp coordinator Bob came to settle up the balance of the rent, which of course I did not have. I hid whatever small amount of remaining loose cash I had, maybe forty dollars. The little I had earned at the café was mostly spent on food, and my pay from the stagehand job would not issue a check for another two weeks. He showed me the total of what I owed, about $300, then confiscated my 35mm camera and my beautiful Schwinn 5 speed bicycle that I had assembled myself with used bike parts. Then he said,

"You can hitch a ride with these other guys. They'll get you to De Moines, Iowa and from there you can take a bus back to Minneapolis. I want your parents to send me a check for the balance when you get there." Thinking me flat broke, he gave me maybe $40 for the bus fare—adding it to the total tab of what was owed.

The three guys and me hopped into their dusty green Nova and headed east. These other guys were all college age –everyone at the camp was older than me. They were all good guys and treated me well and to this day I am both puzzled and thankful they didn't just dump me off at a random truck stop in Nebraska or somewhere. But soon, in the middle of the night we ran out of gas and they woke me up in the back seat. I helped push that Nova across the plains all night under a full moon until we finally got to a gas station just before dawn.

The Unholy Land

I didn't eat much at all on the way home as I was saving as much cash as I could to make sure I would be able to buy that bus ticket back to Minneapolis. Over two days I had a single pack of crackers, a candy bar and one soda. I drank water from the hoses at the gas stations to stay hydrated. I gave the driver five bucks for my part of the gas money when they left me at the bus station in De Moines, then I bought my ticket, made a call home, and was soon back in Minneapolis.

Had I been sixteen, this trip might have been financially fruitful—but no one hires fifteen year olds and Kyle was an idiot for convincing my Mom to send me to Aspen to work over the summer. Let me rephrase that; Kyle was just an idiot. I would never consider sending my fifteen year old son on a trip alone like this, half way across the country and certainly not to a camp run by a Pentecostal zealot. The fact that I made it home at all is a miracle; it's not like we had cell phones, the internet, and GPS. I could have ended up anywhere never to see home again.

Why did this happen? Why would a Christian man trying to help a single parent family do all these crazy things?

Now at fifteen years old, a few of my own friend's parents had privately pulled me aside and let me know their concerns about me and my stage in life. Their conclusion was that there was no plan for my future in Minneapolis. It was not the input I was looking forward to hearing. They suggested that I go and live with my father as he would have a better plan for my life. As disappointed and upset as I was for hearing this, I could not deny the truth; they were right. And so it was in the course of a few minutes, I came to realize that my entire life, the place I called home, was about to be turned upside down and that there was simply no other way. The clock was ticking for me now.

My mother and I were close and the thing I dreaded most of all was breaking the news to her that I was going to have to leave home. I knew she would be heartbroken and upset as any mother would be. In order to avoid this sad confrontation, I formed a plan of my own to leave. Because I lived in south Minneapolis not far from the Mississippi River and I had read Tom Sawyer and Huckleberry Finn, it seemed "doable" to buy a used canoe and float myself down the river to Memphis, TN and then take a bus to Charlotte, NC where my Dad lived. Of course it would have been even easier to just take a bus from Minneapolis all the way to Charlotte, but that would be faster, safer, smart and efficient. Teenage logic is none of those things.

The Unholy Land

I had spent a couple of years fishing the Mississippi River and I could read maps and I understood a surprising amount of "river behavior" such as currents, etc. I had been working part time and could save up enough to buy a used single width canoe and some supplies. I had a National Geographic map of the entire river with its locks and dams, and was able to chart out my stops along the river each night. It would take me a projected three weeks to canoe from Minneapolis to Memphis. What could possibly go wrong? All of this planned in order to avoid telling my mother why I had to go.

But my father wisely advised me to explain to her that I was leaving, so he could form a proper and simpler travel plan. So I did, and it had the predictable results. Having returned from the Aspen debacle, I had only been home for a month or two when I announced to my mother that after being away from my Dad since age two, I wanted to go live with him in North Carolina. She was predictably heartbroken about it. I was much distressed for having to tell her my intentions to leave home. The Reverend Kyle was immediately called in. He came to the house to console her and when he learned why she was so upset he confronted me directly and away from her.

The Reverend Kyle demanded that I tell him why. Why did I want to leave home? Why "go against my mother?" Then he brought the Bible into the matter proclaiming that the Bible says, "children obey your parents." Then he said that my mother told me not to go and I was being disobedient and therefore I "needed discipline and punishment." He asked me why I was being disobedient to my mother and to God. He had decided to "correct me in the name of God" and then proceeded to beat the tar out of me. I was about half his size at the time and no match for him. It remains the worst beating of my life; I permanently lost some hearing in my left ear as a result of Kyle boxing my ear in. I acquiesced and waited until I was sixteen. And with the unspoken threat of legal emancipation, I was finally allowed to move away.

My mother did not see or even know how Kyle mistreated me, and I never said anything at all about it to her. I just accepted it as part of my lot.

Mom used to rationalize that regardless of the outcome that "Kyle meant well." My brother and I always countered this claim by reminding her that Adolf Hitler once "meant well," too. In his mind, Kyle was acting out his Christian faith. His own interpretation of the Bible led him to action and to justify beating up someone else's kid half his size. He certainly gave piety a bad reputation.

The Unholy Land

Kyle's own beliefs about what Christian service was had directed him to become an interruption, hazard, and a nuisance in our home while ignoring the issues in his own life and home. His own pride fueled his motivation for all of this, "Because I am a Believer, I am called to fix these people…" He was indeed acting out his faith…his faith in his own false interpretations of the Bible and faith in himself that he alone could accomplish something whether God wanted him to do it or not. He was his own twisted Pope.

Decades have passed for me now and as a person of the Christian faith, this entire episode is not something for me to be hurt, bitter, or angry about today. I certainly cannot go back and change these things that happened in the 1980's. Rather I look to the fact that some good did come out of all of it; years later I would come to understand that this entire series of events turns out to be a cautionary tale about the hazards of the main un-Biblical pillars of modern Protestantism: Sola Scriptura, religious pride, and personal ambition.

As an adult, the idea of church and dealing with other "church people" was no better for me. I suffered a long series of stressful and painful events at several different denominations across the next few decades. Some of these issues were external or political, many became personal.

At one church we really liked, we soon learned that the pastor was carrying on an affair with a woman in the church. It's probably far more common than we know, but it caused a split this otherwise fine little church, and this issue ruined the pastor's credibility and popularity in the community. The congregation felt as though they had to choose sides between supporting the pastor or not. It was all very ugly. We just left the whole mess.

The next church we joined we soon became attached to. We had a small group of close friends and thought highly of the pastor who was highly educated and a fine orator. Unfortunately, he returned from the denomination's annual conference to announce that the denomination had taken a series of hard Leftist positions on matters of public policy and politics that had absolutely nothing to do with the church, Christ, or the Bible. The Bible was contorted by them into supporting their new Leftist statements for the church. We had to leave that, too.

This denomination has since continued on that path and today supports full-fledged anti-American policies and has aligned itself along Anti-American and Socialist lines of policy. Plenty of Americans still attend there, perhaps completely clueless as to what they truly represent, even if all these measures are published clearly on their website today.

The next church we joined, I started serving on a few boards. Again we enjoyed a relationship with a community of friends there and loved our wonderful pastor. He is a perhaps the best orator of them all, and blessed with a singing voice that outshined the choir. I was eventually forced out of that church because I disagreed with the pastor about the denomination wanting to begin to permit homosexual marriages. When the issue came up, the pastor turned on me, attacking me personally and in public over a period of months for maintaining the same position both he and the church had maintained for decades prior--a conservative position. His defense was never Biblically based in these attacks; all he and the district representative would repeatedly say was, "other people see it differently."

Eventually some 48% of the voting membership DID share the same view as me, but it was not enough to vote the church out of association with their newly Leftist denomination. These two men worked for a year to both "convince us of our error," and to accept the idea, as well as bring in new members who would support their view before a vote could be taken. In this process the pastor used the local media as his soapbox, used fear by placing a long train of "alternative denomination" pastors in the pulpit so as to explore "other affiliations" we might later choose (becoming simply independent was never presented to the church members as an option by him.)

He took time off to write and print a propaganda book on the issue; a book which he later had the church purchase from him and then required all the adult Sunday School classes read as a class study text. This was the man who christened my own children. But in the end, he had hurt me greatly and had damaged our personal friendship and pastoral relationship beyond repair. He utilized all the political mechanisms available to him to further his cause, using the media, procedural delay, fear, propaganda, straw arguments, and many personal attacks which he carried out in public. I was not running for office, but it sure seemed as though he was. I had to go, and so did many others.

My last Protestant church was the most conservative of all that I had tried. At eight or more years, they had asked me to serve on the deacon board. It was not something I had ever considered or wanted, and had truly no idea what was expected of me. I had served on committees before both there and at other churches, but this was different, I thought. I agreed only in the effort to do my part. After the church at large voted and elected me, the deacon board elected me their secretary to keep the minutes and such. When in session, I requested a copy of the church's by-laws. I did not think my request was a big deal. I really wanted to understand what it was I was supposed to be doing in this office and I thought perhaps that the by-laws of the church would define this role. As their secretary and as a deacon, I needed to understand what was expected of me in duties and behaviors. At my request for these by-laws, the room full of deacons fell silent.

The pastor looked at me and said. "I don't think that's a very good idea." This suddenly struck me as odd and...wrong; I replied, "Well I'm not taking a survey or asking for a favor. I do need a copy of the by-laws." It turned out that no one in that room had seen the document in nearly twenty years. Only the pastor himself held a single remaining copy, and he was not about to republish it. What was he hiding and why? I followed up my request in writing to the Chair, but received no reply from him, and no by-laws. What I did receive was unexpected. My request was given to the pastor who became filled with rage at my persistence.

A few days passed and at their vacation Bible school event, the pastor there grabbed me in public, put his hands on me, shook me in anger and said, "I just want to bust your teeth out, and I'm a man who could do it." This was witnessed by others, and a few former deacons present in the room. His conversation after that consisted of a childish rant filled with accusations and name calling. I remained calm and silent so that he could finish yelling at me.

He liked to use the word "coward" a lot. He said "You hide behind your words," whatever that meant. Perhaps he wanted me to wrestle the by-laws from him physically instead of requesting them by letter.(?) When he was finished and out of breath, I replied that I was no coward. I educated him to the fact that a coward would not make a formal request for anything in writing to the appropriate person in the church. A coward would instead go to individuals and start rumors, undermine the pastor and the board and create dissention among the

The Unholy Land

members. I told him it instead takes courage to put thoughts on paper and put your name to it, as I had.

I then addressed this violent encounter and his unacceptable (and unlawful, as throttling another person is assault) behavior to the Chair, again in writing, and received no written reply whatsoever, verbal or otherwise. I then wrote an open letter to the other deacons on these matters, and two of them met me privately off campus, but still nothing was done, and I still could not get a copy of the by-laws. As their entire board had ignored my written repeated verbal and written requests for them to address all these matters, it became clear that it was time to go.

We soon transferred membership to another church of the same denomination a few miles away. Just as we were settling in there, a year or so later my good friend from the former church had started calling me every week to convince me to return. Apparently the pastor had retired, the by-laws had been republished to the members, and the church membership needed to be restored, for other families had dwindled away as well. He said they wanted us back, and needed us back. I eventually agreed and returned, taking my whole family with me. What we discovered was that most of what was going on at that church was not in compliance with their by-laws. It was apparent that the church had become a place operated by the will and preferences of the pastor alone. Now it had to be restored to the proper leadership, programs and governance clearly defined in their by-laws.

Soon, at a regular business meeting, after a brief introduction of the issue, I made a simple motion that that "the church immediately take steps to conform to its published by-laws." Based on the sudden reaction in the room, one would have thought that I had proposed that the church be converted to a Buddhist shrine. I stood in silence as I watched a much heated debate with yelling and screaming between the other members. Soon the vote came and the measure failed. 87% voted against this motion—they would not accept even their own by-laws now. In fact, they quickly started a "commission" to completely rewrite them, the purpose to modify these by-laws to conform to the present errant practices—which they eventually did.

Again, it was time for me to leave the same church in shame for the second time. There was no love at that church, only pride and personal politics supported by mass ignorance. In doing so, the organization has in effect relegated itself to the status of a Christian friendly club, not a holy church. When the standards, organization,

The Unholy Land

structure, doctrine, or dogma of the church can be changed on the fly by a simple majority of local people, this same thing can happen anywhere at any time. There is nothing in Protestantism that is concrete, and certainly not their wildly different "interpretations" of the Bible.

This last episode finally ended any and all future notions or attempts by me to consider joining any church anywhere for any reason. What's the point? Church membership almost always ends badly for me and I am "damaged goods" so far as my candidacy for membership anywhere in my local community—I had become a pariah now and I really could not care any less about a church membership at this point in my life. The quest was complete absurdity. American Christian churches have shown me to the street time and again—so what good are they?

None of these churches were truly holy or even about Christ when the facade was peeled off. Is this the Christian message of love, compassion, hope, and inclusion we have heard so much about? All these many Protestants chasing away Christians from all these churches?

I was taught early in life that "you can't judge God by His people." Right. This is the rationale I once used to tell myself time and time again—every time I had to leave a church. In reality, it is but a rationalization and it is unhealthy. I cannot judge God by His people because I know we are all flawed and only God is perfect. But you'll forgive me for wanting to pass on yet another potentially abusive church episode if I decide not to join one again.

The 1955 book "The Psychology of Personal Constructs" by psychologist George A. Kelly includes a definition for a "disorder" that reads:

"From the standpoint of the psychology of personal constructs we may define a disorder as any personal construction which is used repeatedly in spite of consistent invalidation.[33]"

In layman's terms the familiar adage might be true, that insanity (a disorder) is doing the same thing over and over hoping for a different result. Why in the world after a life filled with serial disappointments and abuses in and by churches and by church people would I ever seek to repeat the experience *yet again*? One would think I would have learned my lesson decades ago.

But according to the definition, every time I join another church with hopes of it being any better, I am only validating the fact that I have a "psychological disorder." I am sure that it is the same for a lot of people, but here I at least own up to it. My psychosis believes that somehow my faith in God will overcome the lousy circumstances repeatedly brought upon me by American "Christian churches." I knew that something had to change.

Perhaps I missed the the advice given in the Bible;

"As a dog that returneth to his vomit, so is the fool that repeateth his folly."

Proverbs 26:11
Douay-Rheims Bible

Perhaps I was not alone. While it had occurred to me during the research of this book that I have hardly ever had a "net positive" experience as a result of any church membership, it also had occurred to me that other Americans might have had similar experiences and so shy away from membership and attendance in the same way. Perhaps the same thing was killing churches. A recent survey indicates that 40% of American churches now see 49 or less attendees on average at their weekly services. The next 27% of churches see less than 124 in attendance.[34]

It would seem to be a logical theory to investigate by some skilled researcher as the statistics seems support this idea, at least on the surface. Is it a trend, a random coincidence or an attempt by me to validate self-pity? I simply don't know.

It is not so much that I have left the church, it's that I feel that the churches have left me, or were never truly "there" for me in the first place—over and over again. I am admittedly a bit jaded against church these days, and I have some advice for you if you are presently considering a new membership in a church.

These are hard lessons I have learned after five decades of church going and might save you some time and frustration. You can choose to be "successful" in a church or you can choose to be "happy" there: You cannot choose both.

To be "successful:"

- In order to be "successful" at a church, be obnoxiously ambitious. Be a superficially polite bully. Have a plan to use the church your way, to use its resources, and use the other members to fulfill your personal agenda regardless of the rules or the dogma of the faith. The weaker or quiet faithful will get out of your way and you'll be free to do whatever you like.
- Do not make any friends there, but if you do, be certain they are the "right" friends, connected to the most popular or wealthiest families. Vet your acquaintances carefully based on the merits of their connections, employment, social status, and resources to discover what they can do for you.
- Do not have an original thought about anything spiritual that conflicts with the pastor's personal view. Instead, try to influence his views by small increments so that he will start saying what you want to hear from the pulpit.
- Engage in a campaign of *virtue signaling*. Help others with food drives and other minor charitable things to make yourself feel better—remember that it's all about you. This also provides the basis upon which you can act more pious in the future, which can come in handy when you run for some church office later on.
- Focus and center your church experience only on your own satisfaction and what the church can do for you. Push to have the church to begin providing services that will benefit you and your family.

To be "happy:"

- Do not read any books not strictly prescribed by the denomination; just stick to the denomination's script. Going outside the lines here will cast suspicion on your faith as viewed by others.
- Remain quiet and do not engage in critical thinking of any kind. Simply indicate that you blindly believe what they say, even when it changes from time to time with the leadership.

- Do not try to help or offer to improve anything at the church; this just makes church people feel threatened because it assumes that whatever is going on there *can* be improved and thus your offer to help or your new idea must mean that you think whatever they are doing is deficient in some way. Because of their pride, they immediately become defensive of their turf. By default, you become a pariah for even suggesting it, so just don't do it.
- Whatever you do, never ask to a church body to operate according to their own church rules, constitution, or their by-laws. Even though they may publish them, it's really just an ignored formality to maintain their tax-free status. No one in the church even pretends to know what it says, and they will often operate however they please regardless of what these documents require of the church. Expecting them to operate according to their own rules is "old fashioned" and "out of step" with modernity. While *your* new ideas make you a pariah, the "church" needs the flexibility to attract new members so whatever others want to do (using that broad rationale) you have to accept it, even when it clearly violates their own by-laws, or even the Bible.
- To be "happy" at church, just do what I have been long advised to: go along with whatever the crowd does, drop a check into the plate, enjoy the various church amenities.
- The more docile and ignorant you are about their dogmas, the happier you will be there. In this case, ignorance is indeed bliss.
- Make your church experience centered on your emotionalism, feelings, comfort, and enjoyment.
- Above all, never forget that when it comes to church, no good deed goes unpunished.

That's just the way they all seem to like it. But there is an issue; none of this has ever been my way of doing anything in life, and certainly not my approach to any Christian church, so I recognize that I am the anomaly, the "problem" anywhere I go.

I'm not angry at God, I am angry at the men who pretend to represent Him. If you do go to church these days, go into church with the understanding that Christ will never abandon you, but the folks in the local church almost always will.

The Unholy Land

With all this pile of uncomfortable personal/religious baggage, am I not completely justified in never once darkening the door of an American church again? Well, let's see how the rest of this exploratory text unfolds before we seal my fate. As the Socratic British writer Gerald Brenan once said, "Wisdom is keeping a sense of fallibility of all our views and opinions."

All of these things and more, I believe, have contributed to a toxic stew of issues that is today driving Americans away from church. But the root causes of these issues go far back into the history of the Christian faith and church. Apparently the Protestant Reformation was not enough to save the church *from itself.* In fact, I will soon demonstrate that Luther's cure was worse than the disease he attempted to treat. My investigation here does not start with my bad church experiences or with all the religious problems in America. We must start at the beginning, with virtue and unity.

3

Virtue and Unity

"Only a virtuous people are capable of freedom. As nations become corrupt and vicious, they have more need of masters."

Benjamin Franklin

The human species is either given into the wildness of their many passions or governed by virtue. Today, it would be a snapshot reflecting our times to say that the application of basic virtues means taking responsibility for your life and actions. It means applying the moral willpower to not have children out of wedlock at age 14. Applying virtues means flat rejecting a life path of drugs, crime, and government funded (taxpayer funded) programs (including prison) and instead the will to apply oneself to actual productive work and independence so much as that is possible. Virtue means that the poor and the widows can rely upon individuals and church bodies (not American government) to assist instead of allowing both churches and politicians to exploit them for political gain generation after generation. It means rejection of false virtue signaling; for example, the new distorted version of virtue pushed by American Leftists would say that buying a new electric car to save the planet is "virtuous."

It is a grand understatement to say that the study of virtue is a deep and complex subject and yet one of paramount importance to America from our founding and today. From what I have seen in the American culture I am left to believe that the whole concept of virtues is wholly misunderstood and mostly forgotten these days. This is probably due to the fact that its very definition and practice not only has evolved as civilization has advanced, but lends itself to a large degree of subjective interpretation now, much like with interpretations of the Bible in modern Christianity.

Society has introduced the concepts of Relativism, Modernism, and Post-Modernism which have had the effect of deconstructing virtue. As a result, many cultural institutions (such as the Boy Scouts of America, for example) and businesses have developed their own "moral and ethical standards" based on their perception of virtue over time, and what behaviors they think will advance their own cause.

It would seem then, that virtue is the source for or connected with morality and ethics—which are unfortunately viewed as somewhat fluid today due to both ignorance and avarice. If virtue, however, is the foundational block of a civilized culture, then from where does true virtue originate? Americans today might well point to Christianity or "religion" or the American laws and legal system. However, this is not the case.

Consider for a moment the question why it was that our Founders and Framers in North America were able to craft a successful civic model, a Constitutional Representative Republic, which raised the standard of living to its highest level on the globe while across the same span of time South America is still plagued with crippling poverty, crime, corruption, and civil unrest.

The motivations for Europeans to explore and establish footholds in the New World (both North and South America) were borne from both religious and political events, and became quickly and solidly driven by economic potential. With the aid of advancing maritime technology, Europeans were able to successfully accomplish their goals in a relatively short period of time.[35]

Both North and South America share these similarities:

- Located in Western Hemisphere
- Abundant natural resources, including fresh water
- Suitable seasons for agriculture
- Access to two oceans and many natural inland waterways

- Similar overall climate variations
- Populated by indigenous people who are intelligent and teachable.
- Possess rich cultural heritages
- Indigenous history present
- Christianity introduced
- Connected to global economies and trade
- Early Colonization by European governments / slave trade issues

With all these similarities, why do we see the dramatic differences in political, economic, and cultural outcomes today? It is because in 1776, the Founders in North America firmly rejected the rule and the controls of the English Monarchy, the corruption of the Church of England and sought a new and different path of self-governance by a representative government and the rule of law instead of the rule of a single man. This had never been tried before. It was to be a grand civic "experiment," as our American Founders wrote, and it has been unrivaled in scope to this day.

For any of this to work for North American colonies, there had to be some common basis of virtue and unity among the Framers of the U.S. Constitution –not 100% unity to be sure, but enough to allow them to carry out the experiment and not devolve into anarchy or revert back to the authority of the Crown. The outcome was a system that allowed free market capitalism for individual citizens as well as giving them the reins of government. It was coupled with an accessible system for legal redress of grievances when the law is broken or in question. They created a system that with some later legal modifications would one day allow equal access to economic opportunities for all Americans. Today we have this and America has been the beacon of that freedom around the world since.

In South America, their leaders have embraced only the greed of Socialism and never stood for the rule of law, no matter how much they pretend to say the words to voters over and over again. It is a collection of nations often completely devoid of virtue and unity at every level of government and across all offices. The culture is now deeply embossed with an intergenerational expectation of control, corruption, and violence. As a result life is cheap and murder is accepted as just part of the South American culture.

The Unholy Land

While successive government regimes attempt to establish one socialist state after another, the result is always the same: bankruptcy, civil unrest, universal poverty and suffering for citizens. Socialism does not create wealth, it consumes it all. This is the inherent legacy of socialism anywhere it has been tried. South America is no different and today they cannot even aspire to embrace some form of virtue on a national level that would lift them out of this depreciative cycle of Socialist hopelessness.

"One of the great tragedies of mankind is that morality has been hijacked by religion. So now people assume that religion and morality have a necessary connection. But the basis of morality is really very simple and doesn't require religion at all."

Arthur C. Clarke

Some American Christians might be surprised to discover that virtue is not the sole propriety of Christianity. Jesus Christ indeed redefined virtue then and now. However, between 33 A.D. and 330 A.D. Christians were a fragmented underground minority group considered as an underclass of rabble and criminals. The Romans, at the instigation of the Jews, were blaming Christians for every wrong in the empire, and persecuting them as punishment for any real or imagined crimes. Christianity, therefore, could not at that time have been the source of the virtue of the Romans, for example. The Romans were pagans and drew much of their virtue from the earlier Greek pattern of gods and goddesses, etc.

Further, it would seem that the earliest examples of what I will call "foundational virtue" are to be discovered in the Bible's Old Testament. At the earliest ages, the pre-Millennial American generations were taught the Ten Commandments. It was a common teaching and there was hardly a church to be found without these on a poster or plaque tacked up in the youth rooms. It was Exodus 20:3-17:

"You shall have no other gods before Me. You shall not make for yourself a carved image—any likeness of anything that is in heaven above, or that is in the earth beneath, or that is in the water under the earth; you shall not bow down to them nor serve them. For I, the Lord your God, am a jealous God, visiting the iniquity of the fathers upon the children to the third and fourth generations of those who hate Me, but showing mercy to thousands, to those who love Me and keep My commandments. You shall not take the name of the Lord your God in vain, for the Lord will not hold him guiltless who takes His name in vain. Remember the Sabbath day, to keep it holy. Six days you shall labor and do all your work, but the seventh day is the Sabbath of the Lord your God. In it you shall do no work: you, nor your son, nor your daughter, nor your male servant, nor your female servant, nor your cattle, nor your stranger who is within your gates. For in six days the Lord made the heavens and the earth, the sea, and all that is in them, and rested the seventh day. Therefore the Lord blessed the Sabbath day and hallowed it. Honor your father and your mother, that your days may be long upon the land which the Lord your God is giving you. You shall not murder. You shall not commit adultery. You shall not steal. You shall not bear false witness against your neighbor. You shall not covet your neighbor's house; you shall not covet your neighbor's wife, nor his male servant, nor his female servant, nor his ox, nor his donkey, nor anything that is your neighbor's."

But contrary to common belief, the foundations of Christian ethics are not limited to the Ten Commandments. We find these passages in Micah and Isaiah, written in the 8th century, BC:

"He has shown you, O mortal, what is good. And what does the Lord require of you? To act justly and to love mercy and to walk humbly with your God."

Micah 6:8

"Wash and make yourselves clean. Take your evil deeds out of my sight; stop doing wrong. Learn to do right; seek justice. Defend the oppressed. Take up the cause of the fatherless; plead the case of the widow."

Isaiah 1:16-17

Even when the word, "virtue" is not expressly used, we see that the Bible lays out a pattern of living for mankind that is what we would consider to be virtuous. I found at least eighteen separate direct references to the words "virtues" and "virtue" in the Bible with only a simple search. Other ancient religious texts from around the globe contain similar ideals, and are beyond the scope of this discussion.

The Unholy Land

We might be surprised to learn that much of our modern Western tradition including our notions of virtue might have its origins in ancient Greece—not with paganist worship like the Romans, but rather with the advent of Greek philosophy. Socrates must be counted as the first or among the first to develop *virtue ethics*, a theory which was later further developed by philosophers Plato and Aristotle.[36] This, of course, predates Christianity by three centuries.

It seems that the original idea of virtue/ethics goes back to a group of normative ethical philosophies that place an emphasis on *being* rather than *doing*. Another way to say this is that in virtue ethics, morality stems from the identity and/or character of the individual, rather than being a reflection of the actions (or consequences thereof) of the individual.

Intrinsic virtues are the common link that unites the disparate normative philosophies into the field known as virtue ethics. Plato and Aristotle's treatment of virtues are not exactly the same. Plato believed that virtue is effectively an end to be sought, for which a friend might be a useful means. Aristotle states that the virtues function more as means to safeguard human relations, particularly authentic friendship, without which one's quest for happiness is frustrated.[37]

In Plato's *Republic* we read a discussion of what were known as the "Four Cardinal Virtues" – wisdom, justice, fortitude, and temperance. Virtue theory was significant to the study of history by more moralistic historians –Livy, Plutarch, Tacitus and others. The Greek idea of the virtues survived in Roman philosophy through Cicero and eventually incorporated into Christian moral theology by St. Ambrose of Milan. The Christian virtue theory was later given broad, comprehensive treatment by St. Thomas Aquinas in his *Summa Theologiae* and his Commentaries on the Nicomachean Ethics.[38] The Church Fathers of the Eastern Christian Church were also deeply engaged in the same kind of thought and writing.

Though the tradition eventually receded into the background of later European philosophical thought, the term "virtue" remained current, and in fact appears prominently in the tradition of classical republicanism or classical liberalism. This tradition was prominent in the intellectual life of 16th-Century Italy, as well as 17th- and 18th-Century Britain and America; indeed the term "virtue" appears frequently in the work of Niccolò Machiavelli, David Hume, the republicans of the English Civil War period, the 18th-Century English Whigs, and the prominent figures among the Scottish Enlightenment and the American Founding Fathers.[39]

In his *Nicomachean Ethics* Aristotle identifies and discusses his lists of virtues that enable a person to reach their human potential in life. He distinguishes virtues pertaining to emotion and desire from those pertaining to the mind.[40] The first he calls "moral" virtues, and the second "intellectual" virtues. Each "moral" virtue is a mean between two corresponding vices, one of excess and one of deficiency. Each "intellectual" virtue is a mental skill or habit by which the mind arrives at truth, affirming what is or denying what is not.[41]

Moral Virtues

Courage in the face of fear

Temperance in the face of pleasure and pain

Liberality with wealth and possessions

Magnificence with great wealth and possessions

Magnanimity with great honors

Proper ambition with normal honors

Truthfulness with self-expression

Wittiness in conversation

Friendliness in social conduct

Modesty in the face of shame or shamelessness

Righteous indignation in the face of injury.

Intellectual Virtues

Nous (intelligence), which apprehends fundamental truths (such as definitions, self-evident principles)

Episteme (science), which is defined as skill with inferential reasoning (such as proofs, syllogisms, demonstrations)

Sophia (theoretical wisdom), which combines fundamental truths with valid, necessary inferences to reason well about unchanging truths.

Aristotle also mentions several other traits:

Gnome (good sense) -- passing judgment, "sympathetic understanding"

Synesis (understanding) -- comprehending what others say, does not issue commands

Phronesis (practical wisdom) -- knowledge of what to do, knowledge of changing truths, issues commands

Techne (art, craftsmanship)

Aristotle's list above is merely one of many made by philosophers over the centuries. As Alasdair MacIntyre observed in *After Virtue*, many have attempted to formalize a list of virtues, including Homer, the Bible's New Testament authors, Thomas Aquinas, and Benjamin Franklin.[42]

In his book, *An Archaeologist Looks at the Gospels*, author James Kelso observes,

"The whole problem of ethics in the ancient world is a fascinating one. As the archaeologist reads the old legal codes, he sees a slow but gradual improvement in ethics. This was not a gradual evolutionary improvement since there were some striking peaks and some sickening depressions in this graph of ethical advance. But the mean average is a gradual improvement in idealism.[43]"

The advancement of ethics and such continued to raise the standards of the civilized world as the centuries rolled past. Eventually, the highest standards of human behavior for the world was delivered to us in eight beatitudes by Jesus Christ, and recorded in the Gospel of St. Matthew 5:3-10:

"Blessed are the poor in spirit, for theirs is the kingdom of heaven. Blessed are they who mourn, for they shall be comforted. Blessed are the meek, for they shall inherit the earth. Blessed are they who hunger and thirst for righteousness, for they shall be satisfied. Blessed are the merciful, for they shall obtain mercy. Blessed are the pure of heart, for they shall see God. Blessed are the peacemakers, for they shall be called children of God. Blessed are they who are persecuted for the sake of righteousness, for theirs is the kingdom of heaven."

Even George Washington, before he was sixteen years old had composed his own "Rules of Civility" which seems to be more about proper manners. This list includes 110 rules to live by and here we see some small nuggets of what may be considered applied virtue. [44]

A partial sampling:

21st: Reproach none for the Infirmaties of Nature, nor Delight to Put them that have in mind thereof.

22d Shew not yourself glad at the Misfortune of another though he were your enemy.

23d When you see a Crime punished, you may be inwardly Pleased; but always shew Pity to the Suffering Offender.

40th Strive not with your Superiers in argument, but always Submit your Judgment to others with Modesty.
41st Undertake not to Teach your equal in the art himself Proffesses; it Savours of arrogancy.

43d Do not express Joy before one sick or in pain for that contrary Passion will aggravate his Misery.

44th When a man does all he can though it Succeeds not well blame not him that did it.

47th Mock not nor Jest at any thing of Importance break no Jest that are Sharp Biting and if you Deliver any thing witty and Pleasent abstain from Laughing there at yourself.

48th Wherein wherein you reprove Another be unblameable yourself; for example is more prevalent than Precepts.

50th Be not hasty to beleive flying Reports to the Disparagement of any.

54th Play not the Peacock, looking every where about you, to See if you be well Deck't, if your Shoes fit well if your Stokings sit neatly, and Cloths handsomely.

56th Associate yourself with Men of good Quality if you Esteem your own Reputation; for 'tis better to be alone than in bad Company.

59th Never express anything unbecoming, nor Act agst the Rules Moral before your inferiours.

61st Utter not base and frivilous things amongst grave and Learn'd Men nor very Difficult Questians or Subjects, among the Ignorant or things hard to be believed, Stuff not your Discourse with Sentences amongst your Betters nor Equals.

63d A Man ought not to value himself of his Atchievements, or rare Qualities of wit; much less of his riches Virtue or Kindred.

65th Speak not injurious Words neither in Jest nor Earnest Scoff at none although they give Occasion.

70th Reprehend not the imperfections of others for that belongs to Parents Masters and Superiours.

71st Gaze not on the marks or blemishes of Others and ask not how they came. What you may Speak in Secret to your Friend deliver not before others.

79th Be not apt to relate News if you know not the truth thereof. In Discoursing of things you Have heard Name not your Author always A Secret Discover not.

81st Be not Curious to Know the Affairs of Others neither approach those that Speak in Private.

82d undertake not what you cannot perform but be carefull to keep your promise.

89th Speak not Evil of the absent for it is unjust.

The Unholy Land

108th When you Speak of God or his Atributes, let it be Seriously & wt. Reverence. Honour & Obey your Natural Parents altho they be Poor.

109th Let your Recreations be Manfull not Sinfull.

110th Labour to keep alive in your Breast that Little Spark of Celestial fire Called Conscience.

Washington's list seems to focus on how to properly deal with everyday issues—except for #59 where he cites what must be another list called the "Rules Moral." Such things as humility, conscience, respect, decency and suppressing personal vanity in dealing with others are addressed. I would again argue that all of these things have their root source in virtue.

Such a copious list would have been a natural thing for a young statesman such as George Washington to want to compile. It was a reflection of how he was raised, what he was taught, and what he saw in his sphere of influence. It was part of the American culture of his day.

But can we assume from this exercise of his that Washington was a Christian? Beyond what he had learned by the age of sixteen, it is not really clear whether Washington was a Christian or not. He refers to God most often as "Providence" (a common practice at the time) and scarcely even mentions Jesus Christ and then only in his public papers[45]. This has given rise to much debate as to whether Washington was a Christian, and all that is really known is that he was very private about his personal religious beliefs.[46]

Upon Washington's retirement from government service, there were those who wondered about his religious beliefs; they wanted to know if he was a Deist or a Christian. This desire sprouted creative attempts to have him finally weigh in on the matter. He would have none of it. Thomas Jefferson reported the event:

"When the clergy addressed General Washington on his departure from the government, it was observed in their consultation that he had never on any occasion said a word to the public which showed a belief in the Christian religion and they thought they should so pen their address as to force him at length to declare publicly whether he was a Christian or not. They did so. However [Dr. Rush] observed the old fox was too cunning for them. He answered every article of their address particularly except that, which he passed over without notice... I know that Gouverneur Morris, who pretended to be in his secrets & believed himself to be so, has often told me that General Washington believed no more of that system [of Christianity] than he himself did.⁴⁷"

Whether Washington and our other Founding Fathers were in fact Christians is not all that critical to our understanding of virtue. There are many both religious and secular paths that lead civilized people to virtue. The tenants of Judaism, Buddhism, Taoism, and so many other religious pursuits present the world with a path that includes a basis for virtue in some form or fashion. Virtue then becomes the general or common thing upon which civilized people can be expected to deal justly with each other—regardless how they arrived there. A "generic" virtue is the common denominator, and the key to a just society.

The Beatitudes aside for a moment, it stands to reason that if anyone can simply create a list of virtues, using whatever sources they choose or notions they imagine—or none as the case may be— then of what absolute value are they aside from the attempt at personal self-governance? What are the consequences of not following such an arbitrary list of virtues? If there are no impactful consequences, then what are they used for?

One man lives by some set of virtues, another does not--or adopts for himself a completely different set of virtues. What purpose do they serve? I liken this to the notion of sitting at the kitchen table and pretending to be the dictator, feverishly crafting a new constitution complete with a full set of written laws—to then attempt to enact them upon a nation that consists only of the house cat.

Pax Americana

The period of time we were living in for the latter half of the 20th century was referred to by historians as the *Pax Americana*, or the "American peace." I don't know what the official period we are living in today, but it doesn't look like much of that "American peace" remains. This period began in 1945 with the conclusion of World War II and was ushered along by the acceptance of postwar American policies around the globe that put America and our values at the center of economic and military objectives across Europe and elsewhere. While that may sound overbearing, it was not certainly not so in the old Roman Empire sense. Why? It is because Americans historically saw themselves as the peacekeepers in the Western World, and that was once viewed as quite a positive thing; less so today. The American writer Roland Hugins noted:

"The truth is that the United States is the only high-minded Power left in the world. It is the only strong nation that has not entered on a career of imperial conquest, and does not want to enter on it. [...] There is in America little of that spirit of selfish aggression which lies at the heart of militarism. Here alone exists a broad basis for 'a new passionate sense of brotherhood, and a new scale of human values.' We have a deep abhorrence of war for war's sake; we are not enamored of glamour or glory. We have a strong faith in the principle of self-government. We do not care to dominate alien peoples, white or colored; we do not aspire to be the Romans of tomorrow or the 'masters of the world.' The idealism of Americans centers in the future of America, wherein we hope to work out those principles of liberty and democracy to which we are committed This political idealism, this strain of pacifism, this abstinence from aggression and desire to be left alone to work out our own destiny, has been manifest from the birth of the republic. We have not always followed our light, but we have never been utterly faithless to it."[48]

He wrote that in 1917; sadly, in a post-9/11 America, it is no longer true in 2025. How would it be possible for American citizens to restore these important values?

The Marshall Plan to rebuild the postwar economy of Western Europe has been seen as "the launching of the *Pax Americana*." [49] It cost American taxpayers $13 billion dollars. The visible political symbol of the *Pax Americana* was NATO itself with an American Supreme Allied Commander.[50] But did this broad postwar American influence affect culture at home? Yes. The Pax Americana would eventually create a political platform for an opposite reaction.

Not surprising, nearly all modern American Leftists continue to criticize our nation's desire for international peace with false charges of "colonialism," "American Imperialism," and so on. The deliberately distorted and misconstrued image of America has driven the Leftists at all levels to an effort to redefine American culture. By the late 20th century, they would embark upon this task starting with undermining the foundations of the traditional American ethos and psyche. Nowhere was this effort more evident, overt or more successful than under both the Obama and Biden Administrations.[51]

American government, on the other hand cannot legislate either virtue or unity—try as it might. This is the folly of American politics today. The American government is a representative republic—*reflective* of the values of the people who elect those who are supposed to do the work of government. Legislators can make all the laws they want—but the actions (or restraint) associated with virtue originate from within a person, not from mere fear of breaking a law. If it were laws alone that were responsible for creating and maintaining virtue, then the jails would be empty.

Which brings us to this central question: do laws make Americans virtuous? We might as well ask if red lights stop cars. The answer is no. Responsible drivers who apply the brakes stop cars. We have many laws prohibiting murder, rape, theft, and so on—and yet all of these crimes, and so many more, are committed every day. Laws are merely the guardrails of society; but laws do not create virtue. Instead, in a free Republic, it is the virtue of the people that constrains bad behavior; their duly elected legislative body only creates just laws and applies them fairly and equally.

For another example; millions of Americans lawfully own firearms in the United States today. Yet we do not see multi-millions of gun crimes committed by these lawful gun owners. Why? Is it fear of the penalty of law alone that prevents them from robbing banks and killing people? No. Malcontents with guns will do bad things regardless of any laws. It is because lawful gun owners not only respect the law, but are not in the least bit inclined to ill use their weapons against their fellow Americans. In fact, many would say they would defend their neighbors if need be. There is virtue there—responsibility, and so on, residing in these people.

Alarmingly, the rule of law in the United States is today being ignored as a two tiered system of justice takes hold across the land. This development was ushered in by the lack of virtue in the nation. In fact the steady but absolute decay of virtues has led America to become the "whatever" state. This condition is not new and effectively highlighted by Lindy Keffer in an article titled, *Absolute Truth:*

"If there is no basis for moral decisions, then *whatever* you choose to do is fine. Of course, most people like to believe that they have *some* basis for the decisions they make. So we've constructed our own standards..."[52]

She mentions three such modern sources for our modern moral decisions:

- *Science and reason* ... "If I can't see it, hear it, smell it, taste it, touch it and test it, it can't be true," they say.
- *Popular opinion.* ..."catch the wave"..."choice of a new generation"..."everyone is doing it" and that you should, too.
- *"Feelings.*" "I did it because I felt like it."

But these of course are not anything to do with virtue as a basis for actual moral decision making. They beg the question, "Where do we find a genuine source of virtue today?"

Other issues often arising from this "whatever" state of our culture are things like moral relativism and Christian nominalism. These are natural outcomes of the successive schools of philosophical thought that dominated the twentieth century in the West, Modernism followed by Postmodernism. We won't spend time here on these two per se but to note that both of these outcomes are problematic to restoring the American cultural fabric. Overreaching "antidiscrimination" laws tend to have the opposite effect of their stated purpose. They cause even more animosity, more division among people, and often contribute to reverse discrimination. Government is not the source of virtue and unity and when it attempts to assume that role, cultural failure is certain.

Alexis De Tocqueville notes that:

"...I am among those who believe that absolute goodness is almost never to be found in laws."

American virtues, then, neither originated with nor resided in American government nor its jurisprudence, but instead rested in the hands of the people.

The Unholy Land

Unity

"So in Christ Jesus you are all children of God through faith, for all of you who were baptized into Christ have clothed yourselves with Christ. There is neither Jew nor Gentile, neither slave nor free, nor is there male and female, for you are all one in Christ Jesus."

Galatians 3:26-28
NIV

I like to believe in a grand, romantic notion that the American nation was founded in unity. I would like to believe that Christian churches are unified under Christ, but in truth, I know better than to believe that it is so—we know it's not. Either of these would be little more than a pleasant fiction. The reality of the historical record simply does not support that idea at all, and in fact proves the opposite was true. America ended its union with England as a result of both the actions and inactions of the Crown that were injurious to the colonists. The Declaration of Independence provides a list of such injuries which is then summed up in this manner:

"In every stage of these Oppressions We have Petitioned for Redress in the most humble terms: Our repeated Petitions have been answered only by repeated injury. A Prince whose character is thus marked by every act which may define a Tyrant, is unfit to be the ruler of a free people.[53]"

The true revolutionaries in America who subscribed to this line of action might at one time been considered the minority. There were the many Tories who lived in the colonies and fiercely loyal to the Crown of England, and in control of most of the institutions of the colonies. The people of the Colonies were politically divided from the start, either by fear, loyalty, ambition, or hope.

But for that small group of revolutionaries who were to be ultimately responsible for setting the nation on its course of perusing Liberty, Benjamin Franklin had this now famous advice:

"We must, indeed, all hang together or, most assuredly, we shall all hang separately."

This may be the only true example of an attempt at American unity then or now. Soon after the Revolution, when it was time for the Constitution of the United States to be ratified, there were unnerving and bitter divisions played out in debates on every point, at every stage. Federalist and anti-federalist factions sparred over so many details. So distrustful were they of each other that both factions kept separate recorded minutes of the meetings.

Divisions in early America were so awful that Alexander Hamilton and Aaron Burr resorted to dueling with pistols which resulted in Hamilton's death in 1804. Even Thomas Jefferson and John Adams were fiercely bitter rivals for a very long time until later in life.

Today, the disunity of the American populace has become the strategy. The modern political class is now manipulating the nation into a hopelessly polarized country. The total lack of unity in America today did not occur by mere accident or some natural anthropological or other cultural process. American politicians and their many allies and accomplices have orchestrated and executed a careful and deliberate plan to divide Americans and keep us at odds with each other on as many levels and for as long as possible. A divided populace is easier to control and pander to than a united one that seeks a common justice and accountability from its own elected government. A divided America is a defeated America. Alexis de Toqueville again states,

"Without common ideas, there is no common action, and without common action men still exist, but a social body does not. Thus in order that there be society, and all the more, that this society prosper, it is necessary that all the minds of the citizens always be brought together and held together by some principle ideas."[54]

Aquinas on unity in government

There was nothing particularly "American" about Saint Thomas Aquinas and his work. An effective and just representative government had not been known since the ancient days of the Roman Republic so it was not a "thing" to be considered in 1265. The status quo was that of a single ruler over all. Five hundred and eleven years later, the American Framers would challenge the norm of the single ruler and introduce the notion that "the best government will come from the rule of law rather than from one ruler." They would craft and codify a mode of government which was exceptional—the exception to the world filled with despots, kings, and emperors ruling over an imprisoned planet.

In spite of the differences in mode of government, Aquinas saw that unity was a key to the purpose of government:

"Management or government is guidance of the governed towards some good end, and involves unity; for no existence is possible without unity."[55]

Aquinas was not a statesman and followed what seemed to be a logical approach to government from his perspective which at the time was Monarchy as the normative system of government;

"Any government of a group aims at unity and peace, and since a number of people can't unify and pacify a group unless they themselves are first united, it seems that the best government will come from one person rather than from many."[56]

That solution might be thought of as a simple one, but history shows it certainly was often not the best solution. By 1265, when he wrote *Summa Theologiæ*, Aquinas and the world already had examples of fallen empires that in his mind might support his view. The Greek system of city-states had fallen away, The Roman Republic had given away to the Roman Empire, which itself fell in 476. Even the Byzantine Empire had been conquered by the Latin Christians of the Fourth Crusade in 1204, and ultimately ended on 29 May, 1453 with the invasion of the Ottoman Turks. Of course these empires were indeed run by "one person" and they had failed. Aquinas was correct that good governance involves unity, but he did not see a better way to unify. It would take the Framers of the American constitution to discover a better way, to craft a "more perfect union," a new American experiment governed by the rule of law, not a single ruler.

4

One Nation Under Gods

"The various modes of worship which prevailed in the Roman world were all considered by the people as equally true; by the philosopher as equally false; and by the magistrate as equally useful."

Edward Gibbon
The Decline and Fall of the Roman Empire

The many civilizations of the ancient world present us with a long history of subjecting themselves and their people to the will or favor of one or more deities. "Appealing to the gods" for health, wealth, victory in battle, or fair weather was always on the minds of the practitioners of the old polytheism of Egypt, Greece and Rome, for example. This would, as one might expect, involve prayers, various elaborate rituals, worship of idols, the erection of temples for worship and various sacrifices to the gods in an effort to get their attention and to curry their favor. Mankind has always sought to be noticed by "the gods."

This often included an earthly king or leader as a god or godlike persona an ancient custom. The notion of a co-gerent godlike ruler was an old concept even to the Romans who employed it. Probably one of the best and earliest examples comes from both Egypt and Assyria, in the latter starting about 1,900 B.C. to around 600 B.C. The god or gods of the Assyrians were not the same one of the Christians centuries later of course, but the process and effect for establishing a "holy ruler" on Earth was similar.[57]

The Romans carried forward this same notion from the Greeks and used the attributes of their various deities in an effort to control and even subjugate their people by attaching these same attributes to their Emperor or projecting them onto desired behaviors for the nation. The Romans in particular, having simply "run out of gods" at some point began to create secondary and tertiary gods called "personifications" which were supposed to espouse those virtues that government wanted their people to subscribe to and to follow.

In addition the nearly sixty Roman gods, there had developed an almost absurd array of these "personifications" to support the various values and approved civil standards. New ideas and personifications such as *Panes,* "goddess/spirits of the pantry," whom was there to support a full pantry of food in the home. It wasn't enough to just tell people, "Hey, it's a good idea to keep a full pantry at home in case the city comes under siege and we are shut in the walls for months." They had created a personification of the home pantry, who could help remind one to keep the pantry fully stocked.

It's difficult for us today with our Western, monotheistic eyes, to accept that anyone should submit prayers, worship or sacrifices to such a wide spectrum of gods or goddesses. But for the Romans, these polytheistic ideals were common and often quite serious matters.

If you were an ancient Roman trying to start a family it was indeed a religious production. There were no less than fourteen gods involved in the process of courtship, intercourse, and conception (sixteen if you add in Venus and Cupid), three gods to determine the correct timing of the birth, eight more gods involved in the act of birthing a child, six more gods to deal with the newborn child, and twenty-three more gods responsible in aiding development of the child[58]. That's fifty-six different gods to whom a Roman would have to maintain his religious practices in order to raise one child if he wanted them to help. As a Roman, you'd need a whole room in your home just to properly house all the small idols, called a *lararium.*

For the Roman Emperors, pagan gods were very useful tools in manipulating the citizens into behaviors favorable to the Roman Empire. No one ever actually saw their gods, even though they considered the weather, volcanic activity, earthquakes, and such as much a series of "signs" of them as anything else. Paganism was "safe" for the Roman Government because there was no physical deity/teacher ever attached to it who contradicted the government's status quo.

A New Faith emerges

Two things shook the old Roman ways. Initially, Judaism, which introduced the concept of the monotheism, was focused on the monotheistic God, Yahweh and offered the idea that there really was only one single God of the universe. Not a "central god" (like Zeus/Jupiter) and hundreds of other gods under him. This actually occurred long before either the Greeks or Romans and alone, was not likely much competition to the established Roman system. What was one more god to a Roman world full of gods? Take your pick.

Later, in the Roman occupied Holy Land, in old Jerusalem things were different. From here, a dusty Roman occupied land, a miserable little outpost of mostly "uncivilized peasants," out of Judaism followed Christianity. It, too, was contrary to the paganism of the day and offered its own radical concept: the same all-powerful central and single God of the Jews who was now seeking to restore His relationship with mankind by way of His human/deity Son to Earth. This claim completely challenged the prevailing paradigm of the religion of the Romans.

The Roman Government did not see much difference between Judaism and Christianity, in practice. But before the Jewish Revolt, Judaism and Christianity were soon viewed as a threat to the power and control of the occupying Romans. The Jewish leadership learned to work with the Romans to avoid conflict and unnecessary bloodshed of their people. And let's remember that both the Jewish and the Roman Governments exerted control upon their peoples using religion as a vehicle.

Christianity was different than both of these systems and began to spread rapidly; challenging both the Jewish and Roman *status quo*. It's a familiar discussion for most Christians.

Author Ramsay McMullen writes,

"From the very beginning, Jesus' disciples followed him instantly, without instruction; new adherents, by supernatural actions, were won to belief, or trust...[59]*"*

Ramsay refers to the first century acceptance of Jesus Christ by voluntary converts, not the later forced "conversions" as inflicted by some future governments. This is a key point, because these First Century Christians were genuinely concerned with the new teachings of Christ. They were not called "Christians" but simply referred to as "the followers of Nazarene" or "the people of the Way." After Christ's Ascension, the church was left into the hands of the Apostles and of His many followers.

Christianity would eventually change everything. Many theologians observe that throughout the history of Christianity this faith is different than other religions in one clear and obvious way. Nearly all other religions are centered on the never-ending quest of mankind seeking their god or gods, or using them to control the populace; Christianity is instead just the opposite— the story of God reaching out and seeking to reconcile with mankind through Jesus Christ, if they wish. It is an important distinction to bear in mind.

Christianity, being a different message of a new faith and hope, was left very much undefined (and civically illegal) at first and so, we discover that because the form was still taking shape that many various sects quickly formed around Christ's teachings—and many of these were not accurate, not faithful to the original teachings, or even good. Many were self-serving. Some were quite nefarious, for example, Jewish men attempting to force Jewish teachings back onto the early Christians as a method of "undoing" Christianity and attempting to make Christians more like the Jews instead of Christ. This might be viewed as an attempt at syncretism. At the time, with little detailed or established doctrine and without any New Testament Bibles, it was a wide-open field to any who wished to claim to start a church as a follower in Christ's name.

Central to the early and proper guidance of this new Christian Church was the Apostle Paul. An unlikely candidate—at first perhaps even *the most* unlikely candidate for such work. He soon proved to quickly become one of the most important and effective. Today we accept that through his travels, his teachings in the churches, and his letters, we discover both the practical instructions and theological support for Christians to operate as a **single** unified church, something that thousands of opposing self-proclaiming Christian denominations and sects lack today.

The Apostle Paul was inspired to expound upon the concepts of both Christian virtue and unity to these fledging outpost churches—it is certainly what was called for. Jesus Christ set the bar for virtue at its highest level for mankind in His landmark Sermon on the Mount. *Christianity, then, is to be the highest standard, not the lowest common denominator.* This one single sermon has spurred endless interpretations as well as centuries of ongoing debate.

Author James Kelso makes the observation that:

"With the coming of Christ, ethics suddenly becomes something completely different, something uniquely new. Now we have Christ Himself and his own standards as par! 'You, therefore, must be perfect, as your heavenly Father is perfect.' Paul caught the essence of the new ethical demand when he said, 'Be imitators of me, as I am of Christ.'"[60]

What exactly was so radically different about Christ-based virtues that were so threatening? Certainly the message was seen as an attempt to challenge not only the content but both entire systems of Roman Paganism and Jewish law and tradition, even though not in a hostile, militant way. Instead it was this idea that some other God and His followers were challenging the Theocracies of both the Roman Emperor/god and the authority of the Hierarchy of the Jewish Temple. The Romans were concerned with an armed uprising of these new Christians; Christ did refer to "His kingdom" which was seen as a potentially direct attempt at usurpation of the Roman Emperor, who only imagined that Christ was speaking of an Earthy Kingdom that was poised to overtake the Romans militarily. The Jews were more concerned with losing their power and with heresy in general. Neither group was prepared to yield their power or control to the followers of the teachings of some poor, falsely accused, convicted, and crucified man from Nazareth.

What were these new values that Christ brought to civilization? Probably the most concise description of the application of Christian based virtue is found in Paul's writings:

The Unholy Land

In the Book of Titus...

"Teach the older men to be temperate, worthy of respect, self-controlled, and sound in faith, in love and in endurance. Likewise, teach the older women to be reverent in the way they live, not to be slanderers or addicted to much wine, but to teach what is good. Then they can urge the younger women to love their husbands and children, to be self-controlled and pure, to be busy at home, to be kind, and to be subject to their husbands, so that no one will malign the word of God. Similarly, encourage the young men to be self-controlled. In everything set them an example by doing what is good. In your teaching show integrity, seriousness and soundness of speech that cannot be condemned, so that those who oppose you may be ashamed because they have nothing bad to say about us...For the grace of God has appeared that offers salvation to all people. It teaches us to say "No" to ungodliness and worldly passions, and to live self-controlled, upright and godly lives in this present age, while we wait for the blessed hope--the appearing of the glory of our great God and Savior, Jesus Christ, who gave himself for us...a people that are his very own, eager to do what is good. These, then, are the things you should teach. Encourage and rebuke with all authority. Do not let anyone despise you. Remind the people to be subject to rulers and authorities, to be obedient, to be ready to do whatever is good to slander no one, to be peaceable and considerate, and always to be gentle toward everyone. At one time we too were foolish, disobedient, deceived and enslaved by all kinds of passions and pleasures. We lived in malice and envy, being hated and hating one another. But when the kindness and love of God our Savior appeared, he saved us, not because of righteous things we had done, but because of his mercy."

...and again in a letter to the Galatians, chapter 5:

13 – 14 "...Rather, serve each other through love. All of Moses' Teachings are summarized in a single statement, 'Love your neighbor as you love yourself.'

...In the letter to the Philippians 4:8 where he wrote

"Finally, brethren, whatever things are true, whatever things are noble, whatever things are just, whatever things are pure, whatever things are lovely, whatever things are of good report, if there is any virtue and if there is anything praiseworthy—meditate on these things"

...from the letter to the Ephesians, 4:32:

"Be kind and compassionate to one another, forgiving each other, just as in Christ God forgave you."

In fact one could copy much of the New Testament in this list should he want to. Why? Because the New Testament writers had to continually lay out corrections and instructions to provide guidance for the behavior of the early Christian church—it was all new and they needed detailed help on how to live as a Christian.

Paul also tells the reader what to expect if Christian values are faithfully observed:

22-24 "But the spiritual nature produces love, joy, peace, patience, kindness, goodness, faithfulness, gentleness, and self-control. There are no laws against things like that. Those who belong to Christ Jesus have crucified their corrupt nature along with its passions and desires."

Apart from Paul, we see other examples, including this one from 2 Peter 1:3-9:

"3 According as his divine power hath given unto us all things that pertain unto life and godliness, through the knowledge of him that hath called us to glory and virtue: 4 Whereby are given unto us exceeding great and precious promises: that by these ye might be partakers of the divine nature, having escaped the corruption that is in the world through lust. 5 And beside this, giving all diligence, add to your faith virtue; and to virtue knowledge; 6 And to knowledge temperance; and to temperance patience; and to patience godliness; 7 And to godliness brotherly kindness; and to brotherly kindness charity. 8 For if these things be in you, and abound, they make you that ye shall neither be barren nor unfruitful in the knowledge of our Lord Jesus Christ. 9 But he that lacketh these things is blind, and cannot see afar off, and hath forgotten that he was purged from his old sins."

The Unholy Land

There are plenty of references to Christian unity that we may discover in the Bible. I won't list them all here for the sake of brevity, but here are a few that come to mind:

"1.Therefore if you have any encouragement from being united with Christ, if any comfort from his love, if any common sharing in the Spirit, if any tenderness and compassion, 2 then make my joy complete by being like-minded, having the same love, being one in spirit and of one mind. 3 Do nothing out of selfish ambition or vain conceit. Rather, in humility value others above yourselves, 4 not looking to your own interests but each of you to the interests of the others .5. In your relationships with one another, have the same mindset as Christ Jesus: 6 Who, being in very nature God, did not consider equality with God something to be used to his own advantage; 7 rather, he made himself nothing by taking the very nature of a servant, being made in human likeness. 8 And being found in appearance as a man, he humbled himself by becoming obedient to death—even death on a cross!"

Philippians 2:1 -8

"Whoever claims to love God yet hates a brother or sister is a liar. For whoever does not love their brother and sister, whom they have seen, cannot love God, whom they have not seen. And he has given us this command: Anyone who loves God must also love their brother and sister."

1 John 4:20-21

As we exit the First Century we are left with the notion that our true Christianity was that of a new direction in religion; one of scope and purpose beyond oneself, structurally redefining both virtue and unity with essentially Paul's writings and others shaping the single, unified, and enduring Christian church. Here we see that that for the Christian, the modern basis for the two things we are after, virtue and unity, can be discovered at the origin of First Century Christianity. Paul writes to the Corinthians:

"Now I beseech you, brethren, by the name of our Lord Jesus Christ, that you all speak the same thing, and that there be no schisms among you; but that you be perfect in the same mind, and in the same judgment."

1 Corinthians 1:10
Douay-Rheims Bible

My immediate task is to ask what happened to this Church, where did it go and can it be found anywhere in the world or the United States today? Or is it just an unobtainable ideal today? Is it an invisible thing, a vapor that cannot be touched but only ever be imagined or hoped for?

5

The Christianity of the Ancient Byzantine East

"The Christian ideal has not been tried and found wanting. It has been found difficult; and left untried"

G.K. Chesterton
From *What's Wrong with the World*

For the first two centuries, Christianity was a religion of social outcasts who were often arrested and executed for their faith; however, with the advent of the Emperor Constantine and the Byzantine Empire, Christianity had finally been legalized, accepted, supported, and its interpretation by laity somewhat more complicated because of its role in the world and with the political realities of tying church and state together. Over the course of centuries, the Byzantines truly shaped the foundations of much of how we observe Christianity in the West today including the Christian Church calendar.[61]

The Unholy Land

If one were searching across the ancient world, looking for an example of how to or how not to practice Christianity as a society, both examples might well be discovered with some of the many emperors of the Byzantines. All might have been well intentioned, but flawed government from the start. One cannot work to support his own political interests and truly serve the Gospels first at the same time, it seems. We soon will see that the political class cannot and should not attempt to meddle with the matters of the Holy Church.

With the advent of Christ and this new Christian set of ethics, there were two possible outcomes: 1) that society would accept the new standards and embrace changes that would result in modifications to law and the moral code, or 2) it would be rejected as a threat to the existing structure and as such, would necessarily be discredited and eliminated as quickly, and as possible. In the case of Christ, both of these events occurred, although centuries apart. His teachings were initially embraced by relatively few followers, as the power structure rejected and eliminated Him, as best they thought they could.

When Constantine the Great established the Eastern Empire that we call Byzantium, he faced a series of challenges in converting the remnants of the time established old pagan polytheism inherited from the old Roman and Greek practices into this new organization that called followers of Christ. Constantine might have initially seemed an unlikely candidate for leadership in the adoption of Christianity. He was not a priest nor a theologian but rather a cunning soldier, a brilliant tactician, and a talented politician. As it turned out, this is exactly the kind of strong leader the Faith needed to secure its advance.

Constantine, however, was not a "nice guy." He'd had his own wife and child murdered, and historians today still do not entirely understand why. As a political and military leader he was a totalitarian. But God uses the vessels of His choosing, and so it was with Constantine. He was bold, effective, and strong. For the first time since the birth of Christ, Christianity had a champion at the highest level of government, and the faith could be practiced without fear of persecution or imprisonment.

With the birth of Constantine, we see how the stage was set for a champion of Christianity to emerge; the period where Christianity is finally validated and begins to expand. The same doctrines and dogmas that the early church had faithfully followed since 33 A.D. were now publicly codified and canonized by the Church as they began to address

The Unholy Land

church structure and defend against the many various heresies. Clergy seemed to have more time now that Christians were not being flogged and fed to lions. Elements in the practice of Christianity become practiced in the open; Gregorian style chant, the use of incense…while the imagery of crucifixes were introduced into the Christian church among other things.

Although Constantine the Great later paved the way for the advancement of Christianity with the Edict of Milan in 313 A.D. by legalizing it, restoring confiscated property back to Christians, and ending the persecutions, it was not until the reign of Theodosius I (AD 379 to AD 395) that Christian ethics and virtue would be fully supported and embraced as the general rule of an empire.

From the start, it was rather inconvenient for Constantine that the Gospels alone do not address or specifically condone the religious assignment of an Emperor to rule over Christians civically with the authority and endorsement of Almighty God— at least from a modern viewpoint. But the Bible does not repudiate it either. Christ tells His followers "to give to Caesar what is Caesars'," but would the expectation under a Christian Emperor versus a pagan one be different?

The role of the new Christian Byzantine Emperor was for a short time perhaps a bit in question at the founding of the empire because of the "newness" of a legalized Christianity. Constantine's solution was to present the people what they were already used to—a continuation of the Roman-styled Emperor who was generally co-equal with "the Gods." Only now it was to be the God of the Christians. The process Constantine instituted to install himself was ultimately little different than the pattern used by his pagan predecessors, but it would be an error to call the arrangement Caesaro-Papism.

"The Byzantine commonwealth was ideally to be governed by two 'ministries.' The imperium and the sacerdotium…The Orthodox believed Christ to be true God and true Man. It is this teaching that they converted to political terms. Thus the [Church] Fathers subordinated the imperium to the sacerdotium, having related the former to the 'humanity' of Christ and the priesthood with His 'divinity.' Together, as a religio-political organism, governed by mutual accord…or diarchy of powers, they would govern the Christian commonwealth."[62]

The Byzantines had crafted a hybrid political system were both Church and State were originally designed to operate as a single unit with separate roles.[63] Metropolitan Timothy Ware explains,

"The life of Byzantium formed a unified whole, and there was no rigid line of separation between the religious and the secular, between Church and State: the two were seen as parts of a single organism. Hence it was inevitable that the Emperor played an active part in the affairs of the Church. Yet at the same time it is not just to accuse Byzantium of Caesaro-Papism, of subordinating the Church to State. Although Church and State formed a single organism, yet within this one organism there were two distinct elements, the priesthood...and the imperial power; and while working in close co-operation, each of these elements had its own proper sphere in which it was autonomous, Between the two there was a 'symphony' or 'harmony', but neither element exercised absolute control over the other." [64]

John I Tzimisces (11 December 969 - 10 January 976 A.D.) was the lover of Empress Theophano, whose adultery led to the murder of Emperor Nicephorus II and John's elevation to the throne. It may seem ironic then to western eyes that here we see John being blessed by the Virgin Mary with the hand of God reaching down to crown the Emperor on the reverse of this gold coin of the period, and the bust of Christ on the obverse. It was treachery that raised him to the throne of Byzantium.
Photo courtesy of www.forumancientcoins.com.

This new style of civic establishment also became part of the public promotion and advertisement of the new Christian Faith. Through this series of rather complicated ecclesiastical gymnastics by the patriarch, Constantine was soon installed as the co-gerent of Christ Himself. A viceroy of Christ for the Byzantines, leaving Christ "in charge" of the heavenly realm while the Byzantine Emperors would be established by God to manage the civil aspects of the inhabited portions of the planet. The Emperor was now invested with the power of God on Earth, His chosen instrument of God's Will to rule civilly in the minds of the Byzantines.[65] Much of this investiture, however, was only appearance and not absolute.

"The legitimacy of the Emperor's sovereignty, civil power and authority was specifically under Christian judgement. The legal status of the Emperors...depended upon their Orthodoxy, good standing in the Church, and obedience to ecclesiastical canons...the Emperor was not a minister of the word and the holy Mysteries. The Emperor could not impose doctrine upon the sacerdotium, let alone Christian society...The somewhat sacerdotal functions of the Emperor were, in fact, a continuation of the fiction of divine appointment which originated with the Roman cæsars..."[66]

To modern Western eyes—and almost certainly to average Americans today, people are unlikely to believe that God needs such an Earthly manager. He's the Almighty, so why would anyone assume that He needs anyone to manage Him and His affairs here on Earth? But things were seen differently in the past. Well defined processes to organize and to manage society were established that still exist to this day, and not only utilized by the Eastern Orthodox and the Roman Catholic Churches.

This, I suspect, may have been the very germ of the flaw that eventually grew incrementally into an irreversible chain of events over the centuries that ultimately contributed to Byzantium's political undoing; the first sin of all sins, pride. Because it was inevitable that there were to be installed "bad" Emperors and usurpers, the applications of religious standards by these might be spuriously suited to fit a forceful Emperor's goals. Mixed with what we know are the insatiable motivations of the political class in general, this would eventually result in a series of subjective civil objectives over time that were crafted to serve some other purpose than support for the Church or beneficial government of the people.

As a result, these interpretations quickly devolve into varying degrees of abusive government policies used against the people to overtax, consolidate power and control to a single ruling group or elite class, more centered on self-aggrandizement instead of focusing on the responsibilities of the office—and quite regardless of the input of the Church.[67] I realize that serious scholars may well disagree with this bit of oversimplification, and I reserve the refuge of the possibility that my assessment may be skewed.

Theology aside, the government of the Byzantine Empire from a political standpoint was not necessarily about Christ's commandment of love or the Beatitudes, but rather an Earthly organization of power to advance political and economic influence and cooperation with the Church. Power corrupts, and absolute power corrupts absolutely, the old maxim goes, and there was to eventually develop certain periods of power struggle and strife between the leaders of the Church and those of the state.

In Constantine's time during the 4th Century, there was a coordinated effort of great magnitude to spread Christianity throughout the empire. Constantine and his immediate successors up to the First Crusade had executed their plan to convert the pagan empire of the Roman West, centered in Rome, into the Christian Empire of the East, centered in Constantinople.

The new ways of Christianity were to be different; after all, Monotheism was nothing like the old known polytheistic pagan religions. "Signs" that today we know as weather and other natural occurrences in the world were no longer attributed to any number of Roman deities. A storm was just a plain storm now, an earthquake was a curiosity again—these events and others were no longer the gods of the Romans speaking to people. People formerly attached to the signs and other symbols of the old religions had to have something new to cling to in Christianity. But how best could this new replacement religion be efficiently and rapidly communicated and taught to pagans throughout the Empire? The production of books was a new technology being developed, but it would be centuries before books were commonly available and accessible to ordinary people. The Bible as we know it today had not yet been organized, or assembled and would not be until after the First Ecumenical Council of the Church in 325 AD and later.The individual books of the Bible had not been canonized by the Church and there were not even chapter or verse numbers added at this time. Even if books had been available, literacy of the public was a

The Unholy Land

secondary concern. There were other forms of effective media that could be employed.

Maximizing media

Pagan symbols were quickly repurposed and adapted for Christianity to be employed as a broad brush on the blank cultural canvas that would become Christendom. There is still much debate and uncertainty over exactly when and how this transition occurred.[68] If we look at just one of the oldest traditional Christian symbols that appeared prior to Constantine, the fish or Ichthys-acrostic, we discover that early Christians were already employing symbols to represent their Faith. The "Christ-fish" appears in places as early as the Second Century, first known to us in the composition of the ancient Greek *Sibyllina Oracula*, which contains compositions of various dates.[69]

Funerary stele of Licinia Amias, one of the most ancient Christian inscriptions. Upper register: dedication to the Dis Manibus and Christian motto in Greek letters ΙΧΘΥC ΖΩΝΤΩΝ / Ikhthus zōntōn ("fish of the living"); middle register: depiction of fish and an anchor; lower register: Latin inscription "LICINIAE AMIATI BE/NEMERENTI VIXIT" ("Licinia Amias well-deserving lived ..."). Marble, early 3rd century CE. From the area of the Vatican necropolis, Rome. Photo: Marie-Lan Nguyen, 2006

There are many theories about how the symbology of the fish translated to become a mark of Christianity. It is perhaps because the five letters that form the word "fish" in Greek are also the initial letters if the phrase, "Jesus Christ, God's Son Savior."[70] Some say it was connected to the commemoration of the miracle of the loaves and fishes. Others say it was because Christ Himself said to His Disciples, "I will make you fishers of men." In any event, the fish as a symbol of Christianity had certainly taken hold even prior to Constantine.

Constantine instead used the sign of the Cross and the now familiar Chi-Rho symbol to represent Christianity after a "heavenly vision" he had in 311 A.D. He and his successors then proceeded to use symbols and imagery created from the Gospels to begin to fill this huge void as a strategy to educate and illuminate the masses about the new Faith. This imagery was communicated and disseminated throughout the known world the same way it had been for centuries prior by the pagans— through the mediums of art, architecture, and especially coinage. Together, these mediums largely served as the many blank canvases upon which the symbols and concepts of Christianity would be spread and supported.

Coinage of Decentius, c. 350 A.D., a Western Roman Emperor featured the Chi-Rho symbol adopted by Constantine; Issued relatively early on in the empire and spread over a broad geography.
Photo courtesy of forumancientcoins.com

The Unholy Land

A Byzantine gold coin c. 976 A.D., featuring Christ holding the Gospels on the obverse, the Imperial family on the reverse. This is classic Byzantine style material of the period.
Photo courtesy of forumancientcoins.com

Constantine and his successors would broadly expand the use of these images in official imperial materials, official document seals, and use the media they knew best could spread the word, coinage.[d] The currency of the day was always an effective medium for the State to use for any message it wanted to spread throughout the Empire. The Romans had used their coinage for propaganda for many centuries prior to the founding of Constantinople. Everyone in the empire and beyond used empirical currency for trade, taxes, and savings. As coinage touched nearly every individual in every walk of life and required little literacy for comprehension, it would be still be an effective medium for the Emperor to spread the Christian message across the land just as it was for the pagan traditions that preceded it. The Emperor also visually attached himself to that message at the same time.

Author Harold Lamb writes of emperor Justinian's approach to the altar at another church, St. Eirene one Christmas Eve,

"While the choirs recited their story, a curtain was drawn back from the dais. There Justinian alone in a simple mantle with diadem, lighted the candles at the altar, and the choirs intoned: 'Now Christ is born, who gave the crown to kings...'[71]"

It took many decades for the fabric of Christianity to be carefully and thoroughly woven into the Byzantine culture this way. Over the next 500 years, almost everything there became Christian

---

[d] For a useful comprehensive survey of this numismatic topic see the monograph by Frederic W. Madden, Christian Emblems on the Coins of Constantine I the Great, His Family and His Successors, Published 1877 – 1878, reprinted.

The Unholy Land

. The images of the old Olympian gods were slowly replaced by Christian ones. Visages of Jupiter were replaced with Christ and the Olympian gods were replaced with the Apostles. Temples of the Olympians were repurposed as Christian churches or torn down and the materials reused elsewhere.

Media messaging was key for the Byzantines to support both their emperors and their Theology. Mosaics and other images like this can be found all across churches and buildings in the former Byzantine territories as well as on their surviving artistry and coinage.

The art and architecture of Byzantium became another large canvas for a new official religion. From the Early Church forward, individual paintings of Mary the Theotokos and the Holy Family and all the Saints (known as holy icons) were used for prayer in homes and churches.

Both art and architecture would be employed extensively throughout the empire to communicate the ideas of this new religion. Magnificent domed churches were erected for the first time—an engineering wonder that world had never before seen.

John Beckwith notes that:

"From the time of Constantine onwards there was a constant stream of precious offerings from the metropolis [Constantinople] to the Holy Places...from the sixth century onwards religious subjects begin to appear on imperial commemorative medallions in gold."[72]

These churches were then filled with the (now) priceless artistry that is truly "iconic" Byzantine material. A mere fraction of this magnificent work survives today. Gilded portraits of Christ and the royal families and courtesans covered everything from ceilings to walls; gold and ivory inlays on furniture; gold, silver and jewel encrusted book covers for their Gospels; complex mosaics filled with Christian symbols; images captured every nuance of emotion and subject of the Christian faith—and at times, the emperor's connection to them.

The Unholy Land

During the Byzantine Period, the architecture of the Christian Church truly takes its classic form. Building so many churches required much public funding though, and by the sixth century the theological (and clearly financial) bond of holy authority with the emperor was clear. Emperor Justinian (ruled from 527 to 565) was a great patron of the Church. He had built the grandest of all churches on Earth—the Hagia Sophia or Church of the Holy Wisdom, or Divine Wisdom.

Example of a Byzantine Icon, Theotokos and Christ child

With the design and construction of this church, first finished in 360 A.D. the Byzantines introduced new concepts in architecture the world had never known prior. These techniques are the Cross-in-square floor plan and the pendentive dome, a construction solution which allows a circular dome to be built atop a rectangular floor plan. While preliminary forms had already evolved in prior examples of Roman dome construction, the first fully developed pendentive dome dates to the reconstruction of the Hagia Sophia in 563.[73] This same church still stands today in what is now Istanbul.

It was such a large church operation at the time, that it required some four hundred to staff it. Justinian describes that the clerical staff of the church would consist of sixty presbyters, one hundred deacons, forty deaconesses, ninety subdeacons, one hundred and ten readers, twenty five singers, and a hundred doorkeepers.[74]

Copies of many of these Christian features and symbols can still be found today, echoing over and over into the Western world and eventually spilling into America. Today you can still see little bits and pieces of Byzantium in the later architecture of America if you know where to look. Saint Nektarios Greek Orthodox Church in Charlotte, North Carolina is actually a miniature copy of the Hagia Sophia, for example.

The Unholy Land

For the Orthodox Church and its faithful scattered across Byzantium, these images and the architecture were not simply artistic expressions as one would discover in any art museum, these were an important part of the very fabric of their faith. Within each image and structure was a ministry of the faith designed for the eyes, just as a sermon heard is ministry to the ears. This was not "art" to the Christians of Byzantium. Everything from the incense to the images and architecture was and is used by the Orthodox Christians to minister to the faithful engaging all five senses to orient the faithful towards Christ and His Holy Church.

Defending the Faith

Even with their new found freedom from persecution, (and perhaps due to that) it became apparent that Christian unity was needed as different sects and new heretical ideas sprouted up under the leadership of various emerging religious upstarts. For this purpose the First Ecumenical Council of Nicaea was called in 325, presided over by none other than Emperor Constantine I himself.

This council gave Christians for the first time, the canonized books of the Bible and soon after, the Nicene Creed in 381, which is still recited in every Eastern Orthodox Church around the world today. The Creed was an attempt to form a single list of the core tenants of the Faith and stamp out the growing heresy of Arianism at the time, a sect which denied the Deity status of Christ[75]. The creed was also useful to verbalize the unity throughout the Christian church then and now:

"We believe in one God, the Father, the Almighty, maker of heaven and earth, of all that is, seen and unseen. We believe in one Lord, Jesus Christ, the only Son of God, eternally begotten of the Father, God from God, Light from Light, true God from true God, begotten, not made, of one Being with the Father. Through him all things were made. For us and for our salvation he came down from heaven: by the power of the Holy Spirit he became incarnate from the Virgin Mary, and was made man. For our sake he was crucified under Pontius Pilate; he suffered death and was buried. On the third day he rose again in accordance with the Scriptures; he ascended into heaven and is seated at the right hand of the Father. He will come again in glory to judge the living and the dead, and his kingdom will have no end. We believe in the Holy Spirit, the Lord, the giver of life, who proceeds from the Father. With the Father and the Son he is worshiped and glorified. He has spoken through the Prophets. We believe in one holy catholic and apostolic Church. We acknowledge one baptism for the forgiveness of sins. We look for the resurrection of the dead, and the life of the world to come. Amen."

The effect of this landmark Council has been summarized as:

"The great council convoked at this juncture was something more than a pivotal event in the history of Christianity. Its sudden, and, in one sense, almost unpremeditated adoption of a quasi-philosophic and non-Scriptural term — homoousion — to express the character of orthodox belief in the Person of the historic Christ, by defining Him to be identical in substance, or co-essential, with the Father, together with its confident appeal to the emperor to lend the sanction of his authority to the decrees and pronouncements by which it hoped to safeguard this more explicit profession of the ancient Faith, had consequences of the gravest import, not only to the world of ideas, but to the world of politics as well."[76]

Saint John Chrysostrom

The ancient Church was shepherded by many different holy men who dedicated their lives to the task of serving the Church. While there were many important early Church Fathers we cannot possibly list them all. But one cannot discuss much of the advancement and application of Byzantine Theology without mentioning the work and influence of Saint John Chrysostom (c.349 – 407).

A Byzantine mosaic of St. John Chrysostom
from the Hagia Sophia, Istanbul, Turkey
(Image public domain)

The Unholy Land

The scope, depth, and volume of St. John Chrysostrom's contributions to ecclesiastical teaching and literature for the Church are both compelling and astounding. As Archbishop of Constantinople, he was an important Father of the Early Church. He was known for his preaching and public speaking and his denunciation of abuse of authority by both ecclesiastical and political leaders.[77]

The epithet Χρυσόστομος (Chrysostomos, anglicized as Chrysostom) means "golden-mouthed" in Greek and denotes his celebrated eloquence in speech. Chrysostom was among the most prolific authors in the early Christian Church and his work forms much of the basis of the Eastern Orthodox tradition today, and echoed by many since. He is certainly a very central figure in Byzantine Theology.[78]

His teachings were centered on the application of that simple and universal First Century Christianity during a period in history where the Church in Rome was beginning to pursue policies of self-aggrandizement, centralization of power and control, building wealth and influence, and often twisting the Gospels to suit political agendas, or ignoring them to avoid facing the obvious errors of ways. His sermons and other writings typify the view of Eastern Orthodoxy even today;

"Consider how [Jesus Christ] teaches us to be humble, by making us see that our virtue does not depend on our work alone but on grace from on high. He commands each of the faithful who prays to do so universally, for the whole world. For he did not say 'thy will be done in me or in us', but 'on earth', the whole earth, so that error may be banished from it, truth take root in it, all vice be destroyed on it, virtue flourish on it, and earth no longer differ from heaven."[79]

"Do you wish to honour the body of Christ? Do not ignore him when he is naked. Do not pay him homage in the temple clad in silk, only then to neglect him outside where he is cold and ill-clad. He who said: 'This is my body' is the same who said: 'You saw me hungry and you gave me no food', and 'Whatever you did to the least of my brothers you did also to me'... What good is it if the Eucharistic table is overloaded with golden chalices when your brother is dying of hunger? Start by satisfying his hunger and then with what is left you may adorn the altar as well."[80]

St. John Chrysostom subscribed to a simpler Christianity, no doubt attributed to the influence of the experienced instructors of ascetic life, the presbyters Flavian and Diodorus of Tarsus from when he was about the age of twenty-five.[81] As a priest, he took Christian service seriously:

"As a priest, Saint John zealously fulfilled the Lord's command to care for the needy. Under Saint John, the Antiochian Church provided sustenance each day to as many as 3,000 virgins and widows, not including in this number the shut-ins, wanderers and the sick."[82]

St. John is honored as a Saint in the Eastern Orthodox, Catholic, and Anglican Churches, as well as in some others. The Eastern Orthodox, together with the Byzantine Catholics, holds him in special regard as one of the Three Holy Hierarchs alongside Basil the Great and Gregory of Nazianzus. In the Roman Catholic Church, he is recognized as a Doctor of the Church. Other churches of the Western tradition, including some Anglican provinces and some Lutheran churches, also recognize him. The Coptic Church also recognizes him as a Saint.[83]

At the same time the competition between the Sees of Constantinople in the east, and Rome in the west was still going on and becoming more pronounced as the years wore on. Today we might compare some of the chain of these events to the period during the 20th century when America engaged the Soviet Union in a great race into space. This was happening concurrently with the Arms Race of the Cold War, in both cases each superpower nation engaged in massive development programs in an effort to keep pace with and outdo the other nation in technological prowess, scope and power of these programs on a global scale.

It was not so different for the Byzantines in their time. The difference is that they were in a race to defend the entire church body against the developing ascendency of the Papacy of Rome, which was gradually trying to usurp the collegiate structure of the canonical Christian Church and establish a religious Monarchy. Of the five Sees of the Christian faith, Rome, Constantinople, Antioch, Jerusalem, and Alexandria, there was a degree of continual competition to establish sway over all Christendom—but none more intense than the competition between Rome and Constantinople.

The Unholy Land

Across the centuries this involved tools such as skills of diplomacy in spreading the faith to new geographies first (establishing a "Greek" or "Latin" church first), wars and skirmishes over a vast territory, and the collection, accumulation, and careful placement of holy relics and the possession of these Christian relics was key. The logic being that the ownership and control over of these relics created a kind of religious *gravitas* for Christians. The relics were (and continue to be) a draw for the people; the more of these relics one had concentrated in an area, the more people who would make pilgrimages to come and see them, venerate them, or pray to be healed by God's Power and Grace when in their presence.

Of course all these Christian pilgrims would require goods and services during their stay and could be taxed. We cannot overlook the potential for economic effects in all of this. The relics had other effects as well; they might well embolden the soldiers defending the empire, and so on.

Constantinople was in direct competition with Rome and the Churches in the capitol city of Byzantium had accumulated or were rumored to have had a staggering number of important Christian artifacts. These numbered some 3,600 different relics of Christ, the Virgin Mary, and 476 Saints, in addition to many Old Testament artifacts.

A very partial list includes:

- The golden vessels, which the Magi brought with their offerings.
- The "swaddling clothes" of the infant Jesus
- Sandals worn by Christ
- Stone jars said to contain the remains of the bread when Christ fed the multitudes.
- The stone well cover where Jesus spoke to the woman at the well.
- A letter written by Christ in his own hand to the King of Edessa (which disappeared in 1185.)
- The small marble table on which Christ celebrated His Supper with the disciples.
- The Cross of Christ's Crucifixion as well as the crosses of the two men crucified alongside Him. (These were eventually chopped into splinters and distributed over centuries.)

The Unholy Land

- The hammer, the gimlet, and the saw, with which the Cross of the Lord was made.
- The pillar against which Christ was scourged
- Christ's Crown of Thorns
- The lance that pierced Christ's side
- Two of the nails used in the Crucifixion (The third nail was thrown into the sea by Constantine's mother to calm a storm)
- A red slab of marble where Christ was laid after the Crucifixion
- A crystal vial containing the blood of Christ –kept at St. Sophia in Constantinople as late as 25 March 866.
- The "holy towel" of Edessa used by Christ to wipe His face
- The Virgin Mary's girdle and robe
- Tombs of St. Andrew, St. Luke, St. Timothy
- The remains of St. James
- The tunic of John the Baptist
- The hair of St. John
- The iron chains of Saint Peter
- The bodies of Prophets Daniel and Isaiah brought to Constantinople from Jerusalem.
- The rod of Moses
- Samuel's horn of oil
- The bronze trumpet of Joshua, who took Jericho.
- Noah's hatchet
- Wood from Noah's Ark used to make the original great, gilded wooden main doors to the church of St. Sophia

What is more, a nation possessing these relics could use them in many different ways. Certainly they were an attraction to Constantinople for Christians. They could impress visiting dignitaries as was often the case in Byzantium. For example, to impress a visiting dignitary, the emperor or patriarch in Constantinople might break off a single thorn from the Crown of Thorns and give as a gift to a visiting king.

When the Byzantines needed to establish an important new satellite church in a remote region of the empire, they might carve off a splinter from the True Cross and encase it in gold and glass to be housed at that church. No other church in the area would have such an important relic. It would assure that the church would continue to draw the faithful in crowds and spread the influence of Byzantine Christianity. People would flock to the town and visit the church hoping to be healed by the grace and power of the Cross. A church so endowed was sure to be successful.

For the same reasons, a local church might apply to the Emperor for a relic to be placed in their church. If the province was faithful to the Emperor, paid their taxes, did not participate in sedition, etc. then perhaps—just maybe—the authorities in Constantinople might send them a relic of their own which would put that little town on the map. Pilgrims would come and stay in the village, improving the economy of the village and the church would likely increase in attendance and contributions. We do see here that the relics could potentially be used for some subtle political manipulation by a calculating emperor.

It is during this entire Byzantine period that the Church faithful continue to work to reflect the entirety of their adoration, reverence, devotion, and respect for Christ and the Virgin Mary (Theotokos) into the practices of the Faith, which is quite evident still today. Christianity here develops into a fine art form, seen in paintings, mosaics, statuary, architecture and music. This collection of arts assumed a trifecta of purposes—these were used in prayer and worship and the holy icons in particular were seen as protection for the church and its capitol city; they served to educate and communicate the details of the faith to the populace; and were used to impress upon the outside world the glory of the Christian God.

Nowhere was this impressive display more evident than at the grand cathedral of Hagia Sophia in Constantinople. In the 10th century, Prince Vladimir of Russia sent an envoy to Constantinople and after having visited the great church, they famously reported back "We no longer knew whether we were in heaven or on earth...nor such beauty, and we know not how to tell of it." The ultimate result of the visit had the intended consequences for the Byzantines:

"The [10th] century ended with the Baptism of Rus into the Orthodox faith - an event that influenced all aspects of Rus from politics and trade to art, music, literature and architecture."[84]

As a result, Russia has been a Christian nation since 988 AD, and by the Grace of God the Orthodox Church survived the attempts of the Soviet Government (who were atheists) to extinguish it for 80 years during the 20th century. Eastern Orthodox Christianity continued on its same path after the Roman See split away from the remaining four

The Unholy Land

churches in 1054. Thereafter, a somewhat uncomfortable situation was made even less comfortable over time.

The 13th Century would begin with the Roman Catholic Latins of the West invading and sacking Constantinople in 1204 with the disastrous Fourth Crusade, an event that that Byzantium would never recover from. Western Latins would then try to run the remains of that empire from Constantinople for 57 years until finally giving it up. But they would not be the last invaders.

By 1453 the Byzantines had regained some small semblance of a nation. A mere fraction of what the empire was at its apogee. The Ottoman Turks, led by Mehmet II, made it clear that Byzantium would soon be at its end. They laid siege to the capitol city in spring of that year. However, Mehmet had sent correspondence to the Emperor stating that he only wanted the city itself. While Mehmet's army outnumbered the Byzantines ten to one, he was not interested in bloodshed. He had even offered safe passage for all the citizens and all their belongings if Constantine XI would simply agree to the peaceful surrender and evacuation of the entire city of Constantinople. The last Emperor of Byzantium flatly refused.

While the army of the Ottoman Turks laid siege to Constantinople in March or April 1453, the Pope in Rome did essentially nothing to send reinforcements to help their Christian brethren in the East, and almost no other kingdoms that the Emperor appealed to had sent any aid. It would appear that Byzantium was out of favors, and the West simply let it happen. Perhaps that old adage is true; the enemy of my enemy is my friend. It was finally over for the Byzantines on May 29, 1453 when the invading army overran the city and the Emperor was killed, still defending the city walls.

Mehmet, however, did not destroy the Christian Church; looted perhaps, but not ruined. He allowed the Greek speaking inhabitants to continue in their faith. This was the genesis of Greek nationalism; the period where civil concerns became imbedded into the faith for the Greeks. For Muslims of the day, there was no distinction at all between holy religion and civil law. Following this pattern, and ignoring the protests by the church officials, the Turks turned the Orthodox Church in Constantinople into a kind of miniature Greek state with the church officials elected to govern over the Greeks as "Entharch" or "ruler of the Greek people." That went on for some time until the Turks eventually saw their own power ending decades later. By this time, the Greeks had "nationalized" Orthodoxy and it has been so ever since

In 1794, the Eastern Orthodox Church in Russia sent missionaries to Alaska and this single mission was responsible for introducing Orthodoxy to North America for the first time.

"Eastern Orthodoxy, though it had an early start on the continent in 'Russian America,' failed to capitalize on its 18th century Alaskan beginnings...Orthodoxy, while in the nation, has yet to move effectively through the bloodstream of the country. Its enclaves remain secluded and isolated; its internal divisions preclude a united voice on national concerns. In all probability, the 21st century will find Orthodoxy, as in the manner of so many other Christian groups that arrived before it, more fully assimilated, more thoroughly engaged in American affairs."[85]

Insofar as America is concerned, The Eastern Orthodox Church is not without its own set of unique challenges of broad public acceptance and fluid assimilation. Orthodoxy continues to be attached (albeit ever more loosely) to some manner of foreign language and ethnicity within the United States and North America as a whole. It is still one church, operating in communion and unity, but with many of the ethnical components of their source region. It is observed that:

"One of the problems that contemporary Orthodoxy faces is the almost complete absence of bridges that would join the church to the outside world. A great number of barriers stand between the church and the person 'on the outside.' These include language, culture, and psychology."[86]

In spite of periodic attacks on the church across the centuries—all of which it has survived intact, the message of faith from the Orthodox Church remains:

"Orthodoxy claims to be universal—not something exotic and oriental, but simple Christianity. Because of human failings and the accidents of history, the Orthodox Church has been largely restricted in the past to certain geographical areas. Yet to the Orthodox themselves their church is something more than a group of local bodies...[they] make what may seem at first a surprising claim: they regard their church as the church which guards and teaches the true belief about God and which glorifies Him with right worship, that is, *as nothing less than the Church of Christ on earth.*"[87]

We generally know this same Church of the Byzantines today as the Eastern Orthodox Church, which survived all the political calamities of the Byzantine Empire and is alive and well. They are organized now as one church with fourteen canonical Sees spread across the globe, each with its own patriarch—but no Pope. Orthodox Christians now comprise about 12% of the world's Christians—fallen from about 20% over the greater course of the 20th century,[88] and we can be certain that the Russian period of persecution from 1917 – 1988, and the Armenian genocide from 1914 -1923 had much to do with that.

Historically as well as today, the Eastern Orthodox Christian Church is a Church of martyrs. No other Christian tradition has suffered more for the Faith of Christ. In spite of so many challenges and attacks that the Orthodox Church has faced, it continues to thrive and serve. While it would be impossible for me to list all the past and current benevolences the Church has provided to the world over the course of millennia, they continue to work to help the needy today under the umbrella of their main charity, the International Orthodox Christian Charities or IOCC, based in Baltimore, Maryland.

On average, since its founding in 1992, the IOCC has used 92 cents of every dollar for direct program services which includes a broad variety of aid programs in Ethiopia, Greece, Georgia, Haiti, The Holy Land, Jordan, Lebanon, Romania, Syria, Uganda, the Western Balkans, Cameroon, Iraq, and the United States.[89]

The IOCC is partnered with the following organizations and agencies[90]:

- Assembly of Canonical Orthodox Bishops of the United States of America
- ACT Alliance
- Agrolink, Association of Consultants
- Al Amal Rehabilitation Society, Rafah
- American Hellenic Educational Progressive Association (AHEPA)
- American Red Cross
- AmeriCorps NCCC
- Andrew and Eula Carlos Foundation, Inc.
- Annunciation Greek Orthodox Cathedral, Houston, TX
- Arabian Medical Relief (AMR)
- Archbishop Iakovos Leadership 100 Endowment Fund
- Armenian Apostolic Church Shirak Diocese
- Armenian Round Table of the Armenian Apostolic Church
- Austrian Development Agency
- Bait Al-Maqdes Community-Based Organization
- Beit Lahiya Development Association, Gaza North
- Bread for the World Institute

The Unholy Land

- Brother's Brother Foundation
- Camp Noah – Lutheran Social Services
- Catholic Charities of Florida
- Cheshire Services Ethiopia
- Chian Federation
- Christian Church Disciples of Christ
- Church World Service (CWS)
- Demery Family Foundation, Inc.
- Diakonie Austria
- Diakonie Katastrophenhilfe (DKH) Germany
- Disabled Child Welfare Association
- DKH Austria City of Vienna
- East Amman Community-Based Organization
- Ecole Orthodox St. Jean de Freres, Haiti
- Ernest C. & Marion R. Karras Family Foundation
- Ethiopian Orthodox Tewahedo Church, Development and Inter-Church Aid Commission (EOC-DICAC)
- Federal Emergency Management Agency (FEMA)
- Federation Filantropia (Romania)
- Finn Church Aid (FCA)
- Footwork
- George and Judy Marcus Foundation
- Georgian Orthodox Church Diocese of Poti and Khobi
- Giorgi Family Foundation
- Good360
- Grateful Hearts Foundation
- Greek Free/Open Source Software Society (GFOSS)
- Greek Orthodox Archdiocese of America
- Greek Orthodox Ladies Philoptochos Society
- Greek Orthodox Patriarchate of Antioch, Department of Ecumenical Relations and Development (GOPA-DERD)
- Greek Orthodox Patriarchate of Jerusalem
- Habitat for Humanity St. Tammany West
- Harper-Eggington Foundation
- HelpAge International
- Holy Metropolis of Guinea and West Africa
- Homeland Security & Emergency Management MN (HSEM)
- Humentum (Formerly Inside NGO)
- InterAction
- IOCC Foundation
- IRN – The Reuse Network
- Jaharis Family Foundation, Inc.
- James & Theodore Pedas Family Foundation
- John C. Kulis Charitable Foundation
- John G. Rangos Sr. Charitable Foundation
- John L. Santikos Charitable Foundation Fund of the San Antonio Area Foundation
- Jordan Hashemite Charity Organization (JHCO)
- Katherine Valone "St. Photini" Water Fund
- Katsaros Family Foundation
- KEMEL (Center of Volunteer Managers in Greece)
- Kerk in Actie – ICCO Cooperation
- KP & Phoebe Tsolainos Foundation, Inc.
- Love of Christ Foundation
- Lutheran World Federation
- Lutheran World Relief (LWR)
- Malbis Memorial Foundation
- Medical Teams International
- MKO Apostoli
- Mutual Fire Foundation, Inc.
- National Podoconiosis Action Network (NaPAN)
- National Voluntary Organizations Active in Disaster (National VOAD)

- NECHAMA Jewish Response to Disaster
- Nicholas J. & Celeste G. Karamatsoukas Family Foundation
- Nicholas J. and Anna K. Bouras Foundation
- Nicholas Tsakalos Family Foundation, Inc.
- Noor Al Hussein Foundation Institute for Family Health
- Norwegian Church Aid (NCA)
- Office of US Foreign Disaster Assistance (OFDA)
- Order of St. Ignatius of Antioch
- Orthodox Christian Mission Center (OCMC)
- Orthodox Vision Foundation
- Orthodox Youth Movement
- Pancretan Association of America
- Paul and Julie Backas Fund
- Paulos Foundation
- Peace Winds Japan (PWJ)
- Red Cross of Republic of Srpska, Bosnia-Herzegovina
- Red Cross of Serbia
- Romanian Orthodox Church
- Rotary District 6200
- Serbian Orthodox Church Diocese of Raška-Prizren and Kosovo-Metohija
- Serbian Orthodox Church Metropolitanate of Montenegro and the Littoral
- St Nicholas Foundation, Inc.
- St. Bernard Project
- St. George Antiochian Orthodox Cathedral, Houston, TX
- St. Ignatius English Medium High School, India
- St. Nektarios Education Fund
- Syriac Orthodox Church in Amman
- Team Rubicon
- The Hellenic Initiative
- Topitzes Family Foundation
- Uganda Orthodox Church
- UN World Food Programme (WFP)
- United Church of Christ of Daytona Beach, FL
- United Methodist Committee on Relief (UMCOR)
- United Nations Children's Fund (UNICEF)
- United Nations Development Program (UNDP)
- United Nations Office for the Coordination of Humanitarian Affairs (UNOCHA)
- United World College USA
- University of Sussex
- US Agency for International Development (USAID)
- US Department of State Bureau of Population, Refugees, and Migration (PRM)
- Volunteer Florida Foundation
- Volusia Interfaith/Agencies Networking in Disaster (VIND)
- World Vision
- Youth Without Border Forum Association, Khan Younis
- Zdravo
- ZOA

As the Eastern Orthodox Church expands into America they are becoming more visible. Recently a pan-orthodox charitable fraternity was organized and established as The Holy Orthodox Order of Saint George the Great Martyr. The objectives of the group are

"...to organize, promote, aid and engage in charitable, humanitarian, educational, religious, medical and chivalric activities, particularly by: aiding the poor, the sick, the needy, the aged, the infirm, the maimed, the mentally ill, the imprisoned and the socially disadvantaged; assisting in the maintenance of holy places including, but not limited to, buildings, monasteries, seminaries, shrines, churches and cathedrals of the Orthodox Faith; establishing and promoting the works of hospitals, medical centers, orphanages, schools and other bona fide Orthodox institutions and/or organizations."[91]

We can hope that Christian efforts such as these will continue to be successful.

6

The Christianity of the Roman West

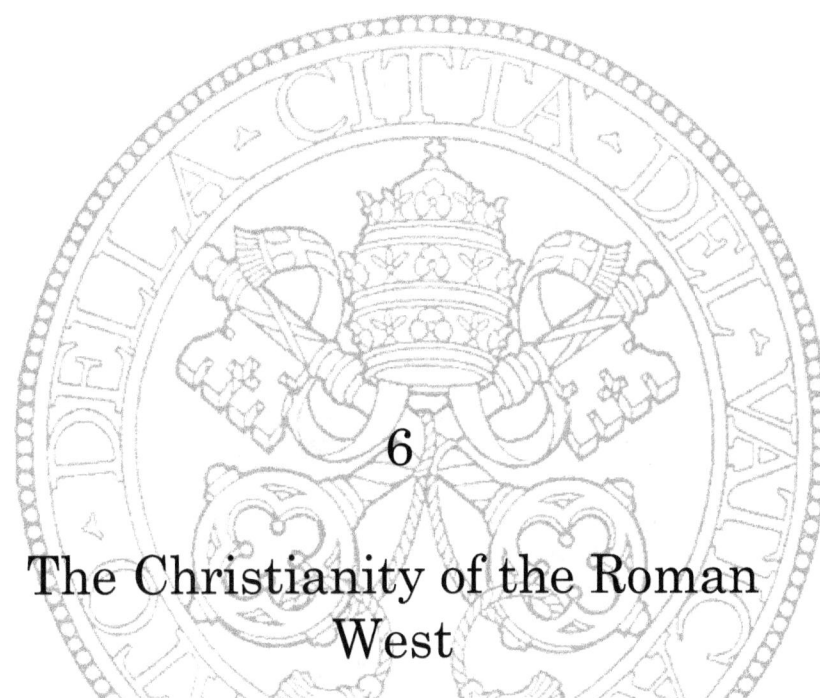

"Civilization will not attain to its perfection until the last stone from the last church falls on the last priest.⁹²"

Émile Zola (1840 -1902)
French novelist

It is an unfortunate and undeniable fact that some of the most egregious problems the world has suffered under the notion of advancing Christendom began in earnest after 1054. The development of Christianity in the central and western parts of Europe presents us with some of the worst examples of war, misery, torture and death by those imagining they were doing so in the name of Christ. It is, of course, beyond the scope of this text to document them all, but I have tried to include many of the salient events, sad as they were to discover. It is a challenge to learn any manner of virtue—Christian or any other—among the historical events of the church in the west after that church split away from the eastern churches in 1054.

The whole of the Christian Church was eventually divided between the Latins of the West centered in Rome, and the Greek speaking churches of the East centered in Constantinople. Geography was a physical divide to be sure, but all these other divisions were over issues both large and small. This division began slowly, almost unperceivably at first.

Iconoclasm, that is, the policy of prohibiting icons to be used in worship was introduced in the East in the 8th century. The first Byzantine Emperor to oppose church icons was Leo III (r.717-741), followed by his son, Constantine V (741-775) who not only destroyed the images, but persecuted the Iconodules (those who venerated the icons.)[93] This put the Byzantines at odds with Rome for quite a long period until Emperor Theophilos permanently restored the veneration of icons in 842. But to many of those in Rome, the damage was done.

Diplomacy between East and West also suffered because of unpopular policy measures. Apparently, the Byzantines had levied taxes into regions of the West and then failed to offer support to defend the West against the advance of the Lombards invading those territories. This failure to support had angered Pope Gregory III (r. 731–741).[94]

Language also became an unfortunate division that eventually grew into a great chasm between East and West. In the West, the language of the church was Latin. In the East, the Byzantine government had adopted Greek and cast aside Latin altogether. Writes Timothy Ware:

"Because the two sides could no longer communicate easily with one another, and each could no longer read what the other wrote, misunderstandings arose much more easily. The shared 'universe of discourse' was progressively lost."[95]

After this, there was a permanent language barrier that contributed to poor communication, errant communications due to questionable translations, and a general feeling of "us and them."[96] The shared culture of a united Christendom was in fact rapidly slipping away and there was little to nothing anyone could do to stop it.

Although Michael Cerularios, the Patriarch of Constantinople was praying for unity between the eastern and western churches, his good intentions were entirely lost in a letter to Pope Leo in Rome due to a poor translation:

"When Patriarch Michael signed the letter as "Ecumenical Patriarch," Pope Leo's staff of translators mistranslated the Patriarch's [Greek] word for "empire" as *universalis*...the Pope was deeply shocked because Cerularios offered, in return for having his name commemorated in the Church of Rome, to see that the Pope's name was commemorated throughout the churches in the whole inhabited earth (*in toto orbe terrarium*). It is most unlikely that Patriarch Michael Cerularios would have claimed to control the churches of the entire world. Cerularios used the word (*ecumene*) in its Byzantine sense of "the empire." The Latins translated the word in its literal sense [meaning] "the whole inhabited world." It was a similar misunderstanding which caused the trouble over the title "Ecumenical Patriarch."[97]

Cardinal Humbert was tasked with providing a response to this letter which surprised and shocked Patriarch Cerularios, writing,

"What a detestable, lamentable, sacrilegious usurpation is thine, when is speech and in writing thou dost call thyself 'universal Patriarch'!"[98]

Then there were other, more important points of division that had quickly developed. These included matters of doctrine, practice, and the issue of Papal Primacy.

With German influence ascending to the papal throne in the 9th Century, came the introduction of the Filioque.[99] The Western Church commonly uses a modified version of the Nicene creed which has the Latin word *filioque* ("and the Son") added after the canonized creed's declaration that the Holy Spirit proceeds from the Father, a change that was not only rejected by the Eastern Churches but remains a divisive barrier between the two churches even today. Depending upon who you talk with, it could amount to a distinction without a difference.

On July 16, 1054, the breaking point had been reached. Cardinal Humbert was part of an official church legate to Constantinople and on this morning he interrupted the Divine Liturgy service in Hagia Sophia and marched in with his colleagues to lay the Pope's letter of excommunication of "the Patriarch and all his followers" on the very altar of the church. Then he and his group turned and marched out. It was this moment in history that the Roman Catholic Church had now separated itself from the Orthodox Church.[100]

The Orthodox Church soon convened a synod on July 24th, 1054 and issued excommunication of Cardinal Humbert and his fellow legates.[101] None of this was necessary; the Pope had died on April 15th and according to Canon Law, no legate may legally act in representation of a deceased Pope.[102] Cardinal Humbert's excommunication order was legally null and void by the time he delivered it. This fact, however, did not change the outcome.

In the West, the political structure and position of the Church was moving towards a Christian Monarchy with the Pope at its head. This was a departure of structure; Byzantium was originally organized as a synthesis between Church and State. There was an Emperor and a Patriarch each with his theoretically separate, defined role; it was not an absolute monarchy. In the East, the four remaining churches (Antioch, Constantinople, Jerusalem, and Alexandria) remained in a collegiate in structure. The Vatican now would no longer be considered "collegiate" like these but rather authoritarian.

To a large degree, many of the Church councils were called to collectively address many new heresies and make some attempts to reconcile these issues. So divisive were these issues between East and West that after 1054 A.D., neither head of the Western Church or the Russian Orthodox Church had met in the same room together for 962 years—until 2016.[103]

There were yet other events that contributed to the growing list of problems. The militant advancement of the Muslim Turks across the East threatened the security of Byzantium and the four Eastern Churches. This would evoke an initial response by Christendom to defend this geography. Christ, however, never specifically instructed His followers to occupy Jerusalem to claim as His city and then to defend it at all costs, slaughtering any and all others. That instruction is not discovered in the Gospels. The Church of the West, often influenced by power hungry Arian Gauls and Franks, funded many diverse groups of militant Crusaders engaged in just such a policy over the course a few hundred years. Many felt they had to in order to prevent the Ottoman Turks and others from invading Europe, and that was probably the case. It may be of importance to consider that the period of these Crusades was also being undertaken during the same long period as that many of the later church councils, starting in 1095 and ending in 1291.

The Unholy Land

Seal of the Knights Templar, a Catholic Military order loyal to the Pope, c. 1119 – c. 1312

It is equally important to understand that the very concept of "crusading." Fighting a holy war is in truth more of an ancient Roman tradition rather than a traditional Christian one. In fact, the rationale for these Christian crusades were not specifically supported by the Gospels or taught by Christ as mentioned. Instead, under a pretense of "taking Jerusalem" the real motivations of pride, greed, and avarice were masked. This begat a series of twelve such crusades:

In 1198, Pope Innocent offers a general amnesty for all sins ("indulgences") to all who pledge and serve in the upcoming crusade. Enlistments were for one year.[e]

1096 - 1099 The First Crusade: The People's Crusade - Freeing the Holy Lands from the occupying Turks. 1st Crusade led by Count Raymond IV of Toulouse and proclaimed by many wandering preachers, notably Peter the Hermit

1144 -1155 The Second of the Crusades led by Holy Roman Emperor Conrad III and by King Louis VII of France

1187 -1192 The Third of the Crusades led by Richard the Lionheart of England, Philip II of France, and Holy Roman Emperor Frederick I. Richard I made a truce with Saladin

1202 -1204 The Fourth Crusade led by Fulk of Neuil French/Flemish advanced on Constantinople with the Venetians. The Western Christians turned on the Eastern Christians and slaughtered them. The Crusaders of the West never made it to Jerusalem but

---

[e] Why pay for an army when you can use Christ to get one for free? Even Napoleon Bonaparte later recognized the deep commitment of men to Christ when he remarked, "I know men and I tell you that Jesus Christ is no mere man. Between Him and every other person in the world there is no possible term of comparison. Alexander, Caesar, Charlemagne, and I have founded empires. But on what did we rest the creation of our genius? Upon force. Jesus Christ founded His empire upon love; and at this hour millions of men would die for Him."

instead deposed the Emperor of Byzantium, completely looted Constantinople, and occupied the former empire for 57 years.

1212 The Children's Crusade led by a French peasant boy, Stephen of Cloyes. It ended as a disaster.

1217 – 1221 The Fifth of the Crusades led by King Andrew II of Hungary, Duke Leopold VI of Austria and John of Brienne

1228 – 1229 The Sixth of the Crusades led by Holy Roman Emperor Frederick II

1248 – 1254 The Seventh of the Crusades led by Louis IX of France

1270 The Eighth of the Crusades led by Louis IX of France

1271 – 1272 The Ninth of the Crusades led by Prince Edward (later Edward I of England)

1291- One of the only remaining Crusader occupied cities in the Holy Land, Acre, fell to the Muslim Mamluks.

There was little chance that any of these military ventures were ever going to succeed, and in fact, most of them failed to a large degree with exception of the First Crusade. While scholars have cited many reasons for their failure, I would point back at the same two things, the lack of virtue and unity within the church. Once the schism occurred and east and west were separated, pride and all the rest can work its way into the hearts of men and obscure the essential work of the Church. That's admittedly a simplification of a very complicated process beyond the scope of this chapter.

The crusaders themselves often lacked virtue and unity. Crusading armies in that time were not comprised of cohesive, disciplined and orderly ranks of well-trained, well-equipped and honorably principled men as we might expect based upon our own standards today. Instead, they were a rag-tag collection of a variety of people, (including their families, and service providers, ordinary pilgrims, etc.), some armed, trained, and healthy, while others not so much. They had a general idea of "taking back Jerusalem for Christendom," with the aid of a few well-equipped knights among them. But there were other objectives on their minds as well.

"A crusading army was an inchoate mass of men moved unpredictably by enthusiasms, fears, ambitions, superstitions, and lusts...the commander of such an army was rather like a man shooting a rapids in a canoe...[104]"

The Unholy Land

One would hope that in time of battle men could unify. It would seem essential to the mission that during the Crusades we would see examples of Christian unity. But even while trying to engage a single common enemy, they were divided and scheming amongst themselves. Just one example:

"During the First Crusade, [Byzantine] emperor Alexios I Komenos negotiated the surrender of Nicaea, despite it being sieged by Crusaders. After the sultan Arslan had retreated, residents of Nicaea wrote a letter to the Emperor, begging for his help. Alexios ordered his general Boutoumites to negotiate the surrender of the city without Crusaders knowing about it. General Tatikios was instructed to join the Crusaders and directly assault the walls, while Boutoumites had to act the same and make it look like Roman soldiers had taken the city. On the 19th of June, Turks surrendered the city to Boutoumites. Crusaders soon found out what happened and they were very angry because they expected to loot the city. Emperor gave them many gifts, money and horses but they still believed they would've gotten more of it if they looted the city. Alexios did not let Crusaders leave Nicaea until they swore an oath to be loyal to the Emperor and return all the rightful Byzantine land they conquer on their way to Jerusalem. Family of the sultan ended up in Constantinople after the reconquest and shortly after sultan paid the ransom.[105]"

Unquestionably, the worst example was the Fourth Crusade. By 1202, the east/west division was the "800 pound gorilla in the room" full of Christians. The Latins now held the Greeks in contempt for the events of the schism of 1054, while the Greeks were distrustful of the Latins—even though the Greek-speaking Byzantines had pleaded for western help to repel the Turks. The Byzantines by now were too financially drained to defend their whole empire by themselves, coupled with the fact that the notion of engaging in a Holy War was both unthinkable and abhorrent to them.[106]

The crusaders of the West responded by hiring the opportunistic Venetians to build, supply, and man 480 ships to deliver the crusading armies to the theater of operation; again with the stated goal to retake Jerusalem for Christendom and to defend the Byzantine frontier against advancing their Ottoman enemies, with the blessing of the Pope.

However, neither the eastern nor western churches nor their governments had enough money to pay the waiting Venetians for their naval services; the army of Crusaders that assembled had been much smaller than expected-by two thirds or more, and so, financial resources came up short.[107]

The short term resolution they reached with the Venetians was this: The Venetians had recently lost control of a coastal city called Zara to the Hungarians. They wanted it back. So if the Crusading army agreed to make a side trip and fight the Hungarians to restore Zara to the Venetians, they would postpone, not forgive, the balance of payment until they reached Constantinople.[108]

Now in all due fairness to the Roman Catholic Church, this wasn't exactly what the Pope had in mind when he called for the Crusade—in no way was he authorizing Crusaders to become a band of mercenaries for the Venetians or any other state. It was, to Pope Innocent III nothing short of outrageous, and instead of the Crusaders receiving the promised absolution, to his credit he immediately excommunicated the entire expeditionary force.[109]

Eventually these Latin Crusaders invaded their fellow Christians in Constantinople, sacking the city to help pay the debt to the Venetians. But at the same time, they raped, pillaged, killed innocents, looted and desecrated the Orthodox Churches. Norwich writes:

"The Fourth Crusade—if indeed it can be so described—surpassed even its predecessors in faithlessness and duplicity, in brutality and greed. By the sack of Constantinople, Western civilization suffered a loss...perhaps the most catastrophic single loss in all history."[110]

Their original mission to take back Jerusalem was all but forgotten, at least for a while. After the sack of Constantinople the Byzantine Emperor was ousted into exile while the Latins set up a government in the city and ran it for 57 years. During that time, Eastern Orthodox Christians in the former empire were obliged to accept the Latin *Filioque* and serve their Divine Liturgy with unleavened bread.[111] The Latin overlords asserted other requirements as well.

It was payday for the Venetians, who hauled everything valuable in Constantinople back to Venice—including disassembling many of the stone buildings to be reconstructed in Venice. The treasury of St. Mark's in Venice which still stands today is mostly constructed with the cut stone and crafted building materials they removed from Constantinople.

The formations, funding, strategy, execution and outcomes of these many Crusades were in general negatively impactful to the Christian Church and all Christendom, the full detail of the subject remains beyond the scope of this work. But neither the many councils nor the Crusades occurred in a vacuum. The beliefs, tenants, and process of western Christianity were being reshaped while territory was being both defended and expanded under the sign of the Cross. The world was spinning at a rapid pace as military, political, religious, and economic events all mixed and congealed. It seems eerily similar to the world today.

By the end of the Byzantine period in 1453, the Roman Catholic Church was in trouble. While outwardly it was gaining power and becoming stronger and more influential, it seems to have strayed so far from the descriptions of the principles of the Apostle Paul's vision of Christian church as to be nearly unrecognizable as something Christian. Soon they would have the baggage of their own unspeakable crimes and sins to drag with them.

Corruption and Torture

The first Inquisition was temporarily established in Languedoc (south of France) in 1184 with the issuance of the Papal Bull *Ad Abolendam*, "On abolition" or "Towards abolishing." Its first line, *Ad abolendam diversam haeresium pravitatem*, or 'To abolish diverse malignant heresies,' was a decretal and bull of Pope Lucius III, issued 4 November 1184.[112] The document prescribes measures to uproot heresy with its chief aim was the complete abolition of all Christian heresy.

The issuance of this order leads directly to the Albigensian Crusade, which lasted from 1209 to 1244. That resulted in at least 200,000 Cathar deaths, and quite possibly many more. The Inquisition was permanently established in 1229, and executed largely by the Dominican order. The gratuitous slaughters of the Albigensian Crusade are well known to many even if today's American population never heard of this event. The Cistercian Abbot and Papal Legate Arnaud Amalric reported the results of the massacre at Béziers in a letter to the Pope in August 1209--and denied that he had any part in it:[113]

"...while discussions were still going on with the barons about the release of those in the city who were deemed to be Catholics, the servants and other persons of low rank and unarmed attacked the city without waiting for orders from their leaders. To our amazement, crying "to arms, to arms!" Within the space of two or three hours they crossed the ditches and the walls and Béziers was taken. Our men spared no one, irrespective of rank, sex or age, and put to the sword almost 20,000 people. After this great slaughter the whole city was despoiled and burnt..."[114]

We can fast-forward to April 26, 1478; Pope Sixtus IV executed a plan to attempt removal of the powerful Medici family from control over Florence. He had allied with the rival family, the Pazzi. On this day *during mass*, in a cathedral filled with 10,000 faithful, Giuliano Medici was murdered during a part of the service known as the *elevation of the host*. It was indeed an assassination rooted in the desire for power and age old greed. The coup was unsuccessful, resulting in more murders as Medici loyalist tracked down the parties involved.[115]

"After the failure of the plot, Pope Sixtus interdicted the city for killing the murderous archbishop and raised an army to crush Lorenzo. The war lasted two years and almost ruined Florence."[116]

In the very same year, Pope Sixtus was actively pursuing slaughter of innocents in Spain, which we know as the Spanish Inquisition. In addition to burning, beating, drowning, and suffocation, there was employed a vast array of new and creative torture devices used on people not just to maim, disfigure, or kill, but to inflict as much agonizing pain and suffering for the victim for as long as possible. This is a rather short list of only a few of the most widely used torture creations.

These devices include such items as the "rack" which was used to slowly and painfully dislocate every joint in the body, one by one, and a cheese grater-like metal surface was used at times on the board where the torso rested to tear the flesh of the body away as the body was stretched.

The common stocks were used to lock the ankles or head and wrists into a fixed board in public where the victim was exposed to the elements and to various abuses of people walking by.

Water torture was used and nothing like "waterboarding" of today:

"In water torture victim's nostrils were first pinched shut, and then about 8 liters of water was forced down the victim's throat with a funnel. In some cases boiling water or vinegar was used to inflict even greater suffering. In the end, victim's stomach would rupture, leading to painful and gruesome death."[117]

The Heretic's Fork was used often and consisted of a sharp, double pronged, double ended, iron fork that was strapped onto the front of the throat vertically. This required the victim to maintain his head erect at all times or else the fork would be forced into piercing the underside of the throat and the base of the neck simultaneously. This method of torture could go on for many weeks because the forks did not damage any vital organs.[118]

The Pear was another iron device often employed on victims of the Spanish Inquisition. Its preferred use was on female victims because the device was inserted into the vagina or mouth where it would be forcefully expanded by twisting a large screw on the outside end. This caused stretching, lacerations, then slow tearing and ripping apart of the flesh from the inside. Torture that involved the Pear almost always had a fatal result.[119]

The Wheel was one of the most popular and cruelest methods used. This giant wooden and spiked wheel had to be operated by several men and was able to break every bone in victim's body as it was slowly turned resulting in an agonizing and slow death.[120]

The Breast Ripper was a large iron device with the appearance of a giant tweezers with sharp forks at the ends. Used almost exclusively on women its main purpose was to tear breasts off the chest.[121]

The Judas Cradle was an elaborate set up where the victim was stripped naked, hoisted and hung over this pointed iron or wooden pyramid or conical device using iron belts. The legs were stretched out frontwards, or their ankles pulled down by weights. The operator would then drop the accused onto the pyramid penetrating the anus or if a woman, the vagina as well. With their muscles constantly contracted and in excruciating constant pain, victims were unable sleep.[122]

Iron Cages were often hung nearby town halls and ducal palaces, as well as the town's hall of justice and cathedrals. The victim would be left naked and exposed inside of the cage and would slowly wither from hunger, thirst, and exposure. The weather could contribute to death by heat stroke and sunburn in the summer and cold and frostbite and frozen extremities in the winter. The victims were often mutilated before being put in the cages and the cadavers remained in the cages until the bones fell apart.[123]

The inquisitions were initiated by the civil government of France and not "specifically" by the church. True, the Church was in support at the beginning but when it became too cruel and bloody, the church eventually condemned it. It was this continuous condemnation that eventually led to the end of the inquisitions. A very truncated version of the series of those events looks like this[124]:

1478- Pope Sixtus IV authorizes the Spanish Inquisition.
1479- Fernando II becomes king of Aragon: Isabella and Fernando begin joint rule.
1480- Inquisition begins operations in Sevilla.
1481- First public *auto de fe* held in Sevilla, meaning "act of faith" which was the ritual of public penance of condemned heretics and apostates that took place when the Spanish Inquisition, Portuguese Inquisition, or Mexican Inquisition had decided their punishment, followed by the carrying out by the civil authorities of the sentences imposed.
1482- War begins with Granada: number of inquisitors enlarged.
1483- Pope Sixtus IV appoints Torquemada first Inquisitor General of Castilla and of Aragon; Jews expelled from Sevilla, Cordoba, and Cadiz.
1484- Inquisition has thirty people burned alive in Ciudad Real.
1485- Rabbis in Toledo ordered to inform on Crypto-Jews.
1491- Rumors circulate of a kidnapped child of La Guardia "murdered by Jews."
1492- Jews expelled from Spain.

1501- Catholic Kings decree that offspring of those condemned by the Inquisition could not hold important positions; Arabic books burned in Granada.
1502- All Muslims in Castilla ordered by the crown to convert Christianity or suffer exile.
1516- Death of Fernando; regency of Cardinal Cisneros begins
1518- Carlos I enhances the judicial power of the inquisition.
1519- Carlos I becomes Carlos V of the Holy Roman Empire.
1525- Royal decree orders all Muslims in Valencia and Aragon to convert to Christianity or suffer exile.
1526- Forty-year agreement between Moriscos, king, and inquisitors.
1572- Fray Luis de Leon arrested by the Spanish Inquisition.
1590- Royal decree forbids for women to wear the veil.
1619- King visits Portugal; gypsies expelled from Castilla.
1621- Death of Felipe III; Felipe IV mounts the throne; Cortes denounces church wealth.
1660- English sailors burned at the stake in Sevilla.
1781- Last victim of the Inquisition burned alive.
1799- Sale of the assets of the inquisition
1826- Last death sentence by the inquisition for heresy.
1834- Inquisition finally abolished.

While I could expound many more pages ripping into the results of all these later Western church rulers and organizations that acted in the name of Christ while introducing modern innovations and ambitious objectives into the Roman Catholic Christian Faith, fortunately I don't have to. The massive body of writings by the many early eastern Church Fathers as well as nearly the entire body of work by the early Protestant Reformers has already done that.

The Reformers were the likes of Jan Hus, Peter Waldo, John Wycliffe, Martin Luther, John Calvin and John Knox. They had identified many other grounds to reject Papal authority far beyond the confines of the abuses of the Inquisition. Any of these actions by the Roman Catholic Church to this point taken alone would be awful to consider, but the tragedy and torment was only intensified with the advent of the Protestant Reformation. From about 1550 to 1700 Europe became embroiled in a period of rampant "witch hunts." Some economists have observed this event as a "non-price competition between the Catholic and Protestant churches for religious market share."[125] Essentially, the Roman Catholic Church was now in direct competition with Protestants for adherents.

The Unholy Land

While Martin Luther was initially focused on the practice of the Church of selling worthless indulgences, he rather bluntly writes later in 1530:

"So out with it, you papal asses! Say that this is the teaching of Christendom: these stinking lies which you villains and traitors have forced upon Christendom and for the sake of which you murderers have killed many Christians. Why each letter of every papal law gives testimony to the fact that nothing has ever been taught by the counsel and the consent of Christendom. There is nothing there but "districte precipiendo mandamus" ["we teach and strictly command"]. That has been your Holy Spirit. Christendom has had to suffer this tyranny. This tyranny has robbed it of the sacrament and, not by its own fault, has been held in captivity. And still the asses would pawn off on us this intolerable tyranny of their own wickedness as a willing act and example of Christendom - and thereby acquit themselves!"[126]

Other Protestant preachers included John Willock, John Row, John Douglas, William Harlaw, and Paul Methven. Patrick Hamilton and George Wishart also began the preaching of Lutheran doctrine in Scotland. Hamilton was martyred in 1528 and Wishart was burned to death in 1546.[127]

The process of sorting it all out was to force the faithful into choosing between the two rival versions of Christianity in Europe. By the end of this period, some 80,000 people were arrested and tried as witches or whatever, with about half ultimately tortured and murdered in the most painful and gruesome of methods—often burned alive.[128] Finally, between May and October 1648, a series of treaties were presented and signed, commonly referred to as the Peace of Westphalia which effectively ended the European witch trials.[129]

The Roman Catholic Church had long ago elevated their Pope to become the "Vicar of Christ." After this happened, the Church could proceed to invent whatever policy it chose "in the name of Christ." They were still controlling the access (and translations) to the Bible, manipulating its content and much more; levying taxes, waging wars, putting masses to the sword, torturing heretics, burning innocent people at the stake, committing murder, supporting false testimonies of and the imprisonment, torture, and supporting murder of the Knights Templar; overthrowing governments, creating and selling "indulgences"

The Unholy Land

to the people,[130] opening the slave trade in West Africa... *Just who were these people?* Where was the Church of Jesus Christ in this litany of Roman Catholic horror? The Vatican seems to act much like an organized crime syndicate during this whole period and not anything that should ever bear the name of Christ. Luther was right.

No wonder so many Protestants and others completely outside of the faith today might see Roman Catholics as both heretics and hypocrites. They preached "peace," but have caused and fought many wars over past centuries. They spoke of Christian love but schemed and usurped emperors, tortured and imprisoned innocents and all the rest while styling their titular head as the "Vicar of Christ." It seems nothing short of an abomination. The centuries of pain, suffering, and destruction that Roman Catholicism has inflicted upon innocents, its own faithful and the heretics alike is well documented. What has changed since that period of the 10th century referred to by historians as the Papal Pornocracy?[131]

These innumerable abuses did not go unnoticed by the world. The eventual response was of course the explosive Protestant Reformation. There we have yet another major split in the church—this time not between east and west, but rather along the lines of the ideological and authoritative split that forever separated Roman Catholics from Protestants. As a result, to this day, Protestants of all denominations it seems are not very welcome at Roman Catholic churches, nor do they desire to join them.

By the 1700's it was obvious to all what the European religious structure had evolved into. Noah Webster commented, "The ecclesiastical establishments of Europe which serve to support tyrannical governments are not the Christian religion but abuses and corruptions of it." Can anyone honestly argue against that position?

Sure, the Roman Catholic leadership knew how Protestants were now running rampant, but what could be done that had not already been tried to arrest it? Protestants in general were still relatively poor and were very soon fragmented—within ten years of Luther's Reformation splits in their churches were already occurring, and so they could never wage an effective rebellion against the Vatican—even though many Protestant groups were backed by nations that no longer wished to submit to the Pope. The competition to the Vatican could be tolerated for now.

The Unholy Land

The Roman Catholics' old rival, the Eastern Orthodox Church, at this time was still operating in Constantinople—now Istanbul, as well as in Greece, and Kiev, where Christian Europe and the Americas alike seemed very distant—still safely isolated from the West by the vast tracts of land, oceans, languages, doctrine, and culture.

It was clear, though that they had lost their monopoly of the Christian Faith. Where the Roman Catholic Church once controlled nearly all access to the Holy Bible in the West prior to the advent of the printing press, soon the Gideons International group formed and began distributing free printed copies of their translated Bible directly to the people starting in 1899—an activity that the Roman Catholics had once made punishable by death. The Roman Catholic Church had banned unauthorized translations of the Bible in 1408.[132]

After the Reformation began, what they really lost was control over the Christian "brand" and the unchecked power of the Vatican to enforce and punish. Where once the Roman Catholic Church could arrest a person who disagreed with their Pope or violated policies and practices; declare them guilty of heresy and have them punished by means of excommunication, torture and burning at the stake, this was now called out as "murder." Eventually, the Vatican could not control and manipulate all the people and their rulers with the policies of their brand of Christianity the old fashioned way; simply by war, taxation, manipulation by selling "indulgences," imprisonment, torture, and executions.

The Roman Catholic Church needed only to worry about the Church of England as serious competition for the control of Christianity in the West, with the petulant Byzantines and their Emperors a very distant memory in the rear-view mirror. But the Vatican was not ending its policy of political involvement and scheming. Perhaps they might achieve the restoration of their power and influence in Europe by proxy.

The Vatican remained active in the global political events of the 20th Century. During the Nazi occupation of Yugoslavia, the Roman Catholic Church even supported those supporting the Nazi regime. The Ustaša, a Croatian fascist, racist, ultranationalist and terrorist organization[133] was active between 1929 and 1945. Its members murdered hundreds of thousands of Serbs, Jews,[134] and Roma as well as an assortment of many other political dissidents.

This terrorist movement functioned prior to World War II[135] and it was founded as a nationalist organization that sought to create an independent Croatian state in 1930[136]. The ideology of the movement was an unholy blend of fascism, Roman Catholicism and Croatian nationalism.[137] However, in April 1941, they were appointed to rule a part of Axis-occupied Yugoslavia as the Independent State of Croatia (NDH), which has been described as both an Italian-German quasi-protectorate,[138] and as a puppet state[139] of Nazi Germany.[140]

With this arrangement, the Ustaša could work with the Nazis as allies toward their mutual goals. Eastern Orthodox Christianity was the predominant faith of the land, but soon errantly identified by the Ustaša as a "nationalist" movement, counter to their own. Once in power, the Ustaše entirely banned the term "Serbian Orthodox faith", requiring instead, "Greek-Eastern faith" to be used in its place.[141] The Ustaše followed a program of forced conversions of many Orthodox Christians to Roman Catholicism, then murdered or expelled 85% of Eastern Orthodox priests.[142] They proceeded to plunder and burn many of the Orthodox Christian churches.[143]

Of course Eastern Orthodox Christianity was an old rival to the Roman Catholic Church since the events leading up to 1054. The head of the Roman Catholic Church in Croatia, the Archbishop Alojzije Stepinac noted this schism when he stated on March 28th, 1941:

"All in all, Croats and Serbs are of two worlds, northpole and southpole, never will they be able to get together unless by a miracle of God. The schism (between the Catholic Church and Eastern Orthodoxy) is the greatest curse in Europe, almost greater than Protestantism. Here there is no moral, no principles, no truth, no justice, no honesty."[144]

On April 28, 1941, he issued a public statement with a letter supporting the new Ustaše controlled state, and he asked the clergy to pray for its Leader, Ante Pavelić.[145] This despite the fact that the Ustaše had already proclaimed a series of anti-Serb and anti-Jewish measures,[146] and he understood that they were preparing Nazi-style Racial Laws, which Pavelić signed only two days later.[147]

The Unholy Land

Ustaše ministers Mile Budak, Mirko Puk and Milovan Žanić declared in May, 1941 that the goal of the new Ustaše policy was an ethnically pure Croatia. The strategy to achieve their goal loosely mirrored Hitler's own goals for his Nazi Germany:[148] One-third of the Serbs were to be killed, one-third were to be expelled, one-third were to be forcibly converted to Catholicism.

Pavelić was motivated and first met with Adolf Hitler on 6 June 1941. Mile Budak, then publicly proclaimed the violent racial policy of the state on 22 July 1941.[149] The Ustaše sent most of their Jews to both Ustaše and Nazi run concentration camps where 80% of the Jews in the Independent State of Croatia, were exterminated.[150]

The regime opened no less than fourteen concentration camps to house upwards of 300,000 to 700,000 prisoners. By the end of World War II, the terrorist Ustaše regime, under Pavelić's leadership, had completed its extermination of what is estimated to be 30,000 Jews, 29,000 Gypsies, and between 300,000 and 600,000 Orthodox Christian Serbs.[151] While the final figures are still disputed either higher or lower depending upon the source, but the point is made.

A Nazi Gestapo report to Reichsführer SS Heinrich Himmler, dated 17 February 1942, states:

"Increased activity of the bands [of rebels] is chiefly due to atrocities carried out by Ustaše units in Croatia against the Orthodox population. The Ustaše committed their deeds in a bestial manner not only against males of conscript age, but especially against helpless old people, women and children. The number of the Orthodox that the Croats have massacred and sadistically tortured to death is about three hundred thousand." [152]

It is known that most of Roman Catholic clergy in Croatia at that time supported the Ustaše regime. Some priests, mostly Franciscans, took part in the many atrocities personally. Priests, including Ivan Guberina served as some of Pavelić's bodyguards; while Dionizije Juričev, responsible for the forced conversion of Serbs in the Ustaše government, wrote that it was no longer regarded as a crime to murder seven-year-olds if they stood in the way of the Ustaše movement.[153]

The Unholy Land

Even though Archbishop Stepinac later objected to some of the Ustaše policies, and assisted some Jews and Serbs, he continued to support the Ustaše regime throughout. He served as the state's War Vicar, and even received a military service medal from Pavelić in 1944.[154]

For the duration of the war, the Vatican maintained in full diplomatic relations with the Ustaše regime through its papal nuncio in Zagreb (the Croatian capital city)—even granting Pavelić an audience. The nuncio was briefed on the efforts of the forced religious conversions of Serbian Orthodox Christians to Roman Catholicism.

After the war ended, many of the Ustaše went underground or fled to countries such as Canada, Australia, Germany and countries in South America, most notably Argentina, with the assistance of Roman Catholic churches. The Ustaše who had managed to escape from Yugoslav territory along with Pavelić, were smuggled to South America. This was largely done through "rat lines" operated by Catholic priests who had previously secured positions at the Vatican.[155]

The 20th Century Revision of the Roman Catholic Canon Law

With all of this blood on their hands, something had to change. This whole process of retooling and reforming the entire operating law the Roman Catholic Church occurred during the Cold War era. Why? What else was going on? They could have accomplished this task a century prior. What was so important and pressing about taking on this task in 1959?

Clues may be discovered by examination of the events of 1958. On July 14, Pope Pius XII published his 39th and final encyclical, *Meminisse juvat;* a publication asking for prayers of the persecuted Church in the East and simultaneously criticizing harmful cultural and military developments *in the West.*[156] He addressed the threat of nuclear proliferation and at the same time supported a modified Marxist cultural perspective:

"By now, of course, that war [World War II] is over, but a just peace does not yet prevail, nor do men live in concord founded on brotherly understanding. For the seeds of war either lurk in hiding or...erupt threateningly and hold the hearts of men in frightened suspense, especially since human ingenuity has devised weapons so powerful that

143

they can ravage and sink into general destruction, not only the vanquished, but the victors with them, and all mankind."[157]

"...Religion teaches mankind that a better distribution of wealth should be had, not by violence or revolution, but by reasonable regulations, so that the proletarian classes which do not yet enjoy life's necessities or advantages may be raised to a more fitting status without social strife."[158]

Pope Pius XII died on October 9th, 1958. He was right about peace not prevailing. Consider here some of the events of 1958:[159]

Jan 7 USSR reduces army to 300,000; focuses resources on its nuclear program.
USSR performs at least 36 nuclear tests in 1958, the U.S. performs about the same number that year.
Mar 27 Nikita Khrushchev becomes Soviet Premier as well as First Secretary of the Communist Party
Mar 31 USSR suspends nuclear weapons tests, and urges US & Britain to do the same. The USSR resumes tests anyway.
Apr 1 Marshal Nikolai Bulganin becomes director of Soviet State Bank
Jun 17 Radio Moscow reports execution of Hungarian ex-premier Imre Nagy
Aug 15 Soviet Marshal Bulganin resigns as director of State Bank
Sep 2 U.S. Air Force C-130A-II is shot down by fighters over Yerevan, Armenia when it strays into Soviet airspace while conducting a mission. All crew lost.
Oct 24 USSR lends Egypt 400 million rubles to build Aswan Dam
Nov 27 USSR abrogates Allied war-time agreements on control of Germany

The picture we see here is one of Soviet aggression, the same events that would worry the rest of the world. Responses to these events were also worrisome. Nobody wanted a global nuclear war. In the midst of all of this, the Roman Catholic Church decided it was time for an overhaul.

The Unholy Land

The Second Vatican Council occurred between October 11, 1962 and December 8, 1965. Even prior to that, on January 25, 1959, Pope John XXIII announced that the Canon Law of the Roman Catholic Church would be revised. A few years later, on March 28, 1963, he appointed a commission of cardinals who would execute the request. Then, on April 17, 1964, Pope Paul VI named the first consultants who would assist.[160]

It would take this body of men many years to complete their task. The proposed changes were sweeping, and the initial process was not completed until 1982. This new second *Codex Juris Canonici* of the Latin rite was declared by Pope John Paul II on January 25, 1983, effective for the Church on November 27, 1983. It contained no fewer than 1,752 canons which were divided among seven different books.[161]

In this entire process of the rewriting of the canons, "An effort was made toward decentralization, with local bishops enjoying more autonomy."[162] Well that sounds nice. We might ask who precisely are these "local bishops" who would now enjoy their new autonomy? Who else might have a vested interest in the complete revision of Canon Law for the Roman Catholic Church?

The Anti-Apostle #1025

A curious piece of literature arrived in bookstores in France in May, 1972. It was a little book credited to a French nurse, Marie Carré (1905 – 1984). The synopsis of this story:

"While working as a nurse in a Paris hospital in the late 1960s, Carré claimed that a severely injured man...was brought in after being in a car accident. Carré tried to communicate with the man to ask him some questions but he didn't or couldn't respond...The man survived for a few hours before he succumbed to his injuries. Having no form of identification Carré was instructed to go through his belongings in order to possibly identify him. She did not succeed in discovering his name, but she did discover...a 100-page-typed memoir."[163]

"The memoir claimed that he was an undercover agent of the Soviet Union ordered to infiltrate the Catholic Church by becoming a priest and to put forth modernist ideas through a teaching position that would undermine the main teachings of the Church during the Second

Vatican Council in subtle ways...No one ever claimed his belongings and Carré eventually decided to publish the memoir."[164]

The book is a result of Carré publishing the agent's document, which claims that around 1,100 such Soviet agents had infiltrated the Roman Catholic Church with the aim to destroy it from within. Ever since its publication, the authenticity of the story had been a source of some debate. Many say it is authentic and that such an infiltration plan was in fact being carried out, while others say that Carré was a "traditionalist" writing a piece of propaganda herself. That argument seems to fall flat because Carré eventually converted to Roman Catholicism and then herself became a nun.

This mild, however, ongoing debate over the authenticity of the account might seem to cast some doubt on whether the book AA-1025 is genuine, but we can be certain that many of the events and outcomes allegedly sought by the Soviet program as described in the book have in fact come to fruition since. History since has proven the text to be more correct and accurate than fantasy. Both publishers of the French and English editions believed that the text reflects an authentic plot as described, the latter remarking in the Publisher's Note section:

"...there is obviously a strong difference in style between Marie Carre's Prologue and her interjected editorial comment...and the text itself...which is strong indication that the story was written by someone else. Also, there is evidence of authenticity in the Memoirs themselves, which discuss a matter that did not take place until approximately 1980 to 1983, namely, the adulation given to Martin Luther in various quarters in the Church-this especially leading up to the 500th centennial of his birth in 1983. It is not reasonable to imagine that a nurse...could have predicted in 1971 or 1972 that various people in the Catholic Church would, within ten years, be extolling Martin Luther as some sort of religious hero. Even if this book were pure fabrication from beginning to end...what it claims to prognosticate has actually come true-unerringly so!"[165]

In this book is laid out the plan of the Cold War Era communist atheists to destroy all Christian churches from within. Here the unnamed agent discusses general plans with his Communist uncle:

The Unholy Land

"'You are right to consider atheism as primordial, as fundamental, but you still have much to learn in this matter.' I agreed with the most perfect bad faith. And while keeping my impassivity, I added, '...Instead of fighting religious sentiment, we ought to prompt it in a utopian direction. You must drive into the head of men...to search for, at any price, a universal religion into which all churches would be melded together. So that this idea could take form and life, in pious people, especially Roman Catholics, a feeling of guilt concerning the unique truth in which they pretend to live...it is essential to strike deeply and definitely at the Catholic Church. It is the most dangerous one.' '...how would you see this Universal Church to which you would like to have all churches run?"...very simple...So that all men could enter it, it could retain a vague idea of a God, more or less Creator, more or less Good, according to the times. Moreover, this God will be useful only in periods of calamity. Then the ancestral fear will fill these temples, but in other times, they will be rather empty...' ...I know that this will not be easy, that we will have to work hard at it, during twenty or even fifty years...By numerous and subtle means. I look at the Catholic Church as if it were a sphere. To destroy it, you must attack it in numerous small points until it loses all resemblance to what it was before. We will have to be very patient..."[166]

"As soon as I entered the seminary, I was supposed to try to discover how to destroy all that was taught to me.... 'It is up to you...to discover the right methods...At the end of a certain time...you will be put into direct action with the network...you will have ten persons under your orders, and each of these ten will also have ten other persons under their orders...[they] will never know you...Thus you will never be denounced. We already have in our service numerous priests in all countries where Catholicism is implanted...One is a bishop...We have spies everywhere and particularly old ones...'"[167]

"'1,024 priests or seminarians have entered this career before me.' 'That is correct;' he answered coldly."[168]

The details of the objectives of the Soviet Communists plan laid out in the text of AA-1025 are indeed frightening and I must agree with the publisher that it appears credible. The Soviet program of destroying the Roman Catholic Church, as well as the other Christian Churches by infiltration seems to have been played out based on the outcomes that we see in our churches today. Who could deny this?

All Christian Churches, from Protestant denominations, Roman Catholics, and the Eastern Orthodox are now expected to accept and adopt the non-Christian doctrines and practices that are in direct opposition to the Christian faith in order to serve the political mandates of the Leftists. If they fail to do so, they are threatened with the consequences of endless and expensive litigation aimed at bankrupting them, or in other cases, having their churches burned to the ground by ANTIFA terrorists while our politicians and the media cheer them on.

The point is that the Cold War was in full swing in 1958 and with the laments and tacit support of the former Pope and the election of a new Pope, the Soviets saw an opportunity to aggressively but incrementally advance their agenda in 1959 and formed plans for doing just that.

Following the Money

In spite of all their atrocities, and perhaps largely because of them, by 1914, it could be argued that the Vatican had built itself up to become the single largest and wealthiest Church organization and network on the planet (and remains so to this day.) It ran organized charities, was (and still is) in possession of vast properties, its buildings and fixtures at the Vatican were all gilded by the finest artisans with precious metals, gems, and fine marble.[169] In the Vatican bank laid untold wealth; Untold because they did not produce a bank statement for 142 years.

To make matters even worse there was the postwar status of the looted blood money to consider. The Ustaše regime had been able to deposit large amounts of gold plundered from their victim Serbs and Jews during World War II into Swiss bank accounts. The Nazis had done the same thing. Switzerland famously remained "neutral" during the war, but that of course is certainly not so. Laundering money and facilitating the security of Axis nation funds might more properly be described as aiding and abetting.

It is obvious that Switzerland while publicly maintaining this thin veneer of "neutrality" had hoped that regardless how the war ended, they would end up on top. If the Axis powers won, then they were "on the right side" for having aided them and if the Axis powers were defeated, the Swiss owned all their assets with few if any records to trace it. It would be "found money" for the Swiss. But this is yet another storyline beyond the scope of the present work.

It is speculated that out of a total of 350 million Swiss francs, an estimated 150 million was seized by British troops; however, the remaining 200 million francs (ca. $47 million) reached the Vatican. In October, 1946 the American intelligence agency SSU alleged that these funds were still held in the Vatican Bank. This issue was the subject of an unsuccessful class-action suit against the Vatican Bank and others.[170]

Alperin v. Vatican Bank was a class action suit brought by Holocaust survivors against the Vatican Bank ("Institute for the Works of Religion" or "IOR") and the Franciscan Order ("Order of Friars Minor") filed in San Francisco, California on November 15, 1999. The case was initially dismissed as a political question by the District Court for the Northern District of California in 2003, but was reinstated in part by the Court of Appeals for the Ninth Circuit in 2005.[171]

A portion of the complaint against the IOR was later dismissed in 2007 on the grounds of sovereign immunity, and the remainder of the claim against that defendant was subsequently dismissed on the ground that the property claim had no nexus to the United States, a decision that was confirmed in February, 2010 by the liberal/leftist leaning Ninth Circuit court. The case against the Franciscan Order, who by then was the sole defendants, ended in March, 2011 when the Ninth Circuit affirmed the district court's judgment dismissing the claim, and the case was not appealed further. No part of the claim, therefore, ever came to trial and none of the plaintiffs' allegations of fact were ever established in court.[172]

The Vatican retains the sole ownership of their portion of any alleged Serbian "blood money" to this day. They still have their own private bank with some 19,000 secret customers[173]. In 2013 this bank finally issued a statement of their accounts; "According to the report, the bank manages $6.8 billion, including more than $4 billion in securities, the majority of which is tied to government index bonds. But the bank also holds $55.9 million in gold, other metals and precious coins as well as a real estate company with two investment properties worth $2.5 million.[174]" This of course is just the Vatican bank assets and excludes all the church accounts and properties abroad.

Several years ago they hired an auditor to review all accounts to help tighten anti-money laundering procedures.[175] This would not have been necessary if it were not allegedly happening; Vatican Bank President at the time, Ernst Von Freyberg stated on Vatican Radio, "We have reviewed our procedures for taking on clients and for dealing with clients to make sure that no money laundering can happen at the institute..."[176] Well, that's certainly reassuring.

"Reuters has learned that as part of the current review, the bank is likely to close all accounts held by foreign embassies, following concerns about large cash deposits and withdrawals by the missions of Iran.[177]"

Was the Vatican Bank involved in money laundering by a terrorist nation at a time when America and her allies were spending money and American blood trying to combat anti-Christian terrorism?

Did not Christ Himself run the moneychangers out of the temple? Here do we have the "Vicar of Christ" operating a bank at the "headquarters" of the Church and potentially involved in illicit financial activity? If only this were the singular problem at the Vatican.

Too Little, Too Late

The Vatican rarely seems to admit any wrongdoing, and when it does, it's centuries late and seems sloppily executed. The deep wounds and innocent blood shed by them during their history are still being felt even today. Eight hundred years would pass before the sitting Pope began to apologize for the misdeeds of the Vatican. On June 29th, 2004, the Pope finally delivered an apology to Bartholomew I, the Ecumenical Patriarch of Constantinople, a leader of the Eastern Orthodox Church, for the Roman Catholic Church's role in plundering and subsequent destruction of Constantinople during the Fourth Crusade in 1204.

Constantinople from that point forward had become permanently crippled and unable to defend herself after the Latin occupation had ended in 1261. After that crusade Byzantium eventually fell to the Ottomans in 1453 and is today known as Istanbul—the apology is in fact too little, too late. The Eastern Orthodox Church left to survive best it might for centuries while the

Vatican amassed untold power, wealth and influence. Many wounds made by the Roman Catholic Church and their old allies, never seem to heal.

Then, on June 17th, 2011, the following report was posted by The Telegraph:

"Knights Templar heirs demand apology from Vatican; The last Grand Master of the warrior monks who fought in the Crusades, Jacques de Molay, was executed in Paris in 1314 on charges of heresy, black magic and idolatry. His death was part of a concerted campaign to suppress the chivalric order by King Philip IV of France....Although it was the French king who ordered de Molay to be put to death, the Templars have for centuries accused the Church in Rome of complicity. Pope Clement V initiated an inquest into the Order which led to many knights being subjected to heresy trials, before disbanding altogether..."[178]

After 697 years in the wrong, the apology seems a bit late, even if it is due.

The abuse of the Faithful

On July 6th 2017, we read the report that at the Vatican Monsignor Luigi Capozzi, 49, was arrested a day earlier by the Vatican gendarmerie in a raid for allegedly "hosting a cocaine-fueled homosexual orgy in a building right next to St. Peter's Basilica...At the time of the arrest, Capozzi was allegedly so high on cocaine that he was hospitalized for detoxification for a short period..."[179]

The article goes on to include witnesses close to the Vatican who relate that the arrest only highlights much larger issues with these kinds of problems within the Roman Catholic Church. But private parties aside, the abuse to the Roman Catholic faithful cannot be overlooked and except for whatever legal remedies the system provides the victims, they are otherwise relatively powerless to affect a correction within the church due to the structure of the organization.

In August, 2018 a grand jury in Pennsylvania issued a report that shook the Roman Catholic Church in America:

The Unholy Land

"A landmark grand jury report on clergy abuse in six Roman Catholic dioceses in Pennsylvania detailed how priests often used religious rituals, symbols of the faith and the threat of eternity in hell to groom, molest and rape children. Pennsylvania Attorney General Josh Shapiro called it the 'weaponization of faith.'"[180]

Investigators discovered that the Roman Catholic Church in Pennsylvania knew that more than 1,000 cases of alleged sexual abuse by its own clergy had occurred over decades by more than 300 men. The revelation clearly shows that the alleged abuses are not isolated incidents. The youngest victim of their alleged sex abuse was eight months old, but no matter the victim's age, the long list of alleged sadistic sexual abuses apparently knows no boundaries whatsoever:

"One priest tied up a victim with rope in the confessional in a 'praying position.' When the victim refused to perform sex, the angered priest used a 7-inch crucifix to sexually assault him."[181]

Not only did the church know about these alleged abuses, but it had allegedly developed a private methodology for *managing them* outside of the law. For the victims and their families, the legal statute of limitations have expired in all but two or three cases, so today there is little liability for the Church. Attorneys General in New York New Jersey, Nebraska, Illinois and Missouri also announced investigations into allegations of clergy abuse and/or cover ups in local dioceses.[182]

An investigation of a series of similar alleged abuses unfolded in Michigan in the same year. All of this after the United States Conference of Catholic Bishops issued their "Charter for the Protection of Children and Young People" in 2002[183]. One has to wonder, why such a charter would be necessary in a church supposedly headed by "The Vicar of Christ?" If the Pope is indeed infallible as they claim, none of this could happen in that organization.

On April 13th, 2018 at a press conference Roman Catholic Bishop Cistone introduced Judge Talbot, a member of the Catholic Lawyers Society Board of Directors.

"Talbot implored other potential victims to speak up. 'I need to hear from those who have hesitated to come forward,' he said during the press conference. "If you have been the victim of an assault of any sort, please come forward.'"[184]

The Unholy Land

What is this? The Roman Catholic Church is asking for the yet unknown alleged victims to come to them so *they* can investigate? Memo to Judge Talbot: The year is 2018 and the place is the United States of America. This is not the 10th century in Europe. But the Church somehow still arrogantly assumes that it can simply take control of a potentially criminal situation and one could suppose, influence or potentially intimidate alleged victims into silence—at least until the legal statute of limitations expires.

Law enforcement in Michigan quickly, forcefully, and properly asserted a different view than the Church after that press conference with their own statement:

"'We respectfully disagree with the procedure of the Catholic Diocese of Saginaw, announced by Bishop Cistone during today's press conference, regarding the handling of allegations of abuse by Diocese officials and employees...' Officials with the investigation team said the Diocese 'cannot and should not be used as a clearing house for the reporting of crimes by victims...That is the function of law enforcement. Any victims of abuse or other crimes should report their allegations directly to law enforcement as opposed to the Diocese or Judge Talbot, its independent delegate.'"[185]

If it is true that a man who was molested when a child cannot become a Roman Catholic priest is there any wonder why child molestation seems to be an accepted standard practice if some group was TRYING to cause the decline of the church? This strategy would force a steady decline in the availability of candidates for new priests. What better way to prevent young men from entering the priesthood than to have them disqualified?

It was just a few years ago that in 2016, the Pope issued a new one hundred page training guide for his clergy which banned homosexuals and anyone supporting what he referred to as 'gay culture' from becoming a Roman Catholic priest.[186] I am guessing the document was issued only in Latin, because based upon the lack of results it would seem that perhaps a lot of priests never read the memo.

The situation is no better in Europe. On February 6th, 2019 the BBC reported a story with the headline, "Pope admits clerical abuse of nuns including sexual slavery." Apparently, Roman Catholic nuns are allegedly being raped by priests and in one case, the woman was used as a sex slave. The report goes on to discuss similar concerns over alleged incidents in France, India, Italy, and Africa. It also refers to another source that states how in some cases pregnant nuns were forced to abort priests' unborn children, a practice strictly forbidden in Roman Catholicism.[187]

With all of this I have described, one might come away with the notion that the Roman Catholics are simply awful people. That is of course not true at all, in spite of all these terrible reports of abuse. I know many devout Roman Catholics and I can without question assure you that they are not terrible people. If you personally take the time and visit any local Roman Catholic parish, perhaps attend their mass, meet the priests, you will see something different. They are comprised by of kind and caring people who are sincere in their faith; people who are dedicated to helping their communities and their neighbors.

As with many organizations (much like the state and federal governments) the leadership at the highest levels with their inevitable human corruption often does not match the sincere values of the people at the "rank and file" levels. It is because local parishes are far removed from the Vatican and all of its centuries of misguided policy and intrigue.

I don't hold the Roman Catholic Church in contempt because they are not my brand of Christianity; it is because the duplicitous heretical actions of their leadership don't seem to reflect any Christian motives or values. Strip away all the pious pomp of the Roman Catholic Church today and throughout history and what you will see remaining is a relatively small group of powerful men acting (mostly in secret) for the purpose of seeking their own power and enrichment at the expense of others instead of serving the mission of Christ as described in the New Testament. The leadership simply uses the Papacy as a means and for all this abhorrent behavior. Do we imagine for one second that Christ would approve of subjugating and enslaving innocent people "in perpetuity" in His name? No other organization on Earth owes the world more than does the Vatican.

Where in any of this is the church that Paul described? Where is virtue and unity? From what high moral ground does the top leadership of this organization preach from? But there is hope.

The Work of the Church

The Roman Catholic Church owes the entire world reparations for their actions, and today on the basis of their abuses, some have argued that the organization ought to be heavily taxed, divested, and completely disbanded. And for the record, I certainly do not hate the Roman Catholics—the faithful people following Christ in a broken world; I have Roman Catholic friends and relatives, and I am sure that they pray for us,. They have needlessly suffered greatly at the hands of their own church leadership for centuries, and it continues today. Even so, the Roman Catholic Church today comprises over 50% of the world's Christians, representing about a 3% increase over the course of the 20th century.[188]

It would be totally unfair and completely irresponsible to conclude an examination of the Roman Catholic Church after looking only at its bloody and troubled history and modern complications. There is another side to the Vatican and it plays a most important role in benevolence around the globe today.

The Roman Catholic Church is today the largest non-government provider of education and medical services on the planet.[189] In 2010, the Catholic Church's Pontifical Council for Pastoral Assistance to Health Care Workers stated that the church now manages 26% of health care facilities in the world, "According to a press release, the Church has '117,000 health care facilities, including hospitals, clinics, orphanages,' as well as '18,000 pharmacies and 512 centers' for the care of those with leprosy."[190]

The Roman Catholic Church has always been involved in education, since the founding of the first universities of Europe. It runs and sponsors thousands of primary and secondary schools, colleges and universities throughout the world[191], and operates the world's largest non-governmental school system.[192]

Religious institutes for women have played a particularly prominent role in the provision of health and education services,[193] as with orders such as the Sisters of Mercy, Little Sisters of the Poor, the Missionaries of Charity, the Sisters of St. Joseph of the Sacred Heart, the Sisters of the Blessed Sacrament and the Daughters of Charity of Saint Vincent de Paul.[194] The renown Roman Catholic nun Mother Teresa of Calcutta, India, founder of the Missionaries of Charity, was awarded the Nobel Peace Prize in 1979 for her humanitarian work among India's poor.[195] In 1996, Bishop Carlos Filipe Ximenes Belo won the same award for "work towards a just and peaceful solution to the conflict in East Timor."[196]

The Church is also actively engaged in international aid and development through organizations such as Catholic Relief Services, Caritas International, Aid to the Church in Need, refugee advocacy groups such as the Jesuit Refugee Service and community aid groups such as the Saint Vincent de Paul Society.[197]

The main fraternity for The Roman Catholics is The Knights of Columbus, boasting a membership of nearly two million Roman Catholic men.[198] It was established by Father Michael J. McGivney, the 29-year-old assistant pastor of St. Mary's Church in New Haven, Connecticut in early 1882.

"Late-19th century Connecticut was marked by the growing prevalence of fraternal benefit societies, hostility toward Catholic immigrants and dangerous working conditions in factories that left many families fatherless. Recognizing a vital, practical need in his community, Father Michael J. McGivney...proposed establishing a lay organization, the goal of which would be to prevent Catholic men from entering secret societies whose membership was antithetical to Church teaching, to unite men of Catholic faith and to provide for the families of deceased members...As a symbol that allegiance to their country did not conflict with allegiance to their faith, the organization's members took as their patron Christopher Columbus — recognized as a Catholic and celebrated as the discoverer of America....In addition to the Order's stated benefits, Catholic men were drawn to the Knights because of its emphasis on serving one's Church, community and family with virtue."[199]

Today the Knights of Columbus are more active than ever supporting many programs,

"charitable activities encompass an almost infinite variety of local, national and international projects. Our own unique charities include the Christian Refugee Relief Fund, Disaster Relief, Ultrasound Initiative, and Coats for Kids. We also partner with international charities including Special Olympics, the Global Wheelchair Mission and Habitat for Humanity."[200]

With these activities in mind, one comes away with a broader, more accurate, and balanced image of the modern Roman Catholic Church and the positive realities of its faithful today. They are no longer burning heretics at the stake, but are committed to supporting a broad network of unmatched international benevolences which the world desperately needs and would sorely miss without them.

7

The Modern Christian Church in America

"My concern is not whether God is on our side; my greatest concern is to be on God's side, for God is always right."

President Abraham Lincoln

When we look to the founding of America, we find that not only do the traditional Christian symbols introduced by the Church endure, but that faith in God was paramount for our Founding Fathers as it also was for just about everyone else at that time. How do we know this? In the world of subjugated peoples, America was different; a nation that ruled *itself.* It was an exception to the rule, an oddity, an experiment. As a result, the ruling classes of the day around the globe at the time had their doubts whether America would succeed and for how long.

It was this concern that motivated Alexis de Tocqueville to visit America in 1831 and examine virtually every facet of American life that he could engage, in order to discover how America even existed and functioned. He had asked the French Revolutionary government to send him to America for the benign purpose of examining our prison system and report on prison reform. His resulting masterpiece work, *Democracy in America,* has eighty-five chapters that cover nearly everything one would want to know about this new nation called

America at that time. Indeed I want to stress that many of the solutions to America's domestic issues today can be gleaned from his work. That is, if we can again discover and understand why America survived its first century, we may come to learn what it is that will correct America's path today. A cultural restoration is in order, to be sure.

Whether technically Christian or not, at America's core is faith in the same God as Noah, Abraham, Moses—and the Byzantines. References to God as "Providence" and "The Creator" are discovered across hundreds of early American Founding texts and speeches. Alexis de Tocqueville observed this general trend in America right away:

"It was religion that gave birth to the Anglo-American societies. This must always be borne in mind. Hence religion in the United States is inextricably intertwined with all the national habits and all the feelings to which the fatherland gives rise. This gives it a peculiar force."[201]

Today, of course, things are different. Our culture is different. I will argue the case that that American organized religion has catastrophically failed to maintain education on virtue in the United States, and is now largely being used by both individuals and political operatives to serve personal and corporate goals and objectives. This is truly an inarguable fact based on the data we see year after year on the subject of religion. Many of the modern denominations do not see the education of Biblical virtues as their mission any longer. Teaching virtue and unity is not exciting, it does not attract new members and their money; and it actually repels folks who enjoy their errant and often sinful ways; teaching the Gospels is now "politically incorrect" and therefore has been cast as unpopular; a losing proposition to a generation of young adults who see little importance and find no purpose for western Christianity.

The Christian Theatre

British author G.K. Chesterton (1874-1936) illustrated what he must have seen as the decline of Christianity in terms that might be expected of one in his trade:

The Unholy Land

"According to most philosophers, God in making the world enslaved it. According to Christianity, in making it, He set it free. God had written, not so much a poem, but rather a play; a play he had planned as perfect, but which had necessarily been left to human actors and stage-managers, who had since made a great mess of it.[202]"

Sometimes you go to a new church and you can't really tell if it's a show or a church service. Sadly, it turns out that the Protestant church services are mostly tailored to the expectations of the crowd they are trying to attract and hold with no thought to reverence, quietness, or even holiness. Do you expect to see a man or woman dressed in white or black robes walking to a row of lit candles while a heavenly choir chants in acapella some time faded early American hymn? You can find a church like that. Do you instead prefer upon your entry into the church an atmosphere of electric guitars and thundering drum solos that approach the likes of a rock band? I have visited a local church that is held in an actual theater and their rock band puts on a concert every Sunday at their services complete with choreographed lights and fog machines. Why not pyrotechnics as well? In either case, WELCOME TO THE SHOW. This is Christian Theater Hour.

Does any of this have anything to do with Christ or the Church Christ founded? Christ was content preaching anywhere He went. From the Jewish temples to the rocky shores of a lake. There was no pomp and circumstance for Christ, no rock music, no fog machines, flashing lights, or the rest of it. In fact, musical instruments were banned for use in the church by the earliest canons of the church...ignored by Protestants altogether.

Further, there are no explicit instructions from Christ or even Paul to turn church services into distracting modern concerts. So why do we do it? I have been to quite a few churches in my life. It seems to me that many Protestant churches often like put on a show for themselves and for the crowd. Their product is not the Gospels, but they sell emotionalism, wrapped in a Bible verse. They want (and need) the people to "feel welcome" and enjoy the atmosphere...and come back next week with more money. The show has to be familiar, interesting, upbeat, loud or exciting. It has to be memorable.

It's difficult to know which elements are designed to merely attract or fulfil the expectations people have about what church should look and feel like today versus what ought to rightfully be practiced in the church for Christ as each has their own custom standards. Now it seems that it's important to provide a distinctive pattern of customized showmanship with various visual and audio elements for the audience that they will remember...I'm talking about important *somatic markers* that make both subtle and deep emotional connections to the human psyche.

Symbols are used across Christianity, lots of symbols; Crosses, Crucifixes, Chi-Rho's, cups and candle sticks, stained glass panels, printed banners, church logos, t-shirts, and embroidered vestments. A mirror-polished brass cross paraded down the aisle. At many churches, the American flag is posted in the sanctuary on the left of the altar space, the Protestant Christian flag posted on the right; patriotism is itself is another important symbol. Have these people forgotten that Christianity trancends lines on a map, or pledges made to a civil government? All these symbols are used to convey ideas and create a specific atmosphere. Their patrons may become trained like Pavlov's dogs only acting upon either the toning of the church bell or the riff of a guitar. They become conditioned to the customized form of Christianity presented to them, and they are comfortable with it.

Both the Roman Catholic Church and the Eastern Orthodox Church use incense at their services, engaging the sense of smell—another powerful somatic marker. The more of the five senses they can engage the more memorable they are.

To complicate matters, so much of these widely varying elements are absolutely genuine practice within Christianity. Consider the view of the (non-Protestant) Orthodox Christians regarding their services:

"All artificiality is foreign to Orthodox worship. There is nothing and must be nothing theatrical or merely entertaining. The rites of the hierarchical services were developed in detail and are not meant to entertain the faithful or distract them from prayer; rather, quite the contrary, they are meant to draw the faithful into the 'theourgic' mystery of the heavenly Eucharist...everything is symbolic, iconic, and significant."[203]

In fact, at the Eastern Orthodox vespers service, an evening service, the choir always sings this as the priest censes the church:

The Unholy Land

"LORD, I cry unto thee: make haste unto me; give ear unto my voice, when I cry unto thee. Let my prayer be set forth before thee as incense; and the lifting up of my hands as the evening sacrifice.,,"

This is directly from Psalm 141. A Reader in the church will read the remaining part of Psalm 141 out loud.

And it may come as a surprise to many Americans that the use of incense in the church is in fact, a Biblical commandment:

"My name will be great among the nations, from where the sun rises to where it sets. In every place incense and pure offerings will be brought to me, because my name will be great among the nations," says the Lord Almighty."

Malachi 1:11 NIV

The American Protestant churches of today have all developed a specific cadence to their shows, and this is also quite deliberate. The details differ much between them, but the framework is similar. They start with music and/or a procession of some kind, they have announcements, they read a passage from the Bible, maybe have some more music, take up an offering, more music, then a sermon, more music, a prayer and then a dismissal. It's eerily similar to a modern corporate board meeting or a meeting of the Masons, but with music added.

At a common board meeting, there is a call to order, minutes are read, the chair makes a statement, others may speak, people contribute to the discussion, and they close the meeting. You see, it's a basic form that is familiar to people. They know it even if they don't notice the similarity consciously. Perhaps this corporate structure was copied from the church, which predated Robert's Rules of Order first published in 1876. But in any event, it makes them comfortable. Not to say it is ALL bad.

Perhaps the root of all this borderline deviant, nontraditional activity in the churches has a more specific and unsuspected contributor--the architects of the buildings. Modern American churches are being designed as public attractions and laid out inside for comfort. One prominent church architect firm states, "We believe in 'architectural evangelism' – that idea that the building itself plays a role in attracting people to your church."[204] The Hagia Sophia was designed with the same aim in the 6th Century. But today have but to ask if all of this for God's glory or for our own comfort and entertainment?

After the legalization of Christianity in 312 AD, Emperor Constantine engaged in a program of building Christian churches in Byzantium. Most of these were quite small in comparison to today's American standards. Not only did this reflect the size of the local populations these parishes were to serve, there was another purpose for this. The Church generally believed that no parish should be so large in number that the priest did not personally know each parishioner. This was to make sure that the priest could effectively do his job to minister to the faithful and that the faithful themselves remained a single, unified, cohesive family of faith--as much as that were possible. This concept is opposite of the American standard today where "megachurches" are being designed larger and larger around attendance of 4,600 people[205] and where no one knows anyone else and there might be ten "associate pastors" attempting to minister to the needs of the massive group not in unity, but piecemeal.

Why would an American church even want 4,600 members? In a an out of control capitalist culture, it is about money. They have structured these churches like a tax-exempt business. The members are in many ways akin to customers who bring their needs and expectations for emotionalism which the church provides and that gives them comfort. The church that accommodates them best to their liking receives their support and donations. It simply was not so in the early churches, nor was it ever intended to be. The largest of all early Christian Churches is the Church of Holy Wisdom, the Hagia Sophia located in Istanbul, Turkey. It was originally built on a smaller scale by Emperor Theodosius II in 415. This church was destroyed during the NIKA revolts, which presented Emperor Justinian I the opportunity to completely rebuild in its near-present form in 532 AD to 537 AD as it took five years to complete it. This church in Constantinople was the center of Christendom and the largest church for a thousand years of Christian history. When we study this remarkable church, its floorplan, its décor, its orientation, and so on, we discover that this church, as with all the other smaller churches, was focused on and designed around the worship of the Christian God; a "Heaven on Earth." Each brick, before firing, was stamped with a verse of Psalms, and the workers paused with every 12th brick they laid to offer prayer. As they built the Hagia Sophia, they enclosed many holy relics in the walls of the sanctuary.[206]

None of these early traditional churches, great or small, were focused on the comfort and amenities to attract "customers" such as being done today with the inclusion of lounges, café's, coffee bars, office suites, sport courts, children's entertainment centers, kitchens and theaters. This has to be done in a world where *competition* for members is the focus. Before Protestantism, there was only ONE choice in Christian Churches because there were no creed-denying "denominations" with churches of their own. In short, modern American church architecture has completely discarded the traditional ministry offered through church architecture and taken on a wholly secular style and appeal. This is a divisive disservice to Christians and a betrayal of the Christian Church because these modern designs present the church as something that it is not.

The Church of Holy Wisdom, the Hagia Sophia. Istanbul, Turkey. Source: http://www.pallasweb.com/deesis/dome-of-hagia-sophia.html

The Cancer of Liberalism and virtue-signaling of artificial "charity"

We are told today by every American Leftist, religious or not, that pushing for wealth redistribution measures ("taxing the rich") is somehow just and charitable because America is "the most wealthy nation in the world." I have already debunked the false narrative about our nation being wealthy as we are a nation approaching $40 trillion in public debt without any means or motivation to do anything about it. A nation so straddled with debt cannot afford to be "charitable." Neither is that false obligation found anywhere in our Constitution.

There is a difference between voluntary charity and forced redistribution of wealth to whatever class the political elites deem worthy to bestow their largesse. Charity never originates from any government; for government has no money of its own. It can only take money from the people by force or borrow money in the name of the people. With this is no virtue or justice whatsoever. Both Socialism and Communism ironically appropriate a Christian sounding message, using the same moral imperatives to subjectively enforce their theft and redistribution. The results are often entirely unjust, unfair, and punitive.

True charity comes from individuals, corporations, and churches that provide support for charitable organizations and individuals. Christianity calls for its adherents to voluntarily help their neighbor, their needy, widows, orphans, elderly, and the poor. This is where virtue is defined and man many show himself a true follower of Christ. Individual voluntary giving and charity is what the great saints of the Christian Church exhorted and expected of us also:

Basil of Caesarea (c. 330-379) established an entire complex around the church and monastery that included hostels, almshouses, and hospitals for infectious diseases. In 368 there was a famine when Basil denounced against profiteers and the indifferent attitudes of the wealthy. He penned a sermon on The Rich Fool, stating:

"Who is the covetous man? One for whom plenty is not enough. Who is the defrauder? One who takes away what belongs to everyone. And are not you covetous, are you not a defrauder, when you keep for private use what you were given for distribution? When some one strips a man of his clothes we call him a thief. And one who might clothe the naked and does not—should not he be given the same name? The bread in your hoard belongs to the hungry; the cloak in your wardrobe belongs to the naked; the shoes you let rot belong to the barefoot; the money in your vaults belongs to the destitute. All you might help and do not—to all these you are doing wrong"

John Chrysostom (c.347 -407) clarified a view of the rich in a more specific tone:

"I am often reproached for continually attacking the rich. Yes, because the rich are continually attacking the poor. But those I attack are not the rich as such, only those who misuse their wealth. I point out constantly that those I accuse are not the rich, but the rapacious; wealth is one thing, covetousness another. Learn to distinguish."

Both men of the church are talking about *individuals* and their roles in society, *not government.* Neither promotes the modern leftist notion of government becoming the clearinghouse of private wealth. That is not charity, its theft. As an Orthodox Christian priest, so rightly observed:

"When the government takes from the rich and gives to the poor, and the government is a secular state, there is no love of Christ in the equation. The rich are not blessed by engaging in an act of charity, because they have no choice in the matter, and the poor have no gratitude to anyone for getting it, and certain do not have the gospel shared with them as a result. I am in favor of helping the poor, and doing it in the name of Christ, not having the government take the love of Christ out of the picture."[207]

For all their artificial cries of "separation of church and state" many Leftist church denominations have used their organization to insert themselves into many political issues, using church resources and influence to achieve political goals instead of focusing on charities and carrying the message and mission of Christ, which is apolitical. They often say they are the same, but their political ambitions and the objectives of Christianity are in fact two different things. Christ is not a politician who set out to change and reshape America into an imaginary Leftist Utopia.

The American Liberals have forever pushed for the largest, bloated, most expensive and incredibly inefficient American government in order to extract money from the citizens and drive the public debt beyond sustainable levels so they can become the primary "keepers" of power in American society, and keep the American people and churches poor. They fill the ranks of government with layers of powerful, uncaring, and often incompetent bureaucrats, promising services that have nothing to do with a Constitutional American Government.

Remember the "Affordable Care Act?" The health insurance premiums were suddenly raised to astronomically high prices—often 500% higher than most families were paying prior to the enactment of the law. It was designed to be unaffordable and a huge financial detriment to Americans. But then there were large subsidies provided only to the preferred class of people whom the Democrats had already identified. The rest of us were expected to pay the confiscatory premiums—and the heavy fines to the government if we did not comply.

How did the Affordable Care Act get passed into law? Why not ask one of its architects Jonathan Gruber:

"Lack of transparency is a huge political advantage...and basically, call it the stupidity of the American voter or whatever, but basically that was really, really critical for the thing to pass...If CBO scored the [individual] mandate as taxes, the bill dies...If you had a law that made it explicit that healthy people are going to pay in and sick people are going to get subsidies, it would not have passed...we could make it all transparent, but I'd rather have this law than not."[208]

And so we learn that it is not benevolent government looking out for our health, but a deceitful government that set up a giant Socialist policy to illicitly transfer wealth from private American citizens to a preferred group; a law that was eventually ruled as a tax by the Supreme Court. Do you need daycare for your child? Government should pay for that. Does your child need education? Government should pay for that. Do you or your kids need to be fed? Government should pay for that. Do the families of their voters need healthcare? Government should pay for that. On and on it goes for only a "qualified" group of targeted democrat voters. The rest of America is largely denied these "benefits" as they are the ones required by taxation to pay for all the rest.

It was nothing short of simple wealth redistribution, massive in scale, forcing some Americans literally into poverty while the Democrats secured votes by pandering to their voter block of illegal aliens and various minorities. Is this government "nanny-state" Socialism supposed to be the virtue and unity of a "Christian nation?" Absolutely not. An educated church would know better and reject it. Socialism is above all, dishonest because it encourages people to take what is not theirs and provides some unjust legal means to permit it;

"Under socialism a ruling class of intellectuals, bureaucrats and social planners decide what people want or what is good for society and then use the coercive power of the State to regulate, tax, and redistribute the wealth of those who work for a living. In other words, socialism is a form of legalized theft."[209]

Someone doubtlessly will argue that these services exist because so many Americans cannot afford health care, child care, education for their children, and basic necessities. That's true, but why is that happening in the "the wealthiest nation in the world?" It is because that same bloated government is bleeding the American citizen dry of the value of the currency through their forever increasing serial taxation and monetary inflation, which amounts to a universal tax.

It is this reason why my grandfather could raise three children, own their house in the city, take vacations and own a car, and retire on a bus driver's salary and today his paycheck would not buy a pair of work boots. Don't be fooled, it is government through use of the Federal Reserve policies and other mechanisms that manipulate the value of the American currency.

For the citizens, it means that saving money and trying to get it to grow for retirement, saving for our children's schooling, and for anything else is now all but impossible. Whatever you are putting into your savings is losing purchasing power more than you are earning on the money every year. Many continue to resort to playing in the Wall Street casino.

It is the American government and its army of bureaucrats having caused the great American poverty we have, and will continue to have. The same government that steps in to promise solutions and services to support the people for the things we can no longer afford on our own.

In Russia, as in other places abroad, it was historically the Orthodox Christian Church and its institutions that cared for society through a vast and successful system of churches, monasteries, schools, hospitals, orphanages, and hospices. The Church was fulfilling the primary social needs of the nation. The Communists are atheists, who came into power by force to replace the role of the church in Russia. To accomplish this, they closed all of these public services and churches, often imprisoned and killed the clergy, tried to destroy the church structure entirely, and fill those roles itself (and poorly) instead. This was done for the purpose of centralizing power and control over the people to a brutal atheist government instead of the benevolent Holy Christian Church. American leftist democrats have done exactly the same thing in the United States to some less obvious degree but with arguably greater success because many if not most American Christians embrace this false "charity."

Liberals in general often point to the many challenges and failures throughout Christianity and its organizations and then promote those failures in their never ending effort to discredit the conservative traditions of the faith and is value to society. They want to judge the God of the Christians by His people and sanctimoniously degrade people of faith as uneducated, ignorant, and irrelevant to the American fabric. Their solution for teaching proper citizenship, taking care of the sick, the poor, the elderly, and so on (what many might call the work of Christ or work of the church) they push to government alone—as "state-ism" or more commonly, Socialism. In order to achieve this goal, they seek to redefine what the Christian Church is and what it teaches. This is a similar ideological process to how the Russian Communists persecuted the Orthodox Church in Russia from 1917 to 1988.

The core principles of leftist/liberalism are actually opposed to the founding principles of both Christianity and our own American Constitution. That's an uncomfortable fact. These liberal principles once unmasked, are really the same principles as socialism, so-called "democratic socialism," communism, and Fascism. Let us ask first what part of the liberal agenda supports constitutionalism? What happens when undereducated or mal-educated Americans are duped into electing liberals into office?

Noah Webster understood exactly the outcome:

"It is alleged by men of loose principles, or defective views of the subject, that religion and morality are not necessary or important qualifications for political station. When a citizen gives his vote to a man of immorality, he abuses his civic responsibility. He sacrifices not only his own interest but that of his neighbor, and he betrays the interest of his country."

"If the citizens neglect their Duty and place unprincipled men in office, the government will soon be corrupted; laws will be made, not for the public good so much as for selfish or local purposes; corrupt or incompetent men will be appointed to execute the Laws; the public revenues will be squandered on unworthy men; and the rights of the citizen will be violated or disregarded."

Right and Wrong

As a result of the deliberate and gradual effort by the Left to "redefine" what American culture is, the Left pushed the notion of moral relativism in all things, where there was no longer any firm standard (biblical or otherwise) for judging right and wrong. They were successful and we now struggle with this basic issue. In a 2014 Pew Religious Landscape Study, 64% of the respondents thought that "right or wrong depends on the situation.[210]" This trend was seen across many religious groups.

What's even worse is that the youngest generation and newest Americans (immigrants) have no moral compass. Only 15% of the respondents in the same study aged 18 – 29 and a scant 12% of immigrants agreed that "there are clear standards for what is right and wrong.[211]"

So-called "higher education" has apparently done much to harm the values of Americans. Only 10% of the respondents in the same study who have completed post-graduate degrees agreed that "there are clear standards for what is right and wrong," while the figure rises to 38% of those with high school or less education[212]"

It should be no surprise that the results of the study show clear differences of opinion between Conservatives and Liberals. Fifty-three percent of conservatives agreed that "there are clear standards for what is right and wrong," while a combined 67% liberal/moderate agreed that "right or wrong depends on the situation [213]" With so great a divide, it would seem impossible to reconcile these two groups, as they are polar opposites on the issue, and reconciliation or unity is not the aim of the Leftists.

God's truth states that there are in fact clear standards for what is right and what is wrong. The religious liberals and "moderates" will need to accept this fact if Christianity is to have any validity. Liberals apparently want to live in a world of moral relativism, defined solely by them. This is contrary to the laws of God and incongruent with the message of Christ as well as the values of our American Founders and statesmen.

It is no wonder that the hard core Leftists despise genuine Christianity. They seek and teach a Christianity of comfort and convenience—one that is there when they need it, and set aside so as not to be in their way when they don't—and has nothing to do with supporting the tenants of a conservative American culture and government. Or worse, they push a political Christianity, one that they craft and use to advance their own political agendas to reshape America.

There are a series of negative results when we ignore God this way. The Apostle Paul clearly lays out what happens when people ignore the message of Christ:

"When you follow the desires of your sinful nature, the results are very clear: sexual immorality, impurity, lustful pleasures, idolatry, sorcery, hostility, quarreling, jealousy, outbursts of anger, selfish ambition, dissension, division, envy, drunkenness, wild parties, and other sins like these. Let me tell you again, as I have before, that anyone living that sort of life will not inherit the Kingdom of God."

Galatians 5: 19- 21 NLT

Are these not the exact things that too often define American cultural landscape of today? Of course they are, and by any and every measure they have continued to get worse with every new generation, spurred on by a media-driven message that teaches our youth that no deviant behavior is unacceptable, and that genuine Christians are just closed-minded racists, sexists, bigoted homophobes and "conservative" Christianity is a farce unless it "changes with the times" to accept and celebrate all manner of sin into its evolving doctrine.

Pushing his party's moral relativism on Americans, Barack Hussein Obama could not help but lecture Christians about the Crusades in order to falsely assert some kind of moral equivalence between conservative Christians today and the modern barbarism of ISIS which, at the time of 2015, was slaughtering Christians around the globe, while he stood idly by and did nothing but play golf. He stated:

"Lest we get on our high horse and think this is unique to some other place, remember that during the Crusades and the Inquisition, people committed terrible deeds in the name of Christ. In our home country, slavery and Jim Crow all too often was justified in the name of Christ. ... So this is not unique to one group or one religion. There is a tendency in us, a sinful tendency that can pervert and distort our faith...I believe that the starting point of faith is some doubt—not being so full of yourself and so confident that you are right and that God speaks only to us, and doesn't speak to others, that God only cares about us and doesn't care about others, that somehow we alone are in possession of the truth."[214]

He is of course, correct in his assessment that terrible things have been done "in the name of Christ," but the Crusades were initially an immediate response to the violent incursion and expansion of Islam into Christian held territories. While Christians were generally supportive of the Crusades, the individual motives of those executing these crusades were often not always Christ-centered... we might ask the Byzantines of 1204 about that. Apparently Obama conveniently forgets the entire Protestant Reformation period which was aimed at addressing the direction, correcting the abuses, and removing the corrupt authority of the Roman Catholic Church at the time.

The Liberal's argument—and Obama's—falls flat in many ways with the simple understanding that while Christ is sinless and perfect, His followers, of course, are not. Obama's invocation of a pre-Reformation series of events that took place on another continent by peoples of other nations to first artificially create and then to invoke a twisted moral equivalence to excuse today's Muslim terrorists slaughter of unarmed Christians is ridiculous, preposterous, and frankly, deeply offensive. Obama has only illustrated his status as a liberal political hack and exposed his apparent deep rooted contempt of Christians.

Where is Unity?

These observations by no means imply that we should ever seek to establish an autocratic Christian Theocracy. Certainly not. Yet virtue and unity must have a solid and specific basis, an origin, and be supported with an organized course of action. Our Founders insisted that our Natural Rights originated from God, and it is past time that we remind our government of this fact.

It is, however, the church then that must teach our citizens about virtues and unity. This means that the fraudulent malfeasance that is pawned off as Christianity now must be "cleaned up" and the message of Christ restored as its centerpiece. It would seem that we need an American Christian Reformation of some kind. Without the standards of something bigger than merely the laws of a few politicians our society will be lost. There seems to be fewer and larger churches today with many teaching dubious messages of nothing more than hope, love, peace, prosperity, and joy—Prosperity Theology.

Many American Protestant churches were at one time quite conservative relative to today's culture. It was this conservatism that Liberals have directly targeted for a bit over a hundred years in the United States. Seeing how ineffective they were at combatting it head on with messaging of "free love" in the 1960's and other cultural stupidity, they decided instead to formulate a plan to destroy the Christian churches from within. (This sounds familiar.)

The Liberal Democrat establishments of today wantonly and deceitfully use Christ and twist the former conservative reputation of the churches to attract and retain many honest Christians who attend out of conscience to worship, who come to learn, and to serve Christ. Once they are "captive" then they are continuously bombarded with both overt and subliminal Liberal messaging, all supported by some misinterpretation and sheer distortion of the Bible. The hoped for result is for young people to become indoctrinated with Liberal thought, ideas, and goals thinking that liberal political ambitions and tenants are actually Christianity—but they are wholly misled.

A large part of the uninformed American public, now almost entirely incapable of problem-solving proficiency[215] (and I would argue also critical thinking) on their own. They accept the liberal messaging and are easily led astray from Christ and His message. They become accustomed to supporting any leftist agenda pushed by the denomination as a part of their "faith," complete with their financial support used for the purpose. The Bible becomes no more holy than any other book the liberals might use to support their twisted agenda of globalism.

"Jesus said, 'Let the little children come to me, and do not hinder them, for the kingdom of heaven belongs to such as these.'"

Matthew 19:14

The nonexistence of the woman's "right" to choose death

The Bill of Rights does not contain an inalienable right for American women to kill their children in the womb. Likewise, the American Constitution has no provision for the Federal Government to approve of infanticide. The government itself is regulated by the enumerated powers, not *unlimited power* to dictate to the American citizens. Here are the specific Constitutional powers the Federal Government presently has:

The list appears in Article One, Section Eight of the Constitution and enumerates the proper objects of congressional legislation.[216]

The U.S. Congress may only:

- ✓ Borrow money, coin money, regulate its value, and punish counterfeiters
- ✓ Regulate commerce with foreign nations, among the states, and with Indian tribes
- ✓ Establish rules for naturalization and bankruptcy
- ✓ Establish Post Offices and Post Roads
- ✓ Issue patents and copyrights
- ✓ Establish courts inferior to the Supreme Court

- ✓ Punish pirates
- ✓ Suppress insurrections, repel invasions, declare war, raise an army, maintain a navy, and make rules for the army and navy
- ✓ Organize the Militia (leaving to the states the appointment of officers and the authority of training the Militias)

Any proposed activity beyond these must be left to the different state governments. The 1870's, however, was not the last time American Federal Government executed a policy of genocide[f] while the American churches turned a blind eye. We were to repeat it again a century later, commencing in 1973 with the Supreme Court's decision on Roe vs Wade—a court decision celebrated and defended by rabid godless liberals then and now. This was to be a quiet genocide, one without soldiers or guns. Since the court ruling in 1973, over 66,313,080 children have been aborted in the U.S. alone.[217] 30% of these children were African American.[218]

When we broaden the scope and look globally, we learn that this "legal" infanticide affects far more lives than just the children of the United States:

"Between 2010–2014, on average, 56 million induced ("safe" and unsafe) abortions occurred worldwide **each year**. There were 35 induced abortions per 1000 women aged between 15–44 years. 25% of all pregnancies ended in an induced abortion."[219]

Since 1980, the number of abortions globally amounts to more than 1,757,192,300.[220] The entire variety of factions involved in the issue of abortion desperately need intervention by the communities of faith.

St. John Chrysostrom wrote:

"To destroy the fetus 'is something worse than murder.' The one who does this 'does not take away life that has already been born, but prevents it from being born."

It was not long after that leaders of the Christian Church met at the Council in Trullo (Constantinople) held in 692 AD. There they concluded many rules, among them was that assisting in abortion or having an abortion became equivalent to murder. At that time the

---

[f] With regards to the Native American Nations.

Christian Church officially became clear on this issue, AND, there was only ONE church.

However, in 21st Century America, the situation has now changed and today not only is the practice legalized but also funded in part with American tax dollars. Sadly, in a recent survey of Christians, 38% disagreed with the statement, "Abortion is a sin."[221]

The following synopsis of church positions on abortion was adapted from a January 16, 2013 PEW article, "Religious Groups' Official Positions on Abortion[222]"

American Baptist Churches in the U.S.A: Though the board opposes abortion "as a primary means of birth control," it does not condemn abortion outright.

Roman Catholicism: In accordance with its widely publicized anti-abortion teachings, the Roman Catholic Church opposes abortion in all circumstances.

The Church of Jesus Christ of Latter-day Saints (Mormons) teaches that "elective abortion for personal or social convenience is contrary to the will and the commandments of God." Therefore, the church says, any facilitation of or support for this kind of abortion warrants excommunication from the church. However, the church believes that certain circumstances can justify abortion, such as a pregnancy that threatens the life of the mother or that has come about as the result of rape or incest.

Episcopal Church: While the Episcopal Church recognizes a woman's right to terminate her pregnancy, the church condones abortion only in cases of rape or incest, cases in which a mother's physical or mental health is at risk, or cases involving fetal abnormalities. The church forbids "abortion as a means of birth control, family planning, sex selection or any reason of mere convenience."

Evangelical Lutheran Church in America: The official position states that "abortion prior to viability [of a fetus] should not be prohibited by law or by lack of public funding" but that abortion after the point of fetal viability should be prohibited except when the life of a mother is threatened or when fetal abnormalities pose a fatal threat to a newborn.

The Lutheran Church-Missouri Synod states that "[s]ince abortion takes a human life, it is not a moral option except to prevent the death of ... the mother."

The National Association of Evangelicals has passed a number of resolutions (more recently in 2010) stating its opposition to abortion. However, the organization recognizes that there might be situations in which terminating a pregnancy is warranted – such as protecting the life of a mother or in cases of rape or incest.

Presbyterian Church (U.S.A.); In 2006, the Presbyterian Church's national governing body, the General Assembly, reaffirmed its belief that the termination of a pregnancy is a personal decision. While the church disapproves of abortion as a means of birth control or as a method of convenience, it seeks "to maintain within its fellowship those who, on the basis of a study of Scripture and prayerful decision, come to diverse conclusions and actions" on the issue.

Southern Baptist Convention; In a 1996 resolution on partial-birth abortion, the Southern Baptist Convention reaffirmed its opposition to abortion, stating that "all human life is a sacred gift from our sovereign God and therefore ... all abortions, except in those very rare cases where the life of the mother is clearly in danger, are wrong."

Unitarian Universalist Association of Congregations; Beginning in 1963, the Unitarian Universalist Association of Congregations passed a series of resolutions to support "the right to choose contraception and abortion as a legitimate expression of our constitutional rights."

The United Church of Christ is a firm advocate of reproductive rights, including the right to a safe abortion.

The United Methodist Church opposes abortion; it affirms that it is "equally bound to respect the sacredness of the life and well-being of the mother and the unborn child." The church sanctions "the legal option of abortion under proper medical procedures" but rejects abortion as a method of gender selection or birth control and stresses that those considering abortions should prayerfully seek guidance from their doctors, families and ministers.

The Unholy Land

Eastern Orthodox Christian Churches generally conclude, "As to abortion, the Church very clearly and absolutely condemns it as an act of murder in every case."[223]

How did this change in values come about? This shift away from valuing the sanctity of life in American churches occurred rapidly, over the course of just a couple of decades and was driven by a variety of mediums in our culture. There were several operatives in the public square: first, there were the hedonists. The group that supported "free love" sprang up in the U.S. in the 1960s' but their philosophy of sex without any responsibility, attachments, or consequences has been around since before Sodom and Gomorrah, and in every civilization since.

In America, our art is but one small reflection into how this change occurred. We often refer to the culture of "sex, drugs, and rock and roll," but at the same time this revolution in music was beginning, a similar pattern was happening in the visual arts as well, and it is a clue to solving this puzzle of the shift in the American ethos.

A Tale of Two Artists; a shift in American Culture

There is an age-old debate whether art depicts life or life is reflecting art. So it is in America. Illustrator and painter Norman P. Rockwell was born in 1894 in Brooklyn, New York. In his 20's he began a successful career in painting original work depicting American life in magazines such as *The Saturday Evening Post*, *Boy's Life*, and *Look*. He would continue his work for the *Post* for forty-seven years, ending in the early 1960's. He would then continue his work for the Boy Scouts of America the rest of his life; he died in November, 1978.[224]

In many ways, Rockwell's work defined and supported our traditional American cultural ideals and helped to keep the American culture grounded. In his work we saw ourselves. Women in particular were depicted as innocent young girls, virtuous wives, and corrective mothers engaged in everyday activities, in average clothes and accessories. They were presented as teachers and nurses. Men were presented as curious and naturally mischievous boys, courageous young men, and often chagrined husbands and fathers. They were painted in occupations of everything from patient barbers and less than honest butchers, to courageous soldiers, aloof doctors, and ambitious architects. These images were supported by other publications like *Better Homes and Gardens* and *Reader's Digest*. Rockwell subconsciously sought to use his art to correct flaws he saw in the American culture, noting once:

"Maybe as I grew up and found the world wasn't the perfect place I had thought it to be, I unconsciously decided that if it wasn't an ideal world, it should be, and so painted only the ideal aspects of it."[225]

Why would Norman Rockwell see a less than "perfect place" or not an "ideal world" in American domestic life? Because, like us, we all understood that it was in fact neither perfect nor ideal. Human nature is what it is, but Rockwell sought to show us a better version of ourselves, perhaps to encourage us to improve.

In contrast, another artistic medium also circulated in America at the same time. The classic pinup depictions of topless women was an old but current medium of the day and coexisted with works like Rockwell's in the American culture all through the 20th century. It was often the same media consumer, and for these men, the genre presented them with an "ideal" image of women that they really liked. The dad, who sat to read the *Saturday Evening Post*, also likely had a pinup calendar in his garage or basement. Nobody really took this medium seriously then or now. It was thought of nothing more than a flash of innocent, gratuitous eye candy.

However, American photography of the 1950's and 1960's soon began to portray American women in a very different way. At first, these images were similar to the pinup calendars. "Glamour photographers" had emerged such as Ron Vogel, one of many who would come to redefine the modern development of an old media.

Instead of seeking to draw attention to and to correct the imperfections in American culture as Rockwell had with his work, this genre cashed in by feeding the source of moral decay more and more of what it wanted. Vogel was born in 1931. By the time he was in his twenties, America was primed for a reaction that became a very public sexual revolution.

Vogel's early imagery was quite racy for the day but incredibly tame by today's standards. He began to present his topless and nude female models in black and white, then later in color. Attractive models were soon shown in a variety of ridiculous and unnatural poses all in the nude; like a nude clinging to a staircase railing while inverted, crawling beneath a coffee table, bending over a piano, sprawled out under a public park children's playset, clinging to a random brick wall for an unknown reason, women climbing trees obviously too small to support themselves, attempting to perch on nightstands, straddling chairs, couch backs, and wheelbarrow handles, pretending to lift barbells, striding unnaturally over furniture like ottomans, writhing around on the floor or lawn, petting goats while nude, and yet other odd poses verging on the bizarre.[226] Women don't normally act this way unless alcohol consumption is involved, and that was precisely the point. This was photography crafted not to depict realism, but to sell an image of women that continued to appeal to men, not created to illustrate some normal behavior or aspect of American life as Rockwell had.

Recall that Norman Rockwell died in 1978 and the conservative American culture he had painstakingly depicted in detail for so many decades had begun to depart with him. In addition to selling magazines to men, the entire genre of Glamour photography exposed young American women to how men were being taught to see them. This began to result in modifying the expectations of both men and women with regards to behavior and gender roles, but there were no longer any guidelines on how these roles would be changed. By the 1960's the genre was both a diversion and a departure from what was before a "safe" and proper conservative understanding about our interpersonal relationships with the opposite sex by outward appearances.

Vogel eventually became a frequent photographic contributor to then current popular magazines such as *Playboy, Modern Man, Rogue* and *Adam* as well as many of the other men's magazines of that era.[227] There was certainly an aggressive appetite for this material by the public. When there was less demand for his earlier glamour style photography of the 1950's and 1960's, Vogel eventually became involved with the production of porn films once glamour photography had evolved into more overtly sexual content in the 1970's and 1980's.[228] In a few short decades following, this genre would advance and morph yet again into the modern digital era of completely unbridled pornography that is everywhere today.

The Unholy Land

As the nature of the Glamour photography became increasingly graphic, it also reflected a further degree of cultural depreciation in the public presentation of the female form, something that Norman Rockwell had long safeguarded against. While topless and nude images of women were certainly not a new innovation, the rapid advancement of this particular media in America was.

Women now saw their bodies apart from their former primary roles of making and raising children while in the photos of Glamour photography their image was reverted from devoted wives and mothers back to two of the most base architypes of women, that of vixen and temptress—two things that naturally appeal to the insatiable sexual psyche of men. Some women would embrace this oversexed image and go for the money, working as models in this lucrative business. It had to be tempting for an 18 or 19 year old female to get into modeling. Good pay, lots of attention and travel, no education required and the hardest thing they had to do was remove clothing and smile. Everyone from the models, photographers, and publishers were all cashing in while the American culture paid the ultimate price. Surely, there were other women who had witnessed the emotional wreckage that resulted from this cultural shift in their own family and were ready to rebel against it.

The Feminists

Because the 1960's American hippie hedonists were often stoned[g], they had little political will or the means to advance the pro-abortion agenda through congress or to form any other coherent agenda for that matter. Most probably didn't really care all that much about the issue. The group that took up the measure almost immediately were the so-called feminists, often also hedonists but on their own terms. There were other social issues in America to deal with at the same time:

"'Women could not apply for credit in [their] own name. There were 'help wanted' ads—help wanted male and help wanted female...Women couldn't go to law school or medical schools in many cases. There was a lot of discrimination going on. And that is why in the late '60s and early '70s, so many women...identified with the feminist movement.'"[229]

---

[g] rather, high on drugs, not stoned to death in the Biblical sense.

Many young American women soon rejected *all* the commercial images of themselves as vixens and temptresses, wives and mothers, and quickly became "feminists," a new role that *they* defined. Their bodies would no longer be a physical or emotional playground for men, and neither would their rights be defined by them. By this new designation they would renounce the objectification of their bodies that the nation was previously sold into accepting, and now became lifelong activists in a maligned and misguided political leftist movement.

In order to help define this new feminist movement and provide young women with some direction, propaganda was needed. *Cosmopolitan* magazine writer, Sue Ellen Browder was one of many who were the instruments of this propaganda.

"Browder...describes what she wrote as 'propaganda.' The goal? To sell women on the idea that sexual liberation is the path to the single woman's personal fulfillment. 'Propaganda is very sophisticated...It's half-truth, selected truth, and truth out of context...Propaganda is used not to sell just products...It's also used to sell ideas.'[230]

For two decades, Browder wrote for the magazine. The negative effects of the magazine's message had on young American women are incalculable. It was with some degree of remorse that Browder's 2015 book describes her role to sell abortion to women, titled, "Subverted: How I Helped the Sexual Revolution Hijack the Women's Movement."[231] Abortion has at times been a convenient way to dispense with an unwanted pregnancy throughout history and of some benefit to the hedonists. We might blame them as the original catalyst for the abortion issue, because before they showed up, there really was no debate about it here in America. Abortion was still murder in nearly all cases. But this was a new era for America.

This group of feminists worked hard to quickly form a wave of new female-leaning divorce laws which passed across all fifty states and are by any measure nothing short of punitive to men. They were soon focused on the woman's right to *choose* to bring the baby in her womb to term or not. They had also formed plenty of heart-tugging rationales to try to support their views; like pointing to the correlation of women with children and poverty abroad. Some would sell the notion that men making women pregnant was a way to "keep women subordinate and in poverty" as a tool of complete subjugation, which often happens with non-Christian cultures abroad. At the end of all their arguments, however, abortion in America was still murder.

Opponents to legalized abortion saw these new pro-abortionists as politically unprepared and simply could not believe that the movement would see much traction. Early on they did not seem to take this movement too seriously which turned out to be a tactical mistake. They simply maintained that the "choice" was made when both men and women consented to intercourse—but the unrelenting feminists insisted that so long as the child was still in their womb it was only mere tissue and should be treated as a possession that belonged to them personally and as such they must be allowed to either maintain it or dispense with it as they see fit (just like one might a mole or tumor)[h].

Through their nonstop shrill, obnoxious political rhetoric and their twisted logic, the constant ear-splitting screams of the so-called feminists eventually won the day. In 1973, the U.S. Supreme Court consented to abortion as an issue of "rights" where none actually exist then or now.[i] They soon had the full support of democrats and the Leftist American media. Now abortion was no longer murder, but simply a medical option fully determined solely by the woman.

On the other hand, the men (and let's not allow feminists to forget that there ARE men involved) really seem to have no rights in the matter of abortion whatsoever. How is it possible that in a nation that operates under the equal application and rule of law, where laws are supposed to be applied equally to all regardless of gender, race economic status, and all the rest, that men have no rights with regards to their unborn children? They cannot invoke the law to save a child of theirs *in vitro* because the issue is all about women, *their* rights, and "*their* bodies."

Where has anyone, anywhere, ever attempted to invoke the man's legal right to intercede to successfully save his unborn child…or conversely under the same rule of law shouldn't it be legal for a man to be able to force an abortion onto his female partner? That's essentially what a woman having an abortion does, right? None of the millions of

---

[h] Even in 2019, they still personally adhere to this notion that the "tissue" is not a child until it is born, which is why Planned Parenthood was able to sell dead aborted babies as "fetal tissue" to the highest bidders in order to continue to fund the organization.

[i] Jane Roe, et al. v. Henry Wade, District Attorney of Dallas County, Citations: 410 U.S. 113 (more) 93 S. Ct. 705, 35 L. Ed. 2d 147, 1973 U.S. LEXIS 159

aborted children were rescued by a legal battle initiated to save them by their fathers. To the feminists, the phrase "unborn child" is itself an oxymoron. If it's not yet born, it can't be a "child," so their twisted logic goes.

The Politicians

Then there are the cowardly, self-serving American politicians. It is common knowledge that these spineless wonders roaming the halls of American government exist for one purpose only—to get themselves reelected. In 1973, it did not take long for them to realize what a hot topic abortion had become. The public was being pummeled with abortion rights stories by the press. But instead of taking an initiative to properly resolve the issue with clearly defined legislation (that is supposed to be the sworn duty of their office) they deferred the issue to the courts entirely in order to simply allow unelected judges (and thuspersons not vulnerable to lose their position on Election Day) to make the final call.

The decision of the Supreme Court would become the default law of the land, unopposed by Congress. Congressmen could go back to their constituents, simply shrug, and tell them to blame the Court if they were unhappy about it. Then they could say, "I'm Conservative, vote for me and I will work to fix it" –for the next 47 years.

The Church

Supreme Court aside, I point all this out to my fellow Christians to illustrate how Christianity failed in this situation, as it has so many times in our nation. Christians failed to successfully and firmly illuminate the minds of our fellow citizens to loudly and forcefully address the flaws in American domestic culture. We failed to face the so-called feminists and to fervently and relentlessly teach that mankind was created in the image of God, that the body is vessel of God, and as such, abortion is a sin of the body and an abomination to God. Of course such a message is absolutely meaningless to the godless.

Christians failed to reach the hedonists of the American sexual revolution of the 1960's, whose god was their genitalia. We failed to reach politicians, who only attempt to invoke the notion of "God" if they perceive that the Almighty can advance their campaign every few years. We failed to demand just policy in the United States that calls for an absolute end to infanticide, eliminates duplicity, and ensures protection of unborn children and the proper application of the rule of law to include the consideration of the rights of both parents as well as the unborn.

American Christians who oppose abortion are now labeled by their opponents as "anti-abortionists" or "extremists" by the media, in the schools, and elsewhere to be further tagged with all manner of negative attributes assigned to them by the ruling Liberal Fascists. Those who oppose abortion today are "against women's health," "against women's rights," "prosecuting a war on women," and so on.

Then we see video snippets of some church members picketing and harassing women who go into the abortion clinics, yelling and screaming at them with hatred. Is this how we should address genocide in process? I suppose it is all we know to do in the absence of a unified Christian message backed by truth and with action to demand an end to state sponsored genocide in America. It's a pathetic, inappropriate, and ineffective response. If there was ever an issue that American Christian churches should have been able to tackle together in a single unified fashion, it should have been abortion.

Modern Politics

Recently in Virginia, a bill was introduced (SB 1637) sponsored by State Sen. Jennifer Boysko, Democrat, which sought to establish a woman's reproductive choice as a right. It was also called the Virginia Human Right Act, and the bill stated that, "Every individual who becomes pregnant has a fundamental right to choose to carry a pregnancy to term, give birth to a child, or terminate the pregnancy."[232]

Virginia Attorney General Mark Herring stated, "I'm going all the way to the Supreme Court if I have to in order to protect Virginians' health care,"[233] The ruse is that abortion is an issue not about "health care," but infanticide and age old gruesome barbarism, which is being supported by certain state governments and pushed into broad acceptance by government and many American Christian denominations. Why does Mr. Herring immediately say he will go to the Supreme Court? Because he knows, as all American Leftists do, that it is easier to get a Leftist-favorable ruling from the court that supports the cause than it is to lobby Congress to pass an unpopular law. Precisely what the strategy was in originally bringing Roe v Wade.

Today, the culture of the American Leftists seems to demand that Christians allow the enemies of the Cross—ISIS, the Islamic State, whomever—to torture and behead as many Christians (and others) as they please while Christians are simply expected to permit it. The barbaric practice of abortion of innocent infants in America (and elsewhere) is scarcely different than this. It is an issue designed and promoted to desensitize Americans to barbarism much like the Nazis had done prior to carrying out the holocaust. I'll let you ponder why.

We can look to the United Nations and the World Health Organization for providing promotion, leadership, and guidance in developing draconian policies and law pushing abortion under the guise of "women's rights," "reproductive rights," "women's health care," and any number of similar innocuous sounding agendas.

I speculate that the purpose for promoting abortion in America is purely a political objective. There is an objective of reducing the amount of legal American citizens by any means possible (including abortion) to make way for an invasion of foreigners, both "legal" and illegal aliens to enter the country. These masses will collectively overwhelm all of the economic, political and cultural systems of America and thereby fundamentally transform America into a European or South American style socialist/fascist state. Far-fetched? Look around and tell me how I'm wrong, and bring your best facts.

Much like the Native American Nations of the 19th Century, today Christians were not then and presently are not now unified to properly, firmly, and effectively address and resolve this issue of infanticide in America or much of anything else. Even when Republicans (who often brand themselves as "Conservative Christians" every election season) held complete control in the House of Representatives, the Senate, and the Presidency under George W. Bush for two years and again for two years during the Presidency of Donald Trump they did not end the practice abortion with legislation, or eliminate the federal funding of it. They clearly lack the political willpower and the courage to do so. But even if they had, it might have well been too late. As I mentioned before, laws do not make people virtuous. Because of the broad moral decay of our nation, abortions might continue on a large scale even if laws were enacted to make the procedure illegal today.

Is Jesus Christ a Liberal Democrat?

Before undertaking the task to compose this book, I had not realized that our Lord Jesus Christ is often viewed as a Liberal Democrat by godless Leftists. It is shameful that people in positions of leadership at these "church" organizations have become so consumed with their own personal political identity and party agendas, that they have no problem whatsoever using their distorted notions of Christ to craft policy and to direct the organizations they serve into serving themselves. These "churches" are nothing more than political campaigns cloaked in the name of Christ. They want the same messages of indoctrination used in our media and the public school systems to be heard again in the church, so no matter where people turn, they will be bombarded with propaganda passed off as "normal." It is of course an entirely false faith and a false reality that they create.

Often introduced into the churches these days are elements of the now familiar false ideologies of anthropological global warming, gender neutrality, transhumanism, virtue signaling, critical race theory, and identity politics. It is not a new phenomenon to be sure, using the cover of the Christian faith to advance political agendas, but one that faces us today nonetheless. Recall the adage that the road to hell is paved with good intentions. In this case, these new ideologies are not "good intentions" at all; they are crafted for the express purpose of the destruction of Christianity and our nation.

"Self-centered indulgence, pride and a lack of shame over sin are now emblems of the American lifestyle.[234]"

Rev. Billy Graham

How do we know that liberals think of Christ as a democrat? Of the plethora of denominations, in the interest of brevity, I will only examine here a few salient examples which illustrate how this concept has manifested in Protestant sects.

The United Methodist Church

The United Methodist Church has adopted many tenets that have nothing to do with either the traditional American or the Christian canonical view of the Bible or the message and mission of Christ. Instead, it appears that they serve to inject their church with politics and to push liberal political agendas to indoctrinate their flocks to the Leftist agenda all in the name of Christ. This only polarizes the broader Christian church by putting them at odds with other churches and perhaps dividing their own conservative and liberal members. In their "social creed" statement they include this:

"We believe in the right and duty of persons to work for the glory of God and the good of themselves and others and in the protection of their welfare in so doing; in the rights to property as a trust from God, collective bargaining, and responsible consumption; and in the elimination of economic and social distress.[235]"

"Collective bargaining?" "Responsible consumption?" "Elimination of economic and social distress?" Their creed includes a commitment to wealth redistribution and support for labor unions? I did not realize that Christ came to establish the Galilean Fisherman's Union, Chapter 1. It is true that you learn something new every day.

Here are only a few excerpts from the rather long list of political positions they are teaching and promoting at the United Methodist Church:

- "Consumers should exercise their economic power to encourage the manufacture of goods that are necessary and beneficial to humanity while avoiding the desecration of the environment in either production or consumption. Consumers should avoid purchasing products made in conditions where workers are being exploited because of their age, gender, or economic status. And while the limited options available to consumers make this extremely difficult to accomplish, buying "Fair Trade Certified" products is one sure way consumers can use their purchasing power to make a contribution to the common good. The International Standards of Fair Trade are based on ensuring livable wages for small farmers and their families, working

- with democratically run farming cooperatives, buying direct so that the benefits and profits from trade actually reach the farmers and their communities, providing vitally important advance credit, and encouraging ecologically sustainable farming practices. Consumers should not only seek out companies whose product lines reflect a strong commitment to these standards, but should also encourage expanded corporate participation in the Fair Trade market.[236]"
- "We affirm the importance of international trade and investment in an interdependent world. Trade and investment should be based on rules that support the dignity of the human person, a clean environment and our common humanity. Trade agreements must include mechanisms to enforce labor rights and human rights as well as environmental standards. Broad-based citizen advocacy and participation in trade negotiations must be ensured through democratic mechanisms of consultation and participation.[237]"
- "We believe war is incompatible with the teachings and example of Christ. We therefore reject war as an instrument of national foreign policy. We oppose unilateral first/preemptive strike actions and strategies on the part of any government. As Disciples of Christ, we are called to love our enemies, seek justice, and serve as reconcilers of conflict. We insist that the first moral duty of all nations is to work together to resolve by
- peaceful means every dispute that arises between or among them. We advocate the extension and strengthening of international treaties and institutions that provide a framework within the rule of law for responding to aggression,
- terrorism, and genocide. We believe that human values must outweigh military claims as governments determine their priorities; that the militarization of society must be challenged and stopped; that the manufacture, sale, and deployment of armaments must be reduced and controlled; and that the production, possession, or use of nuclear weapons be condemned. Consequently, we endorse general and complete disarmament under strict and effective international control.[238]"

Let's see if we can summarize what we have learned here about the United Methodist Church in just these few positions we have examined:

1. They support unionized labor, a well-documented political entity.
2. They give explicit instructions to members on how to shop for "Fair Trade" products. Who controls "The International Standards of Fair Trade" again?
3. They have demonstrated their complete ignorance on how international trade agreements work and why they are formed.
4. They promote the "complete disarmament" of the world, including the United States. Who are these angels that the entire world can trust with their security? "Love your enemies," yes; facilitate the slaughter of half the world's population by disarmament of the just, no.

The United Methodist Church has also adopted a 1,390 word document accepting every anti- Second Amendment policy and position there is, and deferring the authority of the United States on the issue to the United Nations[239]. No surprise there. This Church would do well to remember that the American Bill of Rights is the law of the land here, not some debatable or negotiable concept. Apparently they have ignored that the Lord Himself even called upon his Disciples to prepare to defend themselves in Matthew 22:36-38 "He said to them, 'But now if you have a purse, take it, and also a bag; and if you don't have a sword, sell your cloak and buy one...'"

The early roots of the United Methodist Church go back to the time of the Roe v Wade decision:

"Since the birth of The United Methodist Church in 1968, the Social Principles' paragraph on abortion has been contested. The 1972 paragraph stated: 'We support the removal of abortion from the criminal code, placing it instead under laws relating to other procedures of standard medical practice. A decision concerning abortion should be made only after thorough and thoughtful consideration by the parties involved, with medical and pastoral counsel...'.Following the United States Supreme Court's 1973 Roe v. Wade decision...United Methodism reflected Roe; its 1976 abortion paragraph included this sentence: 'We support the legal option of abortion under proper medical procedures.'"[240]

During the composition of my work, the United Methodist Church became embroiled in divisions over these leftist positions and many others. Consequently the UMC split into two factions by the end of 2023, one UMC sect as far-leftist, the other more conservative.

Facing a 33% decline in attendance, the preparation for their 2020 conference seemed to indicate that the godless Leftists were looking to take over control of the United Methodist Church. They planned to introduce new language that removes the word, "abortion" and replaces it with the sanitized and politically correct language, calling it "Reproductive Health."[241] This totally reframes the discussion from taking the life of an innocent infant to artificially focusing on an imaginary right of a woman to destroy the life of her infant child while calling it "Reproductive Health."

They also plan to completely **remove** these phrases from their current statement:[242]

- "Sanctity of unborn human life."
- "Sacredness of the life and well-being of the mother and the unborn child."
- "We support parental, guardian, or other responsible adult notification and consent before abortions can be performed...."
- "We cannot affirm abortion as an acceptable means of birth control, and we unconditionally reject it as a means of gender selection or eugenics...."
- "We oppose the use of late-term abortion known as dilation and extraction (partial-birth abortion) and call for the end of this practice...."
- "We entrust God to provide guidance, wisdom, and discernment...."
- "We mourn and are committed to promoting the diminishment of high abortion rates." "They [the Church and its congregations] should also support those crisis pregnancy centers and pregnancy resource centers...."
- "We particularly encourage the Church, the government, and social service agencies to support and facilitate the option of adoption... ."

These proposed changes are directly related to what the rabid Leftists are attempting to do legislatively in 2019 by removing ALL restrictions on abortion in America, as had happened in New York. The first thing they have to do is change the language from "abortion" to "Reproductive Health." With that accomplished, then they pit "a woman's right to choose" and "women's access to health care" against anyone who even thinks about opposing abortions at 40 weeks.

My point is that NONE of these things have anything to do with the message or mission of Christ expressed in the Gospels, and are seem to be entirely contrary to it. The Gospels must not be used as a political platform of some party. If they are allocating money and other resources to these and their other political causes, they do Christianity a disservice and are squandering the resources provided to them. They are not using this money to spread and support the message of Christ, but rather to push political propaganda – for which they have twisted the meaning and purpose of the Bible in order to support. It is inexcusable, offensive, and absolutely sickening.

With all these policy positions (and so many more...) the UMC appears to have taken up the entire platform of a Leftist political party. In fact, it would seem that if any group wanted to establish a Byzantine-style empirical theocracy (governed by the United Nations) in America it could be them, according to their own publications.

At a minimum, these Leftist positions deliberately transform this church into one of the "Christian Customizer" churches. If you are a person who believes in the religion of global warming (it is itself a religion, not at all science) then you can find a Methodist church to attend because they not only have a position on it, but will use part of any money you donate to them to address it. It does not make any difference to them that the issue has nothing to do with the Gospels, Christian service, or salvation because they have decided to interpret the Bible in a way that conforms to their political beliefs.

Members of the UMC are apparently content to use their pulpit to push for their politics at a time when Americans can't even tell the difference between right and wrong. The UMC simply uses these simple desires of the members—uses Christ to get them in the door so they can begin the work of warping the message of the Bible to sway support and collect money for their Leftist agenda. It's shameful, wrong, and heretical by any objective Christian theological standard.

What model will the UMC ultimately use locally to save and "transform" its churches into this new liberal progressive standard? We had an example. A UMC church in Cottage Grove, Minnesota was struggling with dwindling membership for years. The Methodists' regional body funded a restart of the church with $250,000 and by installing a special pastor for the task.[243]

The plan was to ask the existing older members to continue to fund the church and serve but not to attend Grove Church[j] in order to change the outward appearance of the congregation from being "old" and to transform the church into the modern progressive vision of the UMC and their programs without resistance from the traditional members. They hired a "restart specialist," a 30-year-old man named Jeremy Peters.

The Pastor, Rev. Dan Wetterstrom:

"It's a new thing with a new mission for a new target and a new culture…"[244]

This pastor should know better, and so should his flock. We are warned about this mindset of "new" things:

"What has been will be again, what has been done will be done again; there is nothing new under the sun." Ecclesiastes 1:9 (NIV)

My question for the UMC and essentially all American Christian churches is this: should the ever-changing American culture drive the message and direction of the church, or should the standards of the church and Christ stand to change the culture? The question is deceptive when it comes to the UMC. Why? Because the "standards" of the UMC have changed and are changing; shifting away from Christ to the standards of the political Leftists so in that sense they ARE working to change the culture—but not to the standards of Christ and the Christian Church. They are becoming a secular association clothed in a heresy, branded and sold as genuine Christian faith. It's so much easier to build your organization with followers when you customize

---

[j] These members were encouraged to attend another local UMC church campus under the same pastor during the transition period.

your message and doctrine to what they want to hear and follow.

The Evangelical Lutheran Church of America

It would appear that the Evangelical Lutheran Church of America (ELCA) has followed a similar pattern as the UMC. They have engaged in a battery of programs that support democrat identity politics and promote leftist propaganda rather than the Gospels. Their "Racial Justice Ministries" are a prime example:

"The Racial Justice Ministries of the ELCA serve as catalysts and bridge builders committed to the work of:

- Equipping leaders to recognize and understand the complexity and implications of racism and racial issues.

- Training and education in the areas of anti-racism and racial justice for leaders in partnership with synods, congregations, associations and social service agencies.

- Building alliances and strategies across race, ethnicity, class, gender, age and sexual orientation to break through barriers of racism and oppression.

- Creating and supporting ecumenical networks that call for and help equip the church to be a multiracial and multicultural community.

- Working together throughout the church in public witness, programs and policies that advance racial justice — locally and globally.

- Developing and sharing educational tools and training models for congregations to use in facing the challenges of racism in a diverse, complex and changing world."[245]

The politics of women's issues are also introduced into the church and promoted by the ELCA by their "Justice for Women" program. These objectives are all the same worn out liberal democrat talking points; create a victim group and service it, here, repackaged to appear as a Christian faith initiative; stating in part,

"The ELCA also recognizes that tending to our neighbors includes not only immediate needs, such as food, shelter and safety, but also changes in social and religious ideas and structures.

What can you do?

Educate for justice.

- Understand patriarchy and sexism.

- Analyze church and society in terms of the effects of patriarchy on all people.

Advocate for change.

- Call for changes in church practices and interpretations, as well as social policy and practice, to support and reflect the full humanity of all people.

- Call for gender justice and theological reflection in programs and policies.

Lead into the future.

- Raise awareness and challenge societal, theological and ecclesial practices and beliefs that are patriarchal.

- Work with a variety of people to create change that leads to gender justice, which affects everyone."[246]

Yeah, that's just what we need; "change church practices and interpretations" for the 30,001st time. That will surely solve it and bring us closer to the truth. Much of their direction frankly appears to be anti-American in nature. They recently published a form letter supporting the invasion of America by illegal aliens, and they ask their members to print off and complete it so that they can send to Congress, stating, in part:

"As a Lutheran and your constituent, I am deeply concerned about policies Congress is considering to provide protection for young Americans without legal status, also known as Dreamers, that would harm vulnerable children and families. No young person should have to choose between their future and the safety of their family, friends or community. Legislation to protect Dreamers, such as the Dream Act (S.1615/H.R. 3440), should pass without additional provisions. Dreamers are pastors, congregants and vital leaders in ministries throughout the Evangelical Lutheran Church in America (ELCA). They should not have to choose between their future and the safety of their family, friends or community. I urge you to voice your support for the passage of the Dream Act without additional provisions that would harm children and families.[247]"

On August 7th, 2019, the ELCA voted itself to become the first North American church denomination to declare itself a "sanctuary church body."[248] The purpose being to support all illegal aliens who are now invading the United States in violation of Federal Law.

Some additional position statements of their church include the following:

- "Only together can we fulfill God's call to be stewards of the earth. Governments at every level, private companies, families and individuals all have steps to take to combat climate change. Here are just a few:
  - WHAT CAN OUR GLOBAL COMMUNITY DO TO COMBAT CLIMATE CHANGE?
    - GOVERNMENTS: CONTINUE COOPERATION AND COMMITMENT TO REDUCE GREENHOUSEGAS EMISSIONS. Countries around the world entered into the Paris Agreement, which went into effect on Nov. 4, 2016. All the countries agreed to work to limit global temperature rise to well below 2oC (a goal of 1.5oC or less). In order to reach this goal,
    - our governments must continue to work together and remain committed to the Agreement.
    - IMPLEMENT ENERGY EFFICIENCY MEASURES AND SWITCH TO RENEWABLE ENERGY SOURCES.
  - INDIVIDUALS: BECOME EDUCATED ABOUT CLIMATE CHANGE, THEN EDUCATE YOUR COMMUNITY.
    - We must become educated about climate change. The U.N. Educational, Scientific and Cultural Organization (UNESCO) has more than 30 programs in the sciences, education, culture and communication to assist in creating knowledge, in educating and in communicating about climate change, and understanding the ethical implications for present and future generations.[249]"

The Unholy Land

- "Budgets are moral documents, and how we reduce future deficits are historic and defining moral choices. As Christian leaders, we urge Congress and the administration to give moral priority to programs that protect the life and dignity of poor and vulnerable people in these difficult times, our broken economy, and our wounded world. It is the vocation and obligation of the church to speak and act on behalf of those Jesus called 'the least of these.' This is our calling, and we will strive to be faithful in carrying out this mission.[250]"
- "Both the House of Representatives and the White House have offered proposals that would make drastic cuts to programs that feed poor and hungry children in our schools and provide food assistance to struggling working families. We call on Congress to:
    - RETAIN THE COMMUNITY ELIGIBILITY PROVISION IN FY18
    - OPPOSE TURNING SNAP INTO A BLOCK GRANT
    - REJECT CUTS TO SNAP[251]"
- "Advocacy: We invite you to join our advocacy efforts to bring about a just and lasting negotiated resolution to the Palestinian Israeli conflict.
    - Call for equal human dignity and rights for all people in the Holy Land.
    - Call for an end to Israeli settlement building and the occupation of Palestinian land, both of which violate international law;
    - Call for a two-state solution, with two viable, secure states living side-by-side.
    - Ask individuals to invest in Palestinian products to build their economy and to utilize selective purchasing to avoid buying products made in illegal Israeli settlements built on Palestinian land.
    - Call for an examination of U.S. military aid to Israel to ensure compliance with U.S. and international human rights law and a possible withholding of aid for noncompliance with those laws.[252]"

In summary of the above, the ELCA

1. Promotes leftist propaganda through their Racial Justice Ministries and Justice for Women program, among others.

2. Fully supports the unlawful invasion of America by illegal aliens who do not share our values and our culture and have no interest in supporting either. These have violated the laws of the United States of America, and have ignored the rule of law in general. Supporting these criminals is in direct conflict with American Jurisprudence and might even be considered seditious. There is no legitimate support for this policy to be found anywhere in the Bible.
3. Again, like the Methodists, support the false religion of "Climate Change."
4. Views the government's budget as their own. They defer to government (taxpayers) the task of caring for the poor by demanding that the American government continue to go into debt in order to fund unaffordable federal entitlements for illegal aliens and others. Government budgets are NOT "moral documents" as they claim. This assertion is flatly absurd.
5. Supports redistribution of wealth by the government in the form of SNAP benefits, and uses its position to tell its members to call congress to continue to support it, regardless of the fact that deficit spending is both irresponsible and unsustainable.
6. Takes a position supporting Palestinians over Israel

However, the dog just won't eat the dog food. The ELCA has suffered a steady decline in attendance and membership since its peak in the 1950's. The further Left they move, the more people they lose or fail to attract. Why is this happening? My mind goes to several possibilities here, none of which I know to be true:

1. The ELCA leadership began to see the initial decline decades ago and tried to gradually "modernize" their doctrines and programs in an initial effort to retain and attract members. This modernization was soon controlled by liberals who wanted to modify the Church to match their own politics out of pride.

2. The ELCA leadership has been consumed by subversive Leftists who know full well that unpopular and unbiblical Leftist policies drummed in by the church will force the decline and ultimate closure of all ELCA churches at some point—akin to the strategy found in the book I mentioned earlier, AA-1025.

3. The ELCA seems to believe that the Holy Gospels exist to serve their political views and have no problem whatsoever modifying their doctrine and funding new programs that attempt to indoctrinate their members to Leftist politics.

Whatever the case may be, the ELCA realizes that it must manage their decline. The various synods have developed plans including a series of options for local churches to adopt according to their situation. A recent internal document of a state synod offers three suggested options:

"Choosing transformation; options include intentional vitality process, redevelopment, and sale of building. Choosing partnership; options include yoking, merger, consolidation, and anchor church models. Choosing resurrection; options include closing and re-opening, word and service mission post, and holy closure."[253]

Sadly, none of these options point to long term, sustained growth or genuine vitality of their denomination. Perhaps converting the ELCA into a political action committee wasn't such a good idea after all. Their strategies appear to be centered upon a losing conclusion, akin to rearranging the deck chairs on the Titanic. One could argue that because of their polarizing politics, they will not be able to drive any form of unity in America.

The Southern Baptist Convention

The Southern Baptist Convention churches do not issue list after list of their individual positions on all political matters. That is likely because they are comprised of many locally independent churches instead of a top-down administrative structure. This works both to their benefit and their detriment.

They do list key beliefs in their statement," The 2000 Baptist Faith & Message[254]," including in part:

"XV. The Christian and the Social Order
All Christians are under obligation to seek to make the will of Christ supreme in our own lives and in human society. Means and methods used for the improvement of society and the establishment of righteousness among men can be truly and permanently helpful only when they are rooted in the regeneration of the individual by the saving grace of God in Jesus Christ. In the spirit of Christ, Christians should oppose racism, every form of greed, selfishness, and vice, and all

forms of sexual immorality, including adultery, homosexuality, and pornography. We should work to provide for the orphaned, the needy, the abused, the aged, the helpless, and the sick. We should speak on behalf of the unborn and contend for the sanctity of all human life from conception to natural death. Every Christian should seek to bring industry, government, and society as a whole under the sway of the principles of righteousness, truth, and brotherly love. In order to promote these ends Christians should be ready to work with all men of good will in any good cause, always being careful to act in the spirit of love without compromising their loyalty to Christ and His truth.

XVI. Peace and War
It is the duty of Christians to seek peace with all men on principles of righteousness. In accordance with the spirit and teachings of Christ they should do all in their power to put an end to war.

The true remedy for the war spirit is the gospel of our Lord. The supreme need of the world is the acceptance of His teachings in all the affairs of men and nations, and the practical application of His law of love. Christian people throughout the world should pray for the reign of the Prince of Peace.

XVII. Religious Liberty
God alone is Lord of the conscience, and He has left it free from the doctrines and commandments of men which are contrary to His Word or not contained in it. Church and state should be separate. The state owes to every church protection and full freedom in the pursuit of its spiritual ends. In providing for such freedom no ecclesiastical group or denomination should be favored by the state more than others. Civil government being ordained of God, it is the duty of Christians to render loyal obedience thereto in all things not contrary to the revealed will of God. The church should not resort to the civil power to carry on its work. The gospel of Christ contemplates spiritual means alone for the pursuit of its ends. The state has no right to impose penalties for religious opinions of any kind. The state has no right to impose taxes for the support of any form of religion. A free church in a free state is the Christian ideal, and this implies the right of free and unhindered access to God on the part of all men, and the right to form and propagate opinions in the sphere of religion without interference by the civil power.

XVIII. The Family
God has ordained the family as the foundational institution of human society. It is composed of persons related to one another by marriage, blood, or adoption.

Marriage is the uniting of one man and one woman in covenant commitment for a lifetime. It is God's unique gift to reveal the union between Christ and His church and to provide for the man and the woman in marriage the framework for intimate companionship, the channel of sexual expression according to biblical standards, and the means for procreation of the human race.

The husband and wife are of equal worth before God, since both are created in God's image. The marriage relationship models the way God relates to His people. A husband is to love his wife as Christ loved the church. He has the God-given responsibility to provide for, to protect, and to lead his family. A wife is to submit herself graciously to the servant leadership of her husband even as the church willingly submits to the headship of Christ. She, being in the image of God as is her husband and thus equal to him, has the God-given responsibility to respect her husband and to serve as his helper in managing the household and nurturing the next generation.

Children, from the moment of conception, are a blessing and heritage from the Lord. Parents are to demonstrate to their children God's pattern for marriage. Parents are to teach their children spiritual and moral values and to lead them, through consistent lifestyle example and loving discipline, to make choices based on biblical truth. Children are to honor and obey their parents."

    The main issue challenging the Baptist organizations is that they are so loosely structured and independent that much of the above is not taken seriously or applied consistently across churches at a local level. They are little more than aspirational statements because they have churches that are all over the map when it comes to implementing and living out these sentiments. Consequently, Baptist churches are often found to be vastly "customized" to local tastes and preferences based on the desires of their local leadership rather than having any consistently firm adherence to the Baptist "Faith & Message," which is quite unfortunate.

America Today

    Unfortunately, 21st century American "Christianity" as seen by non-Christians has the tendency to appear vainly superficial, artificially pious, hopelessly fragmented, often dishonest to their own message, and to some, almost cartoonish in nature. How, for example

, might a county-club style church member explain to a homeless person who has not eaten in three days that they must go and find a homeless shelter downtown because their church does not serve the homeless?

I suppose that he could say that there might have been a shelter built at the church but the plans for their tennis courts took that space. It is the precise outcome aspired by the plans described by the Soviet agents in AA-1025. They were not merely after the neutering of the Roman Catholic Church alone, but ultimately the universal transformation and destruction of all Christian churches.

For our poor handling of our own unified Faith and Message, we as Christians ought to be nothing short of ashamed. If we are not ashamed, we should at least be embarrassed for being such lousy brand managers. It might be effectively argued that Christians are among the worst brand managers in the history of the world. The liberal media today as well as the enemies of the Cross are all too pleased that the state of modern Christianity is so very weak, fragmented, and scattered. The ancient Romans themselves taught that division is a key to conquering.

A disinterested American population today appears to be eerily similar to this description of Europeans nearly 200 years prior:

"There are some nations in Europe whose inhabitants think of themselves in a sense as colonists, indifferent to the fate of the place they live in. The greatest changes occur in their country without their cooperation. They are not even aware of precisely what has taken place. They suspect it; they have heard of the event by chance. More than that, they are unconcerned with the fortunes of their village, the safety of their streets, the fate of their church and its vestry. They think that such things have nothing to do with them, that they belong to a powerful stranger called "the government." They enjoy these goods as tenants, without a sense of ownership, and never give a thought to how they might be improved. They are so divorced from their own interests that even when their own security and that of their children is finally compromised, they do not seek to avert the danger themselves but cross their arms and wait for the nation as a whole to come to their aid. Yet as utterly as they sacrifice their own free will, they are no fonder of obedience than anyone else. They submit, it is true, to the whims of a clerk, but no sooner is force removed than they are glad to defy the law as a defeated enemy. Thus one finds them ever wavering between servitude and license."

"When a nation has reached this point, it must either change its laws and mores or perish, for the well of public virtue has run dry: in such a place one no longer finds citizens but only subjects."

Alexis de Tocqueville
Democracy in America

Alexis de Tocqueville has unwittingly described much of the American condition both then and today. The application of virtue and unity might well go a long way to cure this malaise. But how can modern churches affect this problem if all they do is play in their own petty political dramas?

8

Customizing Christianity

"Some people have a warped idea of living the Christian life. Seeing talented, successful Christians, they attempt to imitate them...But when they discover that their own gifts are different or their contributions are more modest (or even invisible), they collapse in discouragement and overlook genuine opportunities that are open to them. They have forgotten that they are here to serve Christ, not themselves.[255]"

Rev. Billy Graham
Hope for Each Day: Words
of Wisdom and Faith

Even with the Protestant Reformation far behind us, today we witness post-Reformation modern Protestantism everywhere we look. This process has fared even worse in presenting and adhering to the message and mission of Christ and promoting church unity than has the Roman Catholic Church they originally rejected. Instead, the modern Protestants (heterodox) have developed their own problems. Christianity was never intended to be politicized or modernized for the purpose of achieving the objectives of men, and that is precisely what has occurred, rendering their sects as false and useless in the eyes of many. Why do we think that church affiliation and attendance is the lowest it has been in two generations? Were these churches ever the bastion of unity and virtue? Let's go back in history a few decades and find out.

My focus here is mostly on modern American Christianity as it might be considered the original source of American virtue from the start by many, but whether it actually was might be an open question depending upon the context; the perspective and understanding about whom our Framers were and what was happening in America at the time. Most of them were Deists anyway and not Christians.

Abolitionist Frederick Douglass saw the Christian churches in America differently in his day when he properly declared,

"...I therefore hate the corrupt, slaveholding, women-whipping, cradle-plundering, partial and hypocritical Christianity of the land... I look upon it as the climax of all misnomers, the boldest of all frauds, and the grossest of all libels. Never was there a clearer case of 'stealing the livery of the court of heaven to serve the devil in.' I am filled with unutterable loathing when I contemplate the religious pomp and show, together with the horrible inconsistencies, which everywhere surround me. We have men-stealers for ministers, women-whippers for missionaries, and cradle-plunderers for church members. The man who wields the blood-clotted cowskin during the week fills the pulpit on Sunday, and claims to be a minister of the meek and lowly Jesus. . . . The slave auctioneer's bell and the church-going bell chime in with each other, and the bitter cries of the heart-broken slave are drowned in the religious shouts of his pious master. Revivals of religion and revivals in the slave-trade go hand in hand together. The slave prison and the church stand near each other. The clanking of fetters and the rattling of chains in the prison, and the pious psalm and solemn prayer in the church, may be heard at the same time. The dealers in the bodies of men erect their stand in the presence of the pulpit, and they mutually help each other. The dealer gives his blood-stained gold to support the pulpit, and the pulpit, in return, covers his infernal business with the garb of Christianity. Here we have religion and robbery the allies of each other—devils dressed in angels' robes, and hell presenting the semblance of paradise.[256]"

Here we have a completely opposite view of Christianity in America from that of Alexis de Tocqueville who noted, "...Not until I went into the churches of America and heard her pulpits aflame with righteousness did I understand the secret of her genius and power."

Because our modern cultural mores are prismed through the filter of Presentism, we of course judge the past rather harshly. The practice of slavery is both abhorrent and illegal (as it should be) by today's Western cultural, moral, and legal standards, but it was nothing new or unusual back then. Slavery was a standard practice for many cultures for thousands of years across many different cultures prior to the "discovery" of North America by the Europeans. No land was unaffected by the centuries old practice of slavery. Even extending into 17th century Europe we find examples of the Barbary corsairs sacking Baltimore, Ireland in 1631—a 2:00am raid by the corsairs resulting with nearly the entirety of the town's inhabitants taken and sold into slavery.[257]

But here in America, de Tocqueville sees *"Righteousness"* in our churches while Douglass sees blood-stained hypocrisy. Who is correct here, de Tocqueville or Douglass?

    I believe that Douglass understood the history of Christianity in the Roman Catholic tradition in Europe as well as the extension of that religion as post-Reformation Protestantism in America. He clearly understood that the Christian faith was being twisted to serve those who desired power and control in the New World. He knew the depths of the cruelty, greed and perversity of many of the churchmen. Perhaps he learned that it was the Roman Catholic Pope himself who originally authorized the conquest of North America by Christian nations, and not only approved, but *instructed* his Christian followers to engage in and expand the slave trade. You read that correctly.

    It was Pope Nicholas V who issued the *Romanus Pontifex* bull on January 5, 1455. It extended to the Catholic nations of Europe dominion over all discovered lands and sanctified the seizure of non-Christian lands; it also encouraged the enslavement of native, non-Christian peoples everywhere:

"We weighing all and singular the premises with due meditation, and noting that since we had formerly by other letters of ours granted among other things free and ample faculty to the aforesaid King Alfonso -- to invade, search out, capture, vanquish, and subdue all Saracens and pagans whatsoever, and other enemies of Christ wheresoever placed, and the kingdoms, dukedoms, principalities, dominions, possessions, and all movable and immovable goodswhatsoever held and possessed by them and to reduce their persons to perpetual slavery, and to apply and appropriate to himself and his successors the kingdoms, dukedoms, counties, principalities, dominions, possessions, and goods, and to convert them to his and their use and profit -- by having secured the said faculty, the said King

Alfonso, or, by his authority, the aforesaid infante, justly and lawfully has acquired and possessed, and doth possess, these islands, lands, harbors, and seas, and they do of right belong and pertain to the said King Alfonso and his successors."[258]

This Papal Bull was soon followed by another, which created even more justification, rights and clarity to the notion of enslavement in conquered lands:

"The Papal Bull '*Inter Caetera*' issued by Pope Alexander VI on May 4, 1493, played a central role in the Spanish conquest of the New World. The document supported Spain's strategy to ensure its exclusive right to the lands discovered by Columbus the previous year...All others were forbidden to approach the lands...without special license from the rulers of Spain. This effectively gave Spain a monopoly on the lands in the New World."[259]

"The Bull stated that any land not inhabited by Christians was available to be 'discovered,' claimed, and exploited by Christian rulers and declared that 'the Catholic faith and the Christian religion be exalted and be everywhere increased and spread, that the health of souls be cared for and that barbarous nations be overthrown and brought to the faith itself.' This 'Doctrine of Discovery' became the basis of all European claims in the Americas as well as the foundation for the United States' western expansion. In the US Supreme Court in the 1823 case Johnson v. McIntosh, Chief Justice John Marshall's opinion in the unanimous decision held 'that the principle of discovery gave European nations an absolute right to New World lands.' In essence, American Indians had only a right of occupancy, which could be abolished."[260]

Slavery thus began in North America in 1619 at Jamestown, Virginia, 157 years before the United States of America was founded.[261] Once again, we see the Roman Catholic Church and subsequently American Protestant Churches acting in a way not patterned after the teachings of Jesus Christ found in the first century at all, but yet again acting out of political expediency, greed, and self-aggrandizement—just as Douglass had so accurately expressed.

More than a century later, England's King George did not end the practice of slavery in North America and had no intentions of doing so; it had become an approved practice originally authorized by the Roman Catholic Church three hundred odd years prior. Being the primary economic beneficiary of the slave trade would have made all that more difficult for a nation like England, from their perspective, to ever consider ending slavery on some silly "new" moral ideals when they already had the backing of the Church.

Douglass wasn't wrong at all, in fact, he was quite right. He clearly saw a different America surrounding him than what the early Americans saw, just as Chief Seattle and the rest of the Native American Nations would later. He saw an actual America as it plainly was; raw, and cruel—exercising a crafted and modified form of Christianity that was contrary to the message and teachings of Christ. This wasn't the more idyllic and innocent colonial-era America that we might like to ponder when we think of America at our Founding but one that perhaps appeared to be nightmarish at the peak of the slave trade.

This is not to say that the early Americans (1776) were entirely blind to the injustice of the slave trade. During the debates over ratification of the Constitution beginning in September 1787 onward, we see that many American Framers at all levels were concerned about the practice of slavery. Reading the text of these debates reveals that it was apparent to nearly everyone that slavery was an abhorrent practice of the Crown, and would no longer be tolerated in America at some point.

An American Baptist leader, Reverend Isaac Backus was a key supporter for the separation of church and state and the First Amendment.[262] When he addressed the Massachusetts Ratification Assembly on February 4, 1788, he had this to say regarding the slave trade, in part:

"But let us consider where we are, and what we are doing. In the articles of confederation, no provision was made to hinder the importation of slaves into any of these States; but a door is now opened, hereafter to do it; and each State is at liberty now to abolish slavery as soon as they please. And let us remember our former connection with Great Britain, from whom many in our land think we ought not to have revolted: How did they carry on the slave trade! I know that the Bishop of Gloucester, in an annual sermon in London, in February, 1766, endeavoured to justify their tyrannical claims of power over us, by casting the reproach of the slave trade upon the Americans. But at the close of the [Revolutionary] war, the Bishop of Chester, in an annual sermon, in February, 1783, ingenuously owned, that their nation is the most deeply involved in the guilt of that trade, of any nation in the world; and also, that they have treated their slaves in the West Indies, worse than the French or Spaniards have done theirs.—Thus slavery grows more and more odious through the world..."[263]

In practice, slavery during this period was apparently much less affected by any religious concerns than by economics and politics. The immorality of the practice was less important until it finally became an issue. By some accounts, in 1860 no American republican even owned a slave[264] while, "...Democrats like Senator John C. Calhoun invented a new justification for slavery, slavery as a 'positive good.' For the first time in history, American Democrats insisted that slavery wasn't just beneficial for masters; they said it was also good for the slaves."[265]

Alexis de Tocqueville was searching America to find that which holds the republic together, in the absence of a Monarchy. Slavery was apparently not seen as either unusual or a critical moral factor at the time—one way or another. He did not judge the Church as Douglass had. Surely Douglass saw local Christians as hypocrites and Christianity itself a hypocritical sham—and I agree with him. The early American Christians had grown up with the practices of the day as approved by the Churches in Europe for centuries. Revolt for the single purpose of correcting it was not likely to happen. Other factors and public figures had to enter into play for there to be a catalyst for change.

Our own Federal Framers also understood that slavery ultimately had to go. In his writings on American grievances justifying the American Revolution, Thomas Jefferson attacked the British for sponsoring the slave trade into the colonies. In 1778, with Jefferson's leadership, slave importation was banned in Virginia, one of the first jurisdictions worldwide to do so. Jefferson was a lifelong advocate ofending the slave trade and as president led the effort to criminalize the international slave trade with legislation that passed Congress which he signed in 1807, shortly before Britain passed a similar law.[266] The American Constitution prohibited importation of slaves, to begin in

1808 and slave trading became a capital offense in 1819.[267] Even though these measures did not directly free the existing slaves, America was well on its way to eliminating the abhorrent slave trade in North America and the western hemisphere.

We are fortunate to live in a nation where our Framers—in spite of the practice of church-ordained slavery that their nation inherited, wisely crafted a constitution that encourages legal redress and provides a method and means for doing so. The American people were eventually able to completely eliminate the practice of slavery and soon bring equal opportunities and rights to all American citizens—something that King George had absolutely no intentions of doing while we were yet colonies.

The Vatican had originally authorized and encouraged the slave trade in the name of Christ. It is an abomination of the worst kind imaginable. It is equally unfortunate that the same justification for the slave trade became a legal basis for the American extermination of the Native American Nations in the 19th century which I described at the beginning of this text. Why the descendants of formerly enslaved groups of the world seem to spend their energy generally hating white people today instead of storming the Vatican is a mystery to me. That is where the root blame squarely lays.

The Vatican, not surprisingly, has had a bit of a fuzzy memory about how slavery began in the West, acting as if the Roman Catholic Church had been an innocent bystander in the matter. Perhaps sensing the changing public sentiment, the Church recanted its authorization for slavery by the time Pope Leo XIII issued the following statement from Rome, at St. Peter's on November 20, 1890, now repositioning the Church as an historical champion of abolition:

"On Slavery in the Missions...To the Catholic Missionaries in Africa.

"The maternal love of the Catholic Church embraces all people. As you know, venerable brother, the Church from the beginning sought to completely eliminate slavery, whose wretched yoke has oppressed many people. It is the industrious guardian of the teachings of its Founder who, by His words and those of the apostles, taught men the fraternal necessity which unites the whole world. From Him we recall that everybody has sprung from the same source, was redeemed by the same ransom, and is called to the same eternal happiness. He assumed the neglected cause of the slaves and showed Himself the strong champion of freedom. Insofar as time and circumstances allowed, He gradually and moderately accomplished His goal. Of course, pressing constantly with prudence and planning, He showed what He was striving for in the name of religion, justice, and humanity. In this way He put national prosperity and civilization in general into His debt. This zeal of the Church for liberating the slaves has not languished with the passage of time; on the contrary, the more it bore fruit, the more eagerly it glowed. There are incontestable historical documents which attest to that fact, documents which commended to posterity the names of many of Our predecessors. Among them St. Gregory the Great, Hadrian I, Alexander III, Innocent III, Gregory IX, Pius II, Leo X, Paul III, Urban VIII, Benedict XIV, Pius VII, and Gregory XVI stand out. They applied every effort to eliminate the institution of slavery wherever it existed. They also took care lest the seeds of slavery return to those places from which this evil institution had been cut away..."[268]

The statement continues with the requisite platitudes and mentions that monies are to be collected by the church to provide help "for the unfortunate Africans." They must have believed that no one would recall that Pope Nicholas V issued the *Romanus Pontifex* bull on January 5, 1455 supporting the practice of slavery to begin with.

We see here how the churches customized themselves to allow the pious to engage in the abhorrent practice of slavery that predated the foundation of the United States. With the issue of slavery settled long ago, today we see the process of customizing the church with contemporary notions throughout history by some has never stopped. This has resulted in an obvious series of deviations. The fact is that no one seems to notice these deviations as detrimental because frankly, there are so many of them today and they have occurred incrementally over the centuries.

In the United States (and likely elsewhere), it seems that there are two types of Christianity today. "Type One" Christianity adheres to Christ's ministry and the Church that the Apostle Paul was inspired to shape in the first Century A.D. "Type Two" Christianity is the religion of man carried out often falsely in Christ's name and is what we largely have to deal with today. The smallest Christian Churches today may more resemble the "Type One" Christianity in America, while the best funded, well organized, and more prominent Christian entities are almost always "Type Two" constructs; this I will demonstrate. The first of these I'll refer to as the "Frozen Chosen," and the second group as the "Christian Customizers."

The Frozen Chosen

People who are members at long running denominational churches seem to just "like what they like." They actually seem to care little about anything else. Don't present them with any thoughts, ideas, or programs outside of their norm or you'll be ostracized as a "troublemaker." They have their own way they do things (which may or may not have any connection to the Christian standards) and that is that. They are primarily the Wednesday night supper club and I predict that these churches will make fine museums or Mosques one day after a well-earned extinction.

The Frozen Chosen church is not at all committed to or interested in growth or outreach, even if they make a token effort to show they are. They have turned inward and primarily strive to serve the petty whims and preferences of their own membership. You won't change these people or their practices, even if they are Biblically in error. They will always prefer to chase away the guy with the ideas rather than deal with the possibility that they might be wrong or agree that processes could be improved in some way. As a result of these things, they generally become totally ineffective in their communities and risk loss of membership by attrition. These churches could check the obituaries each week to see who is not coming to church that Sunday.

Many of the younger folks who attend these churches are susceptible to being recruited away to more "modern" churches such as I describe in the second group. This is especially true for the folks who are younger and/or likely more educated.

The Christian Customizers

Here, I'll relate a story that is analogous to Christianity. At one time there were some thirty-six employees on the same floor in the office where I worked. At my last count we had about twelve coffee makers on the same floor. The company furnished four of them, the type that will brew a whole pot of coffee in just over two minutes. The balance of these machines were brought in by the employees

The Unholy Land

themselves and are of the type that use individual plastic pods and will brew a single cup of coffee on demand in about 45 seconds.

Coffee must be a popular beverage on the floor to have a ratio of coffee makers to employees of one to three. It tells me that not only do people like their coffee, they don't want to wait for it, and they are not satisfied with the bulk coffee flavors provided by the company, so they created ways to have options of their own –at their own expense. The coffee pods end up costing up to 700% more per cup than if one brewed by the pot the old fashioned way—so there is no economy of scale or efficiency in brewing coffee by the cup. Independent personalization like this is ingrained everywhere in the American culture today. It has become the culture of "ME." Unfortunately that same philosophy doesn't work out so well for Christianity.

One of the strategies that these Christian Customizer churches employ today in order to appease their self-centered members and attract new ones is to constantly customize the interpretation, teachings, and application of Christianity. This is the process of altering the message or doctrine of Christianity to make it more attractive at their church as compared to others, like that stodgy Frozen Chosen church down the street, and it's nothing new.

How denominations and individual churches approach and address popular issues like marriage, homosexuality, divorce, abortion, "LGBTQHSCWPVEMYADF..." rights, modern music in worship, prayer styles, baptism preferences, communion methods—and a host of other issues too long to list— even including today preaching the farces of anthropological global warming and that ignominiously titled subject of "social justice"—results in a seemingly endless color palette of churches for American Christians to choose from. But this is both as much a dubious benefit as it is a serious hazard to the entire cause of the Faith. Who exactly are they attracting to these churches and why are they really there?

In these churches, modern Christianity is approached in sort of the same way as people select their coffee. Forget about any notion of Christian truths, people will often attend a church that has the custom amenities and messages they want rather than tolerate one that is disagreeable to them in some way. For example, look at the split of Protestant churches along the lines of political affiliations. There are denominations that refuse to marry homosexuals and others who not only marry them, but encourage them to serve in the clergy and elsewhere. Some will allow women and divorcees to serve in positions such as Deacon, others will forbid it. On and on it goes...

Christians in general are terrible "brand managers" for the image and direction of the faith. It's true, and this is part of the flaw engrained in modern Protestantism. Christians are also rated poorly at execution of their charge. Where is the unity in the church? I have had Christian pastors tell me that "America needs Jesus" and that "Christianity will heal the nation." If this alone were so, why are the Byzantines now extinct? They were a Christian Empirical Theocracy, the longest running and most dedicated example of a "Christian nation" the planet has ever witnessed—and yet they ultimately failed as an empire, as a nation, even if their church did in fact survive. It is quite apparent that as a Christian Theocracy—Christianity "managed" by a political class—the old Byzantine civil authority became more and more fixated and distracted by man-made political motivations.

It is therefore not enough to say "Christianity will cure the nation." Without the community, guidance, and support of the Genuine Church, without sincere and humble applications of genuine Christianity, Americans who are consumed by pride and trying to individually manage thousands of opposing churches are no better off.

How did this happen in America? It happened gradually at first, then rapidly over the past twenty years or so. People raised in Judeo-Christian homes are often taught to memorize and obey the Ten Commandments at a young age. This is often the first exposure to a formalized, socially (or religiously, if you prefer) -induced set of rules to govern behavior and instill some sense of right, wrong, and ethics in our youth.

Obeying the Ten Commandments as a ten year old in 1970's America was not that difficult. Mom and Dad really did not have to worry too much that their ten year old was going to worship idols or commit adultery. Today the culture is different. We now deal with pre-teen pregnancy in American communities as a commonplace part of the culture. Drug and alcohol abuse is rampant and growing exponentially. Violence and murder are occurring with younger and younger perpetrators and victims. Why?

The answer, I believe lies in two things: first, the simple answer is the deliberate secularization of the culture by our leftist media and secondly, the rationalization of so many non-Christian practices and values in the churches. The godless Left has engaged in a continual battle to remove all references to Christianity and the Christian God in America. It began with eliminating Christian prayer in our public

The Unholy Land

schools, (at the same time encouraging people of other faiths to pray at these very same public schools today.) Public monuments with the Ten Commandments and other Judeo-Christian symbolism and references on them have been removed from across the country, and so on. They want any standard connected to Christ to be absolutely eliminated. They have largely succeeded.

Later in the 20th Century, following 1970's we are reminded by the new liberal churchmen that "the Ten Commandments are in the Old Testament of the Bible." Christians, they say, are living under the "Grace" of the New Testament, and as such, the old laws don't always apply directly to Christians like they used to. They forget that while Christ Himself laid out His commandments of the New Covenant, He did not come to overturn the Law, but to fulfill it.

However, modern churches often fail to effectively teach these tenants and when they do it's not in a way that connects to people. The new standards that Christ laid out for us at the Sermon on the Mount are far more difficult to adhere to that the Ten Commandments. In a culture that continually hammers moral relativism and accommodates personal pride into the American psyche, people are less receptive to humble themselves to accept and follow the high standards of Christ. So it is that many churches simply take the easy path and respond by moderating the message. This leads to rationalization.

Rationalization was key for churches in America throughout our history used to bend the standards of the Bible and of Christ into the acceptance of otherwise obvious and abhorrent sin. Now we are free, they say. There goes the Ten Commandments right out the window in a general sense, along with anything else Christ later taught that is an inconvenience of the new faith they want to push.

The liberals both in the clergy and in the community even point to the Old Testament, Isaiah 1:18 and come up with a whole new acceleration to their rationalization scheme:

"Come now, and let us reason together, saith the LORD: though your sins be as scarlet, they shall be as white as snow; though they be red like crimson, they shall be as wool." (KJV)

This verse, we are often told by the *religious* left, means that God is quite reasonable and flexible. How much so? Reasonable and flexible enough to accept all kinds of secularized deviant practices including homosexuality, transgenderism, or whatever they may be;

and therefore, we must now also. We should be *reasonable*, like God. From this, we get new religious catch phrases from some denominations, like, "Open Hearts, Open Doors, Open Minds.[269]" and, "God is Still Speaking.[270]" I think that these are just catch phrases used to market their church and lead the general public to believe that Christianity is some kind of non-specific, flexible, generic, feel-good spiritualism without any standards.

The seemingly innocent and benevolent position has opened the door to the politically charged "LGBT movement"—a group whose only purpose is to destroy American value systems using the churches, the government, and the courts—by whatever means necessary.

I am sure that "God still speaks," but I am also quite certain that He is not changing His mind about what sin is and all the rest. In fact, Christ was clear in pointing out the cheapening of the Church for both individual and collective gain when He was questioned by the Pharisees:

"Why do thy disciples trangress the tradition of the ancients? For they wash not their hands when they eat bread. But he answering, said to them: Why do you also transgress the commandment of God for your tradition? For God said: Honour thy father and mother: And: He that shall curse father or mother, let him die the death. But you say: Whosoever shall say to father or mother, The gift whatsoever proceedeth from me, shall profit thee. And he shall not honour his father or his mother: and you have made void the commandment of God for your tradition. Hypocrites, well hath Isaias prophesied of you, saying: '*This people honoureth me with their lips: but their heart is far from me. And in vain do they worship me, teaching doctrines and commandments of men.*'"

Matthew 15:2-9
Douay-Rheims Bible

The LGBT "Movement"

What exactly is this LGBT "movement"? It is comprised of a loose collection of various hard-Leftist funded organizations whose range of true ideology spans from generic "democrat" to rabid anarchist. They no more represent the interests "all homosexuals" and "all transgenders" than the Ku Klux Klan represented "all democrats" even though the KKK was largely a democrat-oriented and run organization.[271]

My examination and commentary here is certainly not aimed at individual homosexuals for whom I have compassion and share friendship, but rather this deliberately political "LGBT movement" which is not about "protecting" people's rights or helping their condition, but instead organized as a far leftist political faction whose motivation is to divide and destroy the churches and many other traditional institutions in America and elsewhere. There are dozens of these types of organizations active in the Unites States today:[272]

Accord Alliance
ACT UP
Affirmation: LGBT Mormons, Families & Friends
Against Equality
American Foundation for Equal Rights
American Veterans for Equal Rights
Athlete Ally
Atticus Circle
Bialogue
BiNet USA
Bisexual Resource Center
Campus Pride
Cheer, Dorothy, Cheer!
Children of Lesbians and Gays Everywhere (COLAGE)
Children of LGBTQ parents
Consortium of Higher Education LGBT Resource Professionals
LGBT student centers
El/La Para TransLatinas
Equality Federation
Family Equality Council
Fight OUT Loud
GLBTQ Legal Advocates & Defenders (GLAD)
Gay and Lesbian Medical Association (GLMA)
Homophobia in medicine
Gay & Lesbian Victory Fund
Gay, Lesbian and Straight Education Network (GLSEN)
GetEQUAL
GLAAD
GLIFAA
Global Equality Fund
GSA Network
Human Rights Campaign (HRC)
Immigration Equality
interACT
Integrity USA
International Foundation for Gender Education (IFGE)

Intersex Campaign for Equality (IC4E) formerly OII-USA
Join the Impact
Keshet
LPAC
Lambda Legal
Lavender Menace
Lesbian and Gay Band Association
Lesbian Avengers
Marriage Equality USA
Mattachine Society
Matthew Shepard Foundation
National Black Justice Coalition (NBJC)
National Center for Lesbian Rights (NCLR)
National Center for Transgender Equality (NCTE)
National LGBT Chamber of Commerce (NGLCC)
National Lesbian and Gay Journalists Association (NLGJA)
National LGBTQ Task Force (The Task Force)
National Transgender Advocacy Coalition
National Youth Advocacy Coalition (NYAC)
NOH8 Campaign
North American Conference of Homophile Organizations (NACHO)
ONE National Gay & Lesbian Archives

Out & Equal
OutServe-SLDN
PFLAG
Pride at Work
Queer Nation
Rainbow Sash
Services & Advocacy for GLBT Elders (SAGE)
Soulforce
StartOut

Sylvia Rivera Law Project
Trans Student Educational Resources
Transgender Law Center
Equality Alabama
Center for Artistic Revolution
Californians Against Hate
Courage Campaign
EQCA (Equality California)
Los Angeles LGBT Center
Love Honor Cherish
Trikone
The Pink Panthers
Equality Florida
SAVE Dade
The Pride Center at Equality Park
Georgia Equality
Equality Hawaii
The Civil Rights Agenda
Equality Illinois
Gay Civil Rights (formally Gay Human Rights)
One Iowa
Kansas Equality Coalition
Simply Equal
Fairness Campaign
Kentucky Equality Federation
Forum for Equality
EqualityMaine
Wilde Stein Alliance for Sexual Diversity
Equality Maryland
Gender Rights Maryland
Maryland Coalition for Trans Equality
Harvard Gay & Lesbian Caucus
Knowthyneighbor.org
Massachusetts Transgender Political Coalition
MassEquality
Equality Michigan
OutFront Minnesota
Equality Mississippi
Mississippi Safe Schools Coalition
Missourians for Equality
PROMO
Garden State Equality
African Ancestral Lesbians United for Societal Change
Audre Lorde Project
Empire State Pride Agenda
New York Area Bisexual Network
New Yorkers United for Marriage
Sex Panic!
Sylvia Rivera Law Project
Equality North Carolina
Ten Percent Society
Equality Ohio
Cimarron Alliance Foundation
Basic Rights Oregon
Equality Pennsylvania
Tennessee Equality Project
Tennessee Transgender Political Coalition
Equality Texas
Houston GLBT Political Caucus (HGLBTPC)
Queer Liberaction
Equality Utah
Stonewall Shooting Sports of Utah
Equal Rights Washington
Gay and Lesbian Activists Alliance (GLAA)
Equality Wisconsin

What is their global strategy? For American Leftists who push quasi-religious rot-gut, it is the same strategy as the old twentieth century Soviet Communists had—diminish the Church and replace its tenants with the dogma of the atheist state.[k] When they cannot achieve universal acceptance of their malfeasance within the community or the church, they turn to government to pass and enforce "anti-discrimination" laws that force Christians and their churches to accept not only unbelievers with avowed non-Christian behaviors, but also anti-Christians bent on destroying the church as well.

---

[k] All very similar to the strategy laid out in the book, AA-1025.

Only today in America has perversion been raised from its status as biological abnormality and abhorrent behavior into a plethora of new, imaginary "genders" that the Church is expected to and, they hope, be legally bound to accept and to condone. This is not only wrong, but devastates God's standards and cannot be permitted in any church calling itself Christian. If the Church can be made to change its message and standards, it is no longer a Church that bears Christ's name honestly.

The late Rev. Billy Graham observed:

"Perversion is considered a biological abnormality rather than a sin. These things are contrary to the teaching of God's Word. And God has not changed. His standards have not been lowered. God still calls immorality a sin and the Bible says God is going to judge it.[273]"

We are plainly reminded:

"Fallacies do not cease to be fallacies because they become fashions."
— G.K. Chesterton

What does this mean for Americans? It seems that this mad push to customize the Christian faith has resulted in a bizarre flavor of "Theistic Humanism" where Christ is merely "part of the story" but the dogma and tenants of the faith are almost entirely directed by people based upon their own logic and desires instead of by the Deity. Protestant Christianity has been served up to facilitate sin in America and elsewhere. It has been forced to evolve to the point where God Himself is often reduced and marginalized so as not to interfere with—or worse imagined to support—what is politically correct, popular, or just plain offensive to those who prefer sin and don't want to adhere to God's laws; they don't also want to feel guilty or shunned by those who do. They seek validation and self-justification--by the community, the culture, the government, and ultimately through the Christian churches.

These people seek to create a moral equivalency between what should be a holy faith and an abomination—leading others to accept, condone, and even celebrate their questionable and sinful life choices within a new and strange Christianity—however they choose to twist the doctrine to meet their own standards instead of God's. It was little different for the Popes of Rome or even a few of the less than pious Byzantine Emperors more than a thousand years ago. Instead of Christianity being established and maintained as the highest standard, because of pride and ambition these people intend to make Christianity into the lowest common denominator of mankind—which effectively destroys it.

Contrary to the speculation of the pundits, we recently learned that after three decades of study and genetic analysis of a sample of nearly half a million people, that there is no single "gay gene" that programs human beings as homosexual.[274] But for the Leftists, we can say that they don't let the facts get in the way of the truth. There is now an international effort to force sodomy as a normal behavior and the core leadership for this effort emanates from the United Nations.[1] This is the timeline for the progression of advancing sodomy as a norm across the globe under the umbrella of "Universal Human Rights," according to the UN:

"In 1948, the Universal Declaration of Human Rights was adopted and today forms a key plank of international human rights law. Since the Declaration entered into force, Member States have adopted two major Covenants (on Civil and Political Rights, and on Economic, Social, and Cultural Rights), as well as a number of conventions that safeguard human rights in specific cases and circumstances.

In 2000, the UN Global Compact was unveiled, which specified nine principles by which business should abide (later a tenth principle was added) — among them human rights, labour rights, environmental protection and anti-corruption.

In 2005, John Ruggie was appointed UN Secretary General's Special Representative on Human Rights and Transnational Corporations and other Business Enterprises. In 2011, the UN Human Rights Council endorsed the UN Guiding Principles on Business and Human Rights. The Guiding Principles created the Protect-Respect-Remedy framework, under which the State has the obligation to protect human rights; companies have the responsibility to respect human rights; and access to remedy is essential when rights are violated."[275]

---

[1] Curiously similar to what has historically happened with the sodomy issue in the Roman Catholic Church and others.

These "principles" have echoed in the United States with the Leftists at every level of government adopting and pushing policies to protect sodomy wherever it may be found. Even local governments now attempt to "legally" force Christian pastors to stop preaching the Gospel because it is offensive to those who don't agree with the message. This is precisely what occurred with local churches in Texas.

In Texas and elsewhere in the U.S. Leftists are filing suits using labor laws in order to pit "transgender rights" against the rights of the private Christian churches to exclude hiring LGBTQHSCWPVEMYADFGJKN71429[m] people because it is against the religious policies of the churches, which are based upon Biblical standards and Christian principles.[276]

The Leftists here are applying labor laws and forming policy around the direction and guidance provided from the UN:

"Employment: Companies should recruit staff and extend each individual the same benefits, salaries, opportunities for training or promotion regardless of a candidate's sexual orientation, gender identity, gender expression or sex characteristics, and include reference to non-discrimination on these grounds in vacancy announcements
where legally feasible. Companies should take steps to ensure that LGBTI staff feel fully included in the workforce and avoid them from being forced to either reveal or conceal their identity/status within the workforce. The role of top and middle management in ensuring effective compliance with fair recruiting practices is critical in this regard."[277]

The undermining of Christianity by the Leftists never ends, and never will end— it only advances at a more rapid pace from year to year. On March 13th, 2019 a federal bill fraudulently titled, "Equality Act" HR 5, was introduced and sponsored by Rep. David N. Cicilline, a democrat from Rhode Island. This bill is nothing short of a full frontal assault against all Christians and Christian churches in the United States. Again, it is democrats attempting to divide Americans and pit them against each other as well as to destroy the churches.

---

[m] We had to add letters since the last reference to this political group in the text because additional genders have been discovered and identified in the past few minutes, and we don't want to errantly exclude any group. Numbers are now being employed here because we are nearly out of letters. We don't presently know what specific new genders the numbers refer to, but by the time the text goes to print we are reasonably certain that they will be assigned by the group.

"This bill prohibits discrimination based on sex, sexual orientation, and gender identity in areas including public accommodations and facilities, education, federal funding, employment, housing, credit, and the jury system. Specifically, the bill defines and includes sex, sexual orientation, and gender identity among the prohibited categories of discrimination or segregation...The bill expands the definition of public accommodations to include places or establishments that provide (1) exhibitions, recreation, exercise, amusement, gatherings, or displays; (2) goods, services, or programs; and (3) transportation services...The bill allows the Department of Justice to intervene in equal protection actions in federal court on account of sexual orientation or gender identity."[278]

The bill, if eventually passed and enacted, would require churches everywhere to in every way accommodate, even hire LGBT persons into positions that the Christian faith prohibits, such as clergy, or face the penalty of law. At the end of this frightful train is the true aim of the American liberals and Leftists: a formerly Christian church that simply no longer resembles any form of genuine Christianity or can function as a Christian church without being sued into bankruptcy and dissolution by an "injured party" of sodomites suing because their recently-invented "human rights" were somehow violated.

Some soft minded church members will side with the Sodomites and support their politics in the church while others will fight against the incursion on principle. Local Christian churches will once again become hopelessly divided and become no longer capable of delivering or being allowed to deliver God's message to the people. It is a weakened church, one that serves primarily political purposes by placing the message of the Church under the oversight and jurisdiction of civil authorities. It sounds much like Cold War Era Soviet Union, when the Church there was subject to the brutality of the State for most of the twentieth century.

An example of this would be the establishment of the Association of Welcoming & Affirming Baptists (AWAB) in 1993. Their stated mission:

"As the only organization solely devoted to building the Welcoming and Affirming movement within the Baptist traditions, AWAB has a unique call to be The National Voice for Lesbian, Gay, Bisexual, Transgender, Queer, and Allied Baptists in the US."[279]

They currently list 112 member churches across the United States. It would appear that AWAB seeks to legitimize the Leftist agenda of normalizing homosexuality, sodomy, and the like by targeting otherwise conservative Baptist congregations—places where these issues would never have been considered or accepted before. If accepted, this move will without a doubt create both political and doctrinal tension and division for the Baptists to polarize them to an even greater degree. This is also part of the strategy to be sure.

These divisions will foment animosity and destroy any unity they might have achieved over their history which once again, I think is quite the aim. "Divide and conquer" is not a new strategy, and here it is being done from within as we have seen executed so many times by the Leftists' attempt to erase America, our values, and our culture. They already have completed this task with most of the other denominations, and now are working on the Baptists. If you are a Baptist that holds conservative beliefs, the Leftists are coming to destroy your church from within.

Take for example the recent events shaping up in the State of Texas. In early 2019:

"Left-leaning legislators have formed Texas' first LGBTQ caucus while promising a 'transformative' agenda. This includes a number of proposed 'sexual orientation and gender identity' laws (SOGI) that would attack people of faith so aggressively that they can justifiably be described as 'Ban the Bible' bills."[280]

"These bills would create new government power and protections that ban the free expression of biblically grounded beliefs, especially teaching on marriage and sexuality. Numerous bills seek to force people of faith to conform to others' personal and political activities, while setting aside their own sincerely held religious beliefs. Those who do not comply will face fines, possible jail time, or other criminal charges...These proposals try to fly under the radar as "anti-discrimination" bills... But such so-called anti-discrimination laws turn law-abiding Christians into criminals.... H.B. 244...creates a $100 per day fine for any violation. H.B. 188 includes a Class A Misdemeanor, the same punishment for a DUI or domestic violence, which could lead to a year in jail if the anti-discrimination policy is not followed."[281]

In September, 2019 the State of California also passed legislation dictating pastoral responses to LGBT congregants and medical professionals. It was ramrodded through the legislative process easily with the majority leftist control of the legislative bodies:

"ACR-99 Civil rights: lesbian, gay, bisexual, transgender, or queer people. This measure would call upon all Californians to embrace the individual and social benefits of family and community acceptance, upon religious leaders to counsel on LGBTQ matters from a place of love, compassion, and knowledge of the psychological and other harms of conversion therapy, and upon the people of California and the institutions of California with great moral influence to model equitable treatment of all people of the state....

WHEREAS, The California State Legislature has found that being lesbian, gay, bisexual, transgender, or queer (LGBTQ) is not a disease, disorder, illness, deficiency, or shortcoming; and

WHEREAS, Major professional associations of mental and physical health recognize that being LGBTQ is part of natural variations that occur in sexual orientation and gender identity, and recommend responsive services that foster self-acceptance and skills to cope with social stigma and discrimination; and

WHEREAS, Practices or therapies that attempt to create a change in a person's sexual orientation or gender identity are often referred to as conversion therapy; and

WHEREAS, Some family, caregivers, and communities promote conversion therapy when a person is known or thought to be LGBTQ; and

WHEREAS, California law recognizes that performing conversion therapy on young persons is ineffective, unethical, and harmful; and

WHEREAS, Conversion therapy has been rejected as ineffective, unethical, and harmful by leading medical, mental health, and child welfare organizations in the United States; and

WHEREAS, The stigma associated with being LGBTQ often created by groups in society, including therapists and religious groups, has caused disproportionately high rates of suicide, attempted suicide, depression, rejection, and isolation amongst LGBTQ and questioning individuals; and

WHEREAS, The State of California has a compelling interest in protecting the physical and psychological well-being of minors, including LGBTQ youth, and in protecting its minors against exposure to serious harms caused by family rejection and attempts to change sexual orientation or gender identity; and

WHEREAS, In a pluralistic society, people differing along spectrums of political and religious perspectives share a common responsibility of protecting the health and well-being of all children and vulnerable communities; now, therefore, be it Resolved by the Assembly of the State of California, the Senate thereof concurring, That the Legislature calls upon all Californians to embrace the individual and social benefits of family and community acceptance; and be it further

Resolved, That the Legislature calls upon religious leaders to counsel on LGBTQ matters from a place of love, compassion, and knowledge of the psychological and other harms of conversion therapy; and be it further Resolved, That in addressing the stigma often associated with persons who identify as LGBTQ, we call on the people of California–especially its counselors, pastors, religious workers, educators, and legislators–and the institutions of California with great moral influence–especially its churches, universities, colleges, and other schools, counseling centers, activist groups, and religious centers–to model equitable treatment of all people of the state..."[282]

Where exactly is that "separation of church and state" again? Apparently in both Texas and California, you can only be a "Christian" so long as you strictly conform and obey a political message and actions legislated and mandated by the State and dictated by people who hate the tenants of Christianity and who are actively seeking ways to destroy it. Not much wiggle room for maintaining the "freedom of religion" in there. If the laws are successfully passed (as they already have in California) and duly enacted, churches that conform to these new totalitarian laws will naturally lose membership—which is the goal of these Christ-haters—to make these churches unpalatable for faithful Christians, ultimately driving them away. That will put a dent in the church revenue and ultimately force closures of churches.

It was a similar strategy employed by the Leftists when they attacked the once conservative Boy Scouts of America, first by threatening huge lawsuits over not taking homosexuals, which the BSA could not afford to litigate, then later getting that policy accepted into the organization. Then in 2019 getting the BSA to change its name and accept girls, effectively making the entire organization into something it was not. This has without a doubt caused enrollments to decline, and I think, will ultimately force the organization to one day merge with some other organization to survive or to close altogether—which was the goal for the Leftists from the start; effectively ending another Conservative Christian American institution.

No theological explanation or rational thought applies to the politics of the larger LGBT movement. They seek to do the same damage that all leftists across America and the world are doing: divide the people, destroy the institutions, silence the opposition, and punish the nonconformists. Most Americans were not paying attention to what happened on June 11, 2019 in Ames, Iowa. It might be the least expected public stage for the injustice that was served.

A man named Adolfo Martinez, 30, admitted to taking down a "gay pride" flag from the Ames United Church of Christ, and burning it. The church pastor Eileen Gebbie, who identifies as gay woman, told reporters, "I often experienced Ames as not being as progressive as many people believe it is, and there still is a very large closeted queer community here,"[283]

In November, 2019 Martinez was tried and found guilty of a "hate crime" and other charges. He was sentenced to fifteen years in prison. But make no mistake, his crime was not simply burning a flag—leftists burn the American flag all the time and claim it's their First Amendment right to do so. No, his crime was as the pastor said, "...not being as progressive as many people..." Martinez understood that what he was seeing in his church was wrong and he was just not "drinking the Kool-Aid" there in Ames, Iowa. Now his life is ruined and he is a political prisoner in the United States of America. This is how the leftist LGBT operates.

Abroad, the Orthodox Church continues its mission in faith but is not immune to those who still attempt to divide and use the Church for political gain. This is nothing new to the Church.

The Orthodox Christian Church in Ukraine had recently sought independence (autocephaly) from the traditional and historic Church structure which was centered in Moscow for more than a thousand years. It has been under the patriarch of the Church in Russia since 988 A.D. I mentioned that the greater Orthodox Church consists of fourteen autocephalous jurisdictions serving Christians all over the globe.

Canonical decisions are always collegiate, never to be decided by one single patriarch. But with influence from both the Roman Catholic Vatican, and the U.S., the Ecumenical Patriarch of Constantinople alone decided to allow the Ukrainian Church its autocephaly. He began to make preparations to facilitate the independence of the Ukrainian Church on September 7th, 2018[284]. There was no full Ecumenical Council held by the greater Church to decide, as the rules of the Church require for such a decision.

On December 15th, 2018 "A 'Unification Gathering' was held in Kiev's St Sophia Cathedral to officialize the split of the newly formed government-founded Ukrainian Church from the Moscow Patriarchate."[285]

The move was immediately rejected by the Russian Orthodox Church and many if not most of the other autocephalous jurusdictions. What are the effects of such an action? All this served was to fuel already existing political unrest, and church *disunity*. There are other consequences, according to the former Ukrainian Prime Minster, Nikolai Azarov,

"...by raising the issue on autocephaly (independence) the Kiev authorities plan to destroy the Ukrainian Orthodox Church. 'Unification on the basis of destruction - that's what the Kiev authorities suggest,' he said. 'What's in the future? Forceful seizure of churches, temples, monasteries...Such games may result in blood and killings...' "[286]

It was not long before Ukrainian Security Forces raided the offices of the existing Orthodox Priests in Ukraine with ties to the Russian branch of the Church.[287] These priests were arrested, their property seized, and then they were jailed and interrogated.[288]

The idiotic and duplicitous response from the U.S. State Department not surprisingly, entirely misses the mark:

"The United States congratulates Metropolitan Epifaniy on his election as head of the Orthodox Church of Ukraine. The establishment of the Church was a historic moment for Ukraine. The United States maintains unwavering support for Ukraine and respects the freedom to worship unhindered by outside interference. The right to religious freedom extends to all Ukrainians, including those choosing to join – or not to join – the new Orthodox Church."[289]

While pontificating about respect for "...the freedom to worship unhindered by outside interference," the U.S. Government ignores the specific fact that it and other nations did exactly that...manipulated parties as a primary outside interference.[290] In so doing they have purposefully fueled the fires of disunity and provided just cause in the minds of many for a civil war in Ukraine. The Church did not just split on its own in some natural or canonical way. According to some sources, the United States allegedly paid the Ecumenical Patriarch of Constantinople $25 million to help motivate him to defy the canon of the greater Orthodox Church and declare the Ukrainian Church "autocephalous" on his own.[291]

A government that is nearly $36 trillion in debt seems to have no problem whatsoever finding money to use to manipulate world events as it sees fit, even if it means interfering with the Holy Orthodox Church. Around the world members of the various Orthodox Churches were thrown into confusion and disarray, some leaving parishes and joining others over the issue; more division and hardship courtesy of the arrogant U.S. government. We can conclude that our government understands nothing of the concept of holiness, and respects only its own political interests. America has conveniently forgotten that Russia has been an Orthodox Christian nation since the baptism of Rus in 988 A.D.

But for most Americans, Ukraine is "over there" so why would we care about the issues of the Orthodox Church? It's not your church anyway, right? You should care, we all ought to. If you happen to soon read a headline that says, "Unrest in Ukraine descends into civil war" or some similar tag line, you will know that the United States Government was a major catalyst in causing it. It will be the very same

The Unholy Land

American politicians that will run to the nearest microphone to tell you that we need to "support Ukraine" and to do that they will need to spend billions of tax dollars that our nation does not have. Then they will want to send our sons and daughters in uniform over there to "secure the situation, stabilize the region, and provide humanitarian aid to displaced civilians." Does any of this sound familiar? It should because when it comes to U.S. military operations overseas this is how most of them have begun since 1950.

What we have here is a demonstration that the political class in the United States does not respect the Almighty God by staying out of church matters, but instead elevates politics above holiness and brings foreign heads of state to worship at the altar of the almighty dollar. American officials frame the issue in terms of our own Protestant mindset about "freedom to worship unhindered..." but the religious culture overseas is not like that in America.

The Ukrainian government wasted no time after the new "autocephaly" had been "granted" and then supported by the United States. On December 21st, 2018 they introduced draft legislation to declare war against Russia,[292] no doubt hoping for firm support from their U.S. ally as Ukraine seeks to be more "European" than Russian and America views Russia as an adversary.

Neither did the new church waste time in directing policy. During a phone interview on Christmas Day, "Metropolitan" Epiphany Dumenko, the head of Ukraine's new nationalist church stated,

"Of course, I am for starting reforms in the church, so there wouldn't be conservatism, so we would depart from Russian tradition and so the church would be open and a spiritual guide for the Ukrainian people. Because we are moving towards Europe, and therefore we should depart from the Russian conservative tradition. The church should be more open, because Russian Orthodoxy is very conservative and far from the people. I have the position that we should be with the people. We should understand their problems."[293]

There is now pressure from the European LGBT community to influence this church and force it to accept the principles of the LGBT lifestyle—which would effectively create some strange, heretical, "church." Yes, there would be a building and a clergy, but this is no longer the canonical Holy Orthodox Church.

On the heels of the events in Ukraine, Montenegro also seeks to nationalize its Orthodox Church. On the same Christmas Day we read,

"President Milo Đukanović of Montenegro intends to undertake a push for the recognition of the autocephaly of the schismatic 'Montenegrin Orthodox Church,' as Ukrainian President Petro Poroshenko has done in his country."[294]

The issues of these LGBT movement organizations are not complicated in spite of whatever they would like people to think. When it comes to Christianity, the issue might well be summed up this way:

"Do not accept the delusions and distortions of those who have forsaken the true God and abandoned the wisdom of Christ and the Scriptures. You are not 'gay' or 'homosexual.' You were not 'born this way.' You are men and women created in the image and likeness of GOD!

You were all designed by Him for everlasting life in His Kingdom. You struggle with carnal temptations and spiritual passions, like every single man and woman since the fall of Adam and Eve. In other words you are human."[295]

~

Fr. Ioannes Apiarius

"Christofascism"

Liberals love labels. They can't seem to have enough of them. When they wear out the ones they create, they just keep on making more labels they can use to demonize people they hate, and then mount political or media campaigns against the newly labeled group. "Christofascism" is just such a label, and appears to be one of the latest ones to recently appear in the media.

Parents who are not content to allow their children to be indoctrinated by the Leftist American public schools which are often run by a majority of godless liberals in most areas, can opt for homeschooling. The homeschooling curriculum is often one that follows more conservative viewpoints akin to traditional conservative American and Christian values instead of what passes for education in many of our public school settings today.

The Leftists in America absolutely despise homeschooling and have been attacking it alongside Christianity for many years now. The lessons of conservative values completely contradict those which Leftists push, the same ones indoctrinating our kids with messaging about "man-made global warming," positive messaging of socialism, open borders, anti-"white privilege," pro-abortion, LBGT "rights," "Social Justice" and all the rest of the lies and rot gut spewing from the Democrat Party today. Homeschoolers escape all of that, and being the totalitarian fascists that Leftists are at heart, they won't have it.

They were hard pressed to discover a way to discredit and tarnish homeschooling for a long time. But after the Leftists lost the 2016 national election for the U.S. presidency and having refused to accept the outcome, no, been caught attempting to undermine and even overthrow the new republican president, they looked to blame some nonexistent "Russian collusion" instead. Incredibly, the same formula is now being applied here. They have succeeded in inventing a term that can be plastered all over the homeschoolers: "Christofascists." What's that mean? From the Leftist[296] "Think Progress" website, "a term to refer to fundamentalist Christian ideas used in pursuit of totalitarian rule."[297]

Who in their right mind would ever think of American Christians at totalitarians? As I have been demonstrating, there is no possible way that American Christians are anywhere near unifying on their own, a step that would be necessary if they were ever to be "in pursuit of totalitarian rule." In order that we begin to properly address this complete absurdity, let's be quite clear on something: In America, the Fascists, Socialists, Communists, and hate-filled, anti-American pundits today are not Russians, but all rabid American Leftists, and most of them are ignorant democrats.

Now these same vile people spin a story about homeschooling that is 180 degrees untrue, pretending that evil totalitarian Russians are, from the highest levels of their government creating little totalitarian neo-Nazis out of American homeschoolers—while the real and present danger is an American government owned and operated academia that is indoctrinating children to become violent anti-American Fascists.

Why is it that they are they trying to connect them? This is because a global homeschooling conference was held in Russia in 2018. The Russian co-sponsor of that conference allegedly supports "Russia's 2013 'Anti-Propaganda Law,' which effectively demonizes the entire

LGBTQ community."[298] If you disagree with ANYTHING the LGBTQ people say or want, you are automatically relegated to the rubbish bin of American society today in the eyes of the Leftists. Not only that, but now you are in "collusion" with "evil totalitarian Russians," and conservative Christians are now labeled as totalitarian "Christofascists." It's so crazy a scheme to paint their hated opposition that it just might work.

The strategy to demonize your opposition by accusing them of the very thing you are yourself guilty of is nothing new. The people at ThinkProgress seem to have conveniently forgotten that it was Barack Obama who in 2012 told Mr. Medvedev, Putin's protégé and long considered second in the Russian power structure, "This is my last election ... After my election I have more flexibility," to address Russian concerns about a European missile defense shield. "I will transmit this information to Vladimir," said Medvedev.[299] It was in fact the president of the American Leftists who was cozy with the "evil totalitarian Russians," not conservative Christian homeschooler families.

To be fair, the political Right likewise uses Christianity in many of the same ways that Liberals do. Even Billy Graham noted:

"I don't want to see religious bigotry in any form. It would disturb me if there was a wedding between the religious fundamentalists and the political right. The hard right has no interest in religion except to manipulate it.[300]"

He was correct, of course. It is the tendency of all mankind to use and pervert faith of almost any kind to support personal and political agendas across the ages. For Americans, these matters serve only to keep Christians—Americans—divided against each other. It is an unfortunate truth we must deal with, each of us individually. None of any of this should come as a surprise to Christians. We were told how all this would happen in 2 Timothy 3:

"But mark this: There will be terrible times in the last days. People will be lovers of themselves, lovers of money, boastful, proud, abusive, disobedient to their parents, ungrateful, unholy, without love, unforgiving, slanderous, without self-control, brutal, not lovers of the good, treacherous, rash, conceited, lovers of pleasure rather than lovers of God— having a form of godliness but denying its power. Have nothing to do with such people....They are the kind who worm their way into homes and gain control over gullible women, who are loaded down with sins and are swayed by all kinds of evil desires, always learning but never able to come to a knowledge of the truth. Just as Jannes and Jambres opposed Moses, so also these teachers oppose the truth. They are men of depraved minds, who, as far as the faith is concerned, are rejected. But they will not get very far because, as in the case of those men, their folly will be clear to everyone."

In a place where both Atheists and American Liberals cry for "separation of church and state," they openly support hard-core Leftists who use the "state" to control the churches, and the people who attend them. In so doing, they have made the restoration of virtue and unity as much as a civil and political matter as it is a religious one. This is why American Christians should not and cannot accept these false cries of "separation of church and state." To the Liberals in America who continually cry for that, I say, "you first—keep your hands (or rather your laws) off my church!"

9

The New Religion of the Left

"The Devil has still the same inclination to injure men that he has had since the beginning of the world; and although he does not always do them all the harm he intends, yet he succeeds in doing them a great part of it."

Andronicus II Palaeologos, (1282-1328)
to his grandson Andronicus III

I know people who absolutely believe in anthropological or "man-made" "global warming." They are convinced of it and wonder why and how I can be a "climate denier" when "scientists clearly agree" on the matter. I tell them they are attaching themselves to a new religion of the Left, not a scientific fact or a proven outcome. They of course become uncontrollably upset (as liberals tend to do) when faced with truths that they simply do not accept.

Let us look no further than the entire fact-starved "man-made global warming" crowd—they continue to preach an untruth that mankind—more specifically, Americans are the primary cause for dubious reporting of rising climate temperatures *and* that this rise is both unnatural and detrimental to the planet's survival, *and* that Americans both caused it and can fix it through increased taxation.

To date, there has been no causal link proven scientifically between the activities of mankind and climate change. There is, however, much evidence that datasets used to make this claim were tampered with so as to show fraudulent results to support a political agenda.[301] But closed-minded, self-identified "environmentalists" will accept no debate on the issue—because they have no factual basis whatsoever to actually prove their theory, and any honest debate would quickly and clearly expose this fact. It is their "blind spot" at best, and fraud at its worst.

In the middle of the issue are those non-scientists who are perhaps less informed, who mean well and somehow truly think they can "save the planet" by supporting this farce. If those people, who are likely honest about wanting to help a cause, would accept a person who has a different view rather than only their own "echo chamber" of friends, they might well see their own blind spot and start asking some questions.

Why is the concept of man-made global warming a religion then? Simply this: because it requires faith to believe in it. You read that right. It is a fact that genuine science does not require faith to believe in it or prove it to be fact. Science is a result of factually proven data, and it does not care whether you believe in it or not. Gravity will work every time on this planet whether you believe it is a thing or not. Any attempt to connect mankind to climate change has not yet been scientifically proven. Perhaps science will one day show a causal proof, but today we have to deal with the world in real terms with in what we know, not what we think that we might someday possibly could learn in the future.

What defines science? How does science work? You can discover that through the scientific process which was once taught in public schools in America. The argument of the global warming crowd **cannot pass the basic test of the scientific method**, which used to be taught in grade school. That method looks like this:

1. Purpose- State what we wish to learn about the subject.
2. Research- Discover as much as possible, including all information. (not just select information.)
3. Hypothesis- Try to develop a potential solution to the problem. Another term for hypothesis is 'educated guess'. This is often stated as "If I...(do something) then...(this will occur)."
4. Experiment- Design a repeatable test or procedure to confirm or disprove the hypothesis.
5. Analysis- Record the results of the experiment, the data.
6. Conclusion- Review the data and check to see if the hypothesis was correct. For it to be validated, the experiment **must be repeatable with the same results each time.**

However, the latest liberal premise of pseudo-science is that Americans specifically are the cause for rising climate temperatures and that this rise is both unnatural and detrimental to the planet's survival. The basis of their argument by definition must first insist that there exists some "normal" temperature for the Earth. "Normal compared to what?" an actual scientist would ask. The planet's forces and those forces of our solar system's star, the Sun, are forever in motion, always changing. "Normal" for planet Earth IS CHANGE.

How did the planet end its last two ice ages without Americans there "warming" it up? They cannot say, but we are supposed to accept their even more preposterous convolution that if we agree to give them more of our money through taxes, give up our liberty with more expensive and unneeded regulations, and agree to purchase value-added, high profit margin "green" gadgets and products all of which they promise can somehow fix it. We "must do something" they cry.

The liberal socialists' claim of "American global warming/climate change", et al. fails this basic test every time and is therefore not based upon any actual science but by definition, consensus only. Consensus is not science, and science is not consensus.

Students today are instead told that "scientists agree" on the theory of so-called man-made global warming, including the causes, with the clear intention of making students believe that anthropological global warming is an undeniable fact. Liberals might as well rename their propoganda, "American global warming," because we are apparently the only nation they seek to blame and push for higher taxes, with the exception of Great Britain and maybe a few other first world western nations. Of course it's a complete fabrication when China and India far outstrip the United States in "greenhouse gas emissions."

Students are not taught correctly that when "scientists agree," by definition that alone cannot be defined as "scientific method" – agreement is, by definition, merely consensus.

To illustrate the point another way; what if you had the flu, went to a hospital and five doctors shook your hand to greet you. They perform no diagnostic tests or any physical examination of you whatsoever. They confer together and all agree that you suffer from high blood pressure. Would their consensus about your condition make it true just because they are doctors in agreement? You arrived at the hospital with the flu but unless the doctors take your temperature and perform the necessary tests (which can provide repeatable results) they cannot make a truly accurate diagnosis.

The flu test is repeatable and its results will be the same if you took it once or three times that day. The doctors can discover the other symptoms with information gathered from your diagnostics—temperature, blood pressure, breathing, heart rate, and so on—if they bothered to take them. But leaving the hospital untreated for the flu, and given a bottle of blood pressure medication that will only make you sicker. This sort of mistreatment by the medical community would be considered malpractice today, but somehow we are expected to accept the same practice from so-called "climate scientists."

In the particular case of the liberal messaging of "manmade global warming," or now the more *scientific-sounding* "anthropological climate change", it amounts to nothing short of fascism disguised in the feel-good notion of "saving the Earth" and accomplished by publicly shaming anyone who dares to disagree. It is now supported by and endorsed with the coordinated effort of political, academic, and religious collusion—this could ONLY be a successful stratagem with this arrangement. The Fascist environmentalists accept no debate on the issue—because they have no factual basis whatsoever to prove their theory, and any honest debate would immediately and clearly expose this truth.

I find it quite telling that the same otherwise godless liberals have a difficult time accepting the God of Creation, the Bible, Noah, Moses and Jesus Christ, can somehow willingly thrust themselves into the false belief system of "global warming." The origin of this transformation is important and goes back to the 1960's. An example of the liberal mindset is discovered in an essay written by Lynn White, Jr then, a professor of history at the University of California, Los Angeles:

"What did Christianity tell people about their relations with the environment? ...Christianity, in absolute contrast to ancient paganism and Asia's religions...insisted that it is God's will that man exploit nature for his proper ends. At the level of the common people this worked out in an interesting way. In Antiquity every tree, every spring, every stream, every hill had its own *genius loci*, its guardian spirit...Before one cut a tree, mined a mountain, or dammed a brook, it was important to placate the spirit in charge of that particular situation, and to keep it placated. By destroying pagan animism, Christianity made it possible to exploit nature in a mood of indifference to the feelings of natural objects."[302]

Mr. White concludes his essay with this chilling statement which proves my entire point:

"Both our present science and our present technology are so tinctured with orthodox[n] Christian arrogance toward nature that no solution for our ecologic crisis can be expected from them alone. Since the roots of our trouble are so largely religious, the remedy must also be essentially religious, whether we call it that or not. We must rethink and refeel our nature and destiny. The profoundly religious, but heretical, sense of the primitive Franciscans for the spiritual autonomy of all parts of nature may point a direction. I propose Francis as a patron saint for ecologists."[303]

And so it was that Liberals received their marching orders: **Christianity must be radically altered in order to serve their purpose.**

Why now? Because there is money and power to be had. The "fight against global warming" or "climate change" is never clearly defined and can never end. Why? Because at its base, the movement today is not about saving trees, but rather it is politically motivated. With such a structure in place, they can and will exact untold wealth from the people for all time to come, and claim forever that they need more.

We are allowing the media, our schools, the government, and our churches to indoctrinate an entire generation of people with a newly packaged ancient paganism.[304] They become people who will voluntarily sacrifice money, time and other resources to tax themselves and others into poverty in order to fight an imaginary sinister spook of "global warming" and who, out of their ignorance, will easily surrender the rule of law and our nation's sovereignty to any President or party who asks—all in the deception of "saving the planet."

The modern strain of "environmentalism" is simply cleverly re-bundled socialism, as the former National Columnist the late Dr. Charles Krauthammer explains:

---

[n] Use of the word "orthodox' is not a reference to the Eastern Orthodox Churches here. Another word might be "dogmatic."

"Socialism having failed so spectacularly, the left was adrift until it struck upon a brilliant gambit: metamorphosis from red to green, The cultural elites went straight from the memorial service for socialism to the altar of the environment." [305]

Dr. Krauthammer was right, of course. But while these socialist malcontents refuse to have a sincere debate regarding the environment based upon science instead of consensus, they now move forward to not only silence, but to punish anyone who disagrees with their new environmentalist religion.

A New Gospel

"But I fear lest, as the serpent seduced Eve by his subtilty, so your minds should be corrupted, and fall from the simplicity that is in Christ. For if he that cometh preacheth another Christ, whom we have not preached; or if you receive another Spirit, whom you have not received; or another gospel which you have not received; you might well bear with him."

2 Corinthians 11: 3 – 4
Douay-Rheims Bible

The United Methodist Church, like so many other denominations, has now been co-opted into incorporating a new gospel, the Liberal agenda into their ever cheapened and twisted version of Christianity. They have even adopted this policy for their followers, which encompasses many of the key points of the American Leftist platform:

- "We call upon all to take measures to save energy. Everybody should adapt his or her lifestyle to the average consumption of energy that respects the limits of the planet earth. We encourage persons to limit $CO2$ emissions toward the goal of one tonne per person annually. We strongly advocate for the
- priority of the development of renewable energies. The deposits of carbon, oil, and gas resources are limited and their continuous utilization accelerates global warming. The use of nuclear power is no solution for avoiding $CO2$ emissions. Nuclear power plants are vulnerable, unsafe, and potential

- health risks. A safe, permanent storage of nuclear waste cannot be guaranteed. It is therefore not responsible to future generations to operate them. The production of agricultural fuels and the use of biomass plants rank lower than the provision of safe food supplies and the continued existence for small farming businesses.[306]"
- "We support regulations that protect and conserve the life and health of animals, including those ensuring the humane treatment of pets, domesticated animals, animals used in research, wildlife, and the painless slaughtering of meat animals, fish, and fowl. We recognize unmanaged and managed commercial, multinational, and corporate exploitation of wildlife and the destruction of the ecosystems on which they depend threatens the balance of natural systems, compromises biodiversity, reduces resilience, and threatens ecosystem services. We encourage commitment to effective implementation of national and international governmental and business regulations and guidelines for the conservation of all animal species with particular support to safeguard those threatened with extinction.[307]"

Was this the purpose of Christ's ministry? Is this why He came to Earth to die and resurrect, so that we can submit to the bondage of a paganist religion falsely carried out in His Name? I wonder when they are gazing at a Cross, do these Methodists say to themselves, "Thank you Jesus for your sacrifice, I will sell my SUV and buy a Prius as you instructed. I am sorry for my sin of not recycling that triple A battery last week, and throwing away the empty peanut butter jar because I was too lazy to wash it out; I promise to recycle and buy carbon credits to atone for my environmental sins." That any church calling itself "Christian" could adopt such specific political directives for its members is astonishing to me.

The Bible calls us to be good stewards of the Earth, not to be enslaved by men who invent an imaginary series of events and subsequent onerous rules that pretend to manage it. Did Christ come with instructions for His church to push for a *"commitment to effective implementation of national and international governmental and business regulations and guidelines for the conservation of all animal species with particular support to safeguard those threatened with extinction?"* Not the Christ I am familiar with. Who is this false Christ they use to press their leftist agenda? When the Methodists attend worship, who do they think they are worshipping?

These misguided Methodists would not survive long in an Old Testament world where animals were endlessly slaughtered and sacrificed almost around the clock by God's people. That was not for mankind's entertainment, but a strict requirement of the very same Almighty God they claim to serve today. Would they now, based upon their strong animal-loving policies judge their God for His past treatment of the animals which He created?

The United Church of Christ has considered a similar position, calling on members to support the Leftist's political efforts to enact laws based on no science whatsoever, read it for yourself—it is rationalization in motion:

The following resolution has been received by the Office of General Minister and President prior to the June 9, 2017 deadline established by the Standing Rules of the Thirtieth-first General Synod regarding issues which could not have been anticipated. Receipt of this resolution should not be considered an indication it will come before delegates to the General Synod. The resolution is now being researched by the Board of Director's Committee on Disposition and its staff before consideration by the full Board of Directors prior to the start of the Thirty-first General Synod. Any resolution must meet all of the requirements of the Standing Rules. The Board of Directors will decide prior to the start of Synod whether this resolution meets those requirements and make a determination as to its disposition.

THE EARTH IS THE LORD'S – NOT OURS TO WRECK
IMPERATIVES FOR A NEW MORAL ERA

Submitted by the Southern California, Nevada Conference
A Resolution of Witness

SUMMARY:

God's great gift of Creation – the context in which all life seeks fulfillment – is in crisis. Driven by material aspiration, humanity's use of fossil fuel since the Industrial Revolution has broken Creation's balance. The scale of Creation's demise is dramatically expanding beyond our comprehension. Never has the earth and the climate changed so quickly. While the leaders of every country in the world recognize this reality, our current Administration ignores science, defunds the Environmental Protection Agency, and withdraws from the Paris Climate Accord. As people of faith, recognizing that the earth is the Lord's, it falls upon our generation to embrace the imperatives set forth in this resolution – imperatives that constitute a new moral era. We view the current climate crisis as an opportunity for which the church was born.

BIBLICAL, THEOLOGICAL AND ETHICAL RATIONALE

Psalm 24

John 18:37-38 (NRSV)
[37] Pilate asked him, "So you are a king?" Jesus answered, "You say that I am a king. For this I was born, and for this I came into the world, to testify to the truth. Everyone who belongs to the truth listens to my voice." [38] Pilate asked him, "What is truth?" After he had said this, he went out to the Jews again and told them, "I find no case against him.

TEXT OF THE MOTION

WHEREAS the leaders of over 190 countries have signed the Paris Climate Accord, acknowledging the critical role every country must play if the life-sustaining climate of the earth is to continue to sustain life as we have always known it;

WHEREAS the mayors of 30 American cities, the governors of numerous states and leaders of hundreds of American companies have publicly committed the institutions they lead to reducing greenhouse gas emissions in compliance with the Paris Climate Accord;

WHEREAS over the past 50 years the UCC, along with religious leaders from other faiths and denominations, have issued countless statements on the goodness of Creation and our call to act as responsible stewards, all of which has been an insufficient witness;

WHEREAS the Core Purpose of the United Church of Christ states (in part): "… we serve God in the co-creation of a just and sustainable world as made manifest in the Gospel of Jesus Christ,"

WHEREAS this historic moment provides Christian communities with a powerful opportunity to bear witness to the sacredness of God's Creation and the urgent call to preserve it, and responding to this call expresses the new mission initiative of the UCC known as the three great loves[i], one of which is love of creation;

THEREFORE, BE IT RESOLVED, that the Thirty-first General Synod of the United Church of Christ raises its prophetic voice regarding the urgency of healing the climate of the earth, our home and God's gift for the future of all life, both human and all other life,

BE IT FURTHER RESOLVED, that the Thirty-first General Synod of the United Church of Christ calls upon the whole of the church to prayerfully engage the following imperatives as we seek to initiate a new moral era:

Let our clergy accept the mantle of moral leadership
Now is the time for clergy to speak from their pulpits about the moral obligation of our generation to protect God's creation. Let the world know that whatever the current American administration may say or do, we who follow Jesus will not back away from God's call to protect our common home.

Let all of us incarnate the changes we long for
Now is the time for congregations and for every person of faith to set a moral example through our own words and actions. As individuals and as communities, let us commit to making decisions of integrity in our energy choices, even as we commit to hold our political leaders accountable to do the same.

Let us proclaim truth in the public square
We are now living in a John 18:37 moment, in which we must hold to the truth we understand from our two Testaments and from the sacred book of nature, recognizing that when truth is compromised, only power prevails.
- Let our communities of faith be bold and courageous as we address the greatest moral challenge that the world has ever faced.
- Let us commit to resist all expansion of fossil fuel infrastructure and demand new sources of renewable energy that are accessible to all communities.

92	• Let us do all we can to change America's understanding of the story that our generation is
93	writing. Let us begin a new story – a story that is not dependent on fossil fuel or on
94	wealth for the few and misery for the many.
95	
96	Accepting that it is up to us – we the people – whether in the streets, at the State House, in the
97	halls of power, with our phones and emails, by committing our time, financial resources and
98	prayers – let us pour ourselves out to bend the moral arc of justice, with joy in our hearts, beauty
99	in our sights, and hope for the children.
100	
101	**FUNDING**
102	Funding for the implementation of this Resolution will be made in accordance with the overall
103	mandates of the affected agencies and the funds available.
104	
105	**IMPLEMENTATION**
106	The Collegium of Officers, in consultation with appropriate ministries or other entities within the
107	United Church of Christ, will determine the implementing body.

---

[1] http://www.ucc.org/commentary_three_great_loves_04272017

There are many things in this proclamation that are disturbing coming from a church claiming to follow Christ. First, they say, "We view the current climate crises as an opportunity for which the church was born." REALLY? Christ establishing His Church at Pentecost was done so that the Church could save the Earth from "anthropological global warming?" This is blasphemy and is certainly NOT the reason the church was established.

Then, of course there is the matter of just another church clearly supporting the leftist political agenda. They knock the President by stating, "....the current Administration ignores science..." May I ask, what science, exactly? They must mean consensus or better described, Leftist collusion. But their "Biblical, Theological and Ethical Rationale" is so thin as to be nonexistent if it were not already totally absurd. Ladies and gentlemen, the Unholy Altar of the Environment is now open for business.

Of course the big picture result of all of this misguided political fantasy is a distracted and derailed church. An historically false church that never was is now focused on "the environment" instead of Christ. A church that wastes valuable resources and time to engage in political agendas instead of doing the actual work of Christianity. Every second spent indoctrinating people and their children with this false religion is time taken away from learning God's truth. This is, in fact, Satan's ultimate goal, and who could argue against that conclusion?

In 2019, the course of this climate religion began to be galvanized with the disturbing addition of climate change religious rituals. NBC opened a new website allowing people to post their anonymous "Climate Confessions, directing their followers this way: "Climate Confessions; Even those who care deeply about the planet's future can slip up now and then. Tell us: Where do you fall short in preventing climate change? Do you blast the A/C? Throw out half your lunch? Grill a steak every week? Share your anonymous confession with NBC News."[308]

This sick and twisted religion of the Left sets its own standards of what constitutes "falling short in preventing climate change." The depths of this depravity are difficult even for me to comprehend. If that were not enough, in September 2019, the liberal "Union Theological Seminary" in New York held a service where congregants were encouraged to "confess" environmental sins to house plants in a church setting,[309]

"There's been much discussion online about a Union chapel this week, in which the Union community was asked to engage with the plants, soil, rocks, birds, trees in our lives: confessing harm, hope, love, gratitude. The chapel was held as part of Professor Claudio Carvalhaes' class: "Extractivism: A Ritual/Liturgical Response," in which he and students develop liturgical responses to our climate crisis. It was a beautiful, moving ritual...This is just one expression of worship here at Union. Union Theological Seminary is grounded in the Christian tradition, and at the same time deeply committed to inter-religious engagement."[310]

A "Christian Tradition?" Exactly what traditions are they referring to? It is our foolish Western pride that today even has many believing that most delusional notion of all, "I can save the planet." If you can save the planet, why can't you save the nation? You cannot even save yourself. Their twitter post was even more disturbing:

"We've had many questions about yesterday's chapel, conducted as part of @ccarvalhaes' class, "Extractivism: A Ritual/Liturgical Response." In worship, our community confessed the harm we've done to plants, speaking directly in repentance. This is a beautiful ritual."[311]

Not to be outdone by these efforts and perhaps in coordination with them, Pope Francis publicly supported this agenda in late 2019, throwing the weight of the Roman Catholic Church behind it with this statement on 15 November:

"We must introduce – we are thinking about it – in the Catechism of the Catholic Church the sin against ecology, the ecological sin against the common home, because it is a duty..."[312]

In summary, in an extremely short span of time, this paganism of climate change has:

1. Established its own authority above both men and God.
2. Established standards for determining what "sin" is as defined by the religion (political elites).
3. Created an expectation that believers are guilty of said sin.
4. Developed a means for confession and judgement of said sins.
5. Provided a new false Christian-style ritual as a means for "repentance" of these newly established, imaginary sins.

I am left to ponder what they say happens to someone who is an "unrepentant climate sinner?" My guess is that they are banished to the Republican National Convention during a Presidential election year or something. What exactly is the climate religion's version of "hell?" We may soon find out and I will guarantee that we will not like it.

The goal of this whole crowd, however, is to attract, deceive, and control the gullible while silencing any detractors; not to listen to opposition or negotiate in any way. At its core, it is a dangerous totalitarian regime. Merely calling personal climate violations 'sins" isn't hardly enough. In a letter addressed to Barack Obama, Attorney General Lynch, and OSTP Director Holdren dated September 1, 2015, twenty academics and "climate operatives" (I won't call them scientists) asked the Obama Administration to commence with federal investigations for organizations and other private groups of Americans that disagree with their position on man-made global warming. It was an attempt to punish and silence opposition outside the legal bounds of the rule of law.

"We appreciate that you are making aggressive and imaginative use of the limited tools available to you in the face of a recalcitrant Congress. One additional tool – recently proposed by Senator Sheldon Whitehouse – is a RICO (Racketeer Influenced and Corrupt Organizations Act) investigation of corporations and other organizations that have knowingly deceived the American people about the risks of climate change, as a means to forestall America's response to climate change…
We strongly endorse Senator Whitehouse's call for a RICO investigation….If corporations in the fossil fuel industry and their supporters are guilty of the misdeeds that have been documented in books and journal articles, it is imperative that these misdeeds be stopped as soon as possible so that America and the world can get on with the critically important business of finding effective ways to restabilize the Earth's climate, before even more lasting damage is done."[313]

    The modern socialist now wishes to use American laws designed to prosecute mafia gangsters to persecute any who hold opposing views and would stand in the way of their ultimate goals of consolidating their power and levying higher taxation of the people—and this is really all of it is about. Could these people really be the same folks that told us to "live and let live" in the 1960's?

    It is ironic that while socialists view so-called "climate deniers" (their new fabricated label for anyone who disagrees with them) as either uneducated morons or, in this case, gangsters who seek to conceal the "truth" about climate change to the public, it is in fact the socialists themselves who are in denial regarding the now obvious scientific facts regarding climate change. Little has changed from Medieval days to now; they seek to put the "heretics" away in the tower.

    More to the original point, it's important for us to remember that humans are not aliens. We are as much a part of the natural world as any other plant or creature that populates it. Whether one is a Christian or not, keeping in mind our own limited role in nature forces us to recognize that our Creator is infinitely greater than us. Nature and its processes serve to recall for us of our commonality with both mankind and the natural world across the globe, and makes clear our own mortality—something about which Christianity constantly reminds us.

In contrast, modern liberalism teaches that the only connection we have with nature is to believe in a false paganism, a doctrine that Americans alone are committing sins against the planet, and that we are solely responsible for "destroying" it. We can absolve ourselves and atone for our environmental sins by confessing them, repenting, and paying carbon taxes to Al Gore, buying a Prius, and using mercury-laced lightbulbs, and LED's that end up in the landfill. In the liberal's world, humankind is some sort of otherworldly alien invader, not intelligent beings created in the image of God and formed with a purpose as taught by Christianity and other faiths. We cannot possess rights that may interfere with their belief system. In the end, all they really want is our money, our land, and our Liberty, and for this reason, they will only become more aggressive and violent.

Humans as a species, have no place in the ultimate Liberal Utopian world. The depraved mindset of hard-core liberalism is that man does not belong here, but while the reality is that man is present, they take it upon themselves to direct us as to how we must think and act, what we must eat, where we must live, what we must say or do, and how we must spend our money, all for the false pretense now of "saving the planet."

Embracing nature does not require one to buy an expensive hybrid car to absolve for the imaginary "sins" of ruining a planet, the same goes for all the so-called "green" products on the market today. No one should ever have to pay a "carbon tax" to any government. This proposed tax is the nut of what the eco-terrorists and the liberal leftists are ultimately after with all their phony environmentalism. They want even more of your money, which *is* your liberty.

Even comedian George Carlin concludes,

"I don't know how you feel, but I'm pretty sick of church people. You know what they ought to do with churches? Tax them. If holy people are so interested in politics, government, and public policy, let them pay the price of admission like everybody else. The Catholic Church alone could wipe out the national debt if all you did was tax their real estate.[314]"

A New Leftist Denomination

The church of the leftists even has denominations of its own. If you are one who is not interested in worshipping the plants and confessing your environmental sins, their god of science offers you another path to follow.

In the early months of 2020 the world responded to what was sold as a "pandemic" of an outbreak of a flu-like disease called COVID-19 or Coronavirus. It is a synthetic virus created in a Chinese laboratory and released by same in an American election year. Incumbent president Donald Trump was poised to win reelection without much effective opposition. As a result, the entire handling of the disease was politicized by his opponents; the democrats, ANTIFA, and Black Lives Matter in America, and the various globalists abroad.

The corrupted World Health Organization quickly declared the outbreak as a pandemic; soon after, the world shut down. In a knee-jerk panic, the governors of the fifty states responded by closing down businesses and placing all residents under "quarantine" by restricting us to our homes for most of March and the entire month of April. While government has claimed the authority to quarantine sick people in the past in order to prevent the spread of a deadly disease, the same governments do not have any right whatsoever to "quarantine" the well for any reason. Along with closing businesses, that would constitute a house arrest and violate Fifth Amendment right to not "be deprived of life, liberty, or property, without due process of law"

The president instituted a series of foreign travel bans to keep the infection from being imported from people arriving from affected nations. The media bombarded us with hourly updated on the number of casualties. But when all was tallied, the numbers and death rates were scarcely worse than the seasonal flu we see each year. That is how we knew it was being used as a political tool in an election year.

Most salient were the unlawful and draconian restrictions by primarily leftist democrat governors making every effort to close churches during Lent and Easter. Most churches immediately and willingly complied, moving their services to online video platforms and keeping the physical church locked. These democrat controlled states included California, New York, Kentucky, Michigan, Indiana, Minnesota, and several others. In these states during the month of April, Christians were fined, arrested, charged with misdemeanors, locked out of churches, locked out of parking lots of their churches, dragged out of churches, detained by police, and so on.

The New York City Mayor Bill de Blasio publicly threatened city churches with permanent closures on March 27th,

"Everyone has been instructed that if they see worship services ... going on, they will go to the officials of that congregation...They will inform them they need to stop the services and disperse. If that does not happen, they will take additional action, up to the point of fines and potentially closing the building permanently."[315]

These clear violations of the First Amendment were all unlawfully executed under the false pretense of "preventing the spread of the coronavirus" and they were not without reactions. Protests against these unlawful restrictions erupted in nearly all fifty states. A petition was started in Michigan to recall the governor.[316] Protests in Raleigh, North Carolina were shut down by police and protestor Monica Faith Ussery, 51, was arrested for violating the governor's order. The police claimed that her protesting "was not an essential activity."

"'I have a right to peacefully assemble," she said as officers led her away, her hands bound with a zip tie. "God bless America.'"[317]

She did have every right to peacefully assemble.

The damage inflicted on America as a nation in this campaign by the Leftists to finally unseat the incumbent president whom they hate° was sudden, dramatic, and irreparable. America was at once turned into a police state where inalienable American rights no longer mattered or were protected while despotic governors unlawfully shuttered businesses and locked down their entire states without notice for any reason they saw fit. Once the entire economy was "closed" in late March, unemployment predictably skyrocketed. In the course of less than three weeks, America went from full employment to over 32.75 million people unemployed, or about 24% unemployment.[318] Congress immediately authorized over $7 trillion in emergency relief spending with a series of bills containing the usual political pork, some money for business grants, and worker aid payments in the month of April—money the nation did not have and would be printed, causing massive price inflation from 2022 -2025.

The Liberal Christ haters had achieved their goals. With the nonstop fear mongering over a disease with casualties less than those suffered from the common seasonal flu, they managed to close every church in America for Lent and Easter while most mosques remained open.[319] As a result of all of this, churches too would suffer. Hundreds of smaller struggling churches would now be on the brink of permanent closure due to lack of income. People who are unemployed and underemployed cannot financially support a church.

With the emergency funding authorized by Congress, churches could apply for assistance to help cover payrolls similar to small businesses. But the Congressional democrats inserted requirements that would require churches that receive this aid to comply with federal hiring practices for staff that are incompatible with the Christian faith; again, the Leftist agenda was being broadly institutionalized.

° The Leftists had tried a long series of strategies in multiple attempts to unseat President Trump, including a failed bid for impeachment which was based upon fraudulent information and personal opinions. Each attempt to remove him was grander in scale than the previous one, and the COVID-19 "pandemic" scare was the grandest of them all. This incorporated the collusion of the Chinese Government who created and released the virus. The Chinese Government had good reason to attempt to unseat Trump after his renegotiation of the longstanding unfair trade deals with China.

The Church of Corona

Out of all this coordinated chaos was born a new Leftist church denomination of their father god, Science, who begat the Virus. We might call this new denomination The *Church of Corona*. As with the global warming crowd of plant worshippers, the basis of the Corona Denomination is the same god, Science and scientific studies. Their followers share the same basic ideology and are instructed to repeat their creed, "trust the science" or to speak their confession of faith, "I believe science."

Followers in the Corona Denomination, however, are commanded to bow before their lord, the Virus, for the Virus is also a god, who is omnipresent, omnipotent, invisible, and mysterious. Their god, Virus, demands that specific rituals be publicly and universally followed. These practices include constant handwashing, wearing of useless masks, staying 6' apart from other humans, and avoiding Christian churches and the small businesses often run by people with more independent mindsets. Their lord Virus demands blind obedience to follow every new and various dictate of whatever their master god Science commands; shutdowns of certain places that anger the god of Science, and likely a command for all to be vaccinated with or without their consent with some manner of synthetic poison.

While Christ is the God of Love, their god, Virus, operates entirely by instilling fear with the constant threat of death, and he does demand sacrifices. Even though 99.96% of the population survives the infection inflicted by their lord Virus, people who are "exposed" must submit to testing of the faith, I mean testing of the Virus. Their lives will thereafter be tracked. If one is found to have the antibodies present it means that Virus has chosen them and, they are required to follow a regimen of monastic-style isolation for a ritual of fourteen days. Any believer who is ultimately sacrificed to the Virus and dies, instantly becomes a martyr of the faith. If an unbeliever is killed by Virus, it is punishment for his sins against Science, and his lack of faith in it.

Of course the lord Virus can never be completely appeased, even with the required sacrifices. He is always mysterious and can never be completely understood, even by his creators in the lab. Our knowledge of this god will continue to evolve as their prophets and priests tap into the "new secret knowledge" of research to reveal "the sacred mysteries". Tomorrow's understanding will change based on "new revelations."

The Organization of the Corona Denomination

This new religious denomination has its own holy fathers, saints, and monks who are in fact the scientists and researchers who both created the god Virus in the lab and subsequently created the vaccine. They also bring us the holy and wise words of instruction on how to behave.

The three church Sees of this denomination are located at the World Health Organization, the National Institute of Health, and the Centers for Disease Control.

The Coronites have their evangelists which are the media and many of the health care workers. The Coronites' bishopric and priesthood include such figures as Dr. Anthony Fauci as their Pope, Bill Gates as one of theirs bishop, joined by many others. Followers are required to learn their teachings and follow their words closely.

The holy scriptures of the Corona Denomination are the words of Doctor Fauci himself, the ever-expanding CDC guidelines and all the government health mandates. Anyone who dares to question these scriptures is a heretic who is to be publicly shamed, have his or her life "canceled" by various illicit means, or violently attacked on the street by roving mobs of lawless Coronite enforcers, who are not necessarily part of the Corona faith per se, but are willing to execute enforcement for the denomination none the less. In all truth, the Church of Corona described here is actually a combination of gnostic, scientism, iconoclast, and barlaamite.[p] Its features are being embraced by many formerly Christian denominations across the globe in substitution for their prior faith in Christ.

---

[p] Barlaam overestimated the significance of philosophy for theology, asserting that only through philosophy could humanity arrive at perfection. He thus denied the renewing power of the Holy Spirit. As a humanist, Barlaam placed emphasis on created means of salvation (e.g., philosophy and knowledge).

10

Whose Christianity is it Anyway?

"I like your Christ, I do not like your Christians. Your Christians are so unlike your Christ."

Mahatma Gandhi

It has been said that Christian denominations are the greatest plan ever hatched by Satan to destroy the Christian church, and that could be so. It is estimated by some that there are now in the neighborhood of 43,000 different Protestant Christian denominations that are active today.[320] This seems to highlight the problematic nature of a world religion which is imagined to be simply based in generic love and "freedom." While that figure is disputed (some say 33,000) the point is this: whose Christianity should be put forward as our message to the rest of the world? Which Christianity was and should be the basis, the pattern and lifestyle for our virtue and unity in America? We can try to expound upon the question by examining, in part, how we arrived at this point.

While it appears odd to consider at first, there is a big difference between the Person/Deity of the Lord Jesus Christ our Savior and the modern "Christ" of today's popular "Christianity." While Christ has not changed and never will change, over the past 2,000 years the most well-known Christian churches have never been static since 1054. Throughout history it is shown that the purpose, perception, management, and understanding of church have often changed. Many of these changes were positive; others resulted in great tragedy and war. Nearly all the changes resulted in some permanent alteration to the course of Christendom.

There have been several noted attempts to unify Christians from the start. The first attempt was recorded in the New Testament, the Book of Acts chapter 15, where there needed to be clarity on issues of behavior and Faith by the believers. This was the first council, and it concluded with an instructive letter issued to the Gentile believers in Antioch, Syria and in Cilicia. But even these issues were not about Christians attempting to create their own separate church.

After Christianity was finally recognized and legalized, it was set on a course for expansion. By the 4th Century, there had grown to be differences among individuals concerning issues of orthodoxy, or the correct dogma and doctrine of the faith (defending against several early heresies) and basic Christology which causes divisions across the main churches. As a result, a long series of Church meetings (councils or synods) were called to discuss and resolve these issues. Most of the early councils seemed to be focused on defending the Church against the many errors of heretics who were attempting to pollute and distort Christianity. And so these early councils played a vital role in defense of the faith and strengthening the Church.

In total, they spent centuries confirming the First Century Traditions of the Church which everything from what you can do and eat during Lent to what was to be included in the Bible we have today—this was a good thing. And bear in mind that not every church today recognizes the validity of all these councils. The Orthodox Church recognizes only the first seven Ecumenical Councils, the Roman Catholics far more of them, and the Protestants, almost none of them.

In total there were 45 such meetings held over the course of nearly 1,900 years:

Council at Jerusalem 48-51 AD
Council at Carthage local Council, 251 AD
Council at Elvira local Council, 300-306 AD
Council at Ancyra local Council, 314 AD
Council at Neo-Caesaria local Council, c. 315 AD
First Council at Nicaea - First Ecumenical (Imperial) Council, 325 AD
Synod at Gangra local Council, 340 AD
Council at Sardica 347 AD
Council at Laodicaea local Council, 364 AD
First Ecumenical Council at Constantinople - Second Ecumenical (Imperial) Council, 381 AD
Council in Constantinople local Council, 394 AD
Council at Carthage local Council, 419-424 AD

Council at Ephesus - Third Ecumenical (Imperial) Council, 431 AD
Council at Constantinople local, 448 AD
Council at Ephesus Heretical (known historically as 'Robber Council' 449 AD
Council of Chalcedon - Fourth Ecumenical (Imperial) Council, 451 AD
Council of Orange local Council, never accepted in East, 529 AD
Second Ecumenical Council of Constantinople - Fifth Ecumenical (Imperial) Council, 553 AD
Council of Todelo (Spain) heretical, local Council, 589 AD
Council in Trullo (Constantinople) - Conclusion of Sixth Council, 692 AD
Council in Constantinople heretical Council, 754 AD
Second Ecumenical Council of Nicaea - Seventh Ecumenical (Imperial) Council, 787 AD
Council in Frankfurt heretical, local Council, 794 AD
Council in Aachen heretical, local Council, 809 AD
Council in Constantinople local Council, 861 AD
Council in Constantinople local Council, 867 AD
Council in Constantinople (considered a heretical Council by the Orthodox Church) 869-870 AD
Fourth Ecumenical Council in Constantinople, Eighth Ecumenical (Imperial) Council 879-880 AD
Council in Constantinople local Council, 1082 AD
Synod of Blachernae, in Constantinople local Synod, 1157 AD
Council in Constantinople local Council, 1166 AD
Second Council of Lyons Failed 'reunion Council', 1274 AD
Council at Constantinople local Council, 1285 AD
Council of Constance Roman Catholic Council, 1414-1418 AD
Council of Basel Roman Catholic Council, 1431 AD
Council of Ferrara Failed 'reunion Council', 1438 AD; moved to Florence, 1438 - 1443
Conclusion of Ferrara-Florence after Orthodox departure (1439)
Synod of Jerusalem Pan-Orthodox Council, 1583 AD
Council at Iasi (Romania) local Council, 1642 AD
Council of Jerusalem - Pan-Orthodox Council 1672 AD
Council at Constantinople local Council, 1755 AD
Council at Constantinople local Council, 1772 AD
Council at Constantinople local Council, 1819 AD
Council at Constantinople local Council, 1872 AD
Council at Constantinople Inter-Orthodox Congress, 1923 AD

And after all these Councils, all these meetings of the learned holy men, all the agreement and politicking, Christendom is still more divided today than ever on so many issues. Why? There are churches that have strived to hold Christendom together in the unity of the faith, which historically are the Orthodox and Roman Catholic Churches.

The Unholy Land

What was the practical outcome of all these church councils on the Christian faith? The early councils were often called to defend the church against some new introduction of heresy or a new doctrine that departed from the accepted tradition of the Church, which of course includes the Bible itself. The later councils became a strictly Roman Catholic concern after the Protestant Reformation began to take hold in the 1500's.

Then we have the entirety of Protestantism, which seems to divide itself into new and sects on a near-daily basis. Without the Tradition of the Church, rejecting the Councils and the resulting canon, rejecting the holy Sacramental nature of the Church what do they have left to call "Christian?" While it must certainly be impossible for men to always agree—it is never impossible for the God they serve to restore men in unity to His Truth. What we discover so often is that pride is the both the catalyst and barrier for division in modern Christianity. We'll discuss more about that later.

When we turn our attention to how these events relate to America more than two centuries after the Reformation, we discover that the divisions that had evolved in Christianity were of concern to our own Framers. Thomas Jefferson understood quite clearly what had happened across religions in general, and surely these events had ultimately played well into an unfortunate strategy of division:

"Difference of opinion is advantageous in religion. The several sects perform the office of a Censor morum over each other. Is uniformity attainable? Millions of innocent men, women, and children, since the introduction of Christianity, have been burnt, tortured, fined, imprisoned; yet we have not advanced one inch towards uniformity. What has been the effect of coercion? To make one half the world fools, and the other half hypocrites. To support roguery and error all over the earth. Let us reflect that it is inhabited by a thousand millions of people. That these profess probably a thousand different systems of religion. That ours is but one of that thousand. That if there be but one right, and ours that one, we should wish to see the 999 wandering sects gathered into the fold of truth. But against such a majority we cannot effect this by force. Reason and persuasion are the only practicable instruments. To make way for these, free enquiry must be indulged; and how can we wish others to indulge it while we refuse it ourselves.[321]"

Jefferson saw that using reason and enlightenment of truth was useful rather than resorting to force as the only option to convincing others of the error of their ways. And the way to arrive there was by "free enquiry" or in other words, an open mind. Unfortunately, due to their political polarization, maintaining an open mind on religious matters is not the strong suit of our present American Christian denominations, and herein lays the root of the problem. Once people determine that they "know what they know" they become affixed to whatever dogma they adhere to and are not open for discussing any information (history, doctrine, etc.) that might show them to have been misinformed, and ultimately wrong.

On this subject, John Adams observed:

"And, even since the Reformation, when or where has existed a Protestant or dissenting sect who would tolerate a free inquiry? The blackest billingsgate, the most ungentlemanly insolence, the most yahooish brutality is patiently endured, countenanced, propagated, and applauded. But touch a solemn truth in collision with a dogma of a sect, though capable of the clearest proof, and you will soon find you have disturbed a nest, and the hornets will swarm about your legs and hands, and fly into your face and eyes."[322]

Little or nothing has changed today. I understand this completely, and I learned this the hard way. My question remains, is there a Christian Church where this does not happen? There must be a genuine Church somewhere, or else Christ is a liar.

We still do have this question to deal with from the words of Chief Seattle in the earlier chapter of this text: is Christianity based on the god of the "red man" or the god of the "white man?" Is it the ancient Christianity Paul or of Constantine or of any one of the many patriarchs or successive pontiffs in Rome? Is it the Christianity of Pope Francis of the Roman Catholic Church today, or of the Ecumenical Patriarch of Constantinople Bartholomew of the Eastern Orthodox Church, the Rev. Billy Graham, Joel Osteen, Benny Hinn, Beth Moore, or any number of Christian Church ministers and pastors? It always must be Christ; but where is His Church?

Even Bertrand Russell, the 20th Century British philosopher knew what a person calling himself a Christian should look like:

"Perhaps it would be as well, first of all, to try to make out what one means by the word 'Christian'. It is used these days in a very loose sense by a great many people. Some people mean no more by it than a person who attempts to live a good life. In that sense I suppose there would be Christians in all sects and creeds; but I do not think that that is the proper sense of the word, if only because it would imply that all the people who are not Christians—all the Buddhists, Confucians, Mohammedans, and so on—are not trying to live a good life. I do not mean by a Christian any person who tries to live decently according to his lights. I think that you must have a certain amount of definite belief before you have a right to call yourself a Christian.
The word does not have quite such a full-blooded meaning now as it had in the times of St. Augustine and St. Thomas Aquinas. In those days, if a man said that he was a Christian it was known what he meant. You accepted a whole collection of creeds which were set out with great precision, and every single syllable of those creeds you believed with the whole strength of your convictions."[323]

We must continue to remind ourselves that while God is perfect, His people are irreparably flawed. Nothing we attempt will ever reach the measure of perfection required for absolutely sound religion or government—or quite frankly, anything else. Perfection only comes from God. The best that Americans can do is to make educated decisions about our governance to "form a more perfect union" that is both just and accountable. We have widely strayed from the mark, both in the past and we still do today.

The Denomination Complication

Once, long ago, when I changed jobs the company I was leaving requested an exit interview with me. I obliged and the company president handled it himself. I was in his office for nearly two hours answering questions that were nearly as intensive as the ones I answered when I was first hired.

On his bookshelves in his office, the president of this company had all kinds of popular business management, self-help, and team improvement book titles—written by those whose main goal is to sell books to managers and those who want to be managers but can't make the cut. The interior of his office was crowned with rather large portraits of all his directors, strangely mounted way up high along the crown molding. They were all encircling his office and seemed to be looking down into the room, which was not only odd but downright creepy and unsettling.

Seeing my reaction to the portrait arrangement, the president explained his grand scheme in hiring these people. He said that none of them liked each other, which was by his express design. He said that "this one hates that one, that one wants to fight this other one, everyone is bickering all the time," or something similar to that as he pointed to the various portraits.

Then proudly he reclined and asked me, "Do you know why I hired folks that hate each other and argue all the time?"

"I can't imagine why," I answered. I thought perhaps the answer would be found in one of his many books on business management.

"It's because in management you have to have all kinds of different ideas and views so that you don't end up with blinders on," he remarked. I was unimpressed. "You seem to want to disagree?"

"Yeah, actually I do."

"And why is that? What would you do any different?" he asked me in a decidedly condescending tone.

I explained, "I certainly would not hire folks so different that all they can do is fight against each other. Normally you want a team at that level that can work together on most things. You might designate one of them as a 'Devils' Advocate'—a known curmudgeon among the team who will throw rocks at every idea. He is never fired but is useful in taking the opposing view to show any problems with a plan or idea. Instead, what *you* have created is an entire team of completely dysfunctional 'Devil's Advocates' and that's all."

"But they all bring their different ideas to the table..." he interrupted me.

"Yes, they do, but the problem you have now is that they can't move forward in any one direction together," I concluded. I was referring to the fact that his team, although "diverse," lacked a key ingredient—unity. Each one had his own view and individual purpose to the degree that none could operate together or were willing to help each other towards a common goal.

The company president did not like hearing this from a peon like me, and he never admitted if he thought I was right. I must have struck a chord though; he was the third president I had worked for in that company in my six years there, and he was fired not to too long after our meeting.

Similar to the directors under the President of my former employer, the many Christian churches and denominations are often so different that they work against the unity of the Church as a whole and thus have become ineffective in the very cause of Christianity. St. Constantine himself identified this issue relatively early on—centuries before the Protestant Reformation, and made the first attempt to unify the message and direction of the Church. This was a monumental task to take at that time and one that could not be duplicated today. I am referring to the First Council at Nicaea. Fortunately, Christ issues one main directive for His people: Love one another. This is a simple enough request that all denominations ought to be able to agree upon if they call themselves Christian.

With all the many changes and evolutions of Christian dogmas of the many different denominations one must wonder, can they ever be unified? Perhaps Mark Twain was not far from the truth when he noted,

"'Man is the Reasoning Animal.' Such is the claim. I think it is open to dispute. Indeed, my experiments have proven to me that he is the Unreasoning Animal... In truth, man is incurably foolish. Simple things which other animals easily learn, he is incapable of learning. Among my experiments was this. In an hour I taught a cat and a dog to be friends. I put them in a cage. In another hour I taught them to be friends with a rabbit. In the course of two days I was able to add a fox, a goose, a squirrel and some doves. Finally a monkey. They lived together in peace; even affectionately. Next, in another cage I confined an Irish Catholic from Tipperary, and as soon as he seemed tame I added a Scotch Presbyterian from Aberdeen. Next a Turk from Constantinople; a Greek Christian from Crete; an Armenian; a Methodist from the wilds of Arkansas; a Buddhist from China; a Brahman from Benares. Finally, a Salvation Army Colonel from Wapping. Then I stayed away for two whole days. When I came back to note results, the cage of Higher Animals was all right, but in the other there was but a chaos of gory odds and ends of turbans and fezzes and plaids and bones and flesh--not a specimen left alive. These Reasoning Animals had disagreed on a theological detail and carried the matter to a Higher Court.[324]"

Protestant denominations seem to maintain a separate and often "polite" distance apart from one another. Denominations cannot even agree on the issue of barbaric infanticide—a basic issue of the sanctity of human life. Abortion in America is only one of any number of issues that Christians ought to be fighting to resolve firmly and *together*. Instead, the doctrinal fragmentation and infiltration of Christianity, by what amounts to be political operatives are now at work to support abortion and destroy traditional conservative churches and any hope of unity. Many denominations have adopted firm positions on divisive, modern, political issues which only prevent the Christian churches from moving forward together, and continues to force splits among them. These denominations seem far more interested and invested in carrying out the mission of their particular politics than that of Christ.

Thomas Jefferson summed up the general situation with Protestant Christianity rather succinctly in 1816 when he observed: "When we see religion split into so many thousand of sects, and I may say Christianity itself divided into its thousands also, who are disputing, anathematizing and where the laws permit burning and torturing one another for abstractions which no one of them understand, and which are indeed beyond the comprehension of the human mind, into which of the chambers of this Bedlam would a man wish to thrust himself.[325]"

Even while Thomas Jefferson appreciated the principles taught by Jesus Christ, we could not think him a Christian in a traditional sense. In 1823, he denounced and mocked the faith as a "fable":

"...I can never join Calvin in addressing his god. he was indeed an Atheist, which I can never be; or rather his religion was Dæmonism. if ever man worshipped a false god, he did. the being described in his 5. points is not the God whom you and I acknolege and adore, the Creator and benevolent governor of the world; but a dæmon of malignant spirit. it would be more pardonable to believe in no god at all, than to blaspheme him by the atrocious attributes of Calvin. indeed I think that every Christian sect gives a great handle to Atheism by their general dogma that, without a revelation, there would not be sufficient proof of the being of a god...And the day will come when the mystical generation of Jesus, by the supreme being as his father in the womb of a virgin will be classed with the fable of the generation of Minerva in the brain of Jupiter. But we may hope that the dawn of reason and freedom of thought in these United States will do away all this artificial scaffolding..."[326]

And John Adams had similar lines of thought:

"I almost shudder at the thought of alluding to the most fatal example of the abuses of grief which the history of mankind has preserved - the Cross. Consider what calamities that engine of grief has produced! With the rational respect that is due to it, knavish priests have added prostitutions of it, that fill or might fill the blackest and bloodiest pages of human history."[327]

"But how has it happened that millions of fables, tales, legends have been blended with both Jewish and Christian revelation that have made them the most bloody religion that ever existed?[328]"

We are fortunate that today Christians are no longer "burning and torturing one another" over anything. We are, however, still attempting to deal with our own interpretations about matters of the faith which we do not understand or cannot comprehend—and we remain so much divided over these and socio-political issues. There is never a shortage of heated debate and finger-pointing. Why?

One of my closest friends is a Christian who believes that Noah had dinosaurs on the Ark. He can effectively and persuasively debate the issue. At first I disagreed with him, because I was never taught that. Now I'm not so sure. But here is the realization that is to me the most important; it does not matter today whether Noah had dinosaurs on the Ark. It really doesn't. Whether there were or were not dinosaurs on Noah's Ark does not change, alter, add to, or subtract from the totality of the Word of God. Pressing the difference of opinion on the matter is nonproductive and could be divisive. I guess I file the matter under, "Who Cares?"

There are indeed matters of faith that are essential and important—this one is simply not. I would prefer to try to maintain a relationship with my friend rather than extending a divisive and useless debate on a subject that neither of us can resolve anyway. Denominations have a tendency to fiercely separate themselves over just such petty things, and if they are ever to be able to move the message and mission of Christ forward in a meaningful way, these differences must be set aside. There are indeed "the great Mysteries" of the Faith that we simply cannot understand.

Sola Scriptura

The Bible has been retranslated many times by both the holy and unholy, but when the meaning of it is continually changed in that course it ceases to be the standard of Christianity and instead some other document of historical curiosity. Even if the latest version is found to be suitable, the interpretations of the Bible's meaning and purpose by individuals is always suspect. As if we needed one, I had a personal example of what can happen when Reverend Kyle misconstrued the scripture for his own gratification.

In the decades that followed my thoughts would occasionally return to these episodes with Kyle, remembering the beating I took, the constant harassment, the look on his face when I hadn't fixed the roof, working as a dishwasher and eating garbage in Aspen, Colorado—not knowing if I could ever find my way home again.
What was really going on here? It was this unbiblical concept of Sola Scriptura that allowed a well-meaning Evangelical Reverend named Kyle to interpret the Bible in his own personal way, and acted upon it in good conscience with impunity, even though the law would define his actions as assault and battery of a minor. This is one of the many problems with Luther's Sola Scriptura.

It would appear that the source of most of this modern denominational dysfunction is actually the one thing that set it on its original course, the same *Sola Scriptura*. This new idea was introduced by Martin Luther, to pose the notion that the Bible alone is the source for Christianity, not the Pope in Rome. Here it is important to separate the newly proposed theology from the purpose of the Reformers.

Based on Reformed Protestant Theology, there are actually five solas:
- Sola scriptura, "by Scripture alone"
- Sola fide "by faith alone"
- Sola gratia "by grace alone"
- Solus Christus or Solo Christo "Christ alone" or "through Christ alone"

It seems obvious that when one says, "alone" it means *nothing else with it*. This means that in any intellectually honest discussion, there can really only be *one* of these "solas" as five would be a conflict of no longer being "alone." But for the sake of argument, let's not cloud the modern protestant mind with any such intellectual inconveniences. They have accepted five of them. Where did these come from?

What were the ninety-five things that Luther was addressing in 1517 and why were they important to him? It appears that when we view this document in its historical context of the day, we may come away with a different understanding of why Luther was challenging the Roman Catholic Church. Luther was not attempting to destroy the Roman Catholic Church.

In a world of both small and large kingdoms, headed by varying degrees of good and bad monarchs, the Roman Catholic Church had set itself above them all, as "kingmaker." Kings and kingdoms come and go, but the Church would always succeed any kingdom, as it sees itself as the representing the Kingdom of God on Earth. The Vatican saw itself as the ultimate authority when working with Monarchies and working against them when it suited. The Roman Catholic Church was as much a civic and political authority as it was a religious one. To affect and maintain all of this activity, the Vatican required a large and steady stream of income.

Martin Luther was unhappy with the vast amounts of money being used to build up the Vatican and wrote:

"Why does not the Pope build St. Peter's Minster with his own money since his riches are now more ample than those of Crassus, rather than with the money of poor Christians?"

In addition to the regular tithing and offerings extracted from the people to support the Vatican, As if every day medieval life was not suffering enough just to live and get by, the Vatican invented a senseless structure of "indulgences" –a sliding scale of fees one could pay while alive to be absolved of sin, present and future, so as to escape the other Roman Catholic invention, purgatory. All of this was for the purpose of filling the treasury of the Vatican at the expense of the faithful. Luther would have none of it.

Luther's solution was the introduction of his "Five Solas," which essentially stripped the Church of its abusive authority. These also opened the door for competing theologies resulting in the disarray we see today among the many sects of Protestants. When Luther translated the Bible into German he added text into the Word of God in an effort to conform it to his new Protestant principle, Sola Fide. Luther added the word "alone" to his Bible in Romans 3:28, so it read, "...faith *alone*...". When this practice was discovered, he arrogantly defended his actions with a "why not?" attitude.[329] In a letter dated September 15th, 1530 from Martin Luther, he lays out in plain and even offensive language the motivations of his efforts to support Sola Scriptura with not a little braggadocio:

"Returning to the issue at hand, if your Papist wishes to make a great fuss about the word "alone" (sola), say this to him: 'Dr. Martin Luther will have it so and he says that a papist and an ass are the same thing.' Sic volo, sic iubeo, sit pro ratione voluntas. (I will it, I command it; my will is reason enough) For we are not going to become students and followers of the papists. Rather we will become their judge and master. We, too, are going to be proud and brag with these blockheads; and just as St. Paul brags against his madly raving saints, I will brag over these asses of mine! They are doctors? Me too. They are scholars? I am as well. They are philosophers? And I. They are dialecticians? I am too. They are lecturers? So am I. They write books? So do I.

"I will go even further with my bragging: I can exegete the psalms and the prophets, and they cannot. I can translate, and they cannot. I can read Holy Scriptures, and they cannot. I can pray, they cannot. Coming down to their level, I can do their dialectics and philosophy better than all of them put together. Plus I know that not one of them understands Aristotle. If, in fact, any one of them can correctly understand one part or chapter of Aristotle, I will eat my hat! No, I am not overdoing it for I have been educated in and have practiced their science since my childhood. I recognize how broad and deep it is. They, too, know that everything they can do, I can do. Yet they handle me like a stranger in their discipline, these incurable fellows, as if I had just arrived this morning and had never seen or heard what they know and teach. How they do so brilliantly parade around with their science, teaching me what I grew beyond twenty years ago! To all their shouting and screaming I join the harlot in singing: 'I have known for seven years that horseshoe nails are iron.'

"So this can be the answer to your first question. Please do not give these asses any other answer to their useless braying about that word "sola" than simply "Luther will have it so, and he says that he is a doctor above all the papal doctors." Let it remain at that. I will, from now on, hold them in contempt, and have already held them in contempt, as long as they are the kind of people that they are - asses, I should say. And there are brazen idiots among them who have never learned their own art of sophistry - like Dr. Schmidt and Snot-Nose, and such like them. They set themselves against me in this matter, which not only transcends sophistry, but as St. Paul writes, all the wisdom and understanding in the world as well. An ass truly does not have to sing much as he is already known for his ears."[330]

The Reformation was a much a needed rebellion against the authoritative corruption of the Vatican and its bureaucracy at the time—a discrediting of the unaccountable Pope and a series of longstanding abusive and corrupt church practices. With the invention of the five Solas, Sola Scriptura soon became the bedrock of nearly all Protestant theology that followed, undermining this authority of the visible Church rather than correcting its leadership, as that was neither practical nor possible. Sola Scriptura, however is rooted in the very first among all sins: Pride. How do we know this? Luther forcefully writes, "Sic volo, sic iubeo, sit pro ratione voluntas. (I will it, I command it; my will is reason enough) For we are not going to become students and followers of the papists. Rather we will become their judge and master"...that is what spiritual pride looks like. After this proclamation, pride is sanctioned and we can all become both critic and judge of the Church. Any hope of future unity was destroyed at that point.

What is the correct Purpose and Role of the Holy Scriptures?

At the heart of our difficulties lies our distinct difficulty in finding a common footing on the Holy Scriptures. What are they? What do they mean? What are they used for?

The oldest Christian traditions we have with us today are the Roman Catholic Church and the Eastern Orthodox Church. Prior to the Great Schism of 1054, these were both one Church. Surely we may learn something about the interpretation, purpose, and proper use of the Holy Scriptures from the men who originally canonized the Holy Bible.

For the Orthodox Christians, there are several components of hermeneutics (from Greek *hermeneutikos*) which is the interpretation of a text, particularly the text of Holy Scripture. In the Eastern Orthodox Christian Church, the practice of hermeneutics is according to basic principles, or presuppositions which are manifest in the life of the Church. This is a summary of those principles, expressed here in ten parts[331]:

Orthodox Hermeneutic Principles

1. God is real and is incarnated in our Lord Jesus Christ. Everything pertaining to the Scriptures must be understood Christologically. Jesus Christ, the incarnate Second Person of the Holy Trinity, is the center of all that we as Christians do, and being Himself the very Truth, He is the only gate through which we may enter into understanding of the Bible, both Old and New Testaments (though not all that is contained in the Old Testament is directly relevant for Christians). The Bible ultimately is about Christ and assists us in our union with Him.

2. Only the pure in heart "shall see God." That is, our spiritual state has a direct bearing on our interpretation of the Scriptures. As St. Athanasius said, "One cannot possibly understand the teaching of the saints unless one has a pure mind and is trying to imitate their life." Because the Scripture is a book inspired by the Holy Spirit and given through holy men, one's own holiness is directly relevant to the ability to interpret the book correctly. Unlike any other book, the Bible's words

are "spirit and life," and so we must live spiritually in order to drink from this spiritual well. Clearly, prayer and spiritual discipline are necessary in order to understand Scripture properly.

3. Understanding of the Scripture comes with living its contents. As the quote from St. Athanasius illustrates, one must both have a pure mind and be trying to imitate the saints' lives in order to understand their teaching, a dual principle which applies most of all to the teaching of the saints in the Bible. This life is particularly expressed in terms of living out the commandments and attempting to imitate Christ's life of the Gospel.

4. The primary end of Scriptural hermeneutics is that of the whole Christian life, theosis (deification/divinization). That is, our purpose in attempting to understand the Bible must not be merely for academic inquiry but rather must be in order to become fully divinized human beings, soaked with the life of God, participating in His divine energies, growing to the fullness of the stature of Christ. We interpret Scripture in order to become by grace what Christ is by nature, to "become god."

5. Only within the community of the Church can the Bible be understood. It was written by the Church, in the Church and for the Church. Thus, it is a "family document" which is the highest point of Holy Tradition, taken with faith alongside the writings of the Fathers, the Liturgy, the Icons, the Lives of the Saints, and so on.

6. The Scripture is a witness to the truth, not an exhaustive tome on Christian living. Nowhere in the words of Scripture itself can we find the teaching that it is all-sufficient for Christian life. What we as Orthodox Christians do must always be consonant with the Scriptures, but explicit mention of a practice or teaching in the Scripture is not a requirement for its inclusion in the life of the Church. The Apostle Paul himself mentions the reality of unwritten sources of Church Tradition being equally in force for the believer in II Thessalonians 2:15, that these traditions to which we must "stand fast and hold" may be "by word or by our epistle." Examples of practices not explicit in Scripture are making the Sign of the Cross, triple immersion for baptism, and having monasticism. St. Basil the Great even says that without maintaining the unwritten traditions of the Church, we "mutilate the Gospel."

7. We must respect the integrity of the canon of the Bible as given to us in the Church's Tradition. Searches for other texts written by apostles or prophets may be interesting and of scholarly merit, but they are not part of the hermeneutical project within the Church. Or conversely, attempts to debunk the authorship or authenticity of the books in the canon are also outside the Church's life. If we were to find a verifiable "new" work by St. Paul or to discover that Moses did not in fact write Genesis, neither finding would have any bearing on the canon. It is what it is.

8. We must use every resource at our disposal in interpreting the Scripture to bring ourselves and others to the knowledge of the truth. Certainly, there must be spiritual discernment in knowing how to use those resources, but at least theoretically, anything can be used to come to know the truth better as it is revealed in Holy Writ.

9. We must have humility when approaching Scripture. Even some of the Church's greatest and most philosophically sophisticated saints stated that some passages were difficult for them. We must therefore be prepared to admit that our interpretations may be wrong, submitting them to the judgment of the Church.

10. We may make use in a secondary fashion of the resources of academic scholarship, whether logic, archaeology, linguistics, et cetera. These resources can be helpful in terms of illuminating our understanding of Scripture, but they must always be given only secondary prominence in the project and always only in conjunction with all these other hermeneutic principles. Primary must always be our life in the Church, living, studying and knowing the Bible within that vivified and salvific Holy Tradition.

For the Roman Catholic Church, Holy Scripture is described this way[332]:

SCRIPTURE AND THE CHURCH
Since Scripture is the written word of God; its contents are Divinely guaranteed truths, revealed either in the strict or the wider sense of the word. Again, since the inspiration of a writing cannot be known without Divine testimony, God must have revealed which are the books that constitute Sacred Scripture. Moreover, theologians teach that

Christian Revelation was complete in the Apostles, and that its deposit was entrusted to the Apostles to guard and to promulgate. Hence the apostolic deposit of Revelation contained not merely Sacred Scripture in the abstract, but also the knowledge as to its constituent books. Scripture, then, is an Apostolic deposit entrusted to the Church, and to the Church belongs its lawful administration. This position of Sacred Scripture in the Church implies the following consequences:

(1) The Apostles promulgated both the Old and New Testament as a document received from God. It is antecedently probable that God should not cast his written Word upon men as a mere windfall, coming from no known authority, but that he should entrust its publication to the care of those whom he was sending to preach the Gospel to all nations, and with whom he had promised to be for all days, even to the consummation of the world...

(2) The transmission of the inspired writings consists in the delivery of Scripture by the Apostles to their successors with the right, the duty, and the power to continue its promulgation, to preserve its integrity and identity, to explain its meaning, to use it in proving and illustrating Catholic teaching, to oppose and condemn any attack upon its doctrine, or any abuse of its meaning...It seems plain that, if Scripture cannot be regarded as a private historical document on account of the official mission of the Apostles, on account of the official succession in the Apostolate of their successors, on account of the assistance of the Holy Ghost promised to the Apostles and their successors, the promulgation of Scripture, the preservation of its integrity and identity, and the explanation of its meaning must belong to the Apostles and their legitimate successors...

(3) By virtue of its official and permanent promulgation, Scripture is a public document, the Divine authority of which is evident to all the members of the Church.

(4) The Church necessarily possesses a text of Scripture, which is internally authentic, or substantially identical with the original. Any form or version of the text, the internal authenticity of which the Church has approved either by its universal and constant use, or by a formal declaration, enjoys the character of external or public

authenticity, i.e., its conformity with the original must not merely be presumed juridically, but must be admitted as certain on account of the infallibility of the Church.

(5) The authentic text, legitimately promulgated, is a source and rule of faith, though it remains only a means or instrument in the hands of the teaching body of the Church, which alone has the right of authoritatively interpreting Scripture.

(6) The administration and custody of Scripture is not entrusted directly to the whole Church, but to its teaching body, though Scripture itself is the common property of the members of the whole Church. While the private handling of Scripture is opposed to the fact that it is common property, its administrators are bound to communicate its contents to all the members of the Church.

(7) Though Scripture is the property of the Church alone, those outside her pale may use it as a means of discovering or entering the Church. But Tertullian shows that they have no right to apply Scripture to their own purposes or to turn it against the Church...

(8) The rights of the teaching body of the Church include also that of issuing and enforcing decrees for promoting the right use, or preventing the abuse of Scripture. Not to mention the definition of the Canon, the Council of Trent issued two decrees concerning the Vulgate and a decree concerning the interpretation of Scripture and this last enactment was repeated in a more stringent form by the Vatican Council. The various decisions of the Biblical Commission derive their binding force from this same right of the teaching body of the Church.

We can see from this that there was, and still is a long tradition in both the Eastern Orthodox and the Roman Catholic Churches regarding how the Holy Scriptures are understood and applied. Many, and probably most, Protestant traditions point to the Bible as their only authority in Christianity, or at least their current individual interpretation of it. Unfortunately for them, the principle of Sola Scriptura itself—the theology behind their entire movement, is to be found nowhere in the Bible.[333] The Bible itself does not state "use your own interpretation of the Scriptures alone as the sole authority of your church." The real problem is that Sola Scriptura as promoted by modern Protestantism allows every individual to interpret the meaning scripture for themselves, and then claim that that meaning is the only right one.

What's wrong with that, you say? It's because Sola Scriptura encourages individuals to errantly turn Holy Scripture into whatever they like for it to be, for whatever purposes suit their own objectives and motivations at the time. In contrast, the "other" Catholic Church, the Eastern Orthodox Church has maintained their traditional outlook at the risk of appearing less than well-organized:

"The theology of the Christian West, for both Roman Catholics and Protestants, has a natural tendency to become a system. Definitions are valued and, in the long term, theology tends to become a matter for scholars. On the other hand, the theology of the Christian East sometimes lacks a system, and often lacks clear definition. Theology is preeminently the Church's experience of God, something to be entered into by saints rather than understood by the intelligent....The entire basis of the Western experience, summed up definitively by Descartes as "Cogito ergo sum," ("I think therefore, I am") is, in Orthodox terms, the greatest of deceits. Far from being true, it is actually an expression that perpetuates the very factor that causes the ongoing fragmentation of the human person."[334]

Even the methods by which the Bible is evaluated by Protestants changed as a result of Luther's Sola Scriptura:

"[The] so-called "scientific" biblical criticism is a product of the Protestant world. Such is the irony of fate--that the same religious movement in Christianity which rejected the living voice of the Church...specifically took upon themselves the task of dismantling their own foundations. Feeling for the sanctity of scriptures grew cold among these theologians...Hypothesis followed hypothesis. For the work to be accepted it was necessary to employ "scientific methods of research"...Willingly or unwillingly, for Protestant theology...this meant accepting the methodological principles common to all other sciences."[335]

This scientific approach was and is still accepted as good, but in reality and by definition must reject and discard the supernatural and spiritual elements contained in the Bible in favor of the principles of positivism.[336] These principles negate the intervention of God by His grace and through His sovereignty which is evident throughout all creation, thus undermining the entire biblical narrative. Additionally, it opens the gateway to a host of biblical misunderstandings and bizarre interpretations.

Part of what is at issue here is the inherent conflict between the traditional approach to the scripture and Message of Christ and the traditional American culture of "rugged individualism" which has morphed into self-centered consumerism. While Christ says, "Follow Me," the independent spirit of the American culture makes people think, "I'm free to believe what want and I'm in control of managing my own actions, decisions, and destiny." The applications of these two things are diametrically opposed to one another and cannot coexist in the framework of Christianity unless the individuals commit to use their freedom to follow Christ.

"For you, brethren, have been called unto liberty: only make not liberty an occasion to the flesh, but by charity of the spirit serve one another."

Galatians 5:13

Douay-Rheims Bible

His Eminence, the Most Reverend Metropolitan Kallistos of Diokleia (also known by his lay name, Timothy Ware) is an Eastern Orthodox author who can explain this conundrum more effectively than I can:

"As a Trinity of love, God desired to share his life with created persons in his image, who would be capable of responding to him freely and willingly in a relationship of love. *Where there is no freedom, there can be no love.* Compulsion excludes love...God can do everything except compel us to love him. God, therefore—desiring to share his love—created, not robots who would obey him mechanically, but angels and humans beings endowed with free choice. And thereby...God took a risk: for with this gift of freedom there was given also the possibility of sin...Without freedom there would be no sin. But without freedom man would not be in God's image; without freedom man would not be capable of entering into communion with God in a relationship of love."[337]

Instead of using our freedom in choosing to follow Christ, what has happened is that modern American Christians often do whatever they please in life and merely try to bring Jesus Christ along for the ride—to lead Christ rather than being led by Christ as a result of conforming the meaning of scripture, message, and even prayer—to fit their own plans, motivations, lifestyle, and preferences. They operate their churches in the same manner they operate the civic structures of their counties, towns, and cities—entirely forgetting that the difference is that the Church is holy and the latter are not.[338]

Sola Scriptura and all that it brings with it, instead promises a deceptive kind of Christian freedom apart from any genuine cohesiveness, organization, leadership, or authority of the Christian Church; a liberty which is founded upon the first sin...pride. The Christian individual is quickly deceived into forming Christianity into their own errant state of pseudo-Christianity, and due to the pride that takes hold of them, they celebrate this arrogant individualism. They soon develop personal statements such as,

"I know what's right, the Bible says so."

"I read about _____ in the Bible, and I know the truth."

"I know that Paul meant _____ when that was written..."

"The Bible doesn't say anything about _____ so that can't be true."

The inherent danger in Sola Scriptura lies in its now disastrous results for the Christian Faith; once an individual or a new group imagines that it has the Biblical backing for whatever belief they maintain, all manner of abuses can and will occur— all "justified" by God and the Bible in their minds.

As a result, the scope of common ground among Christian Churches and Christians in general is narrowing all the time. Even as modern Christianity has been fracturing and splitting apart over the centuries in dramatic fashion and efforts have been continually made to try to hold it all together. Philip Schaff (1819-1893) was a Swiss-born, German-educated Protestant theologian and ecclesiastical historian who contributed greatly to the documentation of the history of Christianity. In his exhaustive three volume work, "The Creeds of Christendom" (1877) Schaff lists and explains at least 203 different Christian creeds, catechisms, confessions, declarations, statements and dogmas of the various Christian churches from the time of Christ to his day.[339]

That's how we end up with a Christianity fragmented today, now "mushrooming" into over 43,000 opposing denominations (apparently since 1877) that are rapidly unraveling into even more diluted sects. Sola Scriptura, which is now Solo Scriptura is both the genesis for and the detriment of Protestantism.[340] The Bible does not contain 43,000 different and often conflicting versions of itself and there is exactly one Christ (who formed One Church) who is not divided against Himself.

The rather unfortunate reality is that in spite of all efforts to unify, Americans are not getting closer together in unity as Christians, but rather we are falling further apart, separated by the interjection of personal beliefs and attitudes about the Faith. One Faith now hopelessly divided in tens of thousands of opposing ways.

If the Protestant churches have any aspirations of unifying, there will have to be a reckoning of Sola Scriptura, as well as the rest of Luther's "solae," and that might well prove to be totally impossible. Like the Reverend Kyle, too many American Protestants today "know what they know" and are largely unwilling to explore and accept any truth that conflicts with their understood and long accepted dogmas. They enjoy this comfort at the detriment of Christendom through continued disunity and completely misguided doctrines.

In his book, *That They May Be One*, author Mark Bradshaw points out that while Sola Scriptura is the bedrock of Protestantism, many Protestants today operate as though Sola Scriptura also means "Solo Scriptura," or only scripture. Bradshaw explains that not only is the concept of Sola/Solo Scriptura not found in the writings of the early church fathers, they instead consistently refer to scripture *and tradition* as tenets of Christianity. It is this "Tradition" portion that Protestants seem to completely discard out of hand, even though Orthodox Tradition absolutely includes the Bible,[341] as does the Tradition of the Roman Catholic Church.

Metropolitan Hilarion Alfeyev writes,

"...worship that has lost its original theological content ceases to be a criterion of truth for the faithful. Such worship ceases to be a school of theology and contemplation of God."

This frightful path presented by Sola Scriptura leads to a Christ who becomes whatever people want Him to be on any given day, for any reason whatsoever. Christ is no longer the Deity but more of an ornament, or an object, a "concept" for people to manipulate and manage. In fact, a 2018 survey of American Christians now reveals that 20% of respondents actually ***disagreed*** with the statement, "God is a perfect being and cannot make a mistake."[342]

"We have entirely forgotten that we are the servants of God; we think that we belong to ourselves, and order our lives not in accordance with God's commandments, but in accordance with our own will; we live as we like. And it is owing to this that our life is full of numberless sins."

Righteous JohnWonderworker of Kronstadt   My Life in Christ p.516

Many American churches follow down this path in order to advance their own agenda and little else. It is no wonder, then, that here in the Information Age that Christians around the world are discovering on their own—able to learn and discern just how wrong and distorted the picture of faith presented to them truly is.

It would seem that pastors are partly to blame. Well maybe, but why? It is because whether they know it or not, (and I suspect that they all do) they developed and are now are trapped into a "corporate" church system that is competitive in nature, rather than focusing only on the matters of the faith. This means that the hapless pastor is stuck in this terrible position of choosing to both preach and teach lessons that will attract and retain members in order to provide the funding that the church needs to survive, or instead adhering to a genuine Christian message that may be unpopular and which would threaten the comfort of the membership and risk either getting fired by the laity or losing members to other churches. The members are, of course, able to leave and go to the next church down the street.

Protestant churches are to blame for deliberately forming foundations around these behaviors and beliefs in the misguided attempt to "draw people to Christ" when what they are really attempting is drawing a fictional Christ into conformity to the lives of men. They are guilty of introducing and projecting "new" tenants of Christianity that simply do not exist, while at the same time committing sins of omission (perhaps out of their own ignorance about Christianity) by keeping salient—I will argue critical—knowledge about the history of the Faith away from the believers. Believers who are ignorant of the history of their own Faith prior to Luther are apt to follow anyone claiming to be a Christian. (Go and survey the Protestant landscape today in America for yourself and tell me that I am wrong.)

Consider a modern comparison here: in my state of residence, North Carolina, the state's Department of Motor Vehicles produces a handbook containing all the laws, rules, regulations, and guidelines for operation of a motor vehicle in the state. They have created this book to be the standard that all drivers must adhere to. When you reach the age to drive you are tested on the contents by a trained examiner to make sure that you understand the material and are competent to drive. There are three such tests a prospective driver must pass: the visual test to be sure you can both see and visually identify road markings, the written exam to test whether a person understands the rules of driving, and the road exam, which tests whether a person can manage the equipment—his car.

If we applied Martin Luther's principle of Sola Scriptura to the DMV handbook, then these standards would become meaningless. For if, as with Sola Scriptura, every individual driver was able to take the DMV book and interpret for himself the meaning and application of its contents, even edit parts they disagreed with, while adding other material here or there, then there is no standard at all.

I met a man from India once and he asked me why everyone in North Carolina stops at red lights. I told him, it's because it is the law here, and if you don't stop someone will probably hit your car. He remarked, "Well that is just a custom of your country, but in India we do not have many stops like this." I corrected him, "No it's not a societal *custom* here; it's the law." His sentiment might reflect why developing nations have the highest motor vehicle related death rates in the world, as "many perceive traffic laws more as nuisances than as hard-set rules to live and drive by.[343]"

This is the same way that many churches seem to approach their Christianity. One church observes this or that thing in the Bible, while a different denomination disagrees with that and does it the way they see fit. They organize and govern themselves with a dizzying array of internal political structures. One church is governed by a deacon board, another by a church council, yet another is centralized and instructed by a remote synod. There is no standardization because there cannot be any in Protestantism. This is the Americanization of what is supposed to be the one Holy church. One Christ, one Bible, but 43,000 organizations that can hardly agree on anything and all are convinced that they are correct. It's stunning to consider, really, and few seem to be asking why or how it got this way.

These churches compete among the American public for membership as if their brand of Christianity were somehow reduced to a commodity for sale. Unfortunately, this means modifying the meaning of the Bible to meet these requirements. If the Bible is to be the standard of the faith, then how can its meaning be altered to accommodate individual standards? When that happens as it has, how can we look upon this landscape and say that it is Christian?

11

Separating Church and State

"Leave the Church to its pastors and masters; attend to your own province, the State and the army. If you refuse to do this, and are bent on destroying our faith, know that though an angel came from heaven itself to pervert us we would not obey him. Far less would we obey you."

Abbott Theodore of the Studuim
to the Byzantine Emperor Leo V, 815

One of the many sources of modern church decline in America is a silent killer of churches: the government. The earliest example of this "separation of Church and State" notion did not originate with our American Founders. In fact, we have to go all the way back to A.D. 815 to Constantinople and our cultural ancestors, the Byzantines, and even then the issue probably predates that year.

John Julius Norwich in his magnificent book series on Byzantium does a masterful job of illustration of the history and workings of the Byzantine Empire. From this, the reader can understand why and how an empirical Theocracy divorced itself from the notion of a government that was for centuries symbiotic with the Church. The three volume series is surely worthy of your time to read, but Norwich also condensed his work into a shorter single volume which is a good choice for those who may prefer it.

In Norwich's second installment, *Byzantium, the Apogee*, he details that the Church in the 9th Century was no longer satisfied to accept quasi-ecclesiastical edicts from a head of state, in this case, Leo V. Leo was less of a religious mind than his long train of predecessors but saw that certain doctrines could either calm the waters of the army and the people, or enflame their rage and cause havoc. The Church, for possibly the first time, formally stood before an emperor and stated in no uncertain terms that church matters are not the domain of an emperor. The message was delivered by Abbott Theodore of the Studuim, and appears, in part, at the head of Norwich's chapter on the subject, and above.

I found this issue a rather odd one for Byzantium to have to deal with. It was the same Church under Pope Pelagius who called upon Emperor Justinian's eunuch commander, Narses and his army to force obedience of the bishops in the 6th Century[344].

Was it not a Patriarch or Pope who across 500 years prior had invested the civil powers of Christ into each successive man titled Emperor? The same church that through ordination created an emperor that was "co-gerent" with Christ, endowed to rule the Earth while Christ ruled the heavens? Now, suddenly, the same churchmen wish to tell the emperor to essentially mind his own business? Apparently the lines separating the Byzantine *imperium* and the *sacerdotium* had become blurred.

In any case, Byzantine Emperors were not necessarily focused on carrying out the message of the Gospel of Christ through better government. Of course they could not—they were head of state as well as the then theoretical head of the church. You really can't do both. They claimed to be co-gerent with Christ which put them as leaders in the assumed role of the highest religious leader on Earth, and as such, the ruler over men. It was similar to the old Roman tradition.

This was the triumph of politics over the objectives of a Christ-based religion. It is folly to think that any man could operate a nation as head of state and also be "co-gerent" with Christ to form all national policies around the Gospel. Emperor Justinian generally did not, and neither did most of his predecessors or successors. That cannot happen and it did not happen for the Byzantines—it was never their civil objective. The state instead often used Christianity as a means to control the people, engage in diplomacy with both allies and adversaries, and often as a pretense to conquer its enemies.

While America has long been considered the modern "Christian nation," the American Founders never invested any branch of our own government, including the Executive Branch—the American Presidency, with spiritual powers congruent with or over the church and people. That is true. This separation of church and state owes thanks mostly to the earlier work of English Philosopher John Locke (1632-1704)[345] who paved the way for a system of modern government that was not locked into the machinations of theology. As a result, American government has a distinct and defined role that operates on the basis of the rule of law and the premise that there is equal protection for all citizens under that body of law. That is, that the laws apply to every citizen equally regardless of station in life or perceived favor or discord by agents of the state or Church, and that laws are not enacted to either reward or persecute one group or person.

As a safeguard against a particular theology being made a requirement for public service in America, Article VI, clause 3 of the Constitution clearly states,

"The Senators and Representatives before mentioned, and the Members of the several State Legislatures, and all executive and judicial Officers, both of the United States and of the several States, shall be bound by Oath or Affirmation, to support this Constitution; but no religious Test shall ever be required as a Qualification to any Office or public Trust under the United States."

This is known as the "no religious test" rule.

John Adams even observed that the free examination of the Bible should be excluded from the penalties of law:

"We think ourselves possessed, or at least we boast that we are so, of liberty of conscience on all subjects and of the right of free inquiry and private judgment in all cases, and yet how far are we from these exalted privileges in fact. There exists, I believe, throughout the whole Christian world, a law which makes it blasphemy to deny, or to doubt the divine inspiration of all the books of the Old and New Testaments, from Genesis to Revelations. In most countries of Europe it is punished by fire at the stake, or the rack, or the wheel. In England itself, it is punished by boring through the tongue with a red-hot poker. In America it is not much better; even in our Massachusetts, which, I believe, upon the whole, is as temperate and moderate in religious zeal as most of the States, a law was made in the latter end of the last century, repealing the cruel punishments of the former laws, but substituting fine and imprisonment upon all those blasphemies upon any book of the Old Testament or New. Now, what free inquiry, when a writer must surely encounter the risk of fine or imprisonment for adducing any arguments for investigation into the divine authority of those books? ...I think such laws a great embarrassment, great obstructions to the improvement of the human mind. Books that cannot bear examination, certainly ought not to be established as divine inspiration by penal laws... but as long as they continue in force as laws, the human mind must make an awkward and clumsy progress in its investigations. I wish they were repealed."346

In America, our presidents have claimed a variety of faiths; Deists, Roman Catholic, Episcopalian, Presbyterian, Baptist, Methodist, Unitarian, Disciples of Christ, Dutch Reformed, Quaker, Congregationalist, and United Church of Christ.[q] None of these men really inflicted the nation with radical and strict policies based on their personal faith. The Roman Catholic president, John F. Kennedy, for example, did not carry out the bidding of any Pope against the Protestant churches in the U.S. Five hundred years prior, an Emperor might have made it so, but not here in America today.

The United States, however, is not designed to operate in the same way that the Byzantines had with relation to its churches. For the Byzantines, their emperor was an autocrat who forcefully determined the rules with an appointed puppet senate approving and working out the details of whatever policy was demanded. This of course is an oversimplification of their process, but generally accurate for the short discussion of the point[r].

---

[q] Barack Hussein Obama claimed to be a practicing Christian and was a member of a UCC church until 2008, but the Muslim tradition would define him a Muslim by default as he is the son of a Muslim father.

[r] See History of the Byzantine State by George Ostrogorsky

While it is clear that America was in fact founded upon Judeo-Christian *principles*, we cannot imagine that the United States was based on Christian *practices*. There is a marked difference in these two things. Principles may govern and direct general policy, while practices would force the public into, say, mandatory church attendance, or baptism or some other specific religious activities or rites. American "rugged individualism" had many taking their faith into their own hands as opposed to transplanting European Anglican or Roman Catholic Churches in America. We also must remember that the context of the mindset of the day was a general rejection of England and European authoritarianism.

Benjamin Franklin, for example, composed his own private liturgy of praise, worship and prayers.[347] He included Milton's Hymn to the Creator. Absent from this liturgy is any reference to Jesus Christ or the Holy Spirit.

President Jefferson considered himself a Christian. He was first raised as an Anglican and then influenced by English Deists. Jefferson never seemed to have too much to say about his own deep personal thoughts on religion—so little, in fact, that by the late 1790's, during a particularly nasty political season, Jefferson was even accused of being an atheist. Jefferson, however, saw Christianity in a purer light than the brand of doctrine being advertised and implanted by the Church of England and other organized religions at the time.

Jefferson's Christianity was centered only on the principles and teachings of Christ alone and not His Deity or the piety of the church structured around it. In 1803, Jefferson wrote to Benjamin Rush declaring, "To the corruptions of Christianity I am indeed, opposed; but not to the genuine precepts of Jesus himself. I am a Christian, in the only sense in which he wished any one to be; sincerely attached to his doctrines, in preference to all others; ascribing to himself every human excellence; and believing he never claimed any other."

In 1813 Jefferson wrote to Richard Rush,

"...the subject of religion, a subject on which I have ever been most scrupulously reserved. I have considered it as a matter between every man and his maker, in which no other, & far less the public, had a right to intermeddle."

In 1816 Jefferson wrote to Charles Thomson in his own defense,

"I too have made a wee little book, from the same materials, which I call the Philosophy of Jesus. It is a paradigma of his doctrines, made by cutting the texts out of the book, and arranging them on the pages of a blank book, in a certain order of time or subject. A more beautiful or precious morsel of ethics I have never seen. It is a document in proofthat I am a real Christian, that is to say, a disciple of the doctrines of Jesus, very different from the Platonists, who call me infidel, and themselves Christians and preachers of the gospel, while they draw all their characteristic dogmas from what its Author never said nor saw..."

Jefferson concerned himself with the only the direct teachings of Christ, editing out much of the rest of the New Testament story creating what we know today as "the Jefferson Bible."

By 1819, it was clear that although Jefferson indeed attended church services, he was not a subscriber to denominational organized religion. In a letter that year he wrote, "I am of a sect by myself, as far as I know."

The issue of separation of church and state in America is truly one that boils down to the principles vs. practices notion. Otherwise we would descend into managing our culture and government with events akin to the Salem Witch Trials of 1692.

John Adams makes this clear, stating. "The government of the United States is not, in any sense, founded on the Christian religion.[348]" The godless liberals of today repeat this quote over and over in their endless pursuit to destroying the traditionally conservative culture, undermining key values, and institutions of America. They seem to have forgotten another comment by Adams stating, "Our Constitution was made only for a moral and religious people." It is wholly inadequate to the government of any other.[349]"

Unfortunately this is an important subtlety lost on most young Americans today who are never taught to take the time to learn the difference. All they hear from the media is either a mantra of "we have to keep the religious right from taking over government" or from the opposite camp, "we have to keep the liberals from eliminating God" as if either event could ever entirely occur. This same chorus is repeated over and over to keep Americans divided and make and keep Christians and non-Christians distrustful of each other.

Thomas Jefferson wrote,

"...legitimate powers of government reach actions only, & not opinions, I contemplate with sovereign reverence that act of the whole American people which declared that their legislature should 'make no law respecting an establishment of religion, or prohibiting the free exercise thereof,' thus building a wall of separation between Church & State. Adhering to this expression of the supreme will of the nation in behalf of the rights of conscience, I shall see with sincere satisfaction the progress of those sentiments which tend to restore to man all his natural rights, convinced he has no natural right in opposition to his social duties.[350]"

...and James Madison explained,

"The purpose of separation of church and state is to keep forever from these shores the ceaseless strife that has soaked the soil of Europe in blood for centuries.[351]"

He was referring to the bloodshed in Europe brought by Roman Catholics, Church of England, etc. God is not, however, absent at all from the American fabric. Liberals indeed desire to remove the Christian God from our national fabric, attempting to rewrite history while asserting that God was not part of the conversation at our Founding and should be eliminated from our country and our leadership[352]. While this myth has been completely dispelled, it is still packed, sold, and adhered to by rabid Liberals today. It has been determined that 34% of all quotes of our Founders are directly traceable to the Holy Bible and an overwhelming 94% of direct and indirect quotes and references by our Founders come from the Bible.[353]

Thomas Jefferson, for example, was rather clear about the source of liberty and inherent freedom of religion;

"The God who gave us life, gave us liberty at the same time."[354]

"Under the law of nature, all men are born free, every one comes into the world with a right to his own person, which includes the liberty of moving and using it at his own will. This is what is called personal liberty, and is given him by the author of nature, because necessary [*sic*] for his own sustenance."[355]

The Unholy Land

It is, however, interesting to observe that for all this effort and angst, the matter never seems to be settled. There is always some person or group pushing for either more or less religious involvement in government institutions and for either more or less government involvement in religious institutions. But rather than revisit all the various factions and their arguments of the past century, perhaps it would be a more productive exercise to understand a simpler policy on the matter presented to America by our third President, Thomas Jefferson.

Jefferson's public policies regarding religion and state were as clear and consistent as were his other policy positions. He was a perpetual champion for individual liberties and the concept that the rights of one individual extended only to the point where the rights of another's began. He writes,

"But our rulers can have authority over such natural rights only as we have submitted to them. The rights of conscience we never submitted, we could not submit. We are answerable for them to our God. The legitimate powers of government extend to such acts only as are injurious to others. But it does me no injury for my neighbour to say there are twenty gods, or no god. It neither picks my pocket nor breaks my leg."[356]

In 1802 Jefferson wrote to the Baptist Association of Danbury, Connecticut stating,

"Believing with you that religion is a matter which lies solely between Man & his God, that he owes account to none other for his faith or his worship, that the legitimate powers of government reach actions only, & not opinions, I contemplate with sovereign reverence that act of the whole American people which declared that their legislature should 'make no law respecting an establishment of religion, or prohibiting the free exercise thereof,' thus building a wall of separation between Church & State."

In Jefferson's day the Church of England had continued to apply its authoritative hand in the Commonwealth of Virginia. From 1776 to 1779, Jefferson served as a member of the Virginia House of Delegates where in 1777 he drafted the *Virginia Statute for Religious Freedom*, which was intended to establish freedom of religion and define the separation of church and state. Jefferson saw that the influence of the Church of England had put Virginia at a competitive disadvantage economically compared to the other states not encumbered by the Church. The church demanded a 10% tithe where the other colonies did not.

People immigrating to America could simply choose to live and work in other states not under the influence of the Church of England. As a result, the builders of America— blacksmiths, brick masons, farmers and so on were flooding into other areas of the country and not into Virginia. Educated men who might serve as effective leaders were likewise avoiding Virginia. Jefferson understood that long term, Virginia could not grow at the same pace economically or otherwise as the other states due to this problem.

Entered into the Assembly record of Virginia as Bill No. 82, "A Bill For establishing religious freedom," Jefferson's bill states, in part,

"We the General Assembly of Virginia do enact that no man shall be compelled to frequent or support any religious worship, place, or ministry whatsoever, nor shall be enforced, restrained, molested, or burthened in his body or goods, nor shall otherwise suffer, on account of his religious opinions or belief; but that all men shall be free to profess, and by argument to maintain, their opinions in matters of religion, and that the same shall in no wise diminish, enlarge, or affect their civil capacities."

Bill No. 82 was finally adopted for Virginia in 1785.

In the case of church and state, Jefferson seems to have again gotten it right. Bill No. 82 defines the "separation" for us. Government was to be indifferent to the people's "opinions in matters of religion," neither compelling citizens to practice a specific state mandated religion nor punishing them for not doing so by force of law. Further, citizens were simply free to profess whatever religion they wished "to maintain."

Thomas Jefferson and his peers resolved the issue of the separation of church and state in America a long time ago with Virginia setting the example. He saw America as a place with inexhaustible liberty so long as the people were willing to take the time and effort to maintain it. He worked tirelessly to craft public policy that was clear, concise, and addressed the issues in the simplest and most direct path as possible. He might well be surprised and dismayed by the twisted "separation" policy that we imagine existing today; this modern notion that American government can have nothing to do with Christianity or its founding Christian principles.

Others of course weighed in with their thoughts.

From John Adams:

"The Declaration of Independence laid the cornerstone of human government upon the first precepts of Christianity."

"The highest glory of the American Revolution was this: it connected, in one indissoluble bond, the principles of civil government with the principles of Christianity."

"As the safety and prosperity of nations ultimately and essentially depend on the protection and the blessing of Almighty God, and the national acknowledgment of this truth is not only an indispensable duty which the people owe to Him."

From Patrick Henry:

"It cannot be emphasized too strongly or too often that this great Nation was founded not by religionists, but by Christians; not on religions, but on the Gospel of Jesus Christ."

From Noah Webster:

"The moral principles and precepts contained in the Scripture ought to form the basis of all our civil constitutions and laws."

"No truth is more evident to my mind than that the Christian religion must be the basis of any government intended to secure the rights and privileges of a free people... When I speak of the Christian religion as the basis of government... I mean the primitive Christianity in its simplicity as taught by Christ and His apostles, consisting of a belief in the being, perfections, and government of God; in the revelation of His will to men, as their supreme rule of action; in man's... accountability to God for his conduct in this life; and in the indispensable obligation of all men to yield entire obedience to God's commands in the moral law and the Gospel."

"Every civil government is based upon some religion or philosophy of life. Education in a nation will propagate the religion of that nation. In America, the foundational religion was Christianity. And it was sown in the hearts of Americans through the home and private and public schools for centuries. Our liberty, growth, and prosperity was the result of a Biblical philosophy of life. Our continued freedom and success is dependent on our educating the youth of America in the principles of Christianity."

From Supreme Court Justice Joseph Story:

"I verily believe Christianity necessary to the support of civil society. One of the beautiful boasts of our municipal jurisprudence is that Christianity is a part of the Common Law ... There never has been a period in which the Common Law did not recognize Christianity as lying its foundations."

From Abraham Lincoln:

"In regards to this great Book [the Bible], I have but to say it is the best gift God has given to man. All the good the Savior gave to the world was communicated through this Book. But for it we could not know right from wrong. All things most desirable for man's welfare, here and hereafter, are found portrayed in it."

From Calvin Coolidge:

"The foundations of our society and our government rest so much on the teachings of the Bible that it would be difficult to support them if faith in these teachings would cease to be practically universal in our country."

Americans now have been brainwashed into the popular thinking that local issues like pre-game Christian prayers at a football game, school children saying grace in the school lunchroom, or Nativity scenes on the lawn of a privately owned church are somehow grave and dangerous violations of "the separation of church and state."

Clarity and common sense are again what is needed in today's America. As citizens we must remember that Jefferson showed us that religious tolerance is a two-way street and that indeed it "does me no injury for my neighbour to say there are twenty gods, or no god." One's liberty does not end at the point where another person simply claims to be offended.

Others in American government have clearly demonstrated that the principles of Christ cannot be separated from the civil structure of the United States. There are, however, two problems. These are perhaps the very central problems of all I will discuss in this text.

1. Our American Founders and Framers formed a Constitutional Representative Republic for America. Christianity is NOT a Constitutional Representative Republic, it is a KINGDOM. The Kingdom of God. This kingdom is not a democracy. It is, in many ways, incompatible with many of the ideals of the modern cultural adaptations of "independence" which we have translated into pride. Why? Because in America, we only now possess few actual liberties that have survived from our Founding, We are NOT actually "independent" or free any longer. We have more theoretical freedoms than almost all other nations which makes us "the cleanest shirt in the dirty shirt pile" but America today is not the America of our Founding at all.

In place of this lost liberty, we have backfilled with personal pride which we feed in other ways to prove to ourselves that we are "independent." For example, we buy houses and say "I am a homeowner!" When in reality, the money was merely borrowed on a thirty year mortgage from a bank and we own nothing but the debt until the last payment is made. For the next three decades, we are in servitude to the bank. Even after the loan is repaid, the owner will continue to pay rent to the government for their property in the form of perpetual property taxes.

In our Christian Faith we discover a relatively open field in the United States whereby we can exercise this "liberty." We use it to totally manipulate Christianity into what we think it ought to be for us individually, and anyone who tells us otherwise is just wrong, evil, etc, etc. As long as the IRS approves the organization as a religious organization that's all that matters, The rest of it is wide open for our own definition. Pure political ambitions masquerade as charity, responsibility, and even trump the Gospels in many places. More is read into the Bible than is actually there in order to support a heretical viewpoint. This exercise has played out in hundreds if not thousands of American churches over and over in the exercise of this false liberty that truly is nothing more than pride.

Pontius Pilate asked Christ at his trial, "Art thou the king of the Jews?"[357] Pilate asks this question because if Christ claimed to be a king, that would mean that he intends to assert the authority of a king in some way (Pilate thought in a civic manner) which would be a direct challenge to the authority of Caesar. Because Christians claim to be a part of the Kingdom of God, they must expect to submit themselves completely to the authority of Christ, not to assert their own independent ideals into churches claiming to be Christian.

2. In our Republic, according to Supreme Court Justice Joseph Story, Christianity is necessary to the support of civil society. In America today, we now have reversed this entirely. It is all too common for American Christians to attempt to use a pattern of local civic authority to run their thousands of different churches. The disastrous outcome of this process is plain to any who wish to investigate it.

Controlling the religious in America

Since the beginning of religion itself, government has felt the need to be integral with it or to control it. In America, we have no repository of Holy relics in our churches today as was to be found in Rome, Constantinople and the churches of the Byzantine Empire. But this in no way has prevented the overreach of our government to manipulate churches and their people.

There continues to be endless debate in America over the notion of "the separation of church and state." This has probably occurred more so in the twentieth century than at any time in the course of our history, and it would not be surprising to learn that the issue is likely more related to taxation and public funding than it is to principle. Rather than giving out religious Holy relics owned by the State, the American government wants churches to focus instead on what it will NOT take from them—taxes.

The Unholy Land

For all their grandstanding, the Liberals in America DO want government involved with religion no matter how much they pretend to want "separation of church and state." Their nightmare scenario is for 10,000 new conservative, unified, Bible-focused Christian churches to spring up all over the country. They have taken the opportunity over the decades to craft laws and regulations that control the size, scope, content, activity, growth, and direction of American churches.

Considering that church membership is on the decline, American government interference and control of churches is a plan working remarkably well. Its chief controller is none other than the IRS, which itself is under the direct control of the President of the United States.

The IRS scandal orchestrated by Barack Hussein Obama and his administration clearly illustrated for us how the American government utilizes unconstitutional powers for the purpose of abusive control and punishment of groups that politically opposed his party. Recall that the IRS denied and "slow-walked" applications for conservative groups seeking tax free 501(c)3 status in the effort to prevent them from organizing against liberals prior to the 2012 election.[358] In this they were successful and America would reelect the usurper president. During the same period, the IRS approved over 95% of the same requests for leftist groups. Conservative groups' applications were sorted out and set aside long enough to prevent them from organizing and impacting the campaign.

The United States government itself was designed to be apolitical, or politically neutral. Its agencies are to be impartial and are not themselves to be affiliated with a party or its politics. They are not to be politically self-aware and active in a cause and must be a "disinterested party" in all transactions looking only to the law and courts for operational guidance. No one believes that this is true about America today after the eight years of Barack Hussein Obama's putrefying of America. Deep down, we all now know that "the fix is in" no matter what agency we turn to, including the FBI.

Now we must remember that the same IRS has been using its power of taxation for decades to assert some degree of control over religion in the United States. A church that does not have the specially granted IRS tax-free status may not long survive financially. It seems odd to me that any kind of donation from an individual or a family to anyone else ought to be taxed in the first place. If the donor has already paid taxes on their money why should it be counted as income and taxed again by the recipient, whomever that may be? It is because of the serial taxation structure the IRS maintains in order to scrape off as much money from the people as possible. If you donated $5,000 to a church and they are not designated a tax-free organization by the IRS, it's now "income" again and subject to taxation again.

What if American Christians stopped contributing to a centralized, IRS ordained church bureaucracy, but rather gave in direct support of their neighbors and their community instead? Money need not be funneled into a church bank account as the IRS would prefer, but rather Christians taking only direct individual ownership for helping solve a need. If the church members begin channeling their regular tithe and offerings in this way, without much church overhead to pay for, there would be a lot of money freed up for helping the poor and developing other projects.

Of course, some will say then that the donors lose their IRS tax deduction to charity—which is why this entire procedure is a disincentive to the public. This diabolical structure largely PREVENTS the formation of any charitable plan not blessed by the IRS. The United States government should never have been permitted to use the tax code to manipulate the American public in this way. Instead we see that government has indeed used its authority to control or literally channel charitable giving, the authorization for the establishment of new charities, and by so doing it attempts to make religion into an organization which is a shadow of itself—complete with regulations, reporting, and expensive (and often ineffective) bureaucracy. Not too unlike the Church of England in the 1700's.

The government endows certain "established" religions a tax free status. That means it indeed controls who can be a religious organization and shuts out any it does not deem worthy. Folks who donate to these specially designated groups can deduct portions of the donations from their income taxes. This is a broad control measure that prevents unwanted religious organizations from springing up and funnels the public's donations to the chosen channels, perhaps preventing them from choosing to fund any need outside this tax-blessed structure.

The Unholy Land

Money is what keeps big churches going. The established churches are all too happy to accept and conform to a structure that funnels charitable giving their way while exempting them from paying taxes. What church could survive financially if it had to pay taxes? How many donations might be scattered elsewhere if taxpayers could no longer deduct their charitable donations from their income? Would it be any different for corporate entities and their charitable donations?

The government has figured out, much like the ancient Romans and the Byzantines, that the taxes and taxation structure can and must be used to manipulate behavior and levy super-constitutional controls on the people. In America, this did not start in earnest until February 3rd, 1913 with the passage of the 16th Amendment that permitted broad taxation of the American citizens. Once this was accomplished, government was able to turn the tables against the people and become the provider of exclusions to the taxes. This role has been abused by the government for over 100 years now and there can be no remedy until the debt catches up with the nation and the currency itself hyper-inflates to worthlessness. Only then will national-level financial reforms be necessary.

As Christians, we should carefully examine why it is that we are giving. Is it out of obedience to Christ and to hopefully support Christ-like service in the church and community or is it to get a tax deduction? If it is the latter, then our heart is not in the right place. Christ never mentioned that we should consider the IRS rules before we decide how to help the poor. He said "pay to Caesar what is Caesar's and give to God what is God's." Christ never insisted that a government dole out tax breaks to His ministry. When His disciples had to pay the tax, by faith, He provided it with the coin found in the mouth of the fish. He didn't apply to Caesar for a 501(c)(3).

If you are a proponent of "separation of church and state" then you must accept that this IRS scheme must be completely abandoned. Doing so would be extremely complicated at this stage to be sure, but eliminating government as the keeper of all money (they already control a sizable portion of your income now) and director of charitable giving must be part of the conversation. This is as much a discussion about liberty as anything else. Your money is your liberty. How you choose to use it in a free republic is your business. When government takes your money away through taxation and then manipulates your charitable giving at the same time, they affect this liberty—and they know it.

12

Christianity in Action

"I am convinced that the path to unity isn't a path forward to a new truth, but rather is a path backwards to reconnect with the foundation of our ancient faith.[359]"

Author Mark Bradshaw
From "That They May Be One"

We have now examined both a brief history of the Christian faith and some of the root causes of the failure to maintain both virtue and unity in America. I have implicated the modern American Christian churches for their failure to possess, lead and maintain the cultural standards of the nation which Alexis de Tocqueville and many others thought so important to the survival of our nation. Now we turn to the million dollar question: what does America do about it? How in the midst of a culture centered on "self" can we become retrained to see the larger picture and accept a responsible role in the American society which is greater than our endless pursuit of self-aggrandizement?

If America were a completely godless nation, then the restoration of unity and virtue would be a simple matter of philosophy and politics rather than faith. A dictator would simply rule the nation in "unified" fear, as is the case in North Korea today.

What is the role of the Christian Church? Why do I insist that it is failing in this mission today? These are fair questions. First we must answer the question as to what the role is for the church at large, be it Roman Catholic, Orthodox, or Protestant. They all claim to follow Christ. What did Christ do to set an example for us? He healed the sick, served the poor, and poured out His love for all. He provided for us clear standards and a pattern of living to follow that was holy. He commanded us to love one another. Christ did not come to overthrow either the Jewish or Roman people, their laws, or their government by means of a political agendas pushed by "churches" as we are seeing happen today.

Now we can ask another question, is this the sole focus of the Vatican or of so many Protestant churches? Are they about Christ's mission or simply about brainwashing people with political messaging at the local Wednesday night supper club? These are also fair questions. Christ gave all He had for us. Not so with most of our comfortable churches.

Many Americans now see Socialism as the answer for America's problems and support the false notion that Christianity supports it. I have a friend who stated that America needs to see the value in Socialized medicine. This statement, by definition, makes him a Socialist. There are many problems with Socialism in any form in the United States. The primary problem is that it is in direct opposition to the American Constitution and the rule of law. The Constitution does not permit the American government to force taxes from one group in order to redistribute to another group of the government's choosing. Simply put, it is not the role and scope of the American government. In fact, American government is supposed to protect the private property rights of the citizens, not steal their property.

Left unchecked, Socialism evolves quickly into Communism by design, which is an atheist construct. Communists destroy Christian churches and as such Communism should be considered enemy #1 for all Christians. Secondly, the nation is more than $35 trillion in debt and cannot afford Socialism at any level, period. The debt will soon become unsustainable. Why do I bring this up?

The Church, on the other hand is different. **Every church on the planet is now wealthier than the United States of America.** You read that correctly. If the church has a positive cash flow and a debt less than $35 trillion, they are wealthier than the U.S. government. Not only is it not the job of the American government to carry out any beneficence (if Socialism might be misconstrued by some as that) but also, the churches are actually equipped for the task, and they are not even taxed.

Christian churches are positioned to help. Salient examples of Christian service always come to mind. One story is of the thirty-three-year-old Roman Catholic priest and missionary Father Damien Jones, the son of a Belgian farmer. By May, 1873, some 2,000 of the 40,000 residents of Hawaii had been stricken with leprosy and conditions continued to worsen at a rapid pace. Father Damien arrived with Bishop Monseigneur Maigret on May 4th assigned to serve the leper colony. After Father Damien had seen the horror of late stage lepers for the first time that day, the Bishop offered Father Damien the chance to reconsider his post. Father Damien, though, would have none of it, declaring, "I am ready to be buried alive with those poor wretches," because he had volunteered to serve at Hawaii's leper colony for the remainder of his life. After twelve years of serving the colony, he contracted the disease and died four years later.[360]

For Father Damien, it would be a service of love without any concern for himself. The conditions at the colony were deplorably filthy and even fresh water was not readily available. Writer Dan Graves notes of Father Damien,

"He…organized a bucket brigade to bring water to the settlement. Later, he piped water from a perpetual pool to the settlement's doorsteps…he was strong, energetic, and practical. He burned the filthiest houses, scrubbed out the rest, and built new ones. He laid out farms and a cemetery, opened a dump, and stopped the production of alcohol. Most important of all, he taught the people about Christ. Men who had stolen from the dying or flung others into ditches now repented and sought baptism.[361]"

What about the Protestants? How is this working today? In April 2018, it was reported that Covenant Church in Carrollton, Texas, paid $ 10,551,618 to clear the medical bills of 4,229 Dallas area families. Every American veteran within a 20-mile radius of Covenant's four church campuses had their outstanding bills paid off[362]. This is not government sponsored Socialism; it is the church fulfilling its role in its community.

Similarly, Northview Church in Carmel, Indiana is paying off $7.8 million of medical debt for multiple central Indiana communities. The church says their efforts have led to wiping out medical debt in some entire cities, and the people who received aid did not have to be members of the church.[363]

In November, 2019 a Cincinnati, Ohio megachurch, Crossroads Church, announced that it was similarly paying off $46.5 million in medical debt for more than 45,000 families in Ohio, Kentucky, Tennessee and Indiana.[364]

These are without a doubt, great modern acts of charity and these churches are right to do this. But they are not miracles. None of these churches has the power to heal the sick; the best they might do is pay their medical bills which is a great deed, but not a miracle. Where is the Christian Church where we might see the power of God today? I don't mean the forehead-slapping televangelist crowd. I mean to ask to see the genuine Church where the power of God still resides, and His Grace and Power is present.

The More Perfect Church - Salt and Faith

"You are the salt of the earth, but if salt becomes insipid, with what will it be salted? It is good for nothing except to be thrown outside and to be trodden upon by people."

Matthew 5:13
Aramaic Bible in Plain English

There are more than thirty references to salt in the Bible. Salt these days is inexpensive, underappreciated, even vilified for overconsumption in prepared foods. For a few minutes here, let's put aside the 21st Century and it's now popular hatred for salt and understand what salt was to the ancient world. Was it merely the tasty accent to food?

The Unholy Land

Salt was useful:
- Salt was used broadly as an antiseptic and a food preservative.
- Egyptians may have been the first civilization to preserve fish and meat with salt.
- Salt was used in the military practice of salting the earth by various peoples, beginning with the Assyrians—as a weapon to poison the soil to prevent conquered people from growing crops, resulting in a choice between forced migration and starvation.

Salt was necessary:
- The Egyptians discovered a type of salt in a dry riverbed—an area they called Natrun—that they used in the mummification process—a religious practice.

Salt was important:
- As far back as 6050 BC, salt has been a significant and integral part of the world's history.
- Used as a part of Egyptian religious offerings (as well as mummification.)

Salt was valuable:
- Ancient Greeks exchanged their slaves for salt
- Salt was of high value to the Jews, Greeks, the Chinese, Hittites and other peoples of antiquity.
- Special salt rations given to early Roman soldiers were known as "*salarium argentum*" (Today we say you earn a "salary.")
- Ancient Ethiopians used salt slabs, called amoles, as currency.
- Salt was a valuable trade commodity between the Phoenicians and their Mediterranean empire neighbors.

We see that salt was actually **useful, necessary, important and valuable** in communities spanning millennia prior to the birth of Christ. Is it any accident then how Christians are called to be *the salt of the earth*? Can we honestly say then that today we are useful, necessary, important and valuable in our role in our communities?

Placing ourselves in His service; our words and actions should increasingly reflect the character and priorities of Christ to the exclusion of all else in unity. But even if the issues that separate us as Christians could be either "essential" or "non-essential'—but either way, we need to live in love as Christ commanded, and that includes Christians acting like "brothers and sisters in Christ" across the spectrum of all denominations. Of course this is still not the "unity of the faith," otherwise there would be no "denominations."

On the other hand, we cannot ignore what we read in Mark 9:38-41. Here we read that there is room for unity of the faith even if the name on the building is different than that of the building a block away.

"And John answered him, saying, Master, we saw one casting out devils in thy name, and he followeth not us: and we forbad him, because he followeth not us. But Jesus said, Forbid him not: for there is no man which shall do a miracle in my name, that can lightly speak evil of me. For he that is not against us is on our part. For whosoever shall give you a cup of water to drink in my name, because ye belong to Christ, verily I say unto you, he shall not lose his reward."

This mission cannot happen while Christian churches are themselves often viciously divided over so many opinions or political based differences. In many ways, American Christians seem to want some form of Christianity while rejecting the genuine function of it. They need something to call "Christianity" even if their practices have nothing to do with Christ. How can they worship the Head of the Church, Christ, while separating themselves from the body? Yes, it is an indictment of a system formed by pride that simply does not work.

America today, however, is starving for virtue and unity, and has no idea how to find them. Most of the nation apparently does not have a concept of what these two words even mean, let alone why they are important. The Christian church must be there to feed them. We must learn again that both virtue and unity is the basis for cohesive families and communities, while holding ourselves and government accountable to our nation's just and proper Constitutional standards.

The cultural and social issues of the United States in the 21st Century will not be resolved or improved by our political class in Washington. This has been understood for a long time.

These matters are almost always solved by the people, not by "big government." Sure, American government can provide a nudge of leadership on cultural issues as Ronald Reagan did, but it is the American people who do the work to fix and to accomplish great and small things. In the same way, the needed reconciliations and reformations of the Christian faith today are unlikely to evolve out of "big church."

The Myth of the Flawed Church

As Christians we tend to create our own obstacles. How many times have we been told, "Until Christ's return, there can be no perfect church on this Earth?" Let's examine this statement. After Christ's Ascension, Christians were sent the Holy Spirit at Pentecost—the event that marks the beginning of the Christian Church. The Holy Spirit is part of the Trinity, and as such is all-Holy and has all the perfection of the Deity. Modern Protestants say that churches are believed to be "Spirit-filled" and rely upon the Holy Spirit, and so on.

But somehow when it comes to the church itself modern Christians are expected to believe that the same perfect and powerful Holy Spirit is now incapable and totally incompetent to assure that the church established by Christ remains singularly intact and Holy? Really? Is church merely "amateur hour" for the "Holy Spirit?" I certainly don't believe that, nor can any Christian if they believe the words of the Lord who promised otherwise.

Some time ago I learned that I share the same assessment as Metropolitan Timothy Ware, that the church[s] is not the problem:

"But human sin cannot affect the essential nature of the church. We must not say that because Christians on earth sin and are imperfect, therefore the church sins and is imperfect; for the Church, even on earth, is a thing of heaven, and cannot sin."[365]

It seems quite contradictory to have faith in the Holy Spirit in the most important matters of life but then assume He is unable to maintain a Holy Church. Do we somehow imagine that the omnipotent Holy Spirit *needs* our help? Perhaps this is more telling of these churches than we care to admit.

---

[s] Ware is referring to the Eastern Orthodox Church only.

The Unholy Land

I think the statement really aims to excuse all sinful and flawed acts of people pretending to run a church, when really they are running a Christian-styled social club. This statement invariably leads us down the path to accept practices of sin and mediocrity in our churches, which often lead to division and ultimately failure. Sometimes it ends with abuse and criminal activity.

We assume that the best we can aim for is the "more perfect" church; much like our nation's Founders accepted the creation of a "more perfect union" and not "the perfect union. I have been told all my life that churches will always have church politics, that I should just accept it. To this I say that's also unacceptable. To the extent that the root cause of ambitious politics in a church are driven by greed, ego, favoritism, nepotism, envy, pride, and plain ignorance. I cannot see why anyone should tolerate a church centered on its church politics. Such an organization is not a church at all but
more properly described as a Christ-sympathetic club or association.

Church politics work against church unity and is certainly not rooted in Christ. As a Christian church without Christ is not a church, America without God is nowhere you would want to live. How can this be reconciled? I believe that the American Republic can maintain virtue and unity without fear of becoming a Christian Theocracy. Let the government operate on the basis of the original intent of its Constitution, and the churches operate separately without the interference of government.[t] American Christians must come to the realization that there is a genuine Christian Church out there, somewhere and always has been. It is up to us to have the courage to leave our emotionally and intellectually comfortable "churches" and discover it.

The More Perfect Church we might imagine would not be a church in the sense we are accustomed to seeing today. It is radically different than our present churches and eerily similar to the first century. It would consist of about 25 to 30 members, preferably presided over by a retired pastor, who can afford no to draw a salary form the church members. This church has no need for a "constitution" other than the Bible. It has no man-made oaths, creeds, or committees. No street address of its own, but meets in the homes of the

---

[t] Meaning that government has no role in matters not assigned to it by the Constitution. Churches would pay taxes like any other entity and government would have no role whatsoever in church matters, such as marriages or content of doctrine.

membership, in rotation as needed or at a free room in the local rec center. It collects no money, has no treasury, no officers, no deacon board, no trustees, no bank accounts, and is not a 501 organization. It does not need to report to the IRS, and as such, is not subject to government oversight and control. It has no expenses of its own and everyone, including the pastor, are volunteers.

The way I see it, American Christians basically have three choices today;

1. To stay on the path we are on and watch the "falling away" from the faith continue, continue to permit the leftists to deceive Christians, and witness the nation continue to decline.

2. To attempt to somehow reinvent a unified Christian faith, which seems unlikely with the structures of Protestantism and the Roman Catholic Church.

3. To seek return to the apostolic roots of our faith somehow akin to a generic Orthodoxy. How can this happen? I really do not know.

Restoration of American Virtue and Unity

"Next to the general idea of virtue, I know of no idea more beautiful than that of rights, and, indeed, it would be more accurate to say that the two ideas are indistinguishable. The idea of rights is none other than the idea of virtue introduced into the world of politics."

Alexis de Tocqueville
Democracy in America

Restoring morality in America must be a top priority if our constitutional republic is to survive . C. Bradley Thompson[u] writes in his 1993 publication, "*Socialism vs. Capitalism: Which is the Moral System*,"

"As a consequence of [America's] sixty-year experiment with a mixed economy and the welfare state, America has created two new classes of citizens. The first is a debased class of dependents whose means of survival is contingent upon the forced expropriation of wealth from

---

[u] Assistant Professor of Political Science at Ashland University and Coordinator of Publications and Special Programs at the John M. Ashbrook Center for Public Affairs.

working citizens by a professional class of government social planners. The forgotten man and woman in all of this is the quiet, hardworking, law-abiding, taxpaying citizen who minds his or her own business but is forced to work for the government and their serfs....The return of capitalism will not happen until there is a moral revolution in this country. We must rediscover and then teach our young the virtues associated with being free and independent citizens. Then and only then, will there be social justice in America."[366]

Thompson's last three sentences say it all. This is also precisely why the Leftists in America use the false "separation of church and state" argument as an effort to remove morals and virtue from our communities. They simply must defeat these cultural constructs in order to advance socialism, communism, and wealth redistribution.

It's a fair question to ask of America today, what happened to our virtue? Where did it go? The ancient Greeks and Romans asked the very same questions of themselves. For example, Marcus Tullius Cicero was a Roman politician and lawyer, born in 106 BC, who served as consul in the year 63 BC. He came from a wealthy, municipal family of the Roman equestrian order, and is considered one of Rome's greatest orators and prose stylists. He wrote extensively about government and its role in civilized society, and his work upheld republican values in a time where civil war was destroying the Roman Republic.

Cicero suggests that the introduction of consumerism was to blame:

"It was the Phoenicians who, with their trade and merchandise, first brought greed, luxury, and an insatiable desire for things of all kinds to Greece."

Cicero discovered and lamented that virtue was vacant in his day. He was assassinated on December 7, 43 BC. So much for virtue.

In the later Byzantine Empire, Emperor Justinian's successor, his nephew, Justin II apparently saw that his inherited Byzantine Empire would soon be lost for what was essentially a general lack of virtue. Justin II's personality was steeped in the old Roman traditions which centered upon virtue—and he could now see that without it, the Empire was doomed.

The Unholy Land

But Justin II could not restore this Roman virtue to his empire. Before the end of his reign, he went completely insane, given to fits of uncontrollable rage and violence where he would attack and bite his own chamberlains. He died on 4 October, 578. His successor, Tiberius Constantine, did not fare much better as a ruler. He was poisoned to death and died 13 August 582 —only proving that Justin II's fears had been realized; the empire had completely lost its virtue. Restoring it to the empire would prove difficult.

The Byzantine Empire would see a long period of slow decline over the next 400 years. Emperors came and went; while some of these were notable, many were just plain incompetent. A standout Emperor in the post-Justinian period was Alexius Comnenus who reigned from 1081 until his death in 1118. He was crowned at the age of twenty-four on Easter Sunday at the grandest of Orthodox Churches, the Hagia Sophia in Constantinople.[367]

Alexius was the nephew of Emperor Isaac Comnenus and was brought up in service to the Empire. Even at his young age, He was no stranger to battle, seeing action against the Turks at age fourteen. He quickly became a leader in the Byzantine military and by the time of his ascension to the throne had never lost a battle. He was loved by his soldiers and had earned their trust.[368]

In 1107, Alexius sought reform for the Empire. He wished to restore stability, continuity, and to purify the Empire from religious heresy. He piety was genuine in his Orthodox Christian faith above all. With the aim to affect this national purification and restore true Christian virtues he built a large hospital and hostel for the poor and disabled which he had kept supplied with food, clothing, and the rest. Alexius also had the Church appoint a special order of what amounts to street preachers. These men were assigned by parish as the "guardians of public morals."[369] It was a grand undertaking in the effort to restore the Christian values that had been allowed to decay under the reigns of his predecessors.

If America is to avert a similar fate as empires past, we must restore virtue. The nation is not, however, an autocratic theocracy like Byzantium. How can virtue be restored in the midst of an American culture that now knows nothing of the word? Do more and better laws make us virtuous? Can virtue be purchased? Can we wish for it? Can we sit together around the fireside and hold hands to achieve it? No, none of these things will lead to the restoration of virtue. Fortunately a roadmap to that place has already been laid before us if we choose to take the time to read, comprehend, and apply what we learn.

A Dogma of Virtue

American culture today is infected with the gray fog of ill-defined values. And to be sure, political operatives use this gray area as an opportunity to redefine what they want American virtues to be. Through their use of media, academia, and government they are replacing traditional virtues with their false concepts of "social justice" and slavish Earth worship. What America needs are clearly defined genuine values to teach our children and support a positive culture.

Here, we run into the same brick wall of confusion. The question is how do we figure out what these virtues are, and which ones we should adopt? If the Christian Church was to be the "keepers" of virtues, assigned to the role of keeping these taught in our culture they have not done a good job in doing it. Before we throw church leaders under the bus again, we must remember that the root of the problem is there are so many conflicting ideas about what these virtues are, even for the churches. There are untold hundreds or perhaps thousands of Christian texts that attempt to define and provide guidance for behavior.

The first of these that come to mind was actually a pre-Christian text, the Ten Commandments. Then Christ Himself defined for us an extended set of values, and was followed by men like St. Paul who amplified them. Of course the world became more complex over time and Christians could not live in a vacuum just adhering to their values alone, although the various orders of monks and other ascetics do.

What would our Christian churches tell us today about virtues? Which set of virtues should we each seek to adopt for our families, for our nation? It would take volumes to describe the virtues of the thousands of protestant denominations. However, as I focused on a only a few different churches earlier, I will again do so here.

The United Methodists have formulated their "Social Principles"[370] which are listed as:

The Natural World; All creation is the Lord's, and we are responsible for the ways in which we use and abuse it.

The Nurturing Community; We believe we have a responsibility to innovate, sponsor, and evaluate new forms of community that will encourage development of the fullest potential in individuals.

The Social Community; We affirm all persons as equally valuable in the sight of God's sight. We reject discrimination and assert the rights of minority groups to equal opportunities.

The Economic Community; We claim all economic systems to be under the judgment of God no less than other facets of the created order.

The Political Community; We hold governments responsible for the protection of people's basic freedoms. We believe that neither church nor state should attempt to dominate the other.

The World Community; God's world is one world. We pledge ourselves to seek the meaning of the gospel in all issues that divide people and threaten the growth of world community.

When one explores these "Social Principles" further on their website, it becomes quite clear that these pleasant sounding platitudes are mere headlines of a deception that ends up closely following the platform of the Democrat party.

Good luck to anyone who attempts to discover a single, concise list of simple virtues espoused by the Evangelical Lutheran Church. Instead, they have issued a series of individual "Social Statements" which are rather complex. These include the following topics, which appear to be designed as manifesto and for use as study guides[371]:

- Abortion
- Caring for Creation
- Church in Society
- Criminal Justice
- Death Penalty
- Economic Life
- Education
- Genetics
- Health Care
- Human Sexuality
- Peace
- Race, Ethnicity and Culture
- Sexism

And why is it impossible to discover a clearly defined list of virtues from the ELCA? Because they no longer believe in them. Instead, they have replaced virtues with modern sociopolitical objectives around *issues* with a general sense of redefined "virtue." In so doing, they can frame these issues and define desired behaviors in an effort to manipulate favorable political outcomes. Jeff Mallinson, D. Phil., Professor of Theology and Philosophy, Concordia University, Irvine writes of Lutheran view of virtue today:

"Virtue, despite its emphasis on the individual, focuses less on maintaining the appearance of personal righteousness and more on personal character for the sake of the outside world... when there are no explicit biblical teachings about a given question, a Christian can turn profitably to consequentialism, calculating the best course of action for the greatest good of the greatest possible number of neighbors. ...He or she strives to be the *humane* human they were designed by God to be."[372]

Specifically using the cleverly crafted phrase, "...strives to be the *humane* human..." derails the very concepts of individual virtues and places a person into a new larger space of indefinite "gray area" called "humane behavior." Lutheran leadership can then direct their faithful what this behavior looks like. Drilling down into this further beneath the veneer of bible scriptures plastered over it will uncover that the course for the "humane" thing to do is to support the political objectives of American democrats. This method also creates a useful component of shame for noncompliance; what Christian wouldn't want to be "a humane human?"

Southern Baptists trace their Founding to John Smyth and the Separatist Movement beginning in England in 1608. They are still operated much in the way of the Separatists today. Because the Southern Baptist Convention today is a fellowship of individual congregations instead of a centralized church it is also difficult to find a concise list of their core virtues. The closest we might arrive at is a list of brief statements in their "Baptist Faith & Message 2000" which provides guidance to their member churches and is broken down in this fashion:

I. The Scriptures
II. God
III. Man
IV. Salvation
V. God's Purpose of Grace
VI. The Church
VII. Baptism and the Lord's Supper
VIII. The Lord's Day
IX. The Kingdom
X. Last Things
XI. Evangelism and Missions
XII. Education

XIII. Stewardship
XIV. Cooperation
XV. The Christian and the Social Order

XVI. Peace and War
XVII. Religious Liberty
XVIII. The Family

Like many other denominations, their virtues are contained in a more narrative form. For example, in section XV we read,

"Christians should oppose racism, every form of greed, selfishness, and vice, and all forms of sexual immorality, including adultery, homosexuality, and pornography. We should work to provide for the orphaned, the needy, the abused, the aged, the helpless, and the sick. We should speak on behalf of the unborn and contend for the sanctity of all human life from conception to natural death. Every Christian should seek to bring industry, government, and society as a whole under the sway of the principles of righteousness, truth, and brotherly love. In order to promote these ends Christians should be ready to work with all men of good will in any good cause, always being careful to act in the spirit of love without compromising their loyalty to Christ and His truth."[373]

Their values, while conservative, do not draw their faithful into the mud of identity politics as do the Methodist and the Lutherans.

There are many virtues listed in the catechism of the Roman Catholic Church, which has been taught for many centuries. They are clearly organized into four sections;[374]

Human virtues are firm attitudes, stable dispositions, and habitual perfections of intellect and will that govern our actions, order our passions, and guide our conduct according to reason and faith.

Moral virtues are acquired by human effort. They are the fruit and seed of morally good acts; they dispose all the powers of the human being for communion with divine love.

Cardinal virtues: prudence, justice, fortitude, and temperance.

Theological virtues: Faith, Hope, and Charity (love).

Additionally Roman Catholics describe the seven gifts of the Holy Spirit bestowed upon Christians as wisdom, understanding, counsel, fortitude, knowledge, piety, and fear of the Lord.

The Eastern Orthodox Church talks about virtues this way, in part:

"...all of the human virtues are attributes of God Himself. They are the characteristics of Jesus Christ, the divine Son of God in human flesh. They are the divine properties which should be in all human persons by the gift of God in creation and salvation through Christ...Christian virtues are not all particularly 'Christian' in the sense that only Christians know about them and are committed to attain them. Most, if not all, of the Christian virtues have been honored, respected and recommended by all great teachers of the spiritual life."[375]

The Orthodox Christians have a definitive list of fourteen virtues they teach and adhere to[376]: each of them is carefully defined according to scripture and two millennia of application.

- Faith
- Hope
- Knowledge
- Wisdom
- Honesty
- Humility
- Obedience
- Patience
- Courage
- Faithfulness
- Self-Control
- Kindness
- Gratitude
- Love

With all these various outputs of "virtues" it seems to me that eliminating "gray areas" of teachings might serve Christians best today. We need firm teachings to adhere to, not squishy, loosely defined ideas and concepts that really are not virtues at all. In other words, we can teach our children humility and to love all people instead of teaching them to be immediately offended by someone who doesn't.

St. Thomas Aquinas

Not too long after the disastrous Fourth Crusade, St. Thomas Aquinas, a Dominican friar, penned his *Summa Theologiæ* in 1265. His purpose was to provide a training resource for his students. It became a magnificent sixty-volume work because of its depth, detail, scope and timing. It is the main document I wish to select on the subjects of virtue and unity from a Christian perspective. There are many others, I know, but we could write endless pages from endless sources and accomplish nothing in a lifetime of analysis if I took that path. As a reminder, this was penned 252 years *before* the Protestant Reformation.

Aquinas engages us in a detailed dissection of virtues, morals, prudence, emotions, disciplines, and so on. Many of these discussions can seem to "get into the weeds" diverted from the main course of the road he is taking us down in my observation. Aquinas does include this conclusion:

"Moral virtue then is a disposition to choose a balanced course of action such as a prudent man man's reason would decide is right...Moral virtues are dispositions to make good choices.[377]"

By now we understand that "virtues" are not merely attained by our sitting around and thinking good thoughts while reading a Bible. We see here that attaining virtues requires that a choice be made and a followed through. It is a disposition, a "course of action." This implies that personal choices about how we choose to live are under our control. That they are in fact under our control means that we cannot merely blame any other thing, person, or circumstance for us not following a path that is virtuous.

For example, consider that a robber chooses to rob a bank; he does not do so because he is poor, or because his cohort made him take it, or because he had a bad childhood. He is not robbing because he is a product of his environment. He made a choice and people are not the "helpless victims" of their own crimes. He robbed the bank because he wanted to, he set out to do it, formulated a plan, acquired some means (a weapon, getaway vehicle, etc.) brought himself to the bank, and executed his plans. It was not an accident, a mistake or an order by someone else—it was intentional.

"Good choices require our appetites to be disposed to a goal in accordance with reason, and right choice of means to that good, planned, decided, and commanded by prudent reason...Natural inclinations to the goals of the virtues are only the beginning of virtue, not the achieved fullness. And the stronger such inclinations the more perilous they are unless they are controlled by reason making right choices of means to the desired goal...Virtues are not emotions...emotions can be good or bad, reasonable or unreasonable, whereas virtues dispose us only to good...balanced emotions are virtue's affect, not its substance.[378]"

Virtue is not an emotion of "feeling good" about helping an elderly person across the street. Virtues manifest as a course of action to be used and applied to a thing or a decision. A little later we will apply virtue to the subject of money to see how this all works.

One of the many key points I want to make here first is that no one can force a person to be unvirtuous. Aquinas writes,

"Affections like feeling joyful or sad, loving or hating, are reactions to what we perceive as straightforwardly good or bad, agreeable or disagreeable, pleasurable or painful. Sometimes, however, taking pleasure in something or avoiding pain from it is not within our immediate power and requires effort...to deal with such difficulties we are endowed with emotions that respond to challenges, like boldness, feeling afraid, hoping, and other so-called aggressive emotions.[379]"

I see this as Aquinas illustrating to us that miracle of human spirit so needed and in short supply today, self-control. He says we must exert some "effort" sometimes to overcome that which we may not otherwise be able to deal with. This can mean not only control to not do a thing, but also to use as a proactive measure. Someone who has an estranged relationship with a relative, or is dealing with a grave illness, or a person in poverty, or a wealthy man who has lost himself in the course of building his personal empire—all might benefit from the ability to control their reactions and see their obstacle clearly.

They might choose to be content in a circumstance, not unlike Job or St. Paul of the Bible. Or they may be able to formulate a plan to solve a problem they face. In any event, blaming others (as is so common today) or blaming God is not part of the solution.

The Bible clearly supports this general line of thought:

"...give thanks in all circumstances; for this is God's will for you in Christ Jesus."   1 Thessalonians 5:18   NIV

St. Paul here is telling the Thessalonians to *choose* to be positive, thankful, in spite of whatever happens to them collectively as a church or personally. Why? Probably because they, like other Christians at the time were being persecuted.

Aquinas continues:

"Passion makes us prone to sin only when it's unreasonable; reasonable emotion is virtuous. No one questions the fact that to be morally good we must be in reasonable control of our bodily movements. Since the emotions listen to reason, to be morally good we must also control them. Just as it is better not simply to will good but also to do it externally, so it is morally better to seek good not merely with a will but also with emotion.[380]"

Aquinas here explains that it is reasonable to accept that humans are not merely a product of their own environment as nowadays we are expected to accept as truth. No, each one of us not only has the capability of doing good, but is also in full control of our bodies, our emotions, and our actions. This lie that says we are products of our environment and not wholly responsible for our actions is used by the politicians to excuse away bad behaviors of their own voters. Likewise the same lie is perhaps used by others; those who are wealthy beyond reason might attempt to justify their greed by simply concluding, "I'm from a wealthy family." We can all discover some manner in which to use our own environment to excuse away whatever behavior we wish to ignore.

"When emotions precede the reasoned judgement on which the moral worth of our actions depends, they cloud the judgement and lessen the worth of the action; deeds of charity done merely [from an emotion of] pity are less praiseworthy than those done from choice.[381]"

Here Aquinas indicates that even good things done for the wrong reason or from a questionable motivation are not all that good. For example, attending church every Sunday just to say you were there and in order to be seen by others in the community. These are not necessarily good reasons to be present. Likewise giving to the church or other charity because you need a tax deduction for the calendar year is not a reason for a Christian to give because it is being done to serve your own purpose and not from either the virtue of charity or generosity.

I think that although God has provided us with free will that we are still expected to take actions that are deliberate when we say we are followers of Christ. After all, Christ was very purposeful in His ministry and His sacrifice for us.

Aquinas digs deep into the subject of unity, which is what we need to understand:

"...true love wills good to someone. If the someone is yourself, then love seeks a unity with the good you want; if it is someone else, then love creates a community with him, for you treat him as yourself, willing his unity with the good as you would your own.[382]"

Aquinas explains here in just a few short sentences the example of Christian unity. Just as man is created in God's image, Aquinas' vision of unity is paralleled in the same pattern for the Almighty in his view:

"God's love too seeks unity...and community, since he wills good to others.[383]"

We learn here that according to Aquinas, Christian unity boils down to willing goodness to yourself and others in God's love, which forms a community. Now we know.

There are those who say, "I am an atheist, and all good and bad can be found in humanism," or some other similar argument. I will tell you that I am free to deny the existence, manifestations, and results of gravity. However, that untenable position may one day prove to work towards my own detriment or injure myself and jeopardize the safety of others. Just because I might not believe in gravity does not in any way negate the fact that gravity exists and works regardless of my belief system.

Is Modern American Capitalism compatible with Christianity?

The short answer is in definition and theory, yes, in actual practice—sometimes not so much, but still the best and only system.

America presents the globe with a great paradox that is capitalism. On the one hand capitalism is arguably the best overall economic system to raise the most people out of poverty allowing ordinary people to rise and achieve their full potential in life. On the other hand, left unchecked over time capitalism evolves into an exclusionary club for the elite morphing with government to form an Oligarchy, funded progressively less by consumers and more by taxpayers, or "captive customers."[v] When the economic system transforms into something else, it ceases to be capitalism and should no longer be referred to as such. This is the case in America today—we do not have a free economic system of capitalism and have not had that in a very long time.

Again we turn to C. Bradley Thompson;

"The extraordinary level of material prosperity achieved by the capitalist system over the course of the last two-hundred years is a matter of historical record. But very few people are willing to defend capitalism as morally uplifting... Capitalism is the only moral system because it requires human beings to deal with one another as traders– that is, as free moral agents trading and selling goods and services on the basis of mutual consent. Capitalism is the only just system because the sole criterion that determines the value of thing exchanged is the free, voluntary, universal judgement of the consumer. Coercion and fraud are anathema to the free-market system."[384]

Much of the results or outcomes of capitalism are due either to its proper governance, or lack of governance. For this governance to be justly structured and applied, virtue is absolutely necessary. I mentioned earlier that the human species is either given into its wildest passions or governed by virtue. Aquinas uses common activities to illustrate how virtue works:

---

[v] For example, the "Affordable care Act" or "Obamacare," where citizens were for the first time ever required to purchase services at a great expense as a condition of being a citizen in the United States. Penalties for not purchasing policies were backed by massive fines levied by the government and collected by the IRS.

"There are different kinds of virtue depending on how objects of our opportunities need the control of reason. Certain actions are good or bad in themselves, irrespective of the emotions we deploy in doing them, because they are measured relative to other people. Activities like buying and selling raise the question of what is due others, and require a virtue of their own (justice) to control this.[385]"

This example calls into question the governance of free market capitalism. Aquinas is not saying that free markets are bad, just that justice should be the governing virtue to prevent such things as greed and usury from evolving. Is it just to overcharge for food or medicine just because people are willing to pay for it? Is it just for government to subsidize the U.S. Postal Service with additional taxpayer funds because they set an artificially below market price for their services that does not cover the true cost—creating artificial market competition? In the labor market is it just to pay employees less than they are worth to the company only because they will accept less pay for fear of not having employment?

The American government cannot and should not necessarily have to police all these matters. Elected government is corruptible as we have witnessed in America and all over the world. If the virtue of justice were voluntarily applied by Americans themselves individually in a proper fashion by all in a position to do so then the circumstances would arrive in a balance called moderation by Aquinas. The government creating a progressive taxation structure as "guardrails" does not work and only feeds government more of its addictive drug of choice—money.

In America, the strategy of "taxing the rich" is problematic for many reasons, but two specific ones. First, who is it that is allowed to define "the rich" and decides how much to tax them? Secondly, all this taxation does is drain money from the private sector and feed more money to the political class. This in turn, leads to businesses doing whatever they must to curry favor with lawmakers to sway policies to favor their business sector or specific trade. In this scenario we see it leads directly to corruption.

Indeed what we discover in American commerce is not moderation at all. We seek only market equilibrium instead—the balance of supply and demand that sets the market price for goods, services, and labor. That's difficult to accept in a system where everyone, including the government, attempts to put a thumb on the scale to tip it in their favor. This is what we have been taught to like and to accept, but where is virtue here? Certainly we do not discover virtue in many cases and probably not in most.

The basics of life determine that all people need and seek for their sustenance—food, clothing, shelter, medicine—these things are forever being overpriced to overcharge Americans because in many cases, their price arrives at the highest point that the "free market" will bear, not the lowest when there is collusion or a pseudo monopoly as in the case of medicine. A diabetic person must have insulin and so there exists a constant and growing demand while there isn't any market competition in insulin to drive down the market price. The diabetic must have this product and the pharmaceutical companies can set whatever price they wish without worrying about being priced too high (above the natural market equilibrium price). There is no possibility that insulin consumers will stop consuming insulin regardless of the price set.

What is the solution? Do we nationalize the production of insulin and put government in charge of essentially every lifesaving drug? I'm sure that the political class would love for that to happen. The same government in charge of distributing your social security check would then be in charge of your access to medicine. Seems like a conflict of interest, and further, there are no legal permissions or constitutional mandate for the government to have any control over either.

The motivation for pharmaceutical companies is profit. Do we alternately permit government to place price caps or controls on the manufacturers so they can only charge a certain amount for lifesaving drugs? Again, there is no constitutional authority for government to do so, and if they did, artificially low prices (below the market equilibrium) would cause massive shortages. Manufacturers would produce less or stop producing at all if they are expected to take a loss and bankrupt themselves. New drugs would no longer be developed as there would be no expectation of future profit to be made.

What generally occurs in these cases today is that big government steps in and forces the price to be capped or controlled. Then the company is provided with a government (taxpayer funded) subsidy of some kind to make up the loss, essentially forcing all taxpayers to foot the bill. That's just how the U.S. Postal Service operates today in order to remain artificially competitive with UPS and FedEX.

The real long term danger here is the tendency to permit government overreach. The American Constitution that the Framers laid out for us, along with the Bill of Rights provides us with a series of carefully laid, and firm guard rails which, it was hoped, would prevent the government of the new republic from overreach should the future lack of virtue facilitate governmental deterioration.

The Framers put in place a legislative system designed to create "grid lock" on purpose. They established three separate, equal (and hopefully somewhat opposed) branches of government with the idea that each would keep the other in check. By this method, it was hoped, that no one branch could overtake the government. Some zealot president could not make himself a dictator and congress could not make laws on a whim, while judges would not be able to legislate their own politics into law from the bench.

The Framers apparently did not account for the possibility that two or more of the branches of our government might be corrupted at the same time and so act in collusion to "rubber stamp" oppressive legislation into law, such as what happened with the "Affordable Care Act" aka "Obamacare" legislation among other bills. After all, the Framers delivered to us the "more perfect union," not "the perfect union."

In the case of medicine, there is hardly a top end to what to what people will agree to pay to treat themselves or a loved one. What would you pay to keep your child from dying? As a result, Americans are willing to be overcharged by thousands of percent on many goods and services related to medicine—they pay because they must, and they are used to it. Pharmaceutical companies have long had the practice of loading in the full cost to develop a new drug onto American consumers alone through higher pricing, which is one big reason why the same drugs are far less costly everywhere but the United States.

We already know that government is not the answer. The so-called, "Affordable Care Act" was never designed to be affordable for anyone. Now that we know how the law was carefully crafted with purpose, who crafted it, and why, we can finally understand that the true purpose was to legalize government as controlling agent for the public's access to medicine and as an effective tool used to legally impoverish a broad base of American citizens that the Obama Administration and its political cohorts had long sought to eliminate.

The Unholy Land

The law was truthfully designed to separate Americans from access to health care, leaving elderly citizens without access to care for otherwise treatable ailments, forcing them to perish years earlier than they would if properly treated. This in turn removes the sick and elderly from being a financial burden to Medicare and Social Security, which would generate a "savings" for the program. Under the regulations of the law, the medical treatment "value" assigned to a 16 year old male was "100" and all other ages were a declination from that point. It is the exact same chart used by the 20th Century Nazis in Germany.

This means under the government's Socialized medicine plan they will do all they can to treat a sixteen year old male for any ailment, but hardly anything at all to treat a sixty-two year old woman with pneumonia. This was the source for the conversation about "government death panels" –bureaucrats deciding who should receive how much care and when—by pundits when the law was passed. With a plan like this, we are WAY beyond the lack of virtue. We have veered into the area of a government sponsored systematic genocide in a twisted "ends justify the means" kind of way.

Aquinas again:

"There are two sorts of exchange: those that seek commodities in exchange for other commodities (or for money) in order to maintain life, and those that seek money in exchange for money (or commodities) for the sake of profit. This last is characteristic of people in business, according to Aristotle. The first sort of exchange is praiseworthy because it supplies natural needs, but the second sort can be can be justly criticized for feeding the acquisitive urge, which knows no defined bounds and grows without end. Commerce then as such has something shameful about it, being without any honorable or necessary, is not in itself opposed to virtue. It can be made to serve honorable and necessary goals, and in this way business can be justified. As for example when a business generating modest profits supports a family, or helps the poor, or when commerce ensures that a country doesn't run short of essential supplies, profit not being the goal but a sort of reward for the service provided.[386]"

Aquinas explains here in detail the differences in types of commerce he calls "shameful." There is little, if any shame in the commerce of America today. Some say it is because we have adopted a *laissez-faire* economic system in the United States, but that is simply a myth. The phrase, *laissez-faire* is of course, French; literally, 'let do' and "is an economic system in which transactions between private parties are free from government intervention such as regulation, privileges, tariffs and subsidies.[387]" None of this is the case in American business today. Government has involved itself in every sector of trade in one way or another.

Our American economy operates more along the lines of *caveat emptor* where the buyer must educate himself to make the best choices with his money in an attempt to not be swindled. But American consumers are now accustomed to being financially fleeced generation after generation by government, banks, insurance companies and American businesses in general as well as by each other individually. The lack of shame and acceptance of a high degree of greed as a standard in our commerce is the source of a great and evolving amount of injustice and suffering.

Virtue is a combination of tools used for *proper* management of things in life, including money. If one allowed passions to rule their lives, then in the case of money wild spending might lead ultimately to poverty, while at the opposite end of the spectrum a passion for money might well lead to greed.

"Money requires both generosity to moderate our affection for it, and munificence to deal with challenging projects.[388]"

Here, according to Aquinas, two virtues are applied when it comes to money management: generosity and munificence. No one uses the word, "munificence" anymore so let's just call it frugality for the sake of discussion.

Aquinas does not say here that it is possible for people to earn or own "too much money," which then in turn results in American Leftists insisting that Big Government step in to tax these people into financial oblivion. All that process does is enrich government and grow the bureaucracy—a request which a liberal government is all too happy to oblige. That's not the source of the discourse.

The Unholy Land

But rather, Aquinas explains how the management of money is *governed,* not managed by government, but kept in balance by two virtues. These two virtues, when actively applied, prevent both greed and poverty from happening. Remove these virtues and an imbalance occurs that can cause either greed or poverty. I will call this "applied virtue."

Here is a graphic fictional example of now wealth might be governed over the course of a lifetime by the virtues of frugality and generosity according to Aquinas. This fellow started out relatively poor, and had some success some 20 years into his career. Then he hit some hard times but was able to recover. His recovery was rapid and rewarding, and he found himself with more money than he could ever spend. As net worth exceeds a certain point of the person in this chart (you would have to determine that point) then the virtue of generosity is applied. Likewise for the virtue of frugality at the lower end.

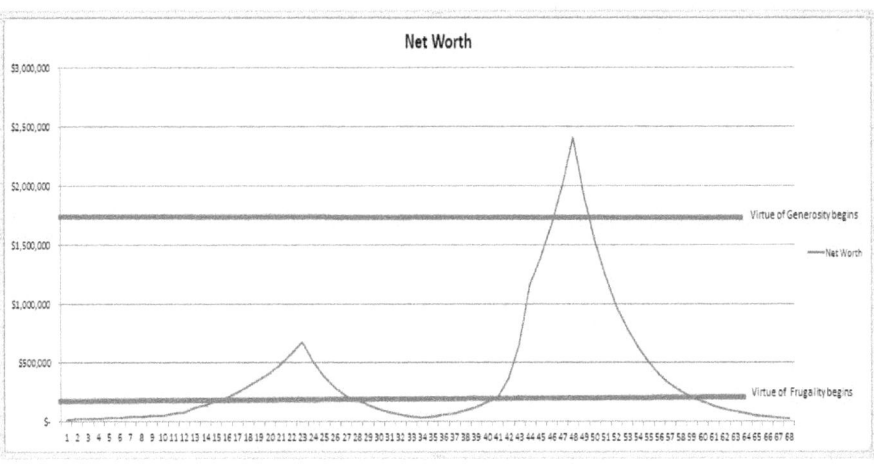

Following Aquinas, if you have achieved a station in life whereby you possess a business or money that is far more than you can ever spend or your children could even need, then the virtue of *generosity* is applied as a kind of "upper guardrail." When that is "hit" it is virtuous to find ways to execute a course of action--of generosity for the amounts above that line. Virtue being applied here prevents personal and corporate greed. (This does not mean writing a check to some art museum in December in order to get a tax deduction.)

At the other end of the spectrum, if money is in short supply in one's life or business, frugality is the virtue to be applied and becomes the "lower guardrail" which is not to be crossed. If your business is in this circumstance, you don't go out and borrow money for a fleet of new company cars, for example. Virtue being applied here prevents personal poverty or corporate bankruptcy. In my opinion, it could have prevented the circumstances that ended up putting American taxpayers on the hook to pay for what is now the $16.8 trillion bank bailout that began in 2008.[389] The subsequent bailout is not so much an example of greed, but actual theft and remains the single largest heist in the history of the civilized world.

This applied virtue may indeed seem a foreign concept for Americans today. If we look at outcomes around us it would be hard to argue against that conclusion. We cannot even be certain that Americans even possessed these Aquinas-defined virtues from the start, the tools that keep and maintain balance in life.

Thomas Jefferson was worried about the pursuit of money and the resultant greed taking over the country as a complete distraction to the maintenance of American liberty when he wrote:

"From the conclusion of this war we shall be going down hill. It will not then be necessary to resort every moment to the people for support. They will be forgotten therefore, and their rights disregarded. They will forget themselves, but in the sole faculty of making money, and will never think of uniting to effect a due respect for their rights.[390]"

Commerce has become so perverse that one can re-translate the Holy Bible—a free and universal text for all mankind— copyright it, print it, market it, and extract profits in exclusivity for a great number of years. Yes, even the marketing of the Holy Scriptures has become a grand profit center for publishers. It's a wonder why we don't have 10,000 "translations" on the market today.

An example of how these virtues are applied: Many liberal politicians in America sell the idea to their voters that government must be empowered to take from the wealthy through taxation to "give to the poor." This of course is the policy of redistribution and breeds a culture of class warfare used to garner votes and enrich government. It is wrong because it is not the constitutional occupation for American government to weaponize the tax code and redistribute wealth. That course is plainly unjust.

Not only that but Americans do not realize that corporations do not pay taxes, but they merely pass them along in their products—goods and services paid for by the consumer. In effect, the consumers pay all corporate taxes. Any person wanting to deal with the greed of corporations though promoting increased taxation is only asking to pay higher prices as a consumer.

What is corporate America to do about these virtues? Do we continue to ignore our own responsibility for it? Most Americans have, but I know one company founder who has not. In spite of the deck being stacked against consumers and average Americans, a few folks are providing examples of leadership in managing business in a just pattern, one where virtue is the rule instead of being ignored.

I had a chance to meet and spend some time with Mr. Bob Moore, the late founder of Bob's Red Mill in Milwaukie, Oregon. The first thing I noticed upon meeting him was that he seemed content and filled with joy. He seemed a happy man, and he had reason to be—at 89, he was achieving his full potential in life, and was helping others do the same. Mr. Moore loved thoughtful conversation, and would engage you in any subject you wish to discuss. Talking with Mr. Moore was always positive; one can tell that even when he talks about his past challenges, he had no regrets. He followed his passion and his hard work at it made him a success.

Mr. Moore was a well-traveled and learned man of many interests, and he had one message for corporate America: *"People Before Profit."* After an active life of working and building his natural foods business against some of the worst odds, he had become successful at milling some of the finest products on the market today. In a time when American business is ruled by corporate greed, Mr. Moore set an example of responsible ownership and just compensation.

Mr. Moore had a remarkable story to tell in his book titled, *"People Before Profits"* by Ken Koopman. In this book we learn of the hard work and setbacks to achieve Mr. Moore's vision. We learn that in 1981, his mill was destroyed by fire and at the age of sixty, he decided to rebuild it all rather than call it quits. This was because of his twenty employees whom he dearly loved, who had helped him build his business would be unemployed if Mr. Moore simply walked away. Miraculously, the only thing of value to survive the fire were his hard to find millstones, covered by piles of loose grain that fell on them during the fire, insulating them from the damaging heat.

At the age of eighty-one, he converted his company to an Employee Stock Ownership Plan or ESOP—he gave it away to his employees, "because it was the right thing to do," he said to me. For this I count him as remarkable, an American hero of business who is not ruled by greed, but governed by the virtue of generosity. Every employee receives a profit sharing check every month in addition to their wages. The company donates to a number of charitable causes and has a full time employee to manage their philanthropy.

It almost seems like Aquinas is describing Bob's Red Mill when he writes about business as being "made to serve honorable and necessary goals." Why? Because this is exactly what Mr. Moore has done with his mill. After seeing it for myself and understanding the organization, I would wish a similar type of business for all Americans if I could. What he has done there is both sustainable and inspiring.

Mr. Moore has set the bar high for corporate America to take notice. Every American corporate officer should read his book. Here we see an example of applied virtue in America, one shining example in a dimly lit world.

American business is likely to take exception to the admonitions of Aquinas and the course of action by Mr. Moore. In fact, we might here personify all "American business" into a general fictional entity called Mr. Business, or simply "Mr. B." so that we can work out some issues here.

Mr. B.: "These are great concepts, but American business can't work that way, Mr. Rundquist."

Me: "Really? Why is that?"

Mr. B: "Because employees lack the investment funds we need to drive growth. Only investors with deep pockets can invest with the capital we need to help us achieve our goals."

Me: "Is that so? Why do you say that employees lack investment funds? What causes that to be so?"

Mr. B. "Well, it's because they are irresponsible with their money."

Me: "I see. A married working couple raising a child or two, which is of a great expense to them (and a benefit to society), is too irresponsible with the large disposable income they have left after paying for the food, clothing, child care, medicine, medical bills, income taxes, property taxes, sales tax, excise taxes, insurance, house payment, home repairs and maintenance, car payment, car maintenance, interest, power bill, water bill, gas bill...."

Mr. B.: "Hey that's not fair! We didn't tell anybody to have children. That was their choice. We give you a job and a paycheck! We pay their wages and contribute 1% to a 401(k) for them. We're the good guys!"

Me: "But without a constant supply of children, demand for your products and services would eventually dry up, right? So you do rely upon Americans having children to sell your products. And wow, you think my paycheck is not 'earnings' for the services I provide, but a 'gift' from you? That's laughable. When someone gives you a gift do you work for it, too? The employee "gives" you over 2,000 irreplaceable and priceless hours of his life every year. As for the 401(k) a person making $40,000 a year before taxes, you give them a whopping $400 for retirement, not much more than a dollar a day—which will also be taxed later. That's not realistic retirement savings there and you well know it. It won't be enough to even pay their property taxes when they get old. Have you ever had to replace a set of tires on your car before winter comes and the kids need new warm clothes at the same time you need to fill the fuel oil for your furnace while all the other bills are still due? Has that ever happened?"

Mr. B: "Well, no, I have a company car, which is entirely tax deductible as a business expense."

Me: "Right you are. And your position is that these families are just bad money managers, right? They are too stupid to manage money? Do you try to hire stupid people?"

Mr. B.: "Well, not particularly, we want the best and the brightest people running our enterprises."

Me: "So are these the same people you claim are irresponsible with their money?"

The Unholy Land

Mr. B: "Well you are twisting my words now. People make choices with money, that's all I'm saying."

Me: "No I'm really not. If these folks truly lack funds as they do, after all their bills and taxes are paid every month, would that not indicate that there is a wage issue?"

Mr. B. "What do you mean 'a wage issue?' We pay the most competitive wages for our sectors. We have no problem hiring or retaining employees."

Me: "So you pay them the minimum they will accept to work for you because that is the market for wages. Wages reach the equilibrium between supply and demand? And you think that is just and honorable because it's a 'fair market price?' "

Mr. B.: "Of course it is. Whatever the market bears. It's the American way!"

Me: "Because the labor market, it's kind of like a market for indentured servants, then? People bid themselves out to whatever they can get for their lives and you just shop for the best deal, right?"

Mr. B: "NO, we want every worker to be compensated fairly."

Me: "Their wages are another tax-deductible expense for you, and you are capitalizing on their labor a hundredfold return from what you pay them. Is this the fairness you mean?"

Mr. B: "You don't understand. Markets are complex and you are oversimplifying things to make a point that simply can't be made."

Me: "Am I? So now I'm also too stupid to be able to formulate a question? You didn't even answer my question."

Mr. B. "What is fair is what I say it is. If I make a million dollars in profit a day and I only have to spend $15,000 a day on all the wages, I think that's fair if they are willing to work. No one is forcing them to work here. And as far as tax-deductions go, we don't even pay any taxes. We just pass along whatever taxes are levied on us directly onto our customers. If we can reduce the impact of taxes with our deductions we do so in order to stay competitive in the marketplace."

Me: "Yeah, right. No one is forcing them to work except their need to eat and provide for their families as best they can. They could choose not work and starve, yes? Just another 'choice,' right?" And we can now add your corporate taxes to the long list of things that the family has to pay when they buy your products.

Mr. B: "Well they can take it or leave it. It's all perfectly legal."

Me: "It's legal because you pay lobbyists to motivate our politicians to get the laws and regulations you need in place to support your business. But no matter what, your employees will never have enough money to be able to stay out of debt or save up. They will never have money to invest by trading hours for dollars—and you'll see to that. That's what keeps them working for you. I am certain that Mr. Bob Moore would beg to differ with you on that opinion."
...

Today there is a renewed debate of Capitalism v. Marxism. The Eastern Orthodox Church, or at least a representative of one jurisdiction has weighed in in this controversy;

"The desire for self-enrichment as the highest goal of life, as well as self-satisfied social egoism, are repugnant to the Christian worldview.
Moreover, the quasi-religiosity ascribed to both capitalism and Marxism is equally unacceptable. For all its talk of creating a paradise on earth, communism and aggressive social justice led to something quite different. We, who have passed the era of communism, know well that the idea of social justice, turned into an aggressive ideology, destroys everything around itself. Hundreds of thousands lawlessly executed for their faith, the creation of a social ghetto for hostile classes—this is the reality of the 'communist paradise on earth.'

However, the capitalist Gospel of accumulation of wealth and goods at any cost is no less dangerous. Any activity, including economic, must be organized on a solid moral basis, which for Christians has always been Holy Scripture and the teachings of the Church, though this is resisted by powerful forces that are ready to use any means to prevent the domination of Divine ideas in the minds of our contemporaries."[391]

His Holiness Patriarch of Moscow and all Russia Kyrill

For the early Christians, it was none other than Christ Himself Who directly addressed this entire issue with the Parable of the Rich Fool

"Someone in the crowd said to him, "Teacher, tell my brother to divide the inheritance with me." Jesus replied, "Man, who appointed me a judge or an arbiter between you?" Then he said to them, "Watch out! Be on your guard against all kinds of greed; life does not consist in an abundance of possessions." And he told them this parable: "The ground of a certain rich man yielded an abundant harvest. He thought to himself, 'What shall I do? I have no place to store my crops."' Then he said, 'This is what I'll do. I will tear down my barns and build bigger ones, and there I will store my surplus grain. And I'll say to myself, "You have plenty of grain laid up for many years. Take life easy; eat, drink and be merry."' "But God said to him, 'You fool! This very night your life will be demanded from you. Then who will get what you have prepared for yourself?' "This is how it will be with whoever stores up things for themselves but is not rich toward God."

Luke 12 13-21

Know that this call to applied virtue is not a suggestion, but for Christians, it is a commandment: "Masters, do to your servants that which is just and equal: knowing that you also have a master in heaven."

Colossians 4:1
Douay-Rheims Bible

Americans should be careful and cautious when dealing with issues and policies around wealth. The nation is slipping into Oligarchy; away from a Representative Republic and the nation is doomed. Plato indicates that an oligarchy, the rule of a few (the wealthy), leads to:

"...a city of the rich and a city of the poor, dwelling together, and always plotting against one another. . . . [The government] will not be able to wage war, because of the necessity of either arming and employing the multitude, and fearing them more than the enemy, or else, if they do not make use of them, of finding themselves on the field of battle . . . And to this must be added their reluctance to contribute money, because they are lovers of money."[392]

Virtue, in a nutshell

My generic description is that virtue derives from the applied will of man to resist his normal sinful and abusive nature and commit each day to place others above self; to value absolute honesty and integrity above corruption; to uphold the common values and principles of the rule of just laws (a republic) instead of clamoring for the easy path of rule by man (a dictatorship).

From virtue springs justice, responsibility, education, accountability, common sense, honesty and liberty. From unity we get courage, community, independence and inter-dependence, charity, compassion, brotherhood, strength, fortitude, and peace.

Should Americans be successful in restoring their virtue, what might be the result? We can use the outline shown at the earlier part of the text to illustrate a best outcome, which is the modern politician's nightmare scenario:

- **Virtue**, contributing to
  - Clear comprehension of the rule of law, contributing to
    - Justice; consistent application of the rule of law
      - Social harmony
    - Ethical standards, contributing to:
      - Clear representation of the law to the public
      - Competent elected officials at all levels
      - The rise of statesmen instead of politicians
        - Effective and just domestic public policies created
          - Political peace
          - Meaningful and tolerant discourse and debate
        - Effective international policy

- - - Peace
      - Fair trade policies
      - Graft and corruption end
      - Public debt is erased methodically
    - Selflessness
  - Charity mindset, contributing to:
    - Corporate generosity
    - Honorable elected officials who are personally generous
    - Stabilization of personal wealth
      - Increase in the standard of living
      - Abortion is reduced as families are able to afford raising children.
        - Systematic infanticide ends.
        - Crime is reduced greatly as jobs are available and preferred over a life of crime.
          - Creation of intergenerational family values
          - Ease on the judicial and penal systems
        - Encourages "hopefulness" which contributes to
          - Home ownership
          - The end of substance abuse and addiction
          - Reduction in Crime (see above)
          - Wise life choices concerned with outcomes.
            - Intergenerational wealth cycle
    - Economic strength
      - Resurrection of the "American Dream" with a new, ever-changing, higher standard.
      - Independence from government for education
        - Increases free thought, speech, and new ideas
        - Outcomes for students are now limitless
        - Factual realities replace "Public opinion" polls
      - Independence from government for subsistence
        - Individual rights and liberty are strengthened

These are precisely the outcomes that American Leftists both fear and work against.

Localizing Unity

The political class in America works overtime to convince us that our neighbor is so diametrically opposed to our views that there is no common ground and we should hate each other. The American people are being played.

I was once asked if I thought relationships with others had impacted my life and if so, how. Well, of course they have. Relationships are both valuable and necessary in life. You may have relationships with people who agree with you and support you. In this case, folks confirm your life choices and direction and that builds confidence.

Confidence empowers you to act boldly towards your goals in life, which is important because that leads to achievement in life—the results of setting reachable goals and doing the necessary work to see them through to completion. But there is something else to consider. Americans might also benefit from relationships with those with whom we somewhat differ.

If all the people in your life agree with everything you say and do all the time, it's easy to create a kind of meaningless echo chamber where all you do is hear how right you are all the time, even when you are demonstrably wrong. This can be hazardous at critical times in your life, and even can cause a blind spot in your thinking or approach to issues. Everyone has these little blind spots, especially when it comes to things like ideology, politics, and religion. We often believe what we want to believe out of convenience, pride, or just personal preference whether there is fact behind it or not. That's not to say that these beliefs are always untrue. Often, they are. But we must learn how to have an honest civil discourse—"just because I don't agree with you doesn't mean that I hate you."

Relationships are also naturally affected by time. When we are born and while being raised, all of our most meaningful relationships are with people older than us. Parents, grandparents, other relatives, pastors, teachers, coaches, and so on all influence our young lives. Later, these relationships end as folks move away, pass away, and so on. The relationships we develop in our own generational group take their place. These must last us the duration of our lives and so, I would argue, that are too valuable to simply throw away over some trivial disagreement on an issue.

I have a best friend who is nearly my political opposite. We don't agree straight down the line on almost anything. The friendship survives because we had established a ground rule a decades ago to "agree to disagree" whenever it becomes apparent that an issue we are discussing is at an impasse. That's ok. We do have many common values, interests, common thought processes, etc. The advantage of the symbiotic relationship is that we are both able to openly bounce thoughts, plans, concepts, ideas against a person who we know may challenge us to perhaps think about something in a different way. This does not always result in agreement of course, but it can be a valuable process leading to adjustment or even correction in plans, or a confirmation that the correct or best option was in motion at the start.

Either way, it's a substantive relationship, even when we must "agree to disagree" on some matters of politics or religion—subjects which neither of us can solve individually anyway. Instead, these issues would become only a matter of will and debate prowess. In such matters, arguing "who's right" or "who's wrong" to the point where we soon devolve to taking bare-knuckled blows makes no sense and would destroy the relationship—over an outcome that doesn't even really matter. We instead place a high value on the friendship—and like what's left of our teeth too much to allow things to go that way.

These values are indeed supported by Jeffersonian thought, when he wrote:

"I never considered a difference of opinion in politics, in religion, in philosophy, as cause for withdrawing from a friend."[393]

This is precisely the kind of process now vacant from the American general social landscape of today. Everyone wants to be "right." Few, if any, will want to stop talking long enough to hear anything that anyone else is saying, let alone take time to consider it. For an extreme example of what happens when people stop listening consider ANTIFA, an enemy of the state comprised of militant left wing Fascists and anarchists. They will listen to nothing and force their voice, and only their voice into the public square.

ANTIFA Members will violently beat down anyone who challenges them. Their followers are people who hate America and accept no debate or discussion on any issue. They are a danger to the country, and they know it, because it is their goal to overthrow it. They use fear and intimidation to silence anyone who would disagree with them or ask them to debate an issue. They don't want any debate; they want conformity to their view alone. We cannot allow America to accept this as a standard.

It is my hope that Americans can develop relationships with an open mind and avoid the comfortable "echo chamber" of familiarity. Don't throw away relationships when you have a disagreement on an issue just because that is the easy path that feels good at the moment. Walking away or pushing your detractors away is not always the best course. Instead, set a standing guideline with that person in the open. Tell them up front, "we may not agree, but when this happens, lets 'agree to disagree' and just let that go" without offense. Both of you are personally better served this way in the long term.

However, even this procedure of "agreeing to disagree" on irreconcilable matters has one major flaw. While it may preserve the relationship it does nothing to actually resolve a problem or improve a permanent unity. Instead, it merely serves to avoid conflict and temporarily pacify emotional responses to conflict

Consider the differences between James and Paul in the Bible. James was head of the Church in Jerusalem where Christian converts (again, "followers of the Nazarene...") were mostly Jewish meaning that they held to the Jewish customs and law at the same time following the message of Christ. They were Jews who were adopting the teachings of Christ, not abandoning Judaism first.

St. Paul, on the other hand, went on to plant churches abroad. His churches were scattered across a non-Jewish pagan landscape. These converts had no interest in following the Jewish customs but were much interested in Christ. So the question quickly arose between James and St. Paul as to whether Christians had to keep the Jewish Law at the same time professing to be Christians. If they merely "agreed to disagree" on the matter and did not finally settle it, the Christian Church today might look quite different.

Likewise, in 1573 the Lutherans contacted the Eastern Orthodox Church in an attempt to unify the Church with them. They soon supplied the Ecumenical Patriarch Jeremias II with a copy of their own new statement of faith, the *Augsburg Confession*—in Greek. But the differences between them were too far to broad. The Eastern Orthodox were still following the ancient Traditions of the faith, including the Nicene-Constantinopolitan Creed which was canonized in A.D. 381--the same one they continue to hold to this day.

The differences with the Lutherans in 1573 centered on the role of sacred Tradition of the Church and the rulings of ecumenical church councils, the *Filioque* clause ("from the son") that the Western church had added to the Nicene Creed, prayer to the saints, veneration of icons, prayers for the dead, and the number of sacraments. (Lutherans accepted only two: Baptism and Communion, while discarding the rest).

After three years of correspondence it became apparent in 1576 that there simply was no way to close the gap between the Lutherans and the Eastern Orthodox Church:[394]

"When Jeremias saw that union was out of the question, he ended the exchange of letters: 'Go your own way, and do not write any more on doctrinal matters; and if you do write, write only for friendship's sake.'"[395]

Of course both Lutheran and Orthodox remain apart today. While the Lutherans created their own dogma and doctrine and continue to modify it, the canonical Eastern Orthodox Christians do not change dogma, doctrine, or any of the Traditions. Their continuity on this has been demonstrated for two thousand years.

Disunity breeds division and despair

In the same vein, Americans simply "agreeing to disagree" would not be good enough at a time when our nation needs a genuine unity above all. We have been separated by pundits and politicians alike into little groups. The largest division of these groups is "Liberal" and "Conservative." They do this out of political expediency so they can manipulate the populace and more effectively assert control by projecting their power. Why? Again, it's "divide and conquer" as we have seen so many times before.

It is this lack of applied virtue that has facilitated intergenerational poverty, all driven by greed and graft. The response from the people is dismay, confusion, hunger, and blame. This is where the Socialists in America step in to answer the call—rather to point the blame at their own political enemies and then proceed to use the people to execute a plan born to destroy the nation that Socialists despise, our Republic. This begins with divisions of classes, races, and so on until the nation is so filled with disunity that the people are incapable of action in a unified manner against an oppressive government.

The Unholy Land

It is not difficult to discover the root cause of disunity in America. It is a seed sown and cultivated by the very same people to whom we entrust to operation of our government; politicians. We have indeed witnessed much disunity in our nation at an increasing rate over the past several decades. This is no accident. Politicians perpetually promise an increasing number of the electorate an ever-expanding menu of "free" things; SNAP benefits, housing subsidies, college loans and grants, and healthcare to name a few. But they also promise to extend these things to the tens of millions of illegal aliens invading our nation. These policies are totally unjust, financially irresponsible, and mathematically unsustainable—and they all know it.

The politicians have promised these things so often that it is now expected by an ever more dependent electorate to hear what more they can expect to get from government if they elect or reelect whatever politician. Who doesn't like "free" stuff? This mindset is not American. In fact, it is the opposite of American. Does anyone recall the words of the once-favorite Democrat President, John F. Kennedy, who famously said in his 1961 Inaugural address:

"And so, my fellow Americans: ask not what your country can do for you — ask what you can do for your country...My fellow citizens of the world: ask not what America will do for you, but what together we can do for the freedom of man...Finally, whether you are citizens of America or citizens of the world, ask of us the same high standards of strength and sacrifice which we ask of you. With a good conscience our only sure reward, with history the final judge of our deeds, let us go forth to lead the land we love, asking His blessing and His help, but knowing that here on earth God's work must truly be our own."[396]

No, modern Washington Democrats have abandoned this statement long ago. They, along with their Leftist pals have reeducated an entire generation of Americans into believing that they are entitled to have some other American pay for everything they need or want. Our youngest generations now fully expect "free everything" because that's what has been taught to the young and gullible, cloaked in the false, unconstitutional Utopian ideals of "equality", "justice," "compassion" and "fairness." A mantra taught by academia, promoted by the media, promised by politicians, and forcibly paid for by others.

Consider the example of the town of Stockton, California. Their Socialist Utopia suffered the predictable bankruptcy in 2012. Not convinced that their Socialist policies failed to produce the promised positive results for the citizens (they apparently blame a series of external forces, like automation), they have now doubled down on Socialism and are instituting a universal "basic wage" by which residents of certain qualifications (read democrat voters) will receive a "basic wage" of $500 per month[397]. The program does not require the recipients to work to receive the money, which is now being privately funded as Stockton is still out of cash. Still, the 27-year old mayor believes that it's a great idea, and why shouldn't he? It's what he just learned from the Socialist teachers in school.

Unfortunately, this Utopian farce can never become reality, financially or otherwise. It is not how the world works, and it never will be because it is not comprised of any sound financial judgement. The facts of life are conservative, and when this promised Utopia never materializes then the affected groups become angry and violent. They are faced with two options: to accept that what they have been taught all their young lives is a complete lie, or to accept that the promises made to them reflect some justifiable mandate to fight any who would oppose it. Those who choose the latter separate themselves from the rest of America ideologically and become their enemies. Disunity has now been institutionalized!

The most extreme of these will march; they protest, they riot, they commit many crimes and pledge to never stop until their demands are met. It's mob rule for these. They trample the flag, trash our Bible, infiltrate our schools, churches, and public offices—and the shred our Constitution while calling for "social justice," and for revolution. They welcome Fascism and anything else if they see it will be useful in their fight, and they act in complete disregard for the laws of the United States and the rights of its citizens. Are these not the same scenes we have witnessed pouring across our TV screens for the past ten years, and daily in 2020 as we watched city after city be burned by them?

What is wrong with my church?

Apart from the aforementioned items, there may be a few serious warning signs to look for at church:

- Is the pastor the focal point or the most popular central figure or focus of your church? Does everyone "love" the pastor and his family and discuss fascinations and minutiae about him more than other people in service to the church? Does the congregation act as though the church "would not be the same" without him? A church that is so centered on its pastor, minister, or priest is by definition not centered on Christ.
- Do the church leaders, deacons, or committees meet or act in secrecy? This is problematic for many obvious reasons. Are they so ashamed of their decisions and policies that they must conceal them from their own church body?
- Are there many groups of opposing factions or "cliques" in the church? Often these divisions occur over questions of doctrine or simple allocations of funds. "A house divided against itself cannot stand."
- Does your church feel the need to have political or civic "statements" addressing proposed legislation, existing laws and other political issues? Do they support or decry any political candidates or public policy measures?
- Does your church follow its own rules, or are the rules (and the Bible itself) bent or ignored? Without firm and defined standards, what is the point in any of it?

These are all common issues found in many Protestant churches in America today, and they are often at the root of what is destroying them. It's why they continue to fragment into more and more protestant churches that oppose each other.

The Christian church seems to have doomed itself to long term failure in America, a result in many cases of simply choosing not to focus on the message and mission of Christ, but rather customizing the message of the Bible to suit lifestyles. Many denominations simply aim to push political messages or to avoid offending people or to simply attract new members and try keep the money flowing.

One would think that these failing strategies would be obvious to the churches as ultimately self-destructive but that has not happened in enough cases to force a true and widespread abandonment of modern Protestantism. We could actually argue that many churches have in fact reformed---they have reformed from Christianity into Political Action Committees, and are allowed a tax-free status to do it, all while pretending the endorsement of Jesus Christ to their members.

When these churches substitute their own plans and motives in place of God's, the result is an unholy affiliation, a secular club instead of a holy church. I can't think that it will end well, either in the short or long term.

Across all these many "versions" of Christianity there is little if any common unity. Think about a secular example here: civics. Could there possibly be 45,000[398] varying versions of the United States Constitution that Americans would attempt to enact? Would that not by definition render the government practically useless? Where is the standard then? The glaring and seemingly unsolvable problem with Christianity is that while there exactly one Christ, and He established one Holy Church, Americans have little notion as to where it is today.

We like to believe, or in some cases pretend, that it's the church down the street which is the one true Church. Why do we do that? If I had to guess, I'd say because it's easy, it's convenient, and frankly, it's comfortable. The pastor there is under some degree of pressure to preach those messages which are acceptable to the members of the church and the community at large. If he goes outside the lines, the church will eventually fire him and hire a pastor that gives them what they want to hear.

In contrast to all these statements and positions is the simple and clear language of the mission statement of the Orthodox Church of America (OCA):

"THE MISSION OF THE ORTHODOX CHURCH IN AMERICA, the local autocephalous Orthodox Church, is to be faithful in fulfilling the commandment of Christ to "Go into all the world and make disciples of all Nations, baptizing them in the name of the Father, and of the Son and of the Holy Spirit, teaching them to observe all [things that He has] commanded" so that all people may be saved and come to the knowledge of the truth: To preach, in accordance with God's will, the fullness of the gospel of the Kingdom to the peoples of North America and to invite them to become members of the Orthodox Church. To utilize for her mission the various languages of the peoples of this continent. To be the body of Christ in North America and to be faithful to the tradition of the Holy Orthodox Church. To witness to the truth, and by God's grace and in the power of the Holy Spirit, to reveal Christ's way of sanctification and eternal salvation to all."[399]

This seems to me to be a refreshing and straightforward approach to the Christian Faith, and unlike many of the approaches of the Protestant organizations we have examined, and of those we have not. The Orthodox apparently did not get the full memo on supporting efforts to end global warming, support for collective bargaining rights, the responsibility in promoting abortion, and all the rest. I'm perplexed as to why only after decades of church-going, I am only now first learning of this.

An Epidemic of Ignorance

There is an old adage that says, "God gave us wars to teach Americans geography." Perhaps God also inflicted us with 45,000 conflicting denominations to teach Christians about faith as well, so that we could eventually ask why and learn our history. In the vacuum of our ignorance, and with the aid of our pride, we eagerly fill the void with our own ideas, doctrines, dogmas, practices, and imagery that serves our own opinions, our decisions by a local majority, and our own denominational preferences rather than follows anything resembling a Holy Christian Church canon.

Both America and the Christian Church are in desperate need of unity. We have managed our own versions of the Faith for the entirety of the American experience and that has gotten us absolutely nowhere. Yes, some "good" has come from churches in America but we are no closer to the Kingdom of God and in many respects seem to have made a mockery of it. Is it possible that this vast array of conflicting denominations no longer attracts and retains people because the lack of authenticity is evident?

Churches were divided long before America and today they have evolved into a plethora of competing groups also promising a litany of fantasy ideals that can never be met by a church. A local church near me states their position in the community this way:

"Neither can we hang a sign outside our church, literally nor symbolically, that says "No fundamentalists" or "No liberals" or "No Doubters" or "Only Those Who Have It All Together" or "Pro-life Only" or "Pro-choice Only" or "No Blacks" or "No Beards." Our attitude must be a sign that invites all to gather here, to seek God, to join in worship, and to share in our small group ministries. We should deliberately invite honest seekers and candid strugglers, including those who may think, act, or look differently than we do. We invite all to consider with us who Jesus Christ is and what he has done, and to study the Scriptures with us as our primary and ultimate authority for faith and life.[400] "

The pastor who wrote this might think he is clever, but Christ called all to repentance, not to modern "inclusiveness" which is a cloak and code for the very social movements aimed at destroying Christianity from within. We need unity if we are to be effective in filling our larger role of educating the public on the desperate need and merits of virtue in the community. We also need to show people what those two words mean for genuine Christians.

However, it is a deceptively positive statement because the crafty author of it writes partly in coded language, "No Liberals" is quite broad, but if he instead listed the dogmas that liberals demand (such as pro-abortion, for example) then the statement for including them and their ideas at your church would not seem so grand. What about people who "look differently than we do," –just who is he talking about? Martians? Extremely tall people? Subterranean survivalists from Utah? Who are these people to him that do not look like normal, average people? Seems like coded language for transgenderism to me, given the political climate we live in.

The problem here is that the meanings of inclusions and diversity today are such that Christians are expected to accept the person *and to accommodate* their habits into the Christian Church. There is no change of behavior expected, no repentance, because the sinful behavior must be accepted, normalized and even adopted by the church, or else the church becomes automatically guilty of the some imaginary (non-Biblical) sin of discrimination or "exclusion." In such cases, the pastors and leaders can be prosecuted under the laws for such things as refusing to marry homosexuals, and so on. The very same liberals who DEMAND a strictly enforced "separation of church and state" then turn around and have Fascist laws passed to have the same government force Christian churches to perform gay weddings and accept gay clergy or suffer the penalty of law. So much for "separation of church and state."

Genuine Christians cannot be expected to sacrifice Christ's standards for the false and popular hope of a politically expedient unity. The cost to the Church in doing so is simply too high—this results in disunity between the churches that move to condone the behaviors and those that will not. There are in fact Biblical standards which rub us the wrong way. That may be considered unfortunate, but we didn't invent the church or write the Bible, so Christians are not in a position to apologize for Christian standards or Biblical content.

For those upset about the Bible and its unchanging standards, they could simply just not bother the Christians and go off to do their own thing at some other religion. But instead, this has led to non-Christians infiltrating churches and demanding that the members accept their ways; same-sex marriage, abortion, and all the rest. This disunity inside the church body tears it apart and destroys it, which we now understand as precisely the aim to begin with.

St. Paul in his letter to the Corinthians explains the same idea, warning the church about the problems with this very thing:

"I wrote to you in an epistle, not to keep company with fornicators. I mean not with the fornicators of this world, or with the covetous, or the extortioners, or the servers of idols; otherwise you must needs go out of this world. But now I have written to you, not to keep company, if any man that is named a brother, be a fornicator, or covetous, or a server of idols, or a railer, or a drunkard, or an extortioner: with such a one, not so much as to eat. For what have I to do to judge them that are without? Do not you judge them that are within? For them that are without, God will judge. Put away the evil one from among yourselves.

1 Corinthians 5:9-13

Douay-Rheims Bible

And I am certain that clever men have been able to explain this away in order to achieve a more popular and inclusive view, as we see evident in the church statement that I quoted above. The man who crafted that statement is just such a sophist.

We are sometimes led to believe that this instruction of St. Paul's to the Corinthians seems to fly in the face of Christianity. Jesus Christ died to defeat the penalty of all the sins of all men. He included us all. He dined with tax collectors and prostitutes. But that is not what this is about. St. Paul is talking about church discipline[401] and focus, not politically correct inclusion and misguided notions of equality that are now used as tool to destroy the church itself by making the Church into something it is not.

Take the present example; the same church that proudly carries this quoted motto is also affiliated with a denomination that supports liberal anti-American political causes, such as illegal "immigrant's rights" and even carved out Sunday, May 6th 2018 as "Immigrant Rights Sunday 2018" where "...congregations are encouraged to...explore avenues to advocate for immigrant justice..." and are offered a list of "...most current issues this year on immigration with potential ways to get involved to limit deportations and unnecessary detentions of immigrants.[402]"

Question: Which of these statements was made by St. John Chrysostrom?

"They say that these are fugitives, foreigners, and wretches; That they've left their homelands in order to gather in our city....How will we be worthy of forgiveness? What kind of defense can we offer, when, through their financial assistance [Paul and Barnabus] fed people living far away and made haste to help them, whereas we want to expel those who've come from afar and we demand detailed explanations?"

Or...

"They say that these are fugitives, foreigners, and wretches; That they've left their homelands in order to gather in our city....How will we be worthy of forgiveness? What kind of defense can we offer? Through their tireless efforts [Paul and Barnabus] worked to help such as these to break the laws of the Romans, they demanded that the Roman government change their immigration laws and abuse Roman taxpayers to feed people living far away; they made haste to protest the nation's laws and to publicity disparage any who would not agree to spend the public treasury and go into debt to help them. Surely we must do more than this to subvert civil authorities and put down the people for the cause we believe in."

Remember that Christ was a respectful of the *civic laws* of the Romans (*"...render unto Caesar what is Caesars..."*) He neither championed the Roman laws, nor led protests for changing them. The religious laws of the Jews were another matter. Immigration laws of the United States are a civic matter. If churches want to support "poor immigrants" let them indeed provide such support as they see fit.

Remember that every single church, including the Vatican presently has more money than the United States Government. Frankly we know that many of these "poor immigrants" are illegal aliens who hate the citizens of the United States and should be considered dangerous as part of an invading force. They do not come to the U.S. to assimilate and accept our culture and our rule of law, they come here to dismantle our institutions and conquer us. That's a fact, not an opinion; ask them.

This denomination also fully embraces marriages of heterosexual, gay, lesbian, bisexual, transgender people, urging their members and leaders to "support equal marriage rights for couples regardless of gender.[403]" Again, as with the other denominations, I could continue to list a whole series of leftist, non-Biblical positions adopted and pushed by this denomination. Is this Church about Christ? Nope. It's just another polluted denomination in the deep swamp of pseudo-Christianity, using the attraction of Christ to push their Leftist political agenda on unsuspecting Americans, and they indeed "speak with forked tongue."

All of this is accepted and condoned by the affected denominations because of the original departure from truth with the principle of Sola Scriptura. Biblical truth now is whatever you want it to be.

A Common Denominator for Americans

If civic unity is all I would propose, then I might be careful what I wish for. Communists are really good at unity, and so were the Fascists and the Nazis of the 20th Century. They instilled unity by fear and force, eliminated outliers with torture and firing squads—but it was "unity" albeit through strict conformity. American unity must instead be again guided by the principles of Christ that were harkened to at our Founding.

While examining the cure for the American cultural decline, we must carefully discard the notion of creating a second Byzantium—an empirical Christian Theocracy. It might sound pretty good on paper, but in practice is contrary to the establishment of a representative republic like America. While Judeo-Christian principles must play a central role in our culture, these cannot be permitted to overtake or replace the rule of law in America. There are a lot of sound and responsible American citizens who are not Christians. We cannot—and should not— install an "American Pope" as our lifelong president—one who is "co-gerent with Christ" as the Byzantines thought their emperors to be.[w] The outcome would be similar to that of the Byzantines (or worse) to be sure.

With many of the American churches on their own steady decline, there is not much probability of this happening anyway unless this "American Pope" is to be of some other single faith that suddenly skyrockets into popularity. Suffice to say it's a bad idea and should be rejected out of hand whenever that discussion arises.

The Founders and Framers of America understood that they could not "legislate" virtue and unity into law via Christianity or by any other religious means. That task is impossible. Rev. Isaac Backus, again addressing the Assembly in 1788 remarked,

"...I shall begin with the exclusion of any religious test. Many appear to be much concerned about it, but nothing is more evident, both in reason, and in the holy scriptures, than that religion is ever a matter between God and individuals, and therefore no man or men can impose any religious test, without invading the essential prerogatives of our Lord Jesus Christ. Ministers first assumed this power under the Christian name, and then Constantine approved of the practice, when he adopted the profession of Christianity, as an engine of state policy. And let the history of all nations be searched, from that day to this, and it will appear that the imposing of religious tests hath been the greatest engine of tyranny in the world."[404]

---

[w] It may be worth understanding that in Protestantism, ever individual has become their own "Pope." This was an outcome of the Reformation.

Of course reverend Backus was correct. Virtue and Unity are maintained in the hearts and minds of the people and supported by the culture of the nation, not through the state's imposition of a religious dictator. Laws proceed from these two things and serve as our "guardrails" of society. Instead we are left with three documents; the Declaration of Independence provides that basis for American unity, and it illustrates why unity in our culture is needed both then and now. It begins this way:

"The unanimous Declaration of the thirteen united States of America, When in the Course of human events, it becomes necessary for one people to dissolve the political bands which have connected them with another, and to assume among the powers of the earth, the separate and equal station to which the Laws of Nature and of Nature's God entitle them, a decent respect to the opinions of mankind requires that they should declare the causes which impel them to the separation."

And it concludes like this:

"And for the support of this Declaration, with a firm reliance on the protection of divine Providence, we mutually pledge to each other our Lives, our Fortunes and our sacred Honor."

Here we see the use of the word "unanimous" and "we." The word, "we" is used several times in the full text. So when was the last time you ever heard congress us the word, "unanimous" to describe anything? You have not, and it is because America is divided, and has been for some time.[405]

If unity is restored, we might expect a whole chain of positives to follow:

- **Unity**, when intact, contributes to
    - Selflessness & purpose.
    - Cultural colorblindness—indifference to all race.
    - Few, if any divisions along other cultural lines contributing to
        - Domestic peace and tranquility.
            - Neighbors that help each other.
                - Easing the strain of law enforcement capacity and training.
        - Harmony between Americans ("We the people" mentality).
        - Legal issues/lawsuits reduced.

- Trust between neighbors with friendships being forged.
- An informed and educated populace.
- Ability of the American people to hold government accountable in a unified manner.
  - Government is defeated in its effort to levy ultimate control over the people.
    - Individual rights are re-established.
      - The Bill of Rights is in practice.
      - Taxation is held in check by the people.
    - Government cannot establish a dictatorship.

Become uncomfortable

Remember that all through the Bible we come to understand so many examples of God's servants made uncomfortable when God wanted them to carry out a mission. In no particular order, Adam might have been a bit uncomfortable after losing a rib when God used his body to form a woman—he was certainly uncomfortable after being separated from the Garden. Noah was uncomfortable because he was not a carpenter, shipbuilder, zookeeper or a deckhand when God called him to build the Ark.

Jonah was particularly uncomfortable but for a series of external reasons. Why did Jonah initially disobey the Lord? Was Jonah simply a rebellious miscreant or could there be more to his motivation? Archaeology might be able to shed some light on why Jonah chose Tarshish instead of obeying God and heading to Nineveh.

During the "golden age" of archaeology in the 19th century, the entire area of the Levant was invaded by archaeologists and treasure hunters from all over Europe and the U.S. From 1845 to 1851 a notable English archaeologist, Austen Henry Layard discovered and excavated the remains of Biblical Nineveh. As a result of Layard's discoveries we have a much better picture of the city Jonah was instructed to preach against.

It turns out that Nineveh was indeed gigantic in scale, confirming the description of the city found in Jonah 3:3. From Layard's work we learn that Nineveh had not one city wall, but three massive walls, two moats, with the largest defensive wall spanning 200 feet high, some thirty feet thick, and fortified by 1,500 imposing watchtowers. Layard uncovered all manner of structures including huge palaces adorned with huge, dangerous looking statues of their gods and many impressive carved stone reliefs. The sheer size, scope, and architecture of Nineveh was second only to Babylon, which made it an extremely intimidating sight to any outsider.

And there was Jonah, instructed by God to preach against the established religion and practices of Nineveh's people. These were certainly not friendly people led by a benevolent government. Jonah was quite uncomfortable.

Abraham was uncomfortable when God promised him a son in his old age, then instructed him to sacrifice the boy.

Moses was uncomfortable, called to become the mouthpiece of God when he was not a leader or a public speaker. Joseph was uncomfortable when his own brothers bullied him and sold him into slavery. Mary and Joseph were uncomfortable when they had to flee to Egypt because Herod was murdering every male child in an effort to find and destroy their son. John the Baptist was uncomfortable opposing Herod's choice in women and most uncomfortable being executed. Christ was uncomfortable in so many ways...and in His ultimate service on the cross to His Father and all of mankind. Paul was uncomfortable being blinded and then imprisoned, beaten, repeatedly shipwrecked, then later executed.

When your own church seeks to make itself and its members comfortable with their doctrine, teachings, programs, traditions, leaders, and music, they may actually be working against the Holy Spirit in order to keep you pleased and attending—and donating. When you are really comfortable in your Christian faith, you might want to question why.

If you really want to see how uncomfortable Christianity is supposed to be, I encourage the reader to delve into The Lives of the Saints. There you will witness thousands of accounts of Christians who served, suffered, and often died in the worst of ways for the faith. One thing they all had in common was the lack of comfort to be sure.

For a practical guide of the application of personal Christianity beyond all of this, one might consider the instructions of Saint Basil, who wrote,

"The world...is the veil of dark flames that surround the heart and shut it out from the tree of life. The world is everything that holds us and satisfies us sensuously: that within us which has not known God (John 17:25). To the world belong our desires and impulses...Weakness for wealth and for collecting and owning things of different kinds; the urge for physical (sensuous) enjoyment; the longing for honour, which is the root of envy; the desire to conquer and be the deciding factor; pride in the glory of power; the urge to adorn oneself and to be liked; the craving for praise; concern and anxiety for physical well-being. All these are of the world; they combine deceitfully to hold us in heavy bonds. If you wish to free yourself, scrutinize yourself with the help of that list and see clearly what you have to struggle against in order to approach God. For friendship with the world is enmity with God, and whosoever therefore will be a friend of the world is the enemy of God (James 4:4). Broad vistas are attained only by leaving the narrow valley and the occupations and pleasures characteristic of the valley."[406]

Here Saint Basil clearly describes a Christianity that is not about our own comfort, but quite the opposite; a selfless religion of prayer, faith, service and obedience to the ways of Christ.[x] Is that not what genuine Christianity is supposed to be?

The Church in America

We all understand that nothing on Earth created by mankind will be perfect, because mankind is inherently flawed. This, however, cannot be accepted as any excuse for the truly un-Christ-like policies, dogmas, and behavior by any church and yet it is precisely what has occurred over two thousand years of Christianity. Many so-called Christian churches that do not follow the Gospels are simply not Christian churches. They are man-made. The stark truth is that modern Americanism and Christianity have very little in common. The genuine Christian Church is not of this Earth.

---

[x] The rest of his piece called, "On the Conquest of the World" is worth reading on your own, and I urge you to do so. It is contained in a short (110 page) collection of works titled, Way of the Ascetics: The Ancient Tradition of Discipline and Inner Growth by Tito Colliander.

The Unholy Land

What are Christians who wish to seek the truth to do? In the history of America we once took bold actions. When the established church in Europe became impossibly corrupt, oppressive, and intolerant, a group of pilgrims formed a company and sailed for a new life on a new continent far beyond the reach of it.

A hundred or so years later, the Colonies on the same continent became an injured party of the English crown. Ignored and mistreated by the monarchy the colonies declared their independence and fought a war for eight years to secure their liberty.

Who then, were the "keepers" of unity and virtue? From who will Americans and others learn these things from? There is an obvious conclusion. If in America it is as deToqueveille and others have observed—that the source of greatness is in the goodness preached from the pulpits of our Christian churches, then those "keepers" are the teachings of those who faithfully served Christ—the many Saints and Martyrs who though their lives and sacrifice for the faith illustrate for us that which we must do to restore unity and virtue in our nation. While not too complicated, the course of learning would require open eyes, an open mind, and a commitment by Americans to apply a personal course that focuses on something other than their own self-centeredness. Egos and pride have to be checked at the door.

Many churches today are plainly on the wrong track. They, like so many others over the centuries simply demand conformity rather than teaching the enlightenment of the Gospel of Christ. Because of this, I call for protesting the forms of our pathetic and politically active "Christian" churches; protesting the falsehoods of thin modern doctrine, banal rules, and useless, irrelevant egoism that excludes and separates people from the message and mission of Christ.

Like the world itself, the present church landscape of America is a flawed environment. It can be filled with self-serving people enforcing useless rules sprung from pride, ego or political agenda or with those who deliberately ignore the sound practices of the Church and the Bible because those standards interfere greatly with their lifestyles.

For as many examples of corporate church malfeasance that we may come across, there are more examples of many Christians acting out of Faith in Christ and completing the mission. This has to be due to the fact that the Christian church managers of all denominations are impossibly outnumbered by those who faithfully commit themselves to the everyday work of carrying out His mission. These are not the pagan "Christians" pretending to save the planet from global warming.

I call upon all fellow American Christians to confront their churches **only once** to abandon these non-Christian constructs and seek out our history; to learn the genuine and traditional Christianity---and I will tell you now that they will not do it in nine out of ten instances. In which case, it past time to boldly walk out and join with others who wish to only focus on the teachings and work of Christ, His Church, and His Word. It is not enough to attend the local church and "go along to get along" anymore.

Or, perhaps, what I have suggested is yet another misguided and terribly weak attempt to fix a church that is not broken. Maybe the notion of a second Reformation is going to result in the very same kind of flaws that Luther injected into the first Reformation. Perhaps it's arrogant for any human to imagine that they can offer "reform" to a holy church that is not itself man-made.

This sad state of affairs derails and obscures the genuine practice of Christianity. American Christians seem to suffer from an epidemic of pride, both personal and corporate which has resulted in an identity crisis for the faithful. Because Eastern Orthodoxy continues to deliver as it always has, a single, unified, and Apostolic Christian standard for the Faithful, it is perhaps, the last, best hope for American Christians to discover the truth of their faith and follow it.

"What is truth?"[407]

That's an excellent question in all of this. Pilate himself was not so sure he knew what the truth was between the testimony of Jesus Christ and the charges that the Jews had brought against Him. Pilate, of course, was in the position of being able to make true whatever he wanted at the moment. A high government official, a Prefect, he could either declare Christ innocent and set him free or condemn him...or make the Jewish community decide. Pilate's truth ended up being whatever he needed it to be in order to absolve himself of the blood of an innocent man.

When it comes to churches in America, we face the very same question today; "What is truth?" Indeed, what is it when it comes to our Christian faith? We have a deep pool of pride from which we draw. There is clouded confusion and a willing desire for self-deception among many of us.

The Unholy Land

For many American Christians, all of this medicine will seem quite difficult to accept. American Christians will never be unified or even normalized until they can replace pride with humility. We have to accept and act upon some basic facts about their own faith:

The genuine Church of Jesus Christ is a real, visible organization and has a defined structure. It is not an "invisible" and "universal church" where anything goes so long as there is a cross posted somewhere in the building. There is order, not chaos. It is a respectful, and calm Holy place standing apart from a world filled with evil, confusion, and turmoil; not at all the kind of commercialized church that we are expected to accept today as Christians. The church is not a venue for entertainment. It is a place where the Cup of Christ is served.

Christians are called to follow Christ and His ways, not to attempt to "lead" Christ into validating their own lifestyles and financial desires. We need not tolerate churches claiming to be of Christ that primarily serve to be politically active and self-important. The madness of power, of money, of egos and of ignorance at these churches must simply be abandoned by the faithful. The American churches, having abdicated their role to teach actual virtue and unity to our American society have failed, come up short, and instead have largely chosen to focus on the matters of men instead of the mission of Christ. They cannot simply change because they are often structured as businesses.

Christianity was not invented in America. It is a wholly "foreign" religion to North America and has had no "roots" in the United States until recently in the history of the Faith. Ninety percent of all the events of Christianity occurred elsewhere before America was ever founded. All attempts to "Americanize" Christianity in church structure, doctrine, or theology are foolhardy ventures by man that only serve to render the practices to little more than club or sect status executed in a building with a cross decorating it.

Likewise Christianity is an ancient faith of a factual substance, with both serious real world benefits and consequences. While genuine Christianity must continuously address the social conditions that affect changes in culture, Christianity itself does not change as a result.

Christianity is the path to the Kingdom of God. It's a *Kingdom*, not a democracy, nor a civic agency, nor a business. We need to think long and hard about this one and what it means for our faith. Christians must consider that the broad and imaginary latitude of liberty within the Protestant paths delivered by Luther and others has injected a sinful pride into the churches. This deception has had the effect of diluting the core message of Christianity; derailing the focus of the church and of the faith as a whole. The Kingdom of God is not a Representative Republic like America. If we imagine that it is, we will be disappointed because Heaven will not necessarily be democratic.

A man named Saint Rufus was a desert dweller in Egypt somewhere between the fourth and fifth centuries. He had a divine vision which revealed to him (and us) this simple truth of our Christian faith:

"Obedience, salvation of all the faithful! Obedience, that gives birth to all virtues! Obedience, that discovers the Kingdom! Obedience, that opens Heaven, enabling men to ascend thereto from earth!"[408]

He's referring to our obedience to God's Law rather than us twisting and perverting the tenants of our Faith into imaginary ones that suit our own times and lifestyles. In America, we don't like to use the word obedience much anymore. We have always preferred the word "independence," or the word "freedom" historically. Obedience to these modernized and invented tenants of the Faith has not worked, is not working, and will continue to dilute and diminish our execution of the mission of Christ. The even larger question this raises is how does anyone really know what the "mission" is these days?

Ask yourself, "what are the standards of my faith? Is it my denominations'? My pastors'? My local churches'?" "My own interpretation of the Bible?" "My own feelings about Christianity?" We are all little independent customized groups, and that must be dealt with by each of us. As a result, much of Protestantism is now the practice of the blind leading the lost.

In this matter of sin, the truths of the Bible and of the Church do not hinge upon opinions or other "feelings" about whether we accept or believe them or not. Sin separates us from God, and because of that it cannot be celebrated in a Christian church. Consider this:

"But now I am writing to you that you must not associate with anyone who claims to be a brother or sister but is sexually immoral or greedy, an idolater or slanderer, a drunkard or swindler. Do not even eat with such people."

1 Corinthians 5:11 (NIV)

If it is our present opinion that as American Christians we can say "live and let live" and that tens of thousands of completely different, opposing, errant, and often sinful doctrines of "Christianity" are somehow acceptable, then we have absolutely missed the mark. With such an attitude, Christianity becomes no longer the Holy standard in the church, but the church becomes a series of mere worldly associations relegated to the domain of (and prone to the error of) men only.

What is perfectly legal in America (such as starting up your own "nondenominational" church) may not be acceptable by the standards of a genuine Christian Church. If we accept the incredulous notion that the Christian Church is "invisible" then how would we ever have a set of standards by which to determine this? While we do of course have free will, it is a freedom to choose to follow Christ and serve in His church or not, but we are not at liberty to invent our own churches and simply call them "Christian."

Christ Himself said,

"Very truly I tell you Pharisees, anyone who does not enter the sheep pen by the gate, but climbs in by some other way, is a thief and a robber. The one who enters by the gate is the shepherd of the sheep. The gatekeeper opens the gate for him, and the sheep listen to his voice. He calls his own sheep by name and leads them out. When he has brought out all his own, he goes on ahead of them, and his sheep follow him because they know his voice. But they will never follow a stranger; in fact, they will run away from him because they do not recognize a stranger's voice.   John 10:1- 5 NIV

The Living God loves us immeasurably and does not want us to live in fear. He does not seek a relationship with us because we fear hell. God does not send us to hell; we could send ourselves there by our own choices.

In America, we are yet still free to have a choice, and we must exercise that right today. In all these things, the effort will not be easy; in fact it will seem quite impossible, certainly uncomfortable, for power generally gives up nothing without a demand. But let our faith remain focused on Christ and not in men and not ourselves. This message need not be nailed to the door of a church, but instead considered by American Christians who may begin to consider the folly of the present state of American Christianity for themselves and are ready to gather the courage and fortitude to act.

American Greed

While Martin Luther would be satisfied today that the long practice of the Roman Catholic Church of selling indulgences in the church has long ended, he might not be surprised that the practice was embraced and refined by entities other than the church.

The capitalist system is by far the best economic system period. The issue becomes equity....what is right. Not some promised Utopian "equality." A company must capitalize on both investment and labor. Capitalizing is one thing. Taking advantage of people is something else, and it's often illegal.

To corporate America, to corporate owners and those in power, I tell you this: your role in America's restoration of virtue and unity must above all, be an active, deliberate, and careful one. Although perhaps not in public office, you are among the leaders of our once great nation. The intergenerational culture of American greed cannot restore the nation and it is largely to blame for its pervasive cultural division, unrest and ills. Likewise doing good things in the wrong places for the wrong reasons does nothing to help.

"To have a right to do a thing is not at all the same as to be right in doing it." — G.K. Chesterton

The American fabric cannot be mended without your willingness to accept and act upon an ethical responsibility that few, like Mr. Bob Moore, seemed to understand. Where is your virtue? Do you know what it means? Do you even care? Trading the soul for the love of money is nothing new, but is that a primary purpose in your life? You must decide, and decide you will. All must answer for their actions sooner or later regardless of their station in life.

In all that I have said, please do not send me letters and fill my email with comments like, "Well, that's wishful thinking, but it can't be done in America." Or, "there is no way I'm changing churches or doing X or Y to correct my own faith." Or better still, "I can't do that, it's just not logical or practical." My experience it is just the direct opposite

. Growing up as I did, I never could see a life beyond age eighteen or so. It was such a clouded and dark future. But I trusted only one thing: that the Lord would do as He saw fit, and He has. If I had demanded of the Lord to reveal to me at age fifteen what my life would be thirty five years in the future (both for good and bad outcomes...), I would not have believed Him at that time. So it is that the Lord reveals plans for us as we are able to receive them.

As Christians, we cannot put ourselves in the place of deciding for God what He can and cannot do with our lives. For when we say, "there's no way, I can't possibly do that," what we are really saying is "I don't ever want to do that, and I hope God doesn't make me do it," very much like Jonah of the Bible. It is pride alone that breeds this attitude. Again pride, the first of all sins, the exact same pride which is rampant among so many American churches today. You may think that by putting God in a box that you imagine that only your control will somehow "work." But what we are really doing is separating ourselves from God, His Holy Church and His plans for our lives. Plans that are infinitely more appropriate, rich, and wise than our own plans could ever be.

To Our Politicians at Every Level:

America has often been the sole beacon of light in a dark and imprisoned modern world. In spite of the mantra of modern politicians, in America, there is not a white America, a black America, an Asian America, an Hispanic America, a young America, an old America, a rich America, or a poor America. There is ONE America painted with all manner of things upon one single canvas that we share. We are knitted together into one nation under God, never intended by our Framers to be separated into all manner of opposing little factions for the political elites to divide and conquer us.

To the American political class; by any measure of your results, you seem to be far more in need of the virtues than any other group in America today. Because of the combination of your actions, inactions, greed, graft, dishonesty, self-aggrandizement, and sheer incompetence, you have driven our fine nation to the brink of financial, civil, and cultural destruction. I understand fully that these are outcomes that you have carefully crafted, measured and insulated yourselves from.

When you have worked only to enrich yourselves in life (*especially* at the expense of others), You may be interested to know that there is a risk that you may have also damned yourselves to an eternal poverty after this life. But that's not for me anyone else to determine, of course.

The scriptures address the matter this way:

"Now listen, you who say, 'Today or tomorrow we will go to this or that city, spend a year there, carry on business and make money.' Why, you do not even know what will happen tomorrow. What is your life? You are a mist that appears for a little while and then vanishes. Instead, you ought to say, 'If it is the Lord's will, we will live and do this or that.' As it is, you boast in your arrogant schemes. All such boasting is evil....Now listen, you rich people, weep and wail because of the misery that is coming on you. Your wealth has rotted, and moths have eaten your clothes. Your gold and silver are corroded. Their corrosion will testify against you and eat your flesh like fire. You have hoarded
wealth in the last days. Look! The wages you failed to pay the workers who mowed your fields are crying out against you. The cries of the harvesters have reached the ears of the Lord Almighty. You have lived on earth in luxury and self-indulgence. You have fattened yourselves in the day of slaughter."   James 4:13...James 5:1-5 NIV

If as Americans we claim to have created a "Christian nation," and we attempt to maintain some resemblance of that notion. It is incumbent upon us to begin acting like it...but we are the problem. In the preface I brought this text from the late Evangelist Billy Graham to your attention:

"We do not fail to enjoy the fruit of the Spirit because we live in a sea of corruption; we fail to do so because the sea of corruption is in us.[409]"

In the Gospels we read that Christ stated, "But Jesus hearing it, said: They that are in health need not a physician, but they that are ill." The Orthodox Christians note that God does His work of salvation when we *need* to be saved. In other words, if a drowning man can swim, he does not need rescuing. He knows what to do and can save himself

The Unholy Land

from his otherwise dire circumstance. But only when we can no longer save ourselves—when we are totally helpless to affect our own rescue can God offer us salvation.[410] It is true.

Our American nation is in fact, "sick" and suffers from the disease of pride. It is pride, the first sin of all that causes us to grope around in the dark of our spiritual blindness as a culture. Pride that allows us believe that we can conform all aspects of Christianity to fit our own comfortable and sinful lifestyles, sending us down a twisted path of a fruitless, futile, and often ridiculous "spiritual journey"- whatever that is supposed to mean.

It is pride that prevents us from forming Christian unity and applying its virtues to the various facets of our own lives. This unity and virtue is learned in the genuine Christian Church. These facts often lead Christians to the obvious conclusions that are as absurd as they are wrong and...entirely logical. It is pride that manifests with people making arrogant, ignorant, and somewhat ridiculous statements such as:

"I don't need a church because I can sit at home and God will just make a house call."

"I find all the God I need when I walk around in the woods."

"We are all on a spiritual journey."

"I can't attend a church I want to because my spouse won't let me."

"We can't look at other churches because the kids won't like to change."

"There is no perfect church so there is no sense in looking for one."

"I have already been saved. I don't need church anymore."

"I'm not the religious type. That would be you."

"All churches are the same, makes no difference which one you go to on any week."

"The original Christian Church died out, so any local church will do."

"We are all going to end up in heaven anyway, so what's the point?"

"I do my own church when I feel like it."

"I'm just too old for all of that."

"I don't have time for church."

...and the excuse which I have often told myself, "I am just done with it."

All of these statements are wrong because they begin from a perspective of denying the establishment and existence of the Christian Church at Pentecost, and they further deny God's power and ability to maintain His holy Church for all time. If these statements are true, then why would Pentecost even have happened?

"Christianity, if false, is of no importance, and if true, of infinite importance. The only thing it cannot be is moderately important."

C. S. Lewis

At the end of all this discussion remains Pontius Pilate's question that still haunts us all today. *What is truth?* Is Jesus Christ the Begotten Son of God and risen King of Kings? If He is, there is but one Christ, one Holy Gospel, and one Holy, visible Church. These would be inescapable truths if we accept Christ, and a series of clear standards of dogma and doctrine that do not change with public opinion or outside political pressures. Or is Jesus Christ merely a representation of a series of concepts and teachings we can use, modify, and selectively apply to support our own set of changing ideas and lifestyles as Thomas Jefferson thought? In this case Christianity has no concrete standards but only general ideas about things that can and often blow with the winds of public opinion. In Christianity, while we are entitled to our own opinions, we are certainly not entitled to our own facts.

"Whosoever revolteth and continueth not in the doctrine of Christ hath not God."

2 John 1:9
Douay-Rheims Bible

American Christianity is a faith that lately has suffered through and been damaged by the changing philosophies of both Modernism, and Postmodernism. The application of these two philosophies in their succession has radically disfigured, distorted, and almost completely obliterated any legacy of genuine Christianity in the greater parts of Protestantism. The result is a self-centered pride. Until American Christians can let go of all of this religious and personal pride and find humility we cannot advance in the faith in America. This also means there is no hope to solve the endemic problems in America.

There is a legitimate reason why Protestants and others cannot simply show up at a Roman Catholic Church or an Eastern Orthodox Church to take communion. It has to do with sanctification and holiness—two main features of Christianity largely lost in America today. This begs the question: have American Christians deceived themselves and diluted the history of our faith so far that too few can now comprehend and accept the basic truths and standards of genuine Christianity? That's the definition of a heresy, and it is the question for each of us to decide every day and that answer may well determine our fate as a nation. It is the very same answer Pilate once sought: "What is truth?"

Those seeking genuine Christianity should know the truth:

"Jesus saith to him: I am the way, and the truth, and the life. No man cometh to the Father, but by me."   John 14:6
Douay-Rheims Bible

The question remains; where can such a truth be found in the fractured and wildly distorted landscape of American Christianity? If the Holy Apostolic Church cannot be found, how then is there any hope for the American restoration of virtue and unity? How are we addressing this problem:

"Every man on earth is sick with the fever of sin, with the blindness of sin, is overcome by the fury of sin; and as sins mostly consist in malice and pride, it is necessary to treat every- one who suffers from the malady of sin with kindness and love. This is an important truth, which we often forget. We often, very often, act in opposition to this truth; we add malice to malice by our anger, we oppose pride to pride."

Righteous John, Wonderworker of Kronstadt[411]

Lord have mercy.

14

Epilogue

"I didn't go to religion to make me happy. I always knew a bottle of Port would do that. If you want a religion to make you feel really comfortable, I certainly don't recommend Christianity."

C.S. Lewis

After four decades of being kicked around in and by churches I was completely miserable—filled with mostly bitter sorrow, some anger, with a healthy dose of frustration. My dejection now teetered on the verge of total despondency. That is when I first began the present work you have just read. All of this had come down to Pilate's question; "What is truth?" An excellent question indeed. Was there really "one holy, catholic, and apostolic Church" in existence today as the early Church had declared with their creed in 381 A.D.? It was time to find out.

As to the disposition of my own troubles expressed by my personal questions raised in the text, I soon came to realize that self-justification is not a path to Divine Sanctification. And, pushing other Christians away is not helpful and certainly won't facilitate the restoration of unity for our nation.

It seems that where the Christian faith is concerned a man requires three things after He has accepted Christ: a map, a compass, and a guide—or if you prefer, the Bible, the Church, and someone trained with both to show you the way. Before I might even contemplate any of these applications, I had to face the reality that I didn't need just "another church," I needed a spiritual hospital.

There was a choice to make.

While I am by no means to blame for those who sinned and pushed me out of churches, it is incumbent upon me to humbly accept the responsibility for my response to these events and to forgive them; and it was still my genuine desire to find the truth. Or I could continue to say to myself, "I'm done with it."

I could choose to be jaded and pretend that Christianity is simply not even a real thing. I might even wallow around in bitterness and self-centered pity for the rest of my life, or conversely... find some other way to continue to seek Him. Why? Because whether I liked to admit it or not, the choice to be made is ever before us so long as we are still drawing breath. We make this choice every single day.

With all I had experienced and all I had learned, I understood that could not return to any Protestant setting—they have made it abundantly clear that I am not welcome time and again across so many denominations where I had been a member in the past. And all of them have demonstrated a breathtaking lack of understanding for their own practice of faith and Christian history.

Apart from my personal struggles, there exists this series of factual issues about modern Protestantism which cannot be resolved. These issues effectively form a "brick wall" of five main concerns that modern Protestantism cannot break itself free from, except by using nothing more than their imaginations about the Bible that was given to them by the same Church which they universally deny:

"1. *The Logic Gap of Denominational Diversity:*
If the Holy Spirit is singular and the Word of God authoritative, the sheer proliferation of tens of thousands of Protestant denominations presents a logical incongruity. The unity promised by the presence of one Holy Spirit seems fragmented by the diversity of doctrinal interpretations and ecclesial divisions among Protestant groups.

Ecclesial identity, in its philosophical essence, should reflect the unified body of Christ as envisioned in the Holy Bible. The Holy Bible speaks of the importance of unity among believers (1 Corinthians 1:10, Ephesians 4:3). Jesus prayed for the unity of His followers in John 17:21, expressing a desire for oneness comparable to the unity within the Holy Trinity.

The philosophical examination of the Christian doctrine posits an inherent unity within the Holy Trinity – the Father, the Son, and the Holy Spirit. The singular essence of the Holy Spirit, as believed in Orthodox Christianity, raises a logical expectation of unity among believers. If the Holy Spirit is singular and the Word of God is authoritative, an intrinsic coherence is anticipated, forming the bedrock for a unified understanding of faith.

The Holy Trinity operates in perfect accord, a symphony of oneness. However, the proliferation of tens of thousands of Protestant denominations introduces a discordant note. The logical progression from a singular Holy Spirit to a myriad of divergent doctrinal interpretations within Protestantism creates a dissonance that warrants philosophical scrutiny.

Coherence in belief systems is expected when deriving teachings from a singular authoritative source – the Word of God. The logical incongruity arises when tens of thousands of Protestant denominations, each claiming fidelity to the authoritative scripture, present divergent doctrines. This divergence challenges the inherent logical progression from a unified source to a multiplicity of interpretations.

2. *The Unintended Division in the Reformation Movement:*

The initial goal of the religious reform movement in the West was to bring about positive change within the Church. However, rather than fostering unity, the Reformation led to long-lasting division. The emergence of myriad Protestant denominations challenges the notion of one unified body of Christ within these religious associations.

St. Paul the Apostle emphasizes the importance of unity in the body of Christ (1 Corinthians 12:12-27). The unintended consequences of division within Protestantism raise questions about adherence to this biblical principle.

3. *Rejection of Tradition and Church Fathers:*

The rejection of the sacred traditions and teachings of Church Fathers and ecumenical councils by certain Protestant denominations has contributed to profound disunity. Orthodox Christianity asserts that the preservation of apostolic traditions is vital for maintaining the integrity of the faith.

St. Paul the Apostle also encourages the preservation of traditions handed down (2 Thessalonians 2:15). The rejection of these traditions in certain Protestant circles raises concerns about departing from biblical guidance.

4. *Assessing the Fruits of Protestant Movements:*

The biblical principle "know the tree by its fruit" urges a critical examination of the outcomes of religious movements. Orthodoxy questions whether the proliferation of denominations and doctrinal variations within Protestantism aligns with the authentic fruit of the Holy Spirit.

Lord Jesus Christ warns about false prophets and identifies them by their fruits (Matthew 7:15-20). Orthodoxy raises concerns about discerning the spiritual origin of the diverse fruits within Protestantism.

5. *Resurgence of Historical Heresies:*

Orthodoxy notes the resurgence of heresies eliminated and condemned in the early centuries of Christianity. Groups like: Jehovah's Witnesses, Mormons, and Seventh-day Adventists, WMSCOG in Korean, Eastern Lightning, Peoples Temple, SCJ, Jesus Morning Star,...associated with Protestantism, revive doctrinal positions that the early Church deemed heterodox.

> *St. Paul the Apostle cautions against false teachings and heresies (2 Peter 2:1, Galatians 1:6-9). Orthodoxy questions how Protestant movements, directly or indirectly, accommodate these historical heresies."* [412]

Unfortunately for me, Roman Catholicism, with all its brutal and often bloody history, ongoing issues with rampant abuse in places, and introduction of some bizarre new doctrines was never even a consideration for me.

The fact is that I suddenly realized that somehow I "knew too much." All those paths were closed to me now. On the morning of Sunday, May 20th, 2018 I had risen early. There was one last try left in me; a singular and final attempt to discover the Christian Church that was promised to us. Only one.

I found myself at the most unlikely of all places. I was standing at the bottom step leading to the door of a small, old, red brick chapel where a local Eastern Orthodox Christian mission meets on Sundays. In my mind, I asked, *"What is this place?"* I just stood there outside…kinda frozen. At that moment I felt like a leaf blowing in the wind that had gotten stuck to the railing of those steps. The few minutes of contemplation there felt like hours to me as my mind raced with so many flooding memories, both good and bad of nearly every church I had ever set foot in from beginning to end, and all the people I had met. I gripped the railing tightly and stared at my feet. It was time to make the call. Do I go inside, or go home?

To my immediate right, only a few yards away there stood the large and modern church building with so many people now bustling through those doors on their way to their Sunday service. Ironically, it was a Lutheran church and they had allowed the Eastern Orthodox to set up a mission in the old chapel they no longer used. I smiled. Yes it was irony; an irony that was apparently lost on everyone but me.

If I veered my feet to the right at this moment, I could go meet the Lutherans. They all seemed friendly enough. But then I'd literally be headed back to "Luther and his Protestants." It would be a far easier step to take. It might even be vaguely familiar. It would be so much more comfortable to try again in yet another Protestant church. I wasn't even upset about Protestant churches anymore. In fact, there was real temptation for me to turn and go that way. It would certainly be the much easier path.

If I instead stepped directly forward, I would be entering a Christian Church entirely foreign to me, one that erases all five hundred years of Protestantism and over nine hundred fifty years of the effects of Roman Catholicism. This decision required more faith and courage than I thought I might be able to muster alone.

There in front of me I faced the last church door I ever intended to open. If this one day ended as all the others there would be no more church for me. It was not a decision made as a last resort, but rather one founded in my ever fervent hope that somehow behind this door was not just another Christian church, but rather *The Church*.

Filled with much trepidation, I reached for the door handle as my eyes welled up with tears. A deep breath. *One last try.* I remembered the scripture...

"Have confidence in the Lord with all thy heart, and lean not upon thy own prudence. In all thy ways think on him, and he will direct thy steps."

Proverbs 3:5-6
Douay-Rheims Bible

I entered the narthex and because I was early there was only one person there, a man who greeted me. I peered into the chapel from the narthex and to once Protestant eyes, the chapel appeared more like a Christian themed museum than a church. There were ancient images of Christ and His saints all over the place. Why was there incense wafting in the air? Why were they burning candles? Although it was confusing, that did not matter to me, I had been confused for years already, so whatever it was, it was. If God wanted me to figure it out He would have to assist, and I accepted that He of course has the power and willingness to do just that because He is not a God of confusion.

It was not difficult for the man to see that I was a visitor.

"Have you ever been to an Orthodox church before?" The man asked.

"I know *absolutely* nothing about Christianity." I replied.

And I meant that plainly and literally. I decided to wipe the slate clean and let go of everything about Christianity that I thought I knew. I had discovered that most of what I thought I knew about my own faith, of Christianity in general, was incomplete, distorted, or just plain wrong. This was new and quite uncomfortable uncharted territory to me; oddly different and entirely uncertain. Now lacking the comfortably warm security blanket of my own pride, I was helpless, and in the Lord's hands. The end of the road for my own religious pride had placed me in exactly the place where He might now begin His work.

Indeed I did discover something there that I have not discovered at any Protestant church in memory. This one thing might be prized over many other things one might find in a church. It seems elusive in the Protestant landscape of America today. After all I had been through it was precisely that one thing which the Lord knew I so desperately needed on that day in May.

Peace.

THE END
of the book, must become the beginning

of America's path to virtue and unity.

Final Notes

This text was several years in the making. It is important to note that the composition was researched, compiled and edited from about 2016 to 2025, and originally scheduled for release in 2020. During this period, Both America and the world at large experienced a deliberate at massive neo-fascist takeover of media, ushered in by the :"pandemic" in 2020. As a result, certain news stories, reports and records of facts and events that occurring during this period have simply "disappeared" from their original online sources and original reporting units as the Left proceeds to sanitize what is now recent history, while claiming that any knowledge of these events and details today is either "misinformation" or "disinformation." Many of the internet web addresses that link to source material listed in the citations section are now dead links, and I am satisfied that I was able to scoop these quotes and use this information before it was scrubbed. Facts do not change simply because the reporting of it is not permitted by a Fascist media or government. This book is now, in part, a testament to the fact that George Orwell warned us all.

Chronology for Historical Context

A short list of events of the Church and its historical context

ca. 27 BC - AD 180	Pax Romana.	26 AD	The Baptism of Jesus Matthew 3:13, Mark 1:9, Luke 3:21
6 BC	Birth of John the Baptist Luke 1, John 1:6	27 AD	Temptation of Jesus Matthew 4, Mark 1:12, Luke 4
6 BC	Roman succession: Gaius Caesar and Lucius Caesar groomed for the throne.	27 AD	Jesus Calls his First Disciples Matthew 4:18, Mark 1:16, Luke 5
6 BC	Augustus Taxes the Roman Empire Luke 2	27 AD	Wedding at Cana John 2
5 BC	Birth of Jesus Matthew 1, Mark 1, Luke 2:6, John 1:14	27 AD	Jesus Teaches Nicodemus John 3
5 BC	Visit of the Magi Matthew 2	27 AD	Jesus Testifies to the Samaritan Woman John 4
5 BC	Escape to Egypt Matthew 2:13	27 AD	Sermon on the Mount Matthew 5 - 7
4 BC	Widely accepted date (Ussher) for birth of Jesus Christ.	28 AD	Instructions on Prayer Luke 11
4 BC	Slaughter of 14,000 Infants Matthew 2:16	28 AD	Jesus Ministers in Galilee Matthew 8, Mark 2, Luke 4:14
4 BC	Return to Nazareth Matthew 2:23	28 AD	The Pool of Bethesda John 5
5 AD	Tiberius's naval expedition to Jutland	28 AD	Jesus Lord of the Sabbath Matthew 12, Mark 3, Luke 6
9 AD	Battle of the Teutoburg Forest, the Imperial Roman Army's bloodiest defeat. Arminius destroy the Roman Legions in Teutoberg Forest - Romans withdraw to the Rhine and Danube frontiers	28 AD	Jesus Answers John's Disciples Matthew 11, Luke 7
		28 AD	Jesus Speaks Many Parables Matthew 13, Mark 4, Luke 8
		28 AD	Jesus Heals a Demoniac Matthew 8:28, Mark 5, Luke 8:26
		28 AD	Jesus Heals a Paralytic Matthew 9
8 AD	The Boy Jesus at the Temple Luke 2:41	29 AD	Jesus Sends out His Twelve Apostles Matthew 10, Mark 6
14 AD	Death of Emperor Augustus (Octavian), ascension of his adopted son Tiberius to the throne.	29 AD	John the Baptist Beheaded Matthew 14, Mark 6:14
ca. 25-26	Death of Joseph the Betrothed.	29 AD	Jesus Feeds the 5,000 Matthew 14:15, Mark 6:30, Luke 9, John 6
ca. 26-28	John the Baptist begins ministry. Matthew 3, Mark 1:4, Luke 3, John 1:15	29 AD	Teachings on Clean and Unclean Matthew 15, Mark 7

The Unholy Land

29 AD	Peter's Confession of Christ Matthew 16, Mark 8, Luke 9:18	30 AD	Jesus' Betrayal, Trial, Crucifixion Matthew 27, Mark 15, Luke 23, John 18, 19 (could be AD. 29, 30, or 33)
29 AD	The Transfiguration Matthew 17, Mark 9, Luke 9:28	30 AD	Jesus' Resurrection Matthew 28, Mark 16, Luke 24, John 20, 21
29 AD	Greatest and Least in the Kingdom Matthew 18	30 AD Acts 1	The Ascension
29 AD	Jesus Sends out the Seventy-two Luke 10	30 AD	Matthias Chosen by Lot Acts 1:12
29 AD	Jesus Teaches at the Feast of Tabernacles John 7	30 AD	The Holy Spirit Comes at Pentecost Acts 2
29 AD	The Woman Caught in Adultery John 8	30 AD	Peter Heals and Preaches Acts 3
29 AD	Jesus Affirms He is the Son of God John 9	30 AD	Peter and John Arrested and Released; Acts 4
29 AD	The Shepherd and His Flock John 10	30 AD	Believers Share All Acts 4:32
30 AD	Jesus Speaks More Parables Luke 12 - 16	30 AD	Deaths of Ananias and Sapphira Acts 5
30 AD	Jesus Cleanses the Ten Lepers Luke 17	30 AD	Apostles Preach and Heal Acts 5:11
30 AD	Jesus Raises Lazarus John 11	ca. 30	Martyrdom of Stephen the deacon, first Christian martyr. Acts 6, 7
30 AD	Final Journey to Jerusalem Matthew 19, 20, Mark 10, Luke 18	31 AD	Saul Persecutes the Church Acts 8
30 AD	The Triumphal Entry Matthew 21, Mark 11, Luke 19, John 12	31 AD	Philip in Samaria Acts 8:3
30 AD	Closing Ministry in Jerusalem Matthew 22 - 25, Mark 12, 13, Luke 20, 21	31 AD	Simon the Sorcerer Acts 8:9
30 AD	Thursday Before Passover Matthew 26, Mark 14, Luke 22, John 13	31 AD	Philip and the Ethiopian Acts 8:26
30 AD	Jesus Comforts His Disciples John 14	34 AD	Saul's Conversion Acts 9
30 AD	Jesus the True Vine John 15	34 AD	Apostle Peter founds See of Antioch.
30 AD	Jesus Promises the Holy Spirit John 16	35 AD	Name "Christian" first used in Antioch
30 AD	Jesus' Intercessory prayers John 17	37 AD	Peter Preaches to the Gentiles Acts 10, 11
		37 AD	Death of Emperor Tiberius, ascension of his nephew Caligula to the throne.

The Unholy Land

37-41	Crisis under Caligula, proposed as the first open break between Rome and the Jews	47	The Church of the East is created by Saint Thomas
40 AD	Rome conquers Morocco.	48-100	Herod Agrippa II appointed King of the Jews by Claudius, seventh and last of the Herodians
40 AD	Apostle Barnabas sent from Jerusalem to Antioch. Acts 11:22	48 AD	Paul's First Missionary Journey Acts 13
41 AD	Emperor Caligula is assassinated by the Roman senate. His uncle Claudius succeeds him.	48 AD	Paul preaches in Pisidian Antioch Acts 13:14
ca. 42	Apostle Paul's ecstasy to the third heaven 2 Cor.12:2-4.	48 AD	Paul and Barnabas in Iconium Acts 14
42 AD	Peter Led from Prison by the Angel Acts 12	48 AD	Paul and Barnabas in Lystra and Derbe Acts 14:8
43 AD	Rome enters Britain for the first time. before 44 Epistle of James if written by James the Great	48 AD	Paul and Barnabas Return to Syrian Antioch Acts 14:21
		48 AD	Return to Syrian Antioch Acts 14:24

44? Saint James the Great: According to ancient local tradition, on 2 January of the year AD 40, the Virgin Mary appeared to James on a pillar on the bank of the Ebro River at Caesaraugusta, while he was preaching the Gospel in Spain. Following that vision, St James returned to Judea, where he was beheaded by King Herod Agrippa I in the year 44 during a Passover (Nisan 15) (Acts 12:1-3).

44 AD	Death of Herod Agrippa I (JA19.8.2, Acts 12:20-23)	48 AD	The Council at Jerusalem Acts 15
44-46?	Theudas beheaded by Procurator Cuspius Fadus for saying he would part the Jordan river (like Moses and the Red Sea or Joshua and the Jordan) (JA20.5.1, Acts 5:36-37 places it before the Census of Quirinius)	49	"Since the Jews constantly made disturbances at the instigation of Chrestus. he [Claudius] expelled them from Rome." Acts 18:2
		49 AD	Paul's ends missionary journey at Antioch; Second Missionary Journey begins. Acts 15:36
		49 AD	Paul in Philippi Acts 16
44 AD	Herod Agrippa Dies Acts 12:20	49 AD	Paul in Thessalonica, Berea, Athens Acts 17
c.44 AD	Paul and Barnabas to Jerusalem on famine relief.	c. 49	Council of Jerusalem and the "Apostolic Decree", Acts 15:1-35, same as Galatians 2:1-10?, which is followed by the Incident at Antioch[8] at which Paul publicly accuses Peter of "Judaizing" (2:11-21), see also Circumcision controversy in early Christianity
45 AD	James Writes his Letter James 1 – 5		
45-49?	Mission of Barnabas and Paul, (Acts 13:1-14:28), to Cyprus, Pisidian Antioch, Iconium, Lystra and Derbe (there they were called "gods ... in human form"), then return to Syrian Antioch.	50 AD	Passover riot in Jerusalem, 20-30,000 killed JA20.5.3,JW2.12.1

50 – 200 AD Revival of the Amber route

The Unholy Land

50-53?	Paul's 2nd mission, (Acts 15:36-18:22), split with Barnabas, to Phrygia, Galatia, Macedonia, Philippi, Thessalonica, Berea, Athens, Corinth, "he had his hair cut off at Cenchrea because of a vow he had taken", then return to Antioch; 1 Thessalonians, Galatians written? Map2. Lydia of Thyatira, a seller of purple, becomes the first European Christian convert Acts 16:11-15
50 AD	Paul establishes a church in Corinth Acts 18
50 AD	Apostle Matthew finishes the Gospel of Matthew in Aramaic.
51 AD	Paul Writes to the Thessalonians 1 Thess. 1 – 5
51-52 or 52-53	Proconsulship of Gallio according to an inscription, only fixed date in chronology of Paul; Paul disputes with philosophers in Athens.
52, November 21	St. Thomas the Apostle lands in India. Establishes churches at Kodungaloor, Palayoor, Paraur, Kottakkav, Kokkamangalam, Nilakkal, Niranam and Kollam
52 AD	Paul Writes again to the Thessalonians 2 Thess. 1 - 3
53-57?	Paul's 3rd mission, (Acts 18:23-22:30), to Galatia, Phrygia, Corinth, Ephesus, Macedonia, Greece, and Jerusalem where James the Just challenges him about rumor of teaching antinomianism (21:21); he addresses a crowd in their language (most likely Aramaic), Romans, 1 Corinthians, 2 Corinthians, Philippians written?
54 AD	Paul in Ephesus Acts 19
54 AD	Paul Writes to the Corinthians 1 Corinthians 1 - 16
54 AD, 57-8?	Paul Writes to the Galatians (or c.50, Galatians 1 – 6
54 AD:	Emperor Claudius dies and is succeeded by his grand nephew Nero.
55?	"Egyptian prophet" (allusion to Moses) and 30,000 unarmed Jews doing The Exodus reenactment massacred by Procurator Antonius Felix (JW2.13.5, JA20.8.6, Acts 21:38)
57 AD	Paul in Macedonia and Greece Acts 20
c. 57 – 58 AD	Paul Writes to the Romans from Corinth Romans 1 - 16
57 AD	Paul Writes again to the Corinthians 2 Corinthians 1 – 13
58?	Paul arrested, accused of being a revolutionary, "ringleader of the sect of the Nazarenes", teaching resurrection of the dead, imprisoned in Caesarea Acts 23-26
59 AD	Paul Returns to Jerusalem Acts 21 – 23
59?	Paul shipwrecked on Malta, there he is called a god Acts 28:6
60 AD	Paul imprisoned in Caesarea Acts 24
60?	Paul in Rome: greeted by many "brothers", three days later calls together the Jewish leaders, who hadn't received any word from Judea about him, but were curious about "this sect", which everywhere is spoken against; he tries to convince them from the "law and prophets", with partial success – said the Gentiles would listen, and spends two years proclaiming the Kingdom of God and teaching "the Lord Jesus Christ" (Acts 28:15-31); Epistle to Philemon written?
60-64?	early date for writing of 1 Peter (Peter as author)
before 62	Epistle of James if written by James the Just
62 AD	James the Just stoned to death for law transgression by High Priest Ananus ben Artanus, popular opinion against act results in Ananus being deposed by new procurator Lucceius Albinus (JA20.9.1)
63-107?	Simeon, 2nd Bishop of Jerusalem, crucified under Trajan
62 AD	Paul Before Festus Acts 25
62 AD	Paul Before Agrippa Acts 26

The Unholy Land

62 AD	Paul Sails for Rome Acts 27		Scrolls found in 1947)destroyed; Syrian troops participate in the First Jewish-Roman War.
62 AD	The Shipwreck Acts 27:13	66 AD	Paul Writes to Titus Titus 1 – 3
62 AD	Paul Ashore at Malta Acts 28	67 AD	Paul Writes Again to Timothy 2 Timothy 1 – 4
62 AD	Paul Preaches at Rome Acts 28:11	c.67	Paul executed in Rome.
62 AD	Paul Writes to the Ephesians Ephesians 1 - 6	67 AD	Peter Writes his Second Letter 2 Peter 1 – 3; Peter crucified upside-down. (Jn 21:18,1 Pet 5:13,
62 AD	Paul Writes to the Philippians Philippians 1 - 4	68 AD	Jude Writes his Letter Jude 1
62 AD	Paul Writes to the Colossians Colossians 1 - 4	68 AD	Emperor Nero commits suicide, prompting the Year of the four emperors in Rome.
62 AD	Paul Writes to Philemon Philemon 1		
63 AD	Paul Writes to Timothy 1 Timothy 1 – 6	69 AD	Ignatius of Antioch consecrated bishop of Antioch.
63 AD	Aristobulus consecrated as first bishop of Britain.	70(+/-10)?	Gospel of Mark, written in Rome, by Peter's interpreter (1 Peter 5:13), original ending apparently lost, endings added c. 400, see Mark 16
64-68	after July 18 Great Fire of Rome, Nero blames and persecutes the Christians (or Chrestians), possibly the earliest mention of Christians, by that name, in Rome, see also Tacitus on Jesus, (Col 1:24,Eph 3:13,2 Tim 4:6-8,1Clem 5:5-7),	70?	Signs Gospel written, hypothetical Greek text used in Gospel of John to prove Jesus is the Messiah
		70-200?	Gospel of Thomas, Jewish Christian Gospels: Gospel of the Ebionites, Gospel of the Hebrews, Gospel of the Nazarenes.
64	Tertullian's Prescription Against Heretics chapter	70 AD	Destruction of Jerusalem by the armies of Titus.
64 AD	Peter Writes his First Letter 1 Peter 1 – 5	71 AD	Apostle Mark introduces Christianity to Egypt.
64 (68?) AD Epistle to the Hebrews written			
64/67(?)-76/79(?) Pope Linus succeeds Peter as Episcopus Romanus (Bishop of Rome)		72, July 3	Martyrdom of St. Thomas the Apostle at Chinnamala, Mylapore, Chennai (Tamil Nadu)
		76/79(?)-88 Pope Anacletus: first Greek Pope, who succeeds Linus as Episcopus Romanus (Bishop of Rome)	
65?	Q document, a hypothetical Greek text thought by many critical scholars to have been used in writing of Matthew and Luke	79 AD	Destruction of Pompeii by the volcano Vesuvius.
66-73	Great Jewish Revolt: destruction of Herod's Temple and end of Judaism according to Supersessionism, Qumran community (site of Dead Sea	80(+/-20)?	Gospel of Matthew, most popular in Early Christianity

375

The Unholy Land

80 AD	Gospel of Luke written by the Apostle Luke; Titus dedicates Colosseum, site of the martyrdom of many early Christians
80(+/-20)?	Pastoral Epistles written (possible post-Pauline authorship)
81-96	Domitian Emperor; renewed persecution of Christians at end of reign.
84 AD	Excommunication of Christians from Jewish synagogue.
85 AD	Acts of the Apostles written by Apostle Luke.
88-90 AD	Didache written
88-101?	Clement, fourth Bishop of Rome: wrote Letter of the Romans to the Corinthians (Apostolic Fathers)
90?	Council of Jamnia of Judaism (disputed), Domitian applies the Fiscus Judaicus tax even to those who merely "lived like Jews"
90(+/-10)?	late date for writing of 1 Peter (associate of Peter as author)
94 AD	Testimonium Flavianum, disputed section of Jewish Antiquities by Josephus in Aramaic, translated to Koine Greek
95 AD	John's Revelation on Patmos Revelation 1 – 22
96 AD	Gospel of John and Epistles of John
96	Nerva modifies the Fiscus Judaicus, from then on, practicing Jews pay the tax, Christians do not
98-117?	Ignatius, third Bishop of Antioch, fed to the lions in the Roman Colosseum, advocated the Bishop (Eph 6:1, Mag 2:1,6:1,7:1,13:2, Tr 3:1, Smy 8:1,9:1), rejected Sabbath on Saturday in favor of "The Lord's Day" (Sunday). (Mag 9.1), rejected Judaizing (Mag 10.3), first recorded use of the term catholic (Smy 8:2).
98:	After a two-year rule, Emperor Nerva dies of natural causes, his adopted son Trajan succeeds him. Cornelius Tacitus pens the Germania
100 AD	Death of Apostle John.
100-150	Larger, better Long ship construction begins to give Vikings some "legs"
100(+/-30)?	Epistle of Barnabas (Apostolic Fathers)
100(+/-25)?	Epistle of James if written by author other than James the Just or James the Great
100(+/-10)?	Epistle of Jude written, probably by doubting relative of Jesus (Mark 6,3), rejected by some early Christians due to its reference to apocryphal Book of Enoch (v14)
100-150?	Apocryphon of James, Gospel of Mary Magdalene, Gospel of James, Infancy Gospel of Thomas, Secret Gospel of Mark.

Key world events prior to and into the early Byzantine period:

107	Martyrdom of Ignatius of Antioch; death of Apostle Symeon.
108-124	Persecution under Emperor Trajan, continuing under Emperor Hadrian (3rd).
120	Beginning of time of the Apologists: Justin Martyr, Aristides, Tatian, Athenagoras of Athens, Theophilus, Minucius Felix, Tertullian and Quadratus.
124	Apostles Quadratus and Aristides present Christian apologies to Emperor Hadrian at Athens.
128	Aquila's Greek translation of the Old Testament.
130	Conversion of Justin Martyr.
132	Jews, led by Bar Kochba, whom some identify as the Messiah, revolt against Rome.

135	Christmas instituted as a feast day in Rome.	ca. 209	Martyrdom of Alban in Britain.
136	Emperor Hadrian crushes Jewish resistance, forbids Jews from returning Jerusalem, and changes city name to Aelia Capitolina; first recorded use of title Pope for the bishop of Rome by Pope Hyginus.	210	Hippolytus of Rome, bishop and martyr and last of Greek-speaking fathers in Rome, writes Refutation of All Heresies (Philosophumena), and Apostolic Tradition.
		215	Conversion of Tertullian to Montanism.
144	Excommunication of Marcion.	225	Death of Tertullian.
150	Justin Martyr describes Divine Liturgy.	ca. 225-250	Didascalia Apostolorum written.
155	Martyrdom of Polycarp of Smyrna.	227	Origen begins Commentary on Genesis, completes work on First Principles.
156	Beginning of Montanism.		
165	Martyrdom of Justin.	235-238	Persecution under Emperor Maximinus Thrax (6th); martyrdom of St. Hippolytus of Rome.
166	Pope Soter inaugurates in Rome a separate annual feast for Pascha, in addition to the weekly Sunday celebrations of the Resurrection, which is also held on a Sunday, in contrast to the Quartodecimans.	238	During reigns of Gordian and Philip the Arab Church preaches openly and increasingly attracts well-educated converts.
ca. 175	Tatian's Diatessaron harmonizes the four canonical gospels into single narrative.	ca. 240	Origen produces Hexapla.
		244	Plotinus founds Neoplatonist school in Rome in opposition to Church.
177-180	Persecution under Emperor Marcus Aurelius (161-180) (4th).	246	Paul of Thebes becomes in Egypt first Christian hermit.
180	Irenaeus of Lyons writes Against Heresies; Dyfan first martyr in British Isles.	247	Rome celebrates thousandth anniversary, witnessing a period of increased persecution of Christians.
180-192	Theodotion's Greek translation of the Old Testament.	248	Origen writes Against Celsus that the Roman Empire was ordained by God.
193-211	Symmachus' Greek translation of the Old Testament.	249-251	Persecution under Emperor Decius (7th).
197	Quartodeciman controversy.	257-260	Persecution under Emperor Valerian (253-260) (8th).
200	Martyrdom of Irenaeus of Lyons.		
202	Emperor Septimus Severus issues edict against Christianity and Judaism; Martyrdom of Haralampus of Magnesia.	258	Martyrdom of Cyprian of Carthage.
		260	Paul of Samosata begins preaching against the divinity of Christ; Synod in Rome condemns Sabellianism and Subordinationism.
202-210	Persecution under Emperor Septimius Severus (193-211) (5th).		
		264	Excommunication of Paul of Samosata.
206	King Abgar IX converts Edessa to Christianity.		

The Unholy Land

265 Homoousios used for first time by Modalist Monarchians of Cyrene.

270 Death of Gregory Thaumaturgus; Porphyry of Tyre writes Against the Christians.

272 Birth of Constantine the Great

274-275 Persecution under Emperor Aurelian (9th).

275? Papyrus 47: 3rd Chester Beatty, ~Sinaiticus, Rev9:10-11:3,5-16:15,17-17:2

276 Mani (prophet), crucified, founder of the dualistic Manichaean sect in Persia

c.280 Gregory the Illuminator converts King Tiridates of Armenia to Christianity.

282-300? Theonas, bishop of Alexandria (Ante-Nicene Fathers)

284 Diocletian becomes Roman emperor, persecutes Church and martyrs an estimated one million Christians; martyrdom of Cosmas and Damian, Andrew Stratelates ("the General") and 2,593 soldiers with him in Cilicia.

285 Anthony the Great flees to desert.

290-345? St Pachomius, founder of Christian monasticism

292: The capital of the Roman empire is officially moved from Rome to Mediolanum (modern day Milan).

296-304 Pope Marcellinus, offered pagan sacrifices for Diocletian, later repented. Name in Martyrology of Bede

300 Christian population reaches about 6,200,000, or 10.5% of the population of the Roman Empire.

301 Gregory the Enlightener converts King Tiridates I of Armenia to the Christian faith.

302, 20,000 Christian Martyrs burned at Nicomedia.

303 Outbreak of the Great Persecution (303-311) (10th); martyrdom of George the Trophy-bearer.

ca. 305-311 Lactantius writes Divinae Institutiones.

ca. 306 Synod of Elvira requires clerical celibacy and sets severe disciplinary penalties for apostasy and adultery, becoming the pattern in the West.

308 Pope Marcellus opposes leniency for Christians who lapsed under persecution.

310 Armenia becomes first Christian nation; persecution of Christians under Persian King Shapur II (310-379).

311 Galerius issues Edict of Toleration, ending persecution of Christians in his part of the Roman Empire; Donatist rebellion in Carthage.

301 Armenia is the first kingdom in history to adopt Christianity as state religion; Diocletian's edict on prices

303-312 Diocletian's Massacre of Christians, includes burning of scriptures (EH 8.2)

303 Saint George, patron saint of Georgia, England and other states

304? Victorinus, bishop of Pettau

304? Pope Marcellinus, having repented from his previous defection, suffers martyrdom with several companions

c.305 Antony of Egypt organizes colony of Christian hermits.

306 Constantine I proclaimed emperor at York; Synod of Elvira prohibits relations between Christians and Jews

310 Maxentius deports Pope Eusebius and Heraclius to Sicily (relapse controversy)

311 Donatist schism begins in N. Africa.

312 Lucian of Antioch, founder of School of Antioch, martyred

312 Vision of Constantine: while gazing into the sun he sees a cross with the words by this sign conquer, see also Labarum, he was later called the 13th Apostle and Equal-to-apostles. He adopts the Christian symbol for his battle standards at the battle of the Milvian Bridge.

313 Edict of Milan: Constantine and Licinius end persecution, establish toleration of all forms of religious worship.

313? Lateran Palace given to Pope Miltiades for residence by Constantine

313? Traditional date for founding of the Brotherhood of the Holy Sepulchre

The Unholy Land

314 King Urnayr of Caucasian Albania adopts Christianity as official religion

314 Catholic Council of Arles, called by Constantine against Donatist schism to confirm the Council of Rome in 313

c.315 Eusebius becomes bishop of Caesarea, church historian, cited Caesarean text-type, wrote Ecclesiastical History in 325

321 Constantine decrees Sunday as state "day of rest" (CJ3.12.2),

324 Constantine becomes sole ruler of the Roman Empire.

325, 20 May- 19 June: The First Council of Nicaea; Constantine called the First Council of Nicaea in 325 to unify Christology, also called the first great Christian council by Jerome, the first ecumenical, decreed the Original Nicene Creed, but rejected by Nontrinitarians such as Arius, Theonas, Secundus of Ptolemais, Eusebius of Nicomedia, and Theognis of Nicaea who were excommunicated, also addressed Easter controversy and passed 20 Canon laws such as Canon VII which granted special recognition to Jerusalem. Council declares Christ is "one in essence with the Father."

325 The Kingdom of Aksum (Modern Ethiopia and Eritrea) declares Christianity as the official state religion, becoming the 2nd country to do so

325 Church of the Nativity in Bethlehem, ordered built by Constantine

326, November 18 Pope Sylvester I consecrates the Basilica of St. Peter built by Constantine the Great over the tomb of the Apostle

328-373 Athanasius, bishop of Alexandria, first cite of modern 27 book New Testament canon

c.330 Macarius of Egypt founds monastery in the desert at Wadi-el-Natrun.

330 Old Church of the Holy Apostles, dedicated by Constantine

330, May 11: Constantinople solemnly inaugurated. Constantine moves the capital of the Roman Empire to Byzantium, renaming it New Rome

331 Constantine commissions Eusebius to deliver 50 Bibles for the Church of Constantinople

335 Council in Jerusalem reverses Nicaea's condemnation of Arius, consecrates Jerusalem Church of the Holy Sepulchre

337? Mirian III of Iberia (present-day Georgia) adopts Christianity.

337, May 22: Constantine the Great dies (baptized shortly prior to his death), leaving his sons Constantius II, Constans I, and Constantine II as the emperors of the Roman Empire

341 Council of Antioch held; Emperor Constans bans pagan sacrifices and magic rituals under penalty of death.

350 Ninian establishes the church Candida Casa at Whithorn in Galloway, Scotland, beginning the missionary effort to the Picts.

351 Apparition of the Cross over Jerusalem.

358 Basil the Great founds monastery of Annesos in Pontus, the model for Eastern monasticism.

359 Councils of Seleucia and Rimini.

360 Martin of Tours founds first French monastery at Liguge; first church of Hagia Sophia inaugurated by Emperor Constantius II.

362 Antiochian schism (362-414).

361-63 Julian the Apostate becomes Roman emperor and attempts to restore paganism.

363 Emperor Jovian reestablishes Christianity as the official religion of the Empire.

364 Council of Laodicea held.

367 Athanasius of Alexandria writes Paschal letter, listing for the first time the canon of the New Testament; death of Hilary of Poitiers.

374 Election of Ambrose as bishop of Milan.

375 Basil the Great writes On the Holy Spirit.

376 Visigoths convert to Arian Christianity.

379 Death of Basil the Great; Emperor Gratian's rescript Ordinariorum Sententias extends power of Bishop of Rome by allowing him authority over bishops within his own jurisdiction.

380 Christianity established as the official faith of the Roman Empire by Emperor Theodosius the

The Unholy Land

Great; Council of Saragossa condemns Priscillianism.

381 Second Ecumenical Council held in Constantinople, condemning Macedonianism/Pneumatomachianism and Apollinarianism, declaring the divinity of the Holy Spirit, confirming the previous Ecumenical Council, and completing the Nicene-Constantinopolitan Creed; Council of Aquileia led by Ambrose of Milan deposes Arian bishops.

382 Pope Siricius of Rome first to bear title Pontifex Maximus.

383 Death of Frumentius of Axum, bishop of Axum and Apostle to Ethiopia.

391-92 Closing of all non-Christian temples in the Empire; Theodosius the Great ends pagan Eleusinian Mysteries by decree and causes surviving pagan sacrifices at Alexandria and Rome to cease.

393 Council of Hippo publishes Biblical canon; Emperor Theodosius bans Olympic Games as a pagan festival.

394 Epiphanius of Salamis attacks teachings of Origen as heretical; Council of Constantinople held; Donatist Council of Bagai in Africa held.

395 Augustine becomes bishop of Hippo in North Africa; placing of the cincture of the Theotokos in the Church of the Virgin in Halkoprateia-Constantinople.

395 Re-division of Empire with death of Emperor Theodosius the Great.

397 Council of Carthage publishes Biblical canon; death of Martin of Tours and Ambrose of Milan.

398 John Chrysostom becomes Archbishop of Constantinople.

ca. 398 Martyrdom of 10,000 Fathers of the Scetis by Patriarch Theophilus of Alexandria.

399 Anastasius I of Rome and other bishops condemn doctrine of Origen.

401 Augustine of Hippo writes Confessions; Pope Innocent I of Rome supports John Chrysostom and condemns Pelagianism..

403 Abduction of Patrick to Irelande; visit of Victricius of Rouen to Britain; Synod of the Oak held near Chalcedon, deposing and exiling John Chrysostom.

404 Martyrdom of Telemachus, resulting in Emperor Honorius' edict banning gladiator fights.

405 Translation of Holy Scriptures into Latin as the Vulgate by Jerome.

407 Death of John Chrysostom in exile.

410 Fall of Rome to the Visigoths under Alaric I; escape of Patrick back to Britain; Emperor Honorius tells Britain to attend to its own affairs, effectively removing the Roman presence.

410 Council of Seleucia declares Mesopotamian Nestorian bishops independent of Orthodox bishops.

411 Pelagius condemned at council in Carthage; Rabbula becomes bishop of Edessa.

412 Cyril succeeds his uncle Theophilus as Pope of Alexandria; Honorius outlaws Donatism; Bishops Lazarus of Aix-en-Provence and Herod of Arles expelled from sees on a charge of Manichaeism; Alexandrian Creation Era date finalized at 25 March, 5493 BC.

414 Resolution of Antiochian division.

418 Foundation of the Arian Visigothic Kingdom, as Emperor Honorius rewards Visigoth federates by giving them land in Gallia Aquitania on which to settle.

426 Augustine of Hippo writes The City of God.

428 Nestorius becomes patriarch of Constantinople.

429 Pope Celestine I dispatches prominent Gallo-Roman Bishops Germanus of Auxerre and Lupus of Troyes to Britain as missionary bishops and to combat the Pelagian heresy; death of Sisoes the Great.

431 Third Ecumenical Council held in Ephesus, condemning Nestorianism and Pelagianism, confirming the use of the term Theotokos to refer to the Virgin Mary, and confirming autocephaly of Church of Cyprus; Pope Celestine sends Palladius to Ireland.

432 Return of Patrick to Ireland to begin missionary work; death of Ninian, Apostle to the Picts.

The Unholy Land

439 Carthage falls to Vandals.

445 Founding of monastery at Armagh in northern Ireland; Emperor Valentinian III issues decree recognizing primacy of the bishop of Rome.

447 Earthquake in Constantinople, when a boy was lifted up to heaven and heard the Trisagion.

449 Robber Synod of Ephesus, presided over by Dioscorus of Alexandria, with an order from the emperor to acquit Eutyches the Monophysite.

450 First monasteries established in Wales; death of Peter Chrysologus.

451 Fourth Ecumenical Council meets at Chalcedon, condemning Eutychianism and Monophysitism, affirming doctrine of two perfect and indivisible but distinct natures in Christ, and recognizing Church of Jerusalem as patriarchate.

452 Proterios of Alexandria convenes synod in Alexandria to reconcile Chalcedonians and non-Chalcedonians; second finding of the Head of John the Forerunner.

457 Victorius of Aquitania computes new Paschalion; first coronation of Byzantine Emperor by patriarch of Constantinople.

466 Church of Antioch elevates bishop of Mtskheta to rank of Catholicos of Kartli, rendering the Church of Georgia autocephalous; death of Shenouda the Great, abbott of White Monastery in Egypt, considered the founder of Coptic Christianity.

475 Emperor Basiliscus issues letter to bishops of empire, supporting Monophysitism.

484 Founding of Mar Sabbas Monastery by Sabbas the Sanctified; Synod of Beth Lapat in Persia declares Nestorianism as official theology of Assyrian Church of the East, effectively separating the Assyrian church from the Byzantine church.

489 Emperor Zeno I closes Nestorian academy in Edessa, which was then transferred under Sassanian Persian auspices to Nisibis, becoming the spiritual center of the Assyrian Church of the East.

490 Brigid of Kildaire founds monastery of Kildare in Ireland.

494 Pope Gelasius I of Rome delineates relationship between Church and state in his letter Duo sunt, written to Emperor Anastasius I.

496 Remigius of Rheims baptizes Franks into Orthodox Christianity.

506 Church of Armenia separates from Chalcedonian Orthodoxy.

507 Clovis I defeats the Arian Visigoths at Battle of Vouillé near Poitiers, ending their power in Gaul.

519 Eastern and Western churches reconciled with end of Acacian Schism.

527 Dionysius Exiguus calculates the date of birth of Jesus incorrectly; foundation of St. Catherine's Monastery on the Sinai peninsula by Justinian the Great.

529 Pagan University of Athens closed and replaced by Christian university in Constantinople; Benedict of Nursia founds monastery of Monte Cassino and codifies Western monasticism; Council of Orange condemns Pelagianism; death of Theodosius the Great.

529-534 Justinian's Corpus Juris Civilis issued.

530 Brendan the Navigator lands in Newfoundland, Canada, establishing a short-lived community of Irish monks.

532 Justinian the Great orders building of Hagia Sophia; death of Sabbas the Sanctified.

533 Mercurius elected Pope of Rome and takes the name of John II, first pope to change name upon election.

534 Roman Empire destroys the Arian kingdom of Vandals.

537 Construction of Hagia Sophia in Constantinople completed.

538 Emperor Justinian the Great, via deportations and force, manages to get all five patriarchates officially into communion.

541 Jacob Baradeus organizes the Non-Chalcedonian Church in western Syria (the "Jacobites"), which spreads to Armenia and Egypt.

543 Doctrine of apokatastasis condemned by Synod of Constantinople.

544 Jacob Baradeus consecrates Sergius of Tella as bishop of Antioch, opening the lasting schism between the Syriac Orthodox Church and the Chalcedonian Church of Antioch; founding of the monastery at Clonmacnoise in Ireland by Ciaran.

The Unholy Land

553 Fifth Ecumenical Council held in Constantinople in an attempt to reconcile Chalcedonians with non-Chalcedonians— Three Chapters of Theodore of Mopsuestia, Theodoret of Cyrrhus, and Ibas of Edessa are condemned for their Nestorianism, and Origen and his writings are also condemned.

554 Church of Armenia officially breaks with West in 554, during the second Council of Dvin where the dyophysite formula of Chalcedon was rejected.

577 Patr. John III Scholasticus is responsible for the first collection of Canon Law, the Nomocanon, of the Orthodox Church.

579 400 Martyrs slain by Lombards in Sicily.

580 Monte Cassino sacked by Lombards, sending its monks fleeing to Rome; Slavs begin to migrate into the Balkans and Greece.

587 Visigoth King Reccared renounces Arianism in favor of Orthodoxy.

589 Council of Toledo adds Filioque to Nicene-Constantinopolitan Creed in an attempt to combat Arianism.

590 Columbanus founds monasteries in France.

593 Anastasius the Sinaite restored as Orthodox Patriarch of Antioch.

596 Gregory the Dialogist sends Augustine along with forty other monks to southern Britain to convert pagans.

598 Glastonbury Abbey founded.

ca. 600 The Ladder of Divine Ascent written by John Climacus; Gregory the Dialogist inspires development of Gregorian Chant through his liturgical reforms.

601 Augustine of Canterbury converts King Ethelbert of Kent and establishes see of Canterbury.

602 Augustine of Canterbury meets with Welsh bishops to bring them under Canterbury.

610 Heraclius changes official language of the Empire from Latin to Greek, already the lingua franca of the vast majority of the population.

612 Holy Sponge and Holy Lance brought to Constantinople from Palestine.

614 Persians sack Jerusalem under Chosroes II of Persia; Church of the Holy Sepulchre damaged by fire, True Cross captured, and over 65,000 Christians in Jerusalem massacred.

617 Persian Army conquers Chalcedon after a long siege.

626 Akathist Hymn to the Virgin Mary written.

627 Emperor Heraclius defeats Sassanid Persians at Battle of Nineveh, recovering True Cross and breaking Sassanid power.

630 Second Elevation of the Holy Cross.

635 Founding of Lindisfarne Monastery by Aidan; Cynegils, king of Wessex, converts to Christianity.

636 Capture of Jerusalem by Muslim Arabs after Battle of Yarmuk.

640 Muslim conquest of Syria; Battle of Heliopolis between Arab Muslim armies and Byzantium opens door for Muslim conquest of Byzantine Exarchate of Africa.

641 Capture of Alexandria by Muslim Arabs.

642 Muslim conquest of Egypt.

646 Alexandria recaptured by Muslim Arabs after Byzantine attempt to retake Egypt fails, ending nearly ten centuries of Greco-Roman civilization in Egypt.

648 Pope Theodore I of Rome excommunicates patriarch Paul II of Constantinople.

649 Arabs invade and conquer Cyprus.

650 Final defeat of Arianism as Lombards convert to Orthodoxy.

653 Pope Martin the Confessor arrested on orders of Byzantine Emperor Constans II.

654 Invasion of Rhodes by Arabs.

669-78 First Arab siege of Constantinople; at Battle of Syllaeum Arab fleet destroyed by Byzantines through use of Greek Fire, ending immediate Arab threat to eastern Europe.

673 Second Council of Hatfield upholds Orthodoxy against Monothelitism.

680-681 Sixth Ecumenical Council held in Constantinople, condemning Monothelitism and

382

The Unholy Land

affirming Christology of Maximus the Confessor, affirming that Christ has both a human will and a divine will; Patr. Sergius I of Constantinople and Pope Honorius I of Rome are both explicitly anathematized for their support of Monothelitism.

685 First monastics come to Mount Athos

685 John Maron elected first Maronite patriarch, founding the Maronite Catholic Church, which embraced Monothelitism, rejected the teaching of the Fifth Ecumenical Council, and separated from the Orthodox Church.

688 Emperor Justinian II and Caliph al-Malik sign treaty neutralizing Cyprus.

ca. 690 Witenagamot of England forbids church appeals to Rome.

691 Dome of the Rock completed in Jerusalem.

692 Quinisext Council (also called the Penthekte Council or Council in Trullo) held in Constantinople, issuing canons completing the work of the Fifth and Sixth Ecumenical Councils, and declaring the Church of Jerusalem to be a patriarchate.

694 Byzantine army of Justinian II defeated by Maronites, who became fully independent.

698 Muslim conquest of Carthage; at Synod of Aquileia, bishops of the diocese of Aquileia end the Schism of the Three Chapters and return to communion with Rome.

710 Pope Constantine makes last papal visit to Constantinople before 1967.

ca. 715 Lindisfarne Gospels produced in Northumbria (Northern England).

715 Grand Mosque of Damascus built over the Cathedral of St. John the Baptist; Al-Aqsa Mosque constructed over site of Church of St. Mary of Justinian; Pictish King Nechtan invites Northumbrian clergy to establish Christianity amongst the Picts.

717-18 Second Arab siege of Constantinople.

726 Iconoclast Emperor Leo the Isaurian starts campaign against icons.

730 Leo the Isaurian orders destruction of all icons, beginning the First Iconoclastic Period.

732 Muslim invasion of Europe stopped by Franks at Battle of Tours, establishing a balance of power between Western Europe, Islam and the Byzantine Empire.

733 Byzantine Emperor Leo the Isaurian withdraws the Balkans, Sicily and Calabria from the jurisdiction of the Pope in response to Pope Gregory III of Rome's support of a revolt in Italy against iconoclasm..

739 Emperor Leo III (717-41) publishes his Ecloga, designed to introduce Christian principle into law; death of Willibrord.

742 After a forty-year vacancy, Stephen IV becomes Orthodox Patriarch of Antioch, at the suggestion of Umayyad caliph Hisham ibn Abd al-Malik.

750 Donation of Constantine accepted as a legitimate document, used by Pope Stephen II to prove territorial and jurisdictional claims.

754 Iconoclastic Council held in Constantinople under the authority of Emperor Constantine V Copronymus, condemning icons and declaring itself to be the Seventh Ecumenical Council; Constantine begins dissolution of monasteries.

756 Donation of Pepin cedes lands including Ravenna that became basis of Papal States.

768 Wales adopts Orthodox Paschalion and other decrees of the Synod of Whitby at teaching of Elfoddw of Gwynedd.

769 Pope Stephen III of Rome holds a council changing papal election procedure and confirming veneration of icons.

772 Charlemagne starts fighting Saxons and Frisians; Saxony is subdued and converted to Christianity.

781 King Charlemagne of the Franks summons Alcuin of York to head palace school at Aachen (Aix-la-Chapelle) to inspire revival of education in Europe.

787 Seventh Ecumenical Council held in Nicea, condemning iconoclasm and affirming veneration of icons; two councils held in England, one in the north at Pincanhale, and the other in the south at Chelsea, reaffirming the faith of the first Six Ecumenical Councils (the decrees of the Seventh having not yet been received), and establishing a third archbishopric at Lichfield.

383

The Unholy Land

793 Sack of Lindisfarne Priory, beginning Viking attacks on England.

794 Charlemagne convenes council in Frankfurt-in-Main, rejecting decrees of Seventh Ecumenical Council and inserting Filioque into Nicene-Constantinopolitan Creed.

800 Charlemagne crowned as Holy Roman Emperor by Leo III of Rome on Christmas day, marking the break of Frankish civilization away from the Orthodox Christian Roman Empire; Book of Kells produced in Ireland.

800 Ambassadors of Caliph Harunu al-Rashid give keys to the Holy Sepulchre to Charlemagne, acknowledging some Frankish control over the interests of Christians in Jerusalem ; establishment of the Western Rite Monastery of Saint Mary in Jerusalem.

810 Pope Leo III bans use of Filioque.

814 Conflict between Emperor Leo V and Patr. Nicephorus over iconoclasm; Leo deposes Nicephorus, Nicephorus excommunicates Leo.

826 Ansgar arrives in Denmark and begins preaching; King Harald Klak of Denmark converts to Christianity.

ca. 829-842 Icon of the Panagia Portaitissa appears on Mount Athos near Iviron Monastery.

843 Triumph of Orthodoxy occurs on first Sunday of Great Lent, restoring icons to churches.

850 Third Finding of the head of John the Forerunner.

858 Photius the Great becomes patriarch of Constantinople.

ca. 860 Christianization of the Rus' Khaganate.

861 Cyril and Methodius depart from Constantinople to missionize the Slavs; Council of Constantinople attended by 318 fathers and presided over by papal legates confirms Photius the Great as patriarch and passes 17 canons.

862 Rastislav of Moravia converts to Christianity.

863 First translations of Biblical and liturgical texts into Church Slavonic by Cyril and Methodius.

863 Venetians steal relics of Apostle Mark from Alexandria.

864 Baptism of Prince Boris of Bulgaria; Synaxis of the Theotokos in Miasena in memory of the return of her icon.

865 Bulgaria under Khan Boris I converts to Orthodox Christianity.

866 Vikings raid and capture York in England.

867 Council in Constantinople held, presided over by Photius, which anathematizes Pope Nicholas I of Rome for his attacks on work of Greek missionaries in Bulgaria and use by papal missionaries of Filioque; Pope Nicholas dies before hearing news of excommunication; Basil the Macedonian has Emperor Michael III murdered and usurps Imperial throne, reinstating Ignatius as patriarch of Constantinople.

867 Death of Kassiani, Greek-Byzantine poet and hymnographer, who composed the Hymn of Kassiani, chanted during Holy Week on Holy Wednesday.

869-870 Robber Council of 869-870 held, deposing Photius the Great from the Constantinopolitan see and putting the rival claimant Ignatius on the throne, declaring itself to be the "Eighth Ecumenical Council."

870 Conversion of Serbia

878 King Alfred the Great of Wessex defeats Vikings; the Treaty of Wedmore divides England between the Anglo-Saxons and the Danes (the Danelaw).

879-880 Eighth Ecumenical Council held in Constantinople attended by 383 fathers passing 3 canons, confirms Photius as Patriarch of Constantinople, anathematizes additions to the Nicene-Constantinopolitan Creed, and declares that the prerogatives and jurisdiction of the Roman pope and the Constantinopolitan patriarch are essentially equal; the council is reluctantly accepted by Pope John VIII of Rome.

885 Mount Athos gains political autonomy.

886 Glagolitic alphabet, (now called Old Church Slavonic) adopted in Bulgarian Empire; St Alfred the Great, King of Wessex, captures London from the Danes.

911 Holy Protection of the Virgin Mary.

912 Normans become Christian; Nicholas I Mysticus becomes Patriarch of Constantinople.

The Unholy Land

927 Church of Bulgaria recognized as autocephalous by Constantinople.

931 Abbott Odo of Cluny reforms monasteries in Aquitaine, northern France, and Italy, starting the Cluniac Reform movement within the Benedictine order, focused on restoring the traditional monastic life, encouraging art and caring for the poor.

944 City of Edessa recovered by Byzantine army, including Icon Not Made By Hands.

957 Olga of Kiev baptized in Constantinople.

960 Emperor Nicephorus II Phocas re-captures Crete for Byzantines; Dunstan becomes Archbishop of Canterbury, reforming monasteries and enforcing rule of Benedict.

962 Denmark becomes Christian nation with baptism of King Harald Blaatand ("Bluetooth"); Holy Roman Empire formed, with Pope John XII crowning Otto I the Great Holy Roman Emperor.

963 Athanasius of Athos establishes first major monastery on Mount Athos, the Great Lavra.

965 Emperor Nicephorus II Phocas gains Cyprus completely for the Byzantines.

969 Emperor Nikephoros II Phokas captures Antioch and Aleppo from Arabs.

972 Emperor John I Tzimiskes grants Mount Athos its first charter (Typikon).

975 Emperor John I Tzimiskes in a Syrian campaign takes Emesa, Baalbek, Damascus, Tiberias, Nazareth, Caesarea, Sidon, Beirut, Byblos and Tripoli, but fails to take Jerusalem.

980 Revelation of the Axion Estin (the hymn "It Is Truly Meet"), with the appearance of the Archangel Gabriel to a monk on Mount Athos.

980-5 The Western Rite Monastery of Amalfion is founded on Mount Athos.

987 Sixth Rus-Byzantine War, where Vladimir of Kiev dispatches troops to the Byzantine Empire to assist Emperor Basil II with an internal revolt, agreeing to accept Orthodox Christianity as his religion and bring his people to the new faith.

988 'Baptism of Rus' begins with the conversion of Vladimir of Kiev who is baptized at Chersonesos, the birthplace of the Russian and Ukrainian Orthodox churches; Vladimir marries Anna, sister of Byzantine emperor Basil II.

995 Olaf of Norway proclaims Norway to be a Christian kingdom.

1000 Conversion of Greenland and Iceland.

1008 Conversion of Sweden.

1009 Patr. Sergius II of Constantinople removes name of Pope Sergius IV of Rome from diptychs of Constantinople, because the pope had written a letter to the patriarch including the Filioque.

1009 Church of the Holy Sepulchre in Jerusalem destroyed by the "mad" Fatimid caliph Al-Hakim bi-Amr Allah, founder of the Druze.

1012 Caliph Al-Hakim bi-Amr Allah issues oppressive decrees against Jews and Christians including the destruction of all Christian and Jewish houses of worship.

1014 Filioque used for first time in Rome by Pope Benedict VIII at coronation of Henry II, Holy Roman Emperor.

1017 Danish king Canute converts to Christianity.

1027 Frankish protectorate over Christian interests in Jerusalem is replaced by a Byzantine protectorate, which begin reconstruction of Holy Sepulchre.

1036 Byzantine Emperor Michael IV makes a truce with the Caliph of Egypt to allow rebuilding of the Church of the Holy Sepulchre by Byzantine masons; Varangian Guard of the Byzantine Emperor sent to protect pilgrims.

1043 Edward the Confessor crowned King of England at Winchester Cathedral.

1045-50 Cathedral of Saint Sophia in Novgorod built, the oldest Orthodox church building in Russia, executed in an architectural style more austere than the Byzantine, reminiscent of the Romanesque.

1048 Re-consecration of Holy Sepulchre.

1054 July 16th; Roman Catholic Cardinal Humbert excommunicates Michael Cerularius, patriarch of Constantinople and all his followers, a major center point in the formation of the Great Schism between East and West; First Letter of Michael Cerularius to Peter of Antioch.

1064 Seljuk Turks storm Anatolia taking Caesarea and Ani, conquering Armenia.

The Unholy Land

1066 Normans invade England flying banner of Pope of Rome, defeating King Harold of England at Battle of Hastings.

1066-1171 Beginning reformation of English church and society to align with Latin continental ecclesiology and politics.

1071 Seljuk Turks defeat Byzantines at the Battle of Manzikert, beginning Islamification of Asia Minor; Norman princes led by Robert Guiscard capture Bari, the last Byzantine stronghold in Italy, bringing to an end over five centuries of Byzantine rule in the south.

1073 Seljuk Turks conquer Ankara.

1075 Dictatus Papae document advances Papal supremacy.

1077 The Seljuk Turks capture Jerusalem and kill 3,000 citizens; Seljuks capture Nicea.

1084 Antioch is captured by the Seljuk Turks.

1088 Founding of monastery of John the Theologian on Patmos

1095 Launching of the First Crusade.

1098 Anselm of Canterbury completes Cur Deus homo, marking a radical divergence of Western theology of the atonement from that of the East.

1098 Crusaders capture Antioch.

1099 Crusaders capture Jerusalem founding the Latin Kingdom of Jerusalem and other crusader states known collectively as "Outremer."

ca. 1131-45 Coptic Pope of Alexandria Gabriel II initiates addition of Arabic as a liturgical language with his Arabic translation of the Liturgy.

1144 Second Crusade; Muslims take Christian stronghold of Edessa.

1149 Crusaders begin to renovate Church of the Holy Sepulchre in Romanesque style, adding a bell tower.

1159 John of Salisbury authors Policraticus, a treatise on government drawing from the Bible, the Codex Justinianus, and arguing for Divine Right of Kings.

1170 Miracle of the weeping icon of the Theotokos "of the Sign" at Novgorod; Anglo-Norman invasion of Ireland; city of Dublin captured by the Roman Catholic Normans.

1176 Sultanate of Rum defeats Byzantine Empire in the Battle of Myriokephalon, marking end of Byzantine attempts to recover Anatolian plateau; Al-Adil I, Muslim ruler of Egypt, suppresses a revolt by Christian Copts in city of Qift, hanging nearly 3,000 of them.

1179 Pope Alexander III convened the Third Lateran Council, which was attended by a certain Nectarios of the important Basilian Monastery of St. Nicholas of Kasoulon near Otranto, under Norman patronage, who made himself the champion of the Greek Church, and vigorously supported their customs and doctrines.[1]

1180 Last formal acceptance of Latins to communion at an Orthodox altar in Antioch.

1182 Maronites, who assisted the Crusaders during the Crusades, reaffirm their affiliation with Rome in 1182; dedication of Monreale Cathedral in Sicily, containing the largest cycle of Byzantine mosaics extant in Italy.

1186 Byzantine Empire recognizes independence of Bulgaria and Serbia.

1187 Saladin retakes Jerusalem after destroying crusader army at Battle of Hattin, and returns Christian holy places to Orthodox Church.

1189 Third Crusade led by King Richard the Lion-Hearted of England, King Philip Augustus II of France, and Emperor Frederick Barbarossa.

1204 Fourth Crusade sacks Constantinople, laying waste to the city and stealing many relics and other items; Great Schism generally regarded as having been completed by this act; Theodore I Lascaris establishes the Empire of Nicaea.

Ca.1207 Stephen Langton divides the Bible into the defined modern chapters in use today.

ca.1220 English Bp. Richard Le Poore is said to have been responsible for the final form of the "Use of Sarum", which had the sterling reputation of being the best liturgy anywhere in the West.

1228 Sixth Crusade results in 10-year treaty starting in 1229 between Holy Roman Emperor Frederick II and Egyptian sultan; Jerusalem ceded to Franks, along with a narrow corridor to the coast, as well as Nazareth, Sidon, Jaffa and Bethlehem.

The Unholy Land

1240 Mongols sack Kiev; Prince Alexander Nevsky defeats Swedish army at Battle of the Neva.

1242 Alexander Nevsky's Novgorodian force defeats Teutonic Knights in Battle of Lake Peipus, a major defeat for the Catholic crusaders.

1244 Jerusalem conquered and razed by Khwarezmian mercenaries (Oghuz Turks) serving under the Ayyubid ruler of Egypt Salih Ayyub, triggering Seventh Crusade.

1247 Ayyubids conquer Jerusalem, driving out the Khwarezmian Turks.

1258 Michael VIII Palaiologos seizes the throne of the Nicaean Empire, founding the last Roman (Byzantine) dynasty, beginning reconquest of Greek peninsula from Latins.

1259 Byzantines defeat Latin Principality of Achaea at the Battle of Pelagonia, marking the beginning of the Byzantine recovery of Greece.

ca. 1259-80 Martyrdom by Latins of monks of Iveron Monastery.

1260 Subjugation of Church of Cyprus to the Roman Catholic Church.

1261 End of Latin occupation of Constantinople and restoration of Orthodox patriarchs; Emperor Michael VIII Palaiologos makes Mystras seat of the new Despotate of Morea, where a Byzantine renaissance occurred.

1268 Egyptian Mamelukes capture Antioch.

1269 Orthodox patriarch returns to Antioch after a 171-year exile and usurpation by Latin patriarch.

1274 Second Council of Lyons held, proclaiming union between the Orthodox East and the Roman Catholic West, but generally unaccepted in the East.

1275 Unionist Patriarch of Constantinople John XI Bekkos elected to replace Patriarch Joseph I Galesiotes, who opposed Council of Lyons; 26 martyrs of Zographou monastery on Mt. Athos, martyred by the Latins.

1281 Pope Martin IV authorizes a Crusade against the newly re-established Byzantine Empire in Constantinople, excommunicating Emperor Michael VIII Palaiologos and the Greeks and renouncing the union of 1274; French and Venetian expeditions set out toward Constantinople but are forced to turn back in the following year due to the Sicilian Vespers.

1291 Fall of Acre; end of crusading in Holy Land.

1298 Ambrose, Augustine, Jerome, and Pope Gregory I are named collectively as the first Great Doctors of the Western Church.

1302 Papal Bull Unam Sanctum issued by Pope Boniface VIII proclaims Papal supremacy.

1326 Metr. Peter moves his see from Kiev to Vladimir and then to Moscow.

1332 Amda Syon, Emperor of Ethiopia begins his campaigns in the southern Muslim provinces, allowing for the spread of Christianity to frontier areas.

1336 Meteora in Greece established as a center of Orthodox monasticism.

1338 Gregory Palamas writes Triads in Defense of the Holy Hesychasts, defending the Orthodox practice of hesychast spirituality and the use of the Jesus Prayer.

1340 Holy Trinity-St. Sergius Lavra founded by Sergius of Radonezh.

1341-51 Three sessions of the Ninth Ecumenical Council held in Constantinople, affirming hesychastic theology of Gregory Palamas and condemning rationalistic philosophy of Barlaam of Calabria.

1349 Prince Stephen Dushan of Serbia assumes the title of Tsar (Caesar); principality of Galicia (Halitsh) comes under Polish control.

1354 Ottoman Turks make first settlement in Europe at Gallipoli.

1379 Western Great Schism ensues, including simultaneous reign of three Popes of Rome.

ca. 1380 English Church reformer John Wycliffe writes that the true faith is preserved only in the East, "among the Greeks."

1382-95 First English Bible translated by John Wycliffe.

1385 Kreva Agreement provides for conversion of Lithuanian nobles and all pagan Lithuanians to Roman Catholicism, joining Grand Duchy of Lithuania with the Kingdom of Poland through a dynastic union.

The Unholy Land

1387 Lithuania converts to Roman Catholicism, while most Ruthenian lands (Belarus and Ukraine) remain Orthodox.

1389 Serbs defeated by Ottoman Turks of Sultan Murad I at the battle of Kosovo Polje; death of Lazar, prince of Serbia.

1390 Ottomans take Philadelphia, last significant Byzantine enclave in Anatolia.

1391-98 Ottoman Turks unsuccessfully besiege Constantinople for the first time.

1410 Iconographer Andrei Rublev paints his most famous icon depicting the three angels who appeared to Abraham and Sarah, the angels being considered a type of the Holy Trinity.

1414-18 Council of Constance in Roman Catholic Church represents high point for Conciliar Movement over authority of pope.

1417 End of Western Great Schism at the Council of Constance.

1422 Second unsuccessful Ottoman siege of Constantinople.

1423-24 Council of Siena in the Roman Catholic Church was the high point of conciliarism, emphasizing the leadership of the bishops gathered in council, but the conciliarism expressed there was later branded as a heresy.

1439 Ecclesiastical reunion with West attempted at Council of Florence, where only Mark of Ephesus refuses to capitulate to demands of delegates from Rome.

1440-41 Encyclical Letter of Mark of Ephesus.

1444 Donation of Constantine proved forgery.

1448 Church of Russia unilaterally declares its independence from the Church of Constantinople.

1452 Unification of Roman Catholic and Greek Orthodox Churches in Hagia Sophia on West's terms, when Emperor Constantine XI Palaiologos, under pressure from Rome, allows the union to be proclaimed.

1453 Constantinople falls to invasion of the Ottoman Turks, ending Roman Empire; Hagia Sophia turned into a mosque; martyrdom of Constantine XI Palaiologos, last of the Byzantine Emperors; many Greek scholars escape to the West with books that become translated into Latin, triggering the Renaissance.

A list of events of the period that shaped Christianity—still during the Byzantine period.

341-379 Shapur II's persecution of Persian Christians

343? Catholic Council of Sardica, canons confirmed by Pope Julius

346 Death of the Abbott Pachomius (Egypt) author of a famous monastic rule.

350? Codex Sinaiticus, Codex Vaticanus Graecus 1209: earliest Christian Bibles, Alexandrian text-type

350? Ulfilas, Arian, apostle to the Goths, translates Greek NT to Gothic

350? Comma Johanneum 1Jn5:7b-8a (KJV)

350? Aëtius, Arian, "Syntagmation": "God is agennetos (unbegotten)", founder of Anomoeanism

355-365 Antipope Felix II, Arian, supported by Constantius II, consecrated by Acacius of Caesarea

357 Council of Sirmium issues so-called Blasphemy of Sirmium or Seventh Arian Confession, called high point of Arianism

359 Council of Rimini, Dated Creed (Acacians); Pope Liberius rejects Arian creed of council

360 Julian the Apostate becomes the last non-Christian Roman Emperor. (He is killed in battle against the Persians in 363.)

363-364 Council of Laodicea: Canon 29 decreed anathema for Christians who rest on the Sabbath;

The Unholy Land

disputed Canon 60 named 26 NT books (excluded Revelation)

366-367 Antipope Ursicinus, rival to Pope Damasus I

367-403 Epiphanius, Bishop of Salamis, wrote Panarion against heresies

370? Doctrine of Addai at Edessa proclaims 17 book NT canon using Diatessaron (instead of the 4 Gospels) + Acts + 15 Pauline Epistles (inc. 3 Corinthians) Syriac Orthodox Church

370 (d. ca.) Optatus of Milevis, who in his conflict with the sectarian Donatists stressed unity and catholicity as marks of the Church over and above holiness, and also that the sacraments derived their validity from God, not from the priest

c.371 Gregory, Bishop of Nyssa; Fl. Gregory of Nazianzus.

374-397 Ambrose, governor of Milan until 374, then made Bishop of Milan

375-395 Ausonius, Christian governor of Gaul

379-381 Gregory Nazianzus, Bishop of Constantinople

380, February 27: Emperor Theodosius I issues the Edict of Thessalonica, declaring Nicene Christianity as the state church of the Roman Empire. Theodosius I declares the Arian faith of Christianity heretical. November 24: Theodosius I is baptized.

381 First Council of Constantinople, 2nd ecumenical: Jesus had true human soul, Nicene Creed of 381; Constantinople is assigned "seniority of honour" after Rome.

382 Catholic Council of Rome under Pope Damasus I sets the Biblical Canon, listing the inspired books of the Old Testament and the New Testaments.

385 Priscillian, first heretic to be executed?

386 Cyril of Jerusalem: wrote compellingly of catholicity of the Church; John Chrysostom preaching at Antioch; Jerome (who translated most of the Bible into Latin) settles into monastery at Bethlehem (d.420)

390? Apollinaris, Bishop of Laodicea, believed Jesus had human body but divine spirit

390 Bishop Ambrose excommunicates the Emperor Theodosius I for the massacre at Thessalonica.

391: The Theodosian decrees outlaw most pagan rituals still practiced in Rome.

394 Theodosius I outlaws the Olympic games as pagan rituals.

395: Theodosius I outlaws all religions other than Catholic Christianity.

395 Augustine, bishop of Hippo (d.430), considered the founder of formalized Christian theology (Nicene and Post-Nicene Fathers). His theological writings against Donatists and Pelagians and his City of God dominate Western thought down to Aquinas. Division of Eastern (Byzantine) and Western Roman Empires

400: Jerome's Vulgate (Latin edition and translation of the Bible) is published

400? Ethiopic Bible: in Ge'ez, 81 books, standard Ethiopian Orthodox Bible

400? Peshitta Bible in Syriac (Aramaic), Syr(p), OT + 22 NT, excludes: 2Pt, 2-3Jn, Jude, Rev; standard Syriac Orthodox Church Bible

405 St. Jerome finishes the Vulgate. The Christian Gospel is translated into Latin.

406 Armenian Bible, translated by Saint Mesrop, standard Armenian Orthodox Bible

410 August 24 Rome is sacked by Alaric, King of the Visigoths. Decisive event in the decline of the Western Roman Empire.

416 Doctrine of Pelagius (a British monk) condemned at council of Carthage.

418-419 Antipope Eulalius, rival to Pope Boniface I

420 St. Jerome, Vulgate translator, Latin scholar, cited expanded ending in Mark after Mark 16:8, Pericope of the Adultress addition to John (John 7:53-8:11) (Nicene and Post-Nicene Fathers)

422-32 Pope Celestine I is said to have sent Palladius to Ireland as its first Bishop.

423-457 Theodoret, bishop of Cyrrhus, noted Tatian's Diatessaron in heavy use, wrote a Church History

The Unholy Land

431 June 22-July 31 Council of Ephesus 3rd ecumenical .Confirmed the original Nicene Creed,and condemned the teachings of Nestorius, Patriarch of Constantinople, that led to his exile and separation with the Church of the East. repudiated Nestorianism, decreed Mary the Mother of God, forbade any changes to Nicene Creed of 381, rejected by the Persian Church, leading to the Nestorian Schism

432 St Patrick begins his mission in Ireland. Almost the entire nation is Christian by the time of his death in a conversion that is both incredibly successful and largely bloodless

440-461 Pope Leo the Great: sometimes considered the first pope (of influence) by non-Catholics, stopped Attila the Hun at Rome, issued Tome in support of Hypostatic Union, approved Council of Chalcedon but rejected canons in 453

449 Second Council of Ephesus, Monophysite: Jesus was divine but not human

450? Codex Alexandrinus(A): Alexandrian text-type; Codex Bezae(D): Greek/Latin Gospels + Acts; Codex Washingtonianus(W): Greek Gospels; both of Western text-type

450? std. Aramaic Targums, Old Testament in Aramaic

450? Socrates Scholasticus Church History of 305-438; Sozomen Church History of 323-425

451 Council of Chalcedon, 4th ecumenical, declared Jesus is a Hypostatic Union: both human and divine in one (Chalcedonian Creed), rejected by Oriental Orthodoxy

455: June 2; Sack of Rome by the Vandals, capture Sicily and Sardinia. Pope Leo the Great negotiates with the Vandals. The spoils of the Temple of Jerusalem previously taken by Titus are allegedly among the treasures taken to Carthage

476, September 4 Emperor Romulus Augustus is deposed in Rome, marked by many as the fall of the Western Roman Empire. Romulus Augustus, last Western Roman Emperor is forced to abdicate by Odoacer, a chieftain of the Germanic Heruli; Odoacer returns the imperial regalia to Eastern Roman Emperor Zeno in Constantinople in return for the title of dux of Italy; most frequently cited date for the end of ancient history. Odoacer deposes the last Roman Emperor Romulus Augustulus. Syria continues under Eastern (Byzantine) Empire.

484-519 Acacian Schism, over Henoticon, divides Eastern (Greek) and Western (Latin) churches

491 Armenian Orthodox split from East (Greek) and West (Latin) churches

495, May 13 Vicar of Christ decreed a title of Bishop of Rome by Pope Gelasius I

496 Clovis I, King of the Franks, baptized

498-499,501-506 Antipope Laurentius, rival of Pope Symmachus, Laurentian schism

c. 500? Incense introduced in Christian church service.

524 Boethius, Roman Christian philosopher, wrote "Theological Tractates", Consolation of Philosophy; (Latin)

c. 524 Boethius writes his Consolation of Philosophy It has been described as the single most important and influential work in the West on Medieval and early Renaissance Christianity.

525 Dionysius Exiguus publishes the Dionysius Exiguus' Easter table. This initiated the Anno Domini era, used for the Gregorian and Julian calendars.; Boethius is executed.

527 August 1 Justinian I becomes Eastern Roman Emperor. Justinian is best remembered for his Code of Civil Law (529), and expansion of imperial territory retaking Italy from the Ostrogoths and N. Africa from the Vandals.

529 Benedict of Nursia founds monastery at Monte Cassino. The first of twelve monasteries founded by Saint Benedict, beginning the Order of Saint Benedict. He writes the Rule of St

530 Antipope Dioscorus, possibly a legitimate Pope.

537-555 Pope Vigilius, involved in death of Pope Silverius, conspired with Justinian and Theodora, on April 11, 548 issued Judicatum supporting Justinian's anti-Hypostatic Union, excommunicated by bishops of Carthage in 550

538 Byzantine general Belisarius defeats last Arian kingdom; Western Europe completely Catholic

c.540 Benedict of Nursia at Monte Casino; here draws up his Monastic rule.

541-542 Plague of Justinian

The Unholy Land

c.542 -78 Jacob Baradaeus, disguised as a beggar, wanders east of Edessa founding Monophysite churches (Jocobite)

543 Justinian condemns Origen, disastrous earthquakes hit the world

544 Justinian condemns the Three Chapters of Theodore of Mopsuestia (died 428) and other writings of Hypostatic Union Christology of Council of Chalcedon

550 St. David converts Wales, crucifix introduced.

553 Second Council of Constantinople, 5th ecumenical, called by Justinian

556-561 Pope Pelagius I, selected by Justinian, endorsed Judicatum

563 Columba goes to Scotland to evangelize Picts, establishes monastery at Iona

563 Saint Columba founds mission in Iona. Constructed an abbey which helped convert the Picts to Christianity until it was destroyed and raided by the Vikings in 794.

568 The Kingdom of the Lombards is founded in Italy. Survived in Italy until the invasion of the Franks in 774 under Charlemagne.

c. 570 Muhammad is born. Professed receiving revelations from God, which were recorded in the Qur'an, the basis of Islamic theology, in which he is regarded as the last of the sent prophets.

589 Catholic Third Council of Toledo: Reccared and the Visigoths convert from Arianism to Catholicism and Filioque clause is added to Nicene Creed of 381

590-604 September 3 Gregory the Great becomes Pope. The missionary work reached new levels during his pontificate, revolutionized the way of worship for the Catholic Church (Gregorian Chants), Seven deadly sins, liturgy, etc., and was soon canonized after his death.

591-628 Theodelinda, Queen of the Lombards, began gradual conversion from Arianism to Catholicism

596 St. Augustine of Canterbury sent by Pope Gregory to evangelize the Jutes

597 Augustine arrives in Kent. Christianization of England (Anglo-Saxons) begins.

600? Evagrius Scholasticus, Church History of AD431-594

604 Saxon cathedral created (by Mellitus) where St Paul's Cathedral in London now stands

609 Pantheon, Rome renamed Church of Santa Maria Rotonda

614 Khosrau II of Persia conquers Damascus, Jerusalem, takes Holy Cross of Christ

622 9 September— 23 September Muhammad Migrates from Mecca to Medina. Event will have designated first year of the Islamic Calendar, as Anno Hegirae. Mohammed founds Islam after fleeing to Mecca. 622 becomes the hegira—year 0 in the Muslim calendar.

624 Battle of Badr, considered beginning of Islamic Empire

628 Babai the Great, pillar of Church of the East, dies

628-629 Battle of Mut'ah: Heraclius recovers Cross of Christ and Jerusalem from Islam until 638

632 June 8 Death of Muhammad. By this point, all of Arabia is Muslim.

632 June 8 Accession of Abu Bakr as first Caliph. Though the period of his caliphate was not long, it included successful invasions of the two most powerful empires of the time.

637 CE Muslim forces defeat the Byzantine army. Syria becomes part of Rashidun Caliphate.

638 Jerusalem captured by the Arab army, mostly Muslims, but with contingents of Syrian Christians.

663 Synod of Whitby. Roman Christianity triumphs over Celtic Christianity in England. Unites Celtic Christianity of British Isles with Roman Catholicism; Roman date for Easter prevails over the Celtic.

674-678 First Arab siege of Constantinople. First time Islamic armies defeated, forestalling Islamic conquest of Europe.

675-700 Composition of Beowulf, and the rise of a Christian literature in Old English

680-681 Third Council of Constantinople, 6th ecumenical, against Monothelites, condemned Pope Honorius I, Patriarch Sergius I of

The Unholy Land

Constantinople, Heraclius' Ecthesis; Council concludes the Christ has "two natural wills."

681-686 Wilfrid converts Sussex

687-691 Dome of the Rock built in Jerusalem

690? Old English Bible translations begin

692 Orthodox Quinisext Council, convoked by Justinian II, approved Canons of the Apostles of Apostolic Constitutions, Clerical celibacy, rejected by Pope Constantine

718-1492 Reconquista: Iberian Peninsula retaken by Roman Catholic Visigoth monarchs

718 Saint Boniface, archbishop of Mainz; an Englishman, given commission by Pope Gregory II to evangelize the Germans

722 Boniface to Rome.

726 Iconoclast movement begun in the Byzantine Empire under Leo III. This was opposed by Pope Gregory II, and an important difference between the Roman and Byzantine churches.

730-787 First Iconoclasm: Byzantine Emperor Leo III bans Christian icons; Pope Gregory II excommunicates him

731 English Church History written by Bede

732 October Battle of Tours. Charles Martel halts Muslim advance. Significant moment that led to the forming of the Carolingian Empire for the Franks, and halted the advancement of the Moors in southwestern Europe.

750 25 January Beginning of Abbasid Caliphate. Would become the longest lasting caliphate, until 1519 when conquered and annexed into the Ottoman Empire.

752? Donation of Constantine, granted Western Roman Empire to the Pope (later proved a forgery)

754 Pepin promises the Pope central Italy. This is arguably the beginning of the temporal power of the Papacy. Martyrdom of Boniface in Frisia.

756 Donation of Pepin recognizes Papal States

768 Beginning of Charlemagne's reign. Charles the Great and Carloman divide the Frankish Kingdom.

772 -- Destruction of the Sacred Tree (Irmiusul) at Easeburg. Charlemagne begins conquest of Saxony. (772 - 804) This is possibly the spark that ignites the coming Viking Raiding activities against Christian Monasteries and the Greater Carolingian Empire.

781 Nestorian Stele, Daqin Pagoda, Jesus Sutras, Christianity in China

787 Second Council of Nicaea, 7th ecumenical: end of the first Iconoclasm period.

800 25 December Charlemagne is crowned Holy Roman Emperor by Pope Leo III . With his crowning, Charlemagne's kingdom is officially recognized by the Papacy as the largest in Europe since the fall of the Roman Empire.

c. 800 Gunpowder was invented (somewhere around 9th century); The book of Kells (Ireland); Beginnings of translating the Bible from Greek to Arabic begin in Baghdad.

814 28 January Death of Charlemagne. Would be a factor towards the splitting of his empire almost 30 years later.

843 Division of Charlemagne's Empire between his grandsons with the Treaty of Verdun. Sets the stage for the founding of the Holy Roman Empire and France as separate states.

855 Antipope Anastasius: Louis II, Holy Roman Emperor appoints him over Pope Benedict III but popular pressure causes withdrawal

863 Saint Cyril and Saint Methodius sent by the Patriarch of Constantinople to evangelise the Slavic peoples. They translate the Bible into Slavonic. Dorestad is abandoned

864 Christianization of Bulgaria.

878 -- Gunthrum and the Great Army capture Chippenham (Jan. 8). Alfred and his thegns are driven into exile; Alfred rallies his forces. Battle of Eddinton: Alfred defeats Gunthrum. Treaty of Wedmore: Gunthrum is given East Anglia (and rules as King Athelstan of East. Anglia after he accepts Christianity and is baptized) and the Vikings withdraw north of the Thames

879-880 Orthodox Fourth Council of Constantinople restores Photius, condemns Pope Nicholas I and Filioque (rejected by Catholics)

885 Arrival of the disciples of Saints Cyril and Methodius in Bulgaria Creation of the Cyrillic script; in the following decades the country became the

The Unholy Land

cultural and spiritual centre of the whole Eastern Orthodox part of the Slavic World.

897, January Cadaver Synod: Pope Stephen VI conducts trial against dead Pope Formosus, public uprising against Stephen leads to his imprisonment and strangulation

910 Cluny Abbey is founded by William I, Count of Auvergne.Cluny goes on to become the acknowledged leader of Western Monasticism. Cluniac Reforms initiated with the abbey's founding.

927 Death of Simeon I the Great. Recognition of the Bulgarian Patriarchate, the first independent National Church in Europe.

962 Otto the Great crowned the Holy Roman Emperor. First to be crowned Holy Roman Emperor in nearly 40 years.

963-964 Otto deposes Pope John XII who is replaced with Pope Leo VIII. Citizens of Rome promise not to elect another Pope without Imperial approval.

965-967 Mieszko I of Poland and his court embrace Christianity, which becomes national religion.

969 John I Tzimiskes the last Byzantium empire and Nikephoros II are being executed. Sultane of Rums are proclaim.

976 Death of John I Tzimiskes; Basil II (his co-emperor) takes sole power. Under Basil II zenith of the power of Eastern Empire after Justinian.

984 Antipope Boniface VII, murdered Pope John XIV, alleged to have murdered Pope Benedict VI in 974

988 Volodymyr I of Kiev embrace Christianity, which becomes national religion. Event known as the Baptism of Rus.

991 Archbishop Arnulf of Rheims accuses Pope John XV of being the Antichrist

996 – 1021 Persecution of Coptic Church in Egypt under Caliph el-Hakim.

997-998 Antipope John XVI, deposed by Pope Gregory V and his cousin Holy Roman Emperor Otto III

989 Peace and Truce of God formed. The first movement of the Catholic Church using spiritual means to limit private war, and the first movement in medieval Europe to control society through non-violent means.

1000 or 1001 Saint Stephen of Hungary crowned; Hungary becomes a Christian country

1001 Byzantine emperor Basil II and Fatimid Caliph Al-Hakim bi-Amr Allah execute a treaty guaranteeing the protection of Christian pilgrimage routes in the Middle East

1009 Caliph Al-Hakim bi-Amr Allah destroys the Church of the Holy Sepulchre, built over the tomb of Jesus in Jerusalem, and then rebuilds it to its current state

1012 Antipope Gregory VI, removed by Henry II, Holy Roman Emperor

1030 Battle of Stiklestad, considered victory of Christianity over Norwegian paganism

1031 Fall of the Islamic caliphate in Cordoba.

1045 Sigfrid of Sweden, Benedictine evangelist.

1046 Council of Sutri: Pope Sylvester III exiled, Pope Gregory VI admits to buying the papacy and resigns, Pope Benedict IX resigns, council appoints Pope Clement II

1049 Pope Leo IX ascends to the papal throne. Leo IX was the pope that excommunicated Patriarch of Constantinople, Michael Cerularius (who also excommunicated Leo), which caused the Great Schism.

1054 The East-West Schism which divided the church into Western Catholicism and Eastern Orthodoxy. Tensions will vary between the Catholic and Orthodox churches throughout the Middle Ages.

1058-1059 Antipope Benedict X, defeated in war with Pope Nicholas II and Normans

1061-1064 Antipope Honorius II, rival of Pope Alexander II

1065 Westminster Abbey consecrated

1067 Pope Gregory VII elevated to the papal throne. This begins a period of church reform.

1073-1085 Pope Gregory VII: Investiture Controversy with Henry IV, Holy Roman Emperor, proponent of clerical celibacy, opponent of simony, concubinage, Antipope Clement III

The Unholy Land

1075 Dictatus Papae in which Pope Gregory VII defines the powers of the pope. Peak of the Gregorian Reform, and an immense factor in the Investiture Controversy.

1077 Holy Roman Emperor Henry IV walks to Canossa where he stands barefoot in the snow to beg forgiveness of the Pope for his offences, and admitting defeat in the Investiture Controversy. This helps establish Papal rule over European heads of state for another 450 years.

1080 Hospital of Saint John the Baptist founded in Jerusalem by merchants from Amalfi and Salerno - serves as the foundation for the Knights Hospitaller.

1095 Pope Urban issues the Crusades to capture the Holy Land, and to repel the Seljuk Turks from the Byzantine Empire from Alexios I Komnenos. This would be the first of 9 Major Crusades, and a number of other crusades that would spread into the late 13th century.

1096 First Crusade. Jerusalem is re-taken from the Muslims on the urging of Pope Urban II. This would lead to the beginning of the Kingdom of Jerusalem, which would last for nearly two centuries; within the era of the Crusades to the Holy Land.

1098 Foundation of the reforming monastery of Cîteaux, leads to the growth of the Cistercian order. The Cistercian Order is founded. Was a return to the original observance of the Rule of St. Benedict.

1093-1109 Anselm, Archbishop of Canterbury, writes Cur Deus Homo (Why God Became Man), a landmark exploration of the Atonement

1099 Crusaders take Jerusalem.

1101 Antipope Theodoric and Antipope Adalbert deposed by Pope Paschal II.

1107 Through the Compromise of 1107, suggested by Adela, the sister of King Henry, the Investiture Struggle in England is ended. This compromise removed one of the points of friction between the English monarchy and the Catholic Church.

1113 Knights Hospitaller confirmed by Papal bull of Pope Paschal II, listing Blessed Gerard (Gerard Thom) as founder, (a.k.a. Sovereign Order of Saint John of Jerusalem of Rhodes and of Malta, Knights of Malta, Knights of Rhodes, and Chevaliers of Malta)

1118 The Knights Templar are founded to protect Jerusalem and European pilgrims on their journey to the city. Becomes the most recognizable, and impactful military orders during the Crusades.

1121 12/25 St. Norbert and 29 companions make their solemn vows marking the beginning of the Premonstratensian Order. This order played a significant role in evangelizing the Slavs, the Wends, to the east of the Holy Roman Empire.

1122 9/23   The Concordat of Worms was drawn up between Emperor Henry V and Pope Calixtus II. This concordat ended the investiture struggle, but bitter rivalry between emperor and pope remained.

1123 3/18-3/27 The First Lateran Council followed and confirmed the Concordat of Worms.

1124 Conversion of Pomerania - first mission of Otto of Bamberg

1125 Lothair of Supplinburg, duke of Saxony, is elected Holy Roman Emperor instead of the nearest heir, Frederick of Swabia. This election marks the beginning of the great struggle between the Guelfs and the Ghibellines.

1128 Holyrood Abbey in Scotland; Conversion of Pomerania - second mission of Otto of Bamberg

1130 Peter of Bruys burned at the stake

1130 12/25 Roger II is crowned King of Sicily, a royal title given him by the Antipope Anacletus II. This coronation marks the beginning of the Kingdom of Sicily and its Mediterranean empire under the Norman kings, which was able to take on the Holy Roman Empire, the Papacy, and the Byzantine Empire.

1131-1138 Antipope Anacletus II

1139 April   The Second Lateran Council declared clerical marriages invalid, regulated clerical dress, and punished attacks on clerics by excommunication. Enforces the major reforms that Gregory VII began to heavily campaign for several decades earlier.

1140? Decretum Gratiani, Catholic Canon law

1147–1149 The Second Crusade was in retaliation for the fall of Edessa, one of the first Crusader States founded in the First Crusade. It was an overall failure. This was the first Crusade to have been led by European kings.

The Unholy Land

1150 Ramon Berenguer IV, Count of Barcelona, married Queen Petronilla of Aragon. They had been betrothed in 1137. This marriage gave the Kingdom of Aragon access to the Mediterranean Sea, creating a powerful kingdom which expanded to control many of the Mediterranean lands.

1152 The Synod of Kells-Mellifont established the present diocesan system of Ireland (with later modifications) and recognized the primacy of Armagh. This synod marks the inclusion of the Irish Church into mainstream European Catholicism.

1154-1159 Pope Adrian IV, first (and to date only) English pope

1155 Theotokos of Vladimir arrives to Bogolyubovo.; Carmelites founded

1168 Conversion of Pomerania - Principality of Rugia missioned by Absalon.

1171 King Henry II of England lands in Ireland to assert his supremacy and the Synod of Cashel acknowledges his sovereignty. With his landing, Henry begins the English claim to and occupation of Ireland which would last some seven and a half centuries.

1173 Waldensians founded

1179 March The Third Lateran Council limits papal candidates to the cardinals alone, condemns simony, and forbids the promotion of anyone to the episcopate before the age of thirty

1184 November Pope Lucius III issues the papal bull Ad Abolendam. This bull set up the organization of the medieval inquisitions.

1187 Saladin recaptures Jerusalem. This event would lead to the Third Crusade.

1189–1192 The Third Crusade follows upon Saladin's uniting the Muslim world and recapturing Jerusalem. Despite managing to win several major battles, the Crusaders did not recapture Jerusalem.

1191 Teutonic Knights founded

1198 Pope Innocent offers a general amnesty for all sins ("indulgences") to all who pledge and serve in the upcoming crusade. Enlistments were for one year.

1199 The Fourth Crusade was an expensive endeavor. Pope Innocent III chose to raise funds by doing something previously unheard of in popes, forcing the entire clergy under his leadership to give one fortieth of their income as a tax in support of the Crusade. This marked the first time a pope ever imposed a direct tax on his clerical subjects.

1202 The Fourth Crusade sacked Croatian town of Zadar (Italian: Zara), a rival of Venice. Unable to raise enough funds to pay to their Venetian contractors, the crusaders agreed to sack the city despite letters from Pope Innocent III forbidding such an action and threatening excommunication. Siege of Zara was the first major Crusade's action and the first attack against a Roman Catholic city by Roman Catholic crusaders.

1204 Sack of Constantinople during the Fourth Crusade. Considered to be the beginning of the decline of the Byzantine Empire. Roman Catholic crusaders attacking Eastern Orthodox Christians.

1204-1261 Latin Empire of Constantinople

1205 Saint Francis of Assisi becomes a hermit, founding the Franciscan order of friars; renounces wealth and begins his ministry; Battle of Adrianople. The Bulgarians under Emperor Kaloyan defeat Baldwin I. Beginning of the decline of the Latin Empire.

1208 Pope Innocent III calls for the Albigensian Crusade which seeks to destroy a rival form of Christianity practiced by the Cathars.

1209 The University of Cambridge is founded; Founding of the Franciscan Order. One of the more significant orders in the Roman Catholic church, founded by Saint Francis of Assisi.

1212 Spanish Christians succeed in defeating the Moors in the long Reconquista campaigns, after the Battle of Las Navas de Tolosa. By 1238, only the small southern Emirate of Granada remained under Muslim control.

1214 Rosary is reportedly given to St. Dominic (who founded Dominican Order) by an apparition of Mary

1215 Catholic Fourth Lateran Council decrees special dress for Jews and Muslims, and declares Waldensians, founded by Peter Waldo, as heretics. One of the goals is the elimination of the heresy of the Cathars Dealt with transubstantiation, papal primacy and conduct of clergy. Pope levies a second income tax which constituted a triennial twentieth. Proclaimed that Jews and Muslims should wear identification marks to distinguish them from Christians.

The Unholy Land

1216 Papal recognition of the Dominican Order.

1219 Francis of Assisi crosses enemy lines during the Fifth Crusade to speak to Sultan al-Kamil; the meeting ends with a meal. James of Vitry writes that Muslim soldiers returned Francis and another friar, Illuminato, "with signs of honor."; Serbian Orthodox Church becomes autocephalous under St. Sava, its first Archbishop.

1231 Charter of the University of Paris granted by Pope Gregory IX

1241 Pope Gregory IX denounced as Antichrist by Eberhard II von Truchsees, Prince-Archbishop of Salzburg, at the Council of Regensburg

1245 Catholic First Council of Lyon

1252, May 15 Ad exstirpanda: Pope Innocent IV authorizes use of torture in Inquisitions

1260 Date at which a 1988 Vatican sponsored scientific study places the origin of the Shroud of Turin

1263, July 20–24 The Disputation of Barcelona is held at the royal palace of King James I of Aragon in the presence of the King, his court, and many prominent ecclesiastical dignitaries and knights, between a convert from Judaism to Christianity Dominican Friar Pablo Christiani and Rabbi Nachmanides

1265 St. Thomas Aquinas work, *Summa Theologæ*

1272-73 The Ninth Crusade occurs. Considered to be the Last Major Crusade to take place in the Holy Land.

1273 29 September Rudolph I of Germany is elected Holy Roman Emperor. This begins the Habsburg de facto domination of the crown that lasted until is dissolution in 1806.

1274 Summa Theologiae, written by Thomas Aquinas, theologian and philosopher, landmark systematic theology which later becomes official Catholic doctrine

1274 Catholic Second Council of Lyon

1291 Last Crusader city (Acre) falls to the Mamelukes

1305 August 23 William Wallace is executed for treason.

1305-1378 Avignon Papacy, Popes reside in Avignon, France

1307 Friday, October 13th The Knights Templar are rounded up and murdered by Philip the Fair of France, with the backing of the Pope. Hastens the demise of the order within a decade; The arrest of many of the Knights Templar, beginning confiscation of their property and extraction of confessions under torture

1307 Beginning of the Babylonian Captivity of the Papacy during which the Popes moved to Avignon. Begins a period of over seven decades of the Papacy outside of Rome that would be one of the major factors of the Western Schism.

1311-1312 Roman Catholic Council of Vienne disbands Knights Templar

1313 Foundation of the legendary Order of the Rose Cross (Rosicrucian Order), a mystic Christian fraternity for the first time expounded in the major Christian literary work The Divine Comedy.

1314 Jacques de Molay, last Grandmaster of Knights Templar, burned at the stake

1341-1351 Orthodox Fifth Council of Constantinople

1347 The Black Death ravages Europe for the first of many times. An estimated 20% - 40% of the population is thought to have perished within the first year. The first of many concurrences of this plague, This was believed to have wiped out as many as 50% of Europe's population by its end.

1378 The Western Schism during which three claimant popes were elected simultaneously. The Avignon Papacy ends.

1380-1382 Wycliffe's Bible, by John Wycliffe, eminent theologian at Oxford, NT in 1380, OT (with help of Nicholas of Hereford) in 1382, translations into Middle English, 1st complete translation to English, includes deuterocanonical books, preaches against abuses, expresses anti-Catholic views of the sacraments (Penance and Eucharist), the use of relics, and clerical celibacy.

1381 Peasants' Revolt in England. Quickest-spread revolt in English history, and the most popular revolt of the Late Middle Ages; The Bible is translated into English by John Wycliffe. First print published in English (Vulgate)

The Unholy Land

1396 The Battle of Nicopolis. The last great Crusade fails.

1408 Council of Oxford forbids translations of the Scriptures into the vernacular, unless and until they are fully approved by church authority.

1409 Council of Pisa declares Roman Pope Gregory XII and Avignon Pope Benedict XIII deposed, elects Pope Alexander V (called the Pisan Pope)

1414-1418 Catholic Council of Constance asks Gregory XII, Benedict XIII, Pisan Pope John XXIII to resign their papal claims, then elects Pope Martin V; condemns John Wycliffe and Jan Hus, who is burned at the stake

1417 The Council of Constance ends. The Western Schism comes to a close, and elects Pope Martin V as the sole pope.

1419 Hussite Wars begins after 4 years after the death of Jan Hus in central Europe, dealing with the followers of Jan Hus and those against them. Although the war was a stalemate (ended around 1434), it was another factor that[clarification needed] between the Catholics and Protestants before the Protestant Reformation.

1423-1424 Council of Siena.

1425 Catholic University of Leuven

1431-1445 Catholic Council of Basel-Ferrara-Florence.

1431 30 May Trial and execution of Joan of Arc. Death of the woman who helped turned the Hundred Years' War in favor of the French over the past two years--burned at the stake.

1439 Johannes Gutenberg invents the printing press. Literature, News, etc. becomes more accessible throughout Europe.; Notre-Dame de Strasbourg, highest building in the world until 1874

1452 Dum Diversas, papal bull issued on 18 June 1452, credited with ushering in the West African slave trade in Europe and the New World

1453 May 29th Constantinople falls to the Ottoman Turks after a 53 day siege of the capitol city. This ended the Byzantine Empire (or Eastern Roman Empire); Constantinople becomes capital of Ottoman Empire; During the same year, the Hundred Years' War ends. England's once vast territories in France is now reduced to only Calais, which they eventually lose control of as well

The summary historical points of the timeline of Church history since 1453[413] with a few contextual listings about the Roman Catholic Church:

1456-1587 Byzantine Church of Theotokos Pammakaristos became the seat of the Ecumenical Patriarchate.

1492 Millennialist movements in Moscow, due to end of church calendar (year 7,000, according to the Byzantine Date of Creation).

1503 Possessor and Non-Possessor controversy.

1516 Desiderius Erasmus publishes "Textus Receptus" of New Testament on the basis of six late manuscripts of the Byzantine text-type.

1517 Maximus the Greek invited to Russia to translate Greek service books and correct Russian ones; Ottomans conquer Jerusalem, Antioch and Alexandria.

1529 First Ottoman Siege of Vienna, marking Ottoman Empire's apex and end of Ottoman expansion in central Europe.

1551 Council of the Hundred Chapters in Russia.

1555 Abp. Gurian begins mission to Kazan.

1568 Pope Pius V recognizes four Great Doctors of the Eastern Church, John Chrysostom, Basil the Great, Gregory of Nazianzus, and Athanasius.

1569 Union of Lublin unites Kingdom of Poland and Grand Duchy of Lithuania into a single state, the Polish-Lithuanian Commonwealth, placing the Ruthenian Orthodox lands of Belarus, and modern Ukraine under direct Roman Catholic rule.

1571 Restoration of Church of Cyprus to Orthodox rule.

1573-81 Correspondence of Patr. Jeremias II of Constantinople with Lutherans.

1575 Church of Constantinople grants autonomy to Church of Sinai.

1582 Institution of the Gregorian Calendar by Pope Gregory XIII.

1583 Sigillion of 1583 issued against Gregorian Calendar by council convened in Constantinople.

1587-Present. The relatively modest Church of St George in the Phanar district of Istanbul becomes the seat of the Ecumenical Patriarchate.

1589 Autocephaly and canonical territory of Church of Russia recognized, as Patr. Jeremias II of Constantinople raises Metr. Job of Moscow to the rank of Patriarch of Moscow and of All Russia.

1596 Union of Brest-Litovsk, several million Ukrainian and Byelorussian Orthodox Christians, living under Polish rule, leave the Church of Constantinople and recognize the Pope of Rome, without giving up their Byzantine liturgy and customs, creating the Uniate church.

ca. 1600-1700 Conversion of Albania to Islam mainly through discriminatory tax system, the Djize.

1625 *Confession of Faith* by Metrophanes Kritopoulos written.

1627 Pope Cyril Lucaris of Alexandria presents Codex Alexandrinus to King Charles I of England for safe keeping.

1633 Ethiopian emperor Fasilides expels Jesuits and other Roman Catholic missionaries from Ethiopia.

1642 Council of Jassy (Iași) revises Peter Mogila's confession to remove overtly Roman Catholic theology and confirms canonicity of certain deuterocanonical books.

1646 Union of Uzhhorod joins 63 Ruthenian Orthodox priests from the Carpathian Mountains to Roman Catholic Church on terms similar to Union of Brest.

1652-1658 Patriarch Nikon of Moscow revises liturgical books to bring them into conformity with the Greek liturgical customs, leading to mass excommunication and schism of dissenters, who become known as Old Believers.

1672 Synod of Jerusalem convened by Patr. Dositheos Notaras, refuting article by article the Calvinistic confession of Cyril Lucaris, defining Orthodoxy relative to Roman Catholicism and Protestantism, and defining the Orthodox Biblical canon; acts of this council are later signed by all five patriarchates (including Russia).

1682 The *Sabaite Typikon* was published in its final form in Russia; from 1682 to 1888 the Greek and Russian Churches shared a common Typikon.

1685-87 The Slavic Greek Latin Academy is organized as the first higher education establishment in Moscow on the premises of the Zaikonospassky Monastery with over 70 students.

1685 Orthodoxy introduced in Beijing by Church of Russia.

1698 Consecration of the first Orthodox Church in China, in the name of Sophia (Divine Wisdom), when Emperor Kangxi ordered a Buddhist temple to be cleared for Russian inhabitants in Beijing.

The Unholy Land

1700 The Creation Era calendar in Russia, in use since AD 988 was changed to the Julian Calendar by Peter the Great.

1700-02 Submission of the dioceses of Lemberg (Lviv) and Luzk (Lutsk) in the Galician area of Ukraine to Roman Catholic Church completes Union of Brest-Litovsk, so that two-thirds of the Orthodox in western Ukraine had become Greek Catholic.

1715-1956 Russian Ecclesiastical Mission in China.

1721 Czar Peter I of Russia replaces Russian patriarchate with a ruling holy synod.

1724 Melkite schism, in which many faithful from the Church of Antioch become Uniates.

1728 The Ecumenical Patriarchate formally replaced the Creation Era (AM) calendar with the Christian Era (AD).

1754 Hesychast Renaissance begins with the Kollyvades Movement.

1755 Synod of Constantinople declares Roman Catholic baptism invalid and ordered baptism of converts from Roman Catholicism.

1756 Sigillion of 1756 issued against the Gregorian calendar by Patr. Cyril V of Constantinople.

1767 Ottoman Empire legally divides Church of the Holy Sepulchre among claimants.

1767-1815 Suppression of the Jesuits in Roman Catholic countries, subsequently finding refuge in Orthodox nations, particularly in Russia.

1768 Jews are massacred during riots in Russia-occupied Poland.

ca. 1770 About 1,200 Kiev region Uniate churches return to Orthodoxy under political pressure from Russia.

1774 Russia and Ottoman Empire sign treaty of Kuchuk-Kainarji, bringing Russia for the first time into the Mediterranean as the acknowledged protector of Orthodox Christians.

1782 First publication of *Philokalia*; autonomy of Church of Sinai confirmed by Church of Constantinople.

1793-95 Over 2,300 Uniate churches became Orthodox under Tsarina Catherine the Great.

1794 Missionaries, including Herman of Alaska, arrive at Kodiak Island, bringing Orthodoxy to Russian Alaska; death of Paisius Velichkovsky of Moldova and Mt. Athos.

1796 Nicodemus the Hagiorite publishes Unseen Warfare in Venice.

1798 Patriarch Anthimus of Jerusalem contended that the Ottoman Empire was part of the Divine Dispensation granted by God to protect Orthodoxy from the taint of Roman Catholicism and of Western secularism and irreligion.

1800 *The Rudder* published and printed in Athens.

1811 Autocephaly of the Church of Georgia revoked by the Russian imperial state after Georgia's annexation, making it subject to the Church of Russia.

1819 Council at Constantinople endorses views of Kollyvades fathers.

ca. 1830 Slavophile movement begins in Russia.

1831 Return of 3,000,000 Uniates with the Orthodox Church at Vilnius in 1831.

1832 Church of Serbia becomes de facto autocephalous.

1833 Church of Greece declares autocephaly, making it independent of the Constantinople; death of Seraphim of Sarov.

1839 Synod of Polotsk abolishes Union of Brest-Litovsk in all areas under Russian rule as Greek Catholic dioceses in Lithuania and Belarus re-enter the Orthodox Church.

1848 Encyclical of the Eastern Patriarchs sent by the primates and synods of the four ancient patriarchates of the Orthodox Church, condemning the Filioque as heresy, declaring the Roman Catholic Church to be heretical, schismatic, and in apostasy, repudiating Ultramontanism and referring to the Photian Council of 879-880 as the "Eighth Ecumenical Council."

1850 Church of Constantinople recognizes autocephaly of Church of Greece.

1851 Translation into English of *Septuagint* by Lancelot C. L. Brenton; Ottoman Empire recognizes France as supreme Christian authority in Holy Land and grants it possession of the Church of the Nativity.

1852 Ottoman Empire makes division of Church of the Holy Sepulchre permanent.

1853-56 Crimean War fought between Russia and the Ottoman Empire together with Britain and France, beginning over which church would be recognized as the "sovereign authority" of the Christian faith in the Holy Land.

1854 Immaculate Conception declared dogma by Roman Catholic Church.

1859 Constantin von Tischendorf discovers *Codex Sinaiticus* at St. Catherine's Monastery.

1864 First Orthodox parish established on American soil in New Orleans, Louisiana, by Greeks.

1865 Church of Romania declares its independence from the Church of Constantinople.

1869 Russian synod authorizes corrected text of Western Rite liturgy and Benedictine offices.

1870 Papal Infallibility declared Roman Catholic dogma necessary for salvation by First Vatican Council.

1871 Nikolai Kasatkin establishes Orthodox mission in Japan.

1872 Council in Jerusalem declares phyletism to be heresy; Church of Bulgaria gains de facto autocephaly by a decree of the Sultan.

1875 Uniate diocese of Chelm in Poland incorporated into Russian Orthodox Church under Alexander II, with all of the local Uniates converted to Orthodoxy.

1879 Church of Constantinople recognizes autocephaly of Church of Serbia; death of Innocent of Alaska.

1882 Mitrophan Ji becomes the first Chinese ordained a priest in the Church of China.

1885 Church of Constantinople recognizes autocephaly of Church of Romania; English Revised Version published; Archbishop of Canterbury officially removes all of Apocrypha from King James Bible.

1888 *Typikon* of the Great Church of Christ is published with revised church services, prepared by Protopsaltis George Violakis, issued with the approval and blessing of the Ecumenical Patriarch, while the Sabaite (monastic) *Typikon* continues to be used in Russia.

1889 Federation of Old Catholic Churches, not in communion with Rome, at the Union of Utrecht.

ca. 1890 *Unseen Warfare* further revised by Theophan the Recluse.

1898 Last ethnically Greek patriarch of Antioch deposed; Western Rite diocese organized in Czechoslovakia by Church of Russia.

The Unholy Land

1899 Restoration of Arabs to the Patriarchal throne of Antioch.

1900 Martyrdom of Orthodox Christians in Chinese Boxer Rebellion (Yihetuan Movement).

1901 "Evangelakia" riots in Athens Greece in November, over translations of New Testament into Demotic (Modern) Greek, resulting in fall of both government and Metropolitan of Athens.

1904 Ecumenical Patriarchate publishes the "Patriarchal" Text of the Greek New Testament, based on about twenty Byzantine manuscripts; petition to Russian synod by Abp. Tikhon (Belavin), Bp. Raphael (Hawaweeny), and Fr. John Kochurov to permit adaption of services taken from Anglican Book of Common Prayer for use by Orthodox people.

1905 Death of Apostolos Makrakis; Tsar Nicholas Romanov's decree on freedom of religion results in about 250,000 Ruthenians returning to Uniatism; seat of Russian Orthodox bishop in America moved from San Francisco to New York, as immigration from Eastern Europe and the reception of ex-Uniates shifts the balance of Orthodox population to eastern North America.

1908 Fr. Nikodemos Sarikas sent to Johannesburg, Transvaal, by Ecumenical Patriarchate as first Orthodox priest there, leaving after a short time for German East Africa (later Tanzania) because of the opposition of Johannesburg Greeks to mission among Africans.

1917 Bolshevik Revolution throws Church of Russia into chaos, effectively stranding the fledgling Russian Orthodox mission in America; restoration of Moscow Patriarchate with Tikhon as patriarch; Church of Georgia's autocephaly restored de facto by political chaos in Russia.

1917-40 Persecution of the Orthodox Church in Russia begins, with 130,000 priests arrested, 95,000 of whom were executed by firing squad.

1918 Tsar Nicholas II of Russia murdered together with his wife Alexandra and children.

1919-1922 Greco-Turkish War; a million refugees flee to Greece joining half a million Greeks who had fled earlier; Pontic Greek Genocide eliminates the Christian population of Trebizond.

1920 Death of Nektarios of Aegina; publication of Encyclical Letters by Constantinople on Christian unity and on the Ecumenical Movement.

1921 Constantinople renounces all claims to jurisdiction in any part of Africa, with Alexandrian primate thenceforth known as Pope and Patriarch of Alexandria and All Africa; Greek Archdiocese of America formed; the Ukrainian Autocephalous Orthodox Church (UAOC) (as yet unrecognized) is declared independent from the Moscow Patriarchate (MP).

1922 Church of Albania declares autocephaly from Constantinople; formation of the Russian Orthodox Church Outside Russia; Solovetsky Monastery converted by Lenin's decree to the "Solovki Special Purpose Camp", one of the earliest forced-labor camps of the Gulag where 75 bishops died, along with tens of thousands of laity; the predominantly Christian city of Smyrna is destroyed, ending 1900 years of Christian civilization.

1923 Church of the Czech Lands and Slovakia granted autonomy by Church of Constantinople; Treaty of Lausanne affirmed the international status of the Ecumenical Patriarchate, with Turkey guaranteeing respect and the Patriarchate's full protection.

401

The Unholy Land

1924 Church of Constantinople recognizes autocephaly of Church of Poland.

1925 Church of Romania becomes a patriarchate; first Africans in sub-Saharan Africa baptized in Tanganyika by Fr. Nikodemos Sarikas; death of Tikhon of Moscow.

1926 Polish Catholic National Church received as a Western Rite diocese in Poland of Church of Russia.

1927 Bishops of Russian church in America authorize formation of American Orthodox Catholic Church, including a Western Rite missionary outreach.

1929 Kingdom of Italy and Papacy ratify Lateran Treaty, recognizing sovereignty of Papacy within the new state of the Vatican City.

1931 Reception of Patriarchal Exarchate for Orthodox Parishes of Russian Tradition in Western Europe into the Ecumenical Patriarchate, led by Metr. Eulogius (Georgievsky) of Paris.

1932 Daniel William Alexander travels to Uganda to meet Reuben Spartas, establishing African Orthodox Church there.

1933 Church of Greece bans Freemasonry.

1934 Daniel William Alexander travels to Kenya, establishing African Orthodox Church led by Arthur Gathuna; episcopal consecration of John Maximovitch.

1935 Critical edition of *Septuagint* published in Gottingen Germany by Alfred Rahlfs at the Septuaginta-Unternehmens (Institute).

1935-40 Italian forces occupy Ethiopia and begin intermittent persecutions of the Ethiopian Orthodox Church.

1936 Ukase of Moscow Patriarchate establishes Western Orthodox Church in France using Western Rite.

1936-37 Many Russian Orthodox Clerics die in Joseph Stalin's Great Purge.

1937 Church of Constantinople recognizes autocephaly of Church of Albania.

1938 American Carpatho-Russian Orthodox Diocese founded, when a group of 37 Carpatho-Russian Eastern Catholic parishes, under the leadership of Fr. Orestes Chornock, were received into the jurisdiction of the Ecumenical Patriarchate.

1941 Martyrdom of Gorazd (Pavlik) of Prague by Nazis.

1941-45 Nazi-backed Croatian Ustasa terrorists kill 500,000 Orthodox Serbs, expel 250,000 and force 250,000 to convert to Catholicism.

1943 Church of Russia recognizes autocephaly of Church of Georgia; first constitution of the African Orthodox Church in East Africa. Joseph Stalin meets with hierarchs of Russian Orthodox Church to establish a "patriotic union," granting concessions to the church, including the gathering of the Holy Synod and the election of Sergius I as patriarch of Moscow.

1943-44 Hundreds of Orthodox priests of the Ukrainian Orthodox Church eliminated, tortured and drowned by Organization of Ukrainian Nationalists - Ukrainian Rebel Army, aided by Uniate Metr. Josyf Slipyj who was a spiritual leader of Nazi military units that were later condemned by the Nuremberg tribunal, and who was imprisoned by Soviet authorities for aiding the UPA.

The Unholy Land

1945 Church of Bulgaria's autocephaly generally recognized; library of early Christian texts discovered at Nag Hammadi in Egypt; Soviet Union annexes Czechoslovakia; Church of Russia claims jurisdiction over the Church of the Czech Lands and Slovakia.

1945-90 Persecution of the Orthodox Church in Albania.

1946 Reuben Spartas of the African Orthodox Church visits Alexandria; Holy Synod of the Church of Alexandria officially recognizes and accepts the African Greek Orthodox Church in Kenya and Uganda; state-sponsored synod is held at Lviv, Ukraine in March, which officially dissolves the Union of Brest-Litovsk and integrates the Ukrainian Greek Catholic Church into the Russian Orthodox Church, Soviet authorities arresting resisters or deporting them to Siberia.

1948 Church of Russia re-grants autocephaly to the Church of Poland (after having revoked it in the aftermath of World War II); World Council of Churches is founded; Council of Moscow is held on the occasion of the 500th anniversary of the independence of the Russian Church from Constantinople, with representatives of the local Orthodox Churches rejecting all participation in the World Council of Churches.

1949 Soviet authorities revoke the Union of Uzhhorod of 1646, creating the Orthodox Eparchy of Mukachiv-Uzhhorod, under the Patriarch of Moscow.

1950 Roman Catholic Pope Pius XII proclaims the Bodily Assumption of the Virgin Mary as a dogma.

1951 Church of Russia grants autocephaly to the Church of the Czech Lands and Slovakia; 1500th anniversary celebration of the Patriarchate of Jerusalem.

1952-60 With the Mau-Mau Movement in Kenya (British East Africa Protectorate), the Orthodox Church is banished by the Colonial Government.

1953 Metr. Antony (Bashir) accepts three Western Rite parishes into Syrian Metropolitanate in America.

1957 Church of Russia grants autonomy to Church of China.

1958 Patriarch of Antioch adopts provisions of Russian synods of 1879 and 1907 for use by Western Rite in America.

1959 Autocephaly granted to the Church of Ethiopia by Coptic Pope Cyril VI (Atta) of Alexandria.

1961 Creation of Western Rite Vicariate in the Antiochian Orthodox Christian Archdiocese of North America; consecration of first Orthodox Church in Uganda; first Pan-Orthodox Conference in Rhodes.

1963 Second Pan-Orthodox Conference in Rhodes; 1000th anniversary celebration of founding of Mount Athos.

1964 Meeting of Pope Paul VI of Rome and Patr. Athenagoras I (Spyrou) of Constantinople in Jerusalem; third Pan-Orthodox Conference in Rhodes; Synaxis of the Saints of Rostov established by resolution of His Holiness Patriarch Alexis I and the Holy Synod of the Russian Orthodox Church.

1965 Pope Paul VI of Rome and Patriarch Athenagoras I (Spyrou) of Constantinople mutually nullify the excommunications of 1054.

1966 The Cultural Revolution almost totally destroyed the young Chinese Orthodox Church.

1967 Church of Macedonia unilaterally declares its autocephaly, making it independent of the Church of Serbia (as yet unrecognized); Albania is declared an atheist state, closing all religious institutions and forbidding any religious practices.

1968 fourth Pan-Orthodox Conference in Chambesy, Switzerland.

1970 Russian-American Metropolia reconciles with Church of Russia and is granted autocephaly, renamed as the Orthodox Church in America, returning control of Church of Japan to Moscow, which grants it autonomy; Abp. Makarios III (Mouskos) of Cyprus baptizes 10,000 into the Orthodox Church in Kenya.

1971 Halki Seminary is closed by Turkish authorities.

1975 Division in the Antiochian church in North America overcome; Joint Commission of Orthodox and Old Catholic theologians is established.

1976 First Pre-Synodal Pan-Orthodox Conference at Orthodox Centre of the Ecumenical Patriarchate in Chambesy, Switzerland.

1979 Joint Commission of Orthodox and Roman Catholic Churches for Theological Dialogue is established by Pope John Paul II and Patr. Demetrius I (Papadopoulos) of Constantinople.

1981 Lutheran-Orthodox Joint Commission meets for the first time in Espoo, Finland.

1982 Orthodox-Roman Catholic Joint Commission publishes in Munich first official common document, "The Mystery of the Church and of the Eucharist in Light of the Mystery of the Holy Trinity"; second Pre-Synodal Pan-Orthodox Conference in Chambesy, Switzerland.

1986 Third Pre-Synodal Pan-Orthodox Conference in Chambesy, Switzerland.

1987 Orthodox-Roman Catholic Joint Commission issues common document "Faith, Sacraments and the Unity of the Church"; visit by Patr. Demetrius I (Papadopoulos) of Constantinople to Vatican.

1987 Group of twenty parishes of the Evangelical Orthodox Church, originally formed by former Campus Crusade for Christ leaders Peter Gillquist and Jon Braun, are received into Antiochian Archdiocese in US, becoming the Antiochian Evangelical Orthodox Mission; Lutheran-Orthodox Joint Commission issues the statement "Scripture and Tradition."

1988 1000th anniversary of Orthodoxy in Russia; Orthodox-Roman Catholic Joint Commission publishes common document "The Sacrament of Order in the Sacramental Structure of the Church"

1989 Church of Constantinople recognizes autocephaly of the Church of Georgia; Elder Ephraim begins founding Athonite-style monasteries in North America; Uniate Ukrainian Greek Catholic Church legalized, with Greek Catholics beginning seizure of property from Russian Orthodox Church, which they claimed as theirs prior to the synod of 1946.

1990 Ukrainian Orthodox Church-Kiev Patriarchate (UOC-KP) self-proclaims its independence from the UAOC (both groups unrecognized).

1991 Representatives of Eastern and Oriental Orthodox Churches meet in Chambesy, Switzerland, discussing relations with World Council of Churches.

1993 Orthodox-Roman Catholic Joint Theological Commission meets in Balamand, Lebanon, issuing common document "Uniatism: Method of Union of the Past, and Present. Search for Full Communion" (the "Balamand document"); Lutheran-Orthodox Joint Commission issues statement "The Ecumenical Councils."

1993 Church of Cyprus condemns Freemasonry; Orthodox Study Bible: New Testament and Psalms published; Eritrean Orthodox Tewahedo Church becomes autocephalous.

1994 Ligonier Meeting in Western Pennsylvania at Antiochian Village held by the majority of Orthodox hierarchs in North America votes to end the notion of Orthodox Christians in America being a "diaspora".

1995 Patr. Bartholomew I visits Vatican; Lutheran-Orthodox Joint Commission issues statement "Understanding of Salvation in the Light of the Ecumenical Councils"; Pope John Paul II issues encyclical Orientale Lumen, encouraging reunion between East and West.

1996 Greek Orthodox Archdiocese of North and South America reorganized by the Ecumenical Patriarchate, dividing the administration of the two continents into four parts.

1998 Church of Constantinople, not recognizing Russia's right to issue a tomos of autocephaly in 1951, issues its own tomos for the Church of the Czech Lands and Slovakia; Thessaloniki Summit held to discuss Orthodox participation in WCC.

1999 Numerous Serbian Orthodox sites in Kosovo and Metohia destroyed and desecrated during NATO peacekeeping presence.

2000 Orthodox-Roman Catholic Joint Theological Commission meets in Baltimore, discusses text on "The Ecclesiological and Canonical Implications of Uniatism," but is suspended.

2001 Church of Armenia celebrates 1700th Anniversary of Christianity in Armenia (in 301 AD, King Tiridates III declared Christianity as Armenia's state religion); Pope John Paul II of Rome apologizes to Orthodox Church for Fourth Crusade.

2002 Patr. Bartholomew I (Archontonis) of Constantinople and Pope John Paul II co-sign Venice Declaration of Environmental Ethics.

2003 Orthodox Churches in Europe commemorated the 550th anniversary of the fall of Constantinople in May; Antiochian Orthodox Christian Archdiocese of North America granted "self-rule" (Autocephaly, similar but not identical to autonomy) by Church of Antioch.

2004 Pope John Paul II returns relics of John Chrysostom and Gregory the Theologian to Church of Constantinople.

2006 Pope Benedict XVI visits Ecumenical Patriarchate, drawing criticism from the Orthodox on Mount Athos; Abp. Christodoulos (Paraskevaides) of Athens visits Vatican.

2007 Restoration of full communion between Moscow Patriarchate and ROCOR; synod of over 50 bishops of the Church of Ukraine announce that the UOC-MP is "an autonomous, historical part of the Russian Orthodox Church"; Orthodox-Roman Catholic Joint Commission meets in Ravenna, Italy, agreeing upon a joint document consisting of 46 articles providing an ecclesiastical road map in discussing union; Russian delegation walks out of Ravenna talks in protest.

2008 Orthodox Study Bible (with Septuagint) published; Pan-Orthodox meeting in Constantinople in October of the Primates of the fourteen Orthodox Churches, signing a document calling for inter-orthodox unity and collaboration and "the continuation of preparations for the Holy and Great Council".

2009 The 4th Pan-Orthodox pre-conciliar consultation was held in Chambésy on June 6-13.

Bibliography and Additional Materials

On the Subjects of Antiquity:

History's Timeline: 40,000 Year Chronology of Civilization by Jean Cooke
Publisher: Crescent Books: NY February 11, 1981
- ISBN-10: 0517340003
- ISBN-13: 978-0517340004

The Era of the Crusades (The Great Courses, Ancient & Medieval History) Format: DVD
- University Professor Kenneth W. Harl
- Number of discs: 6
- The Great Courses The Teaching Company 2003

(Note: This is an in-depth and highly comprehensive college-level course)

Accounts of Medieval Constantinople: The Patria by Albrecht Berger
- Series: Dumbarton Oaks Medieval Library (Book 24)
- Publisher: Harvard University Press; November 1, 2013
- ISBN-10: 067472481X
- ISBN-13: 978-0674724815

Early Christian and Byzantine Art by John Beckwith
- Publisher: Penguin, 1979
- ISBN -10: 0140560335

A Short History of Byzantium by John Julius Norwich
- Publisher: Vintage; Reprint ed. December 29, 1998
- ISBN-10: 0679772693
- ISBN-13: 978-0679772699

(Note: This is the abridged version of the work. The unabridged text is in three volumes.)

The Shorter Cambridge Medieval History by Charles William Previte-Orton
- Publisher: University Press; First Ed. 1952

History of the Byzantine Empire: Vol. 1, 324-1453 by Alexander A. Vasiliev
- Publisher: University of Wisconsin Press; 2, Second Ed. April 15, 1958
- ISBN-10: 0299809250
- ISBN-13: 978-0299809256

History of the Byzantine Empire: Vol. 2, 324-1453 by Alexander A. Vasiliev

- Publisher: University of Wisconsin Press; 2, Second English Ed. April 15, 1958
- ISBN-10: 0299809269
- ISBN-13: 978-0299809263

History of the Byzantine State (Rutgers Byzantine series) Revised Edition by George Ostrogorsky
- Publisher: Rutgers University Press; Revised ed. October 1969
- ISBN-10: 0813505992
- ISBN-13: 978-0813505992

John Skylitzes: A Synopsis of Byzantine History, 811-1057: Translation and Notes by John Skylitzes, John Wortley
- Publisher: Cambridge University Press; February 16, 2012
- ISBN-10: 1107404746
- ISBN-13: 978-1107404748

The Oxford Illustrated History of Medieval Europe by George Holmes
- Publisher: Oxford University Press; 1st Ed. May 19, 1988
- ISBN-10: 0198200730
- ISBN-13: 978-0198200734

A History of the Crusades (Complete in Three Volumes) The First Crusade, The Kingdom of Jerusalem, The Kingdom of Acre by Steven Runciman

The Oxford Illustrated History of the Crusades by Jonathan Riley-Smith
- Publisher: Oxford University Press; Illustrated ed. October 19, 1995
- ISBN-10: 0198204353
- ISBN-13: 978-0198204350

The Concise History of the Crusades 3rd Ed. by Thomas F. Madden
- ISBN-13: 978-1442215757
- ISBN-10: 1442215755

1453: The Holy War for Constantinople and the Clash of Islam and the West by Roger Crowley
- Publisher: Hachette Books; Reprint Ed. August 15, 2006
- ISBN-10: 1401308503
- ISBN-13: 978-1401308506

From Christ to Constantine by Michael A. Smith
- Publisher: Inter-Varsity Press; 1st ed. October 21, 1971
- ISBN-10: 0877847584
- ISBN-13: 978-0877847588

Coins and Christianity by Kenneth A. Jacob

- Publisher: Numismatic Fine Arts Intl; 2nd Enlarged ed. June 1985
- ISBN-10: 090065273X
- ISBN-13: 978-0900652738

The Crusades: A Reader, Second Edition by S.J. Allen (Editor), Emilie Amt
- Publisher: University of Toronto Press, Higher Education Division; 2 ed. April 21, 2014
- ISBN-10: 1442606231
- ISBN-13: 978-1442606234

Christian Slaves, Muslim Masters: White Slavery in the Mediterranean, The Barbary Coast, and Italy, 1500-1800 by Robert C. Davis
- Publisher: Palgrave Macmillan; September 16, 2003
- ISBN-10: 0333719662
- ISBN-13: 978-0333719664

Chronicles of the Crusades by Joinville / Villehardouin (many formats available)

forumancientcoins.com, Ancient coin dealer with ancient Greek and Roman coins, Byzantine coins, and other ancient coins in a huge online catalog. Articles, discussion forum and tools. A treasure trove of free education is offered by Forum.

On the Subject of the Christianity and the Church:

Luther's Small Catechism with Explanation by Martin Luther
- Publisher : Concordia Publishing (January 1, 2008)
- ISBN-10 : 0758616473
- ISBN-13 : 978-0758616470

Catechism of the Catholic Church: Complete and Updated by U.S. Catholic Church
- Publisher : USCCB Publishing
- ISBN-10 : 0385479670
- ISBN-13 : 978-0385479677

The Longer Catechism of the Eastern Orthodox Church: The Catechism of St. Philaret of Moscow by St. Philaret Drozdov of Moscow.
- ISBN-13 : 979-8686378803

Orthodox Christianity Volume I: The History and Canonical Structure of the Orthodox Church by Metropolitan Hilarion Alfeyev
- Publisher : St Vladimirs Seminary Pr (February 4, 2011)
- ISBN-10 : 0881418781
- ISBN-13 : 978-0881418781

The Unholy Land

The Oxford Illustrated History of Christianity by John McManners
- Publisher: Oxford University Press; Annotated ed. November 29, 1990
- ISBN-10: 0198229283
- ISBN-13: 978-0198229285

History of the Christian Church, 8 vols. by Philip Schaff
- Publisher: Hendrickson Publishers, Inc.; 3rd edition (July 1, 2006)
- ISBN-10: 156563196X
- ISBN-13: 978-1565631960

The Early Church (The Penguin History of the Church) by Henry Chadwick
- Publisher: Penguin; Revised ed. October 1, 1993
- ISBN-10: 0140231994
- ISBN-13: 978-0140231991

That They May Be One: An Invitation for Protestants to Encounter the Ancient Church by Mark Bradshaw
- ISBN-10: 1521161631
- ISBN-13: 978-1521161630

In Search of Ancient Roots: The Christian Past and the Evangelical Identity Crisis by Kenneth J. Stewart
- Publisher: IVP Academic
- ISBN-10: 0830851720
- ISBN-13: 978-0830851720

The Church in Ancient Society: From Galilee to Gregory the Great (Oxford History of the Christian Church) 1st Edition by Henry Chadwick
- ISBN-13: 978-0199265770
- ISBN-10: 0199265771

From Christ to Constantine by Michael A. Smith
- Publisher: Inter-Varsity Press; 1st ed. October 21, 1971
- ISBN-10: 0877847584
- ISBN-13: 978-0851105703

Christianizing the Roman Empire (A.D. 100-400) by Ramsay MacMullen
- Publisher: Yale Univ Press, October 1984
- ISBN-10: 0300032161
- ISBN-13: 978-030003216

The Rise of Christianity: How the Obscure, Marginal Jesus Movement Became the Dominant Religious Force in the Western World in a Few Centuries by Rodney Stark
- Publisher: Harper San Francisco; May 9, 1997
- ISBN-10: 0060677015
- ISBN-13: 978-0060677015

Josephus the Complete Works by Josephus translated by William Whiston
- Publisher: Thomas Nelson; First Trade Paper ed. edition (July 30, 2003)
- ISBN-10: 0785250506
- ISBN-13: 978-0785250500

Private Religious Foundations in the Byzantine Empire by John Philip Thomas Series: Dumbarton Oaks Studies (Book 24)
- Publisher: Dumbarton Oaks Research Library and Collection (January 1, 1988)
- ISBN-10: 0884021645
- ISBN-13: 978-0884021643

Christianity at the Crossroads: How the Second Century Shaped the Future of the Church by Michael J. Kruger
- Publisher: IVP Academic
- ISBN-10: 0830852034
- ISBN-13: 978-0830852031

The Apostolic Fathers: Greek Texts and English Translations 3rd Ed. Michael W. Holmes (editor)
- ISBN-13: 978-0801034688
- ISBN-10: 080103468X

Summa Theologiae: A Concise Translation; by St. Thomas Aquinas (Author), Timothy McDermott (Editor)
- Publisher: Christian Classics; December 1989
- ISBN-10: 0870611704
- ISBN-13: 978-0870611704

The VATICAN. Its History. Its Treasures. (1914) by Ernesto – Editor Begni

An Archaeologist Looks at the Gospels by James L. Kelso
- Publisher:Word Books (1969)

The Creeds of Christendom (3 Volume Set) by Phillip Schaff
- Publisher: Baker; 6th Edition (1998)
- ISBN-10: 0801082323
- ISBN-13: 978-0801082320

The First Seven Ecumenical Councils (325-787): Their History and Theology by Leo D. Davis SJ
- Publisher: Michael Glazier, January 1, 1988
- ISBN-10: 0814656161
- ISBN-13: 978-0814656167

The Byzantine Legacy in the Orthodox Church by John Meyendorff
- Publisher: St Vladimirs Seminary Press, August 9, 2000

- ISBN-10: 0913836907
- ISBN-13: 978-0913836903

On Free Choice of the Will by Saint Augustine of Hippo, Thomas Williams
- ISBN-13: 978-0872201880
- ISBN-10: 0872201880

The Spanish Inquisition: A Historical Revision, Fourth Edition by Henry Kamen
- ISBN-13: 978-0300180510
- ISBN-10: 0300180519

Spanish Inquisition, 1478-1614: An Anthology of Sources by Lu Ann Homza
- ISBN-13: 978-0872207943
- ISBN-10: 0872207943

The Inquisition in New Spain, 1536–1820: A Documentary History by John F. Chuchiak IV
- Publisher: Johns Hopkins University Press (April 18, 2012)
- ISBN-10: 1421403862
- ISBN-13: 978-1421403861

Ancient Christian Worship: Early Church Practices in Social, Historical, and Theological Perspective by Andrew B. McGowan
- Publisher: Baker Academic; Reprint Ed. January 5, 2016
- ISBN-10: 0801097878
- ISBN-13: 978-0801097874

Popes and Patriarchs: An Orthodox Perspective on Roman Catholic Claims by Michael Whelton
- Publisher: Conciliar Press, June 1, 2006
- ISBN-10: 1888212780
- ISBN-13: 978-1888212785

AA-1025: The Memoirs of a Communist's infiltration in to the Church by Marie Carre
- Publisher: TAN Books; English edition May 1, 1972
- ISBN-10: 0895554496
- ISBN-13: 978-0895554499

The Orthodox Church: An Introduction to Eastern Christianity by Timothy Ware
- Publisher: Penguin Books; 3rd Revised ed. October 6, 2015
- ISBN-10: 014198063X
- ISBN-13: 978-0141980638

The Christian History Institute, http://christianhistoryinstitute.org/

On the Subject of America and Culture:

http://www.nlnrac.org/ The Witherspoon Institute's online center for Natural Law, Natural Rights, and American Constitutionalism. An online resource and repository for the philosophy and documentation of the above.

The Debate on the Constitution : Federalist and Antifederalist Speeches, Articles, and Letters During the Struggle over Ratification : Part One, September 1787-February 1788 (Library of America) by Various , Bernard Bailyn
- Publisher: Library of America (June 1, 1993)
- ISBN-10: 0940450429
- ISBN-13: 978-0940450424

The Debate on the Constitution : Federalist and Antifederalist Speeches, Articles and Letters During the Struggle over Ratification, Part Two: January to August 1788 (Library of America)
by Various , Bernard Bailyn
- Publisher: Library of America (June 1, 1993)
- ISBN-10: 9780940450646
- ISBN-13: 978-0940450646

People Before Profit: The Inspiring Story of the Founder of Bob's Red Mill by Ken Koopman
- Publisher: Inkwater Press; First ed. March 1, 2012
- ISBN-10: 1592997260
- ISBN-13: 978-1592997268

If Aristotle Ran General Motors by Tom Morris
- Publisher: Holt Paperbacks; 1st ed. November 15, 1998.
- ISBN-10: 0805052534
- ISBN-13: 978-0805052534

Tears for Byzantium; The Entropic Course of American Exceptionalism by Daniel B. Rundquist
- Publisher: New Plymouth Press, LLC, December 1, 2017
- ISBN-13 978-0-9862967-5-8

America's God and Country: Encyclopedia of Quotations revised Ed. by William J. Federer
- ISBN-13: 978-1880563090

The Unholy Land

- ISBN-10: 1880563096

De Tocqueville: Democracy in America (Library of America)
by Alexis de Tocqueville, Arthur Goldhammer (Translator)
- Series: Library of America (Book 147)
- Publisher: Library of America; 1st ed, February 9, 2004
- ISBN-10: 1931082545
- ISBN-13: 978-1931082549

Christianity and the Constitution: The Faith of Our Founding Fathers
by John Eidsmoe D. Kennedy
- Publisher: Baker Book House, June 1987
- ISBN-10: 0801034442
- ISBN-13: 978-0801034442

The Constitutional Thought of Thomas Jefferson by David N. Mayer
- Publisher: University of Virginia Press, September 8, 1995
- ISBN-10: 081391485X
- ISBN-13: 978-0813914855

John Adams's Republic: The One, the Few, and the Many by Richard Alan Ryerson
- Publisher: Johns Hopkins University Press , July 26, 2016
- ISBN-10: 142141922X
- ISBN-13: 978-1421419220

Two Treatises of Government and A Letter Concerning Toleration by John Locke (Author), Ian Shapiro (Editor)
- ISBN-13: 978-0300100181
- ISBN-10: 9780300100181

Separation of Church & State: What the Founders Meant
by David Barton
- Publisher: WallBuilder Press; 1st ed. May 8, 2007
- ISBN-10: 1932225412
- ISBN-13: 978-1932225419

The Myth of Separation: What Is the Correct Relationship Between Church and State? by David Barton
- Publisher: Baker Book House, June 1987
- ISBN-10: 0801034442
- ISBN-13: 978-0801034442

When a Nation Forgets God: 7 Lessons We Must Learn from Nazi Germany by Erwin W. Lutzer
- Publisher: Moody Publishers; New Ed. January 1, 2010
- ISBN-10: 0802446566
- ISBN-13: 978-0802446565

What's Wrong with the World by G.K. Chesterton
- ISBN-10: 1619491834
- ISBN-13: 978-1619491830

Liberal Fascism: The Secret History of the American Left, From Mussolini to the Politics of Change by Jonah Goldberg
- Publisher: Crown Forum; June 2, 2009
- ISBN-10: 0767917189
- ISBN-13: 978-0767917186

Citations and Endnotes

[1] There are eight levels of control that must be obtained in order to create a social state according to Saul Alinsky. The first is the most important. 1) Healthcare – Control healthcare and you control the people. 2) Poverty – Increase the poverty level as high as possible; poor people are easier to control and will not fight back if you are providing everything for them to live. 3) Debt – Increase the debt to an unsustainable level. That way you are able to increase taxes and this will produce more poverty. 4) Gun control – Remove people's ability to defend themselves from the government. That way you are able to create a police state. 5) Welfare – Take control of every aspect of people's lives (food, housing and income). 6) Education – Take control of what people read and listen to; take control of what children learn in school. 7) Religion – Remove the belief in God from the government and schools. 8) Class warfare – Divide the people into the wealthy and the poor. This will cause more discontent and it will be easier to take from (tax) the wealthy with the support of the poor. See Saul D. Alinsky, "Rules for Radicals: A Practical Primer for Realistic Radicals"
[2] http://www.goodreads.com/author/quotes/40328.Billy_Graham?page=4 accessed 1/28/18 from Billy Graham in Quotes.
[3] Extract from Thomas Jefferson's Argument in the Case of Howell vs. Netherland [ca. April 1770] sourced at http://tjrs.monticello.org/letter/45 accessed 1/14/2018
[4] See Tears for Byzantium, the Entropic Course of American Exceptionalism by Daniel B. Rundquist. New Plymouth Pres, LLC 12/1/2017
[5] "The Impact of Christianity" Faithfacts.org http://www.faithfacts.org/christ-and-the-culture/the-impact-of-christianity accessed 11/28/18
[6] Thom S. Rainer, Autopsy of a Deceased Church; 12 Ways to Keep Your Alive. Pg. 7 B&H Publishing Group, 2014.
[7] Some dates and events may be listed twice or even approximate due to different or even conflicting sources. This information was collected over many years from very many sources and studies, including, but not limited to The Oxford Illustrated History of Medieval Europe by George Holmes and The Oxford Illustrated History of Christianity by John McManners. Nevertheless the overall information is thought to be generally useful for the purposes of this book. No single chronology is ever complete as new historical facts are being discovered and corrected all the time.
[8] "Anyone who is capable of speaking the truth but remains silent, will be heavily judged by God, especially in this case, where the faith and the very foundation of the entire church of the Orthodox is in danger. To remain silent under these circumstances is to betray these, and the appropriate witness belongs to those that reproach (stand up for the faith)." --St. Basil the Great.
[9] President Thomas Jefferson, First Annual Message, December 8, 1801.
[10] AUTHENTIC TEXT OF CHIEF SEATTLE'S TREATY ORATION 1854 Version 1, which appeared in the Seattle 'Sunday Star' on October 29, 1887, in a column by Dr. Henry A. Smith.
[11] http://www.goodreads.com/author/quotes/40328.Billy_Graham?page=5 accessed 1/28/18
[12] "Module 05: Industrialization and Its Discontents: The Great Strike of 1877" https://www.dhr.history.vt.edu/modules/us/mod05_industry/resources.html accessed 7/9/2019
[13] "The Trail Of Tears: Government-Approved Ethnic Cleansing That Removed 100,000 Native Americans From Their Ancestral Lands By Daniel Rennie. All That's Interesting. Published January 16, 2019 Updated August 5, 2020. https://allthatsinteresting.com/trail-of-tears Accessed 9/18/2020.
[14] Alexis de Tocqueville, Democracy in America, Introduction, pg 13, Library of America, 2004
[15] "What Would You Do For A Raise? | 35% of Americans Would Give Up the Right to Vote" by Mike Brown April 3, 2018 LendEDU http://lendedu.com/blog/what-would-you-do-for-a-raise/ accessed 4/7/18

[16] http://www.goodreads.com/quotes/search?commit=Search&page=21&q=religion&utf8=%E2%9C%93 Accessed 2/1/2018

[17] Thomas Jefferson, Letter to Mathew Carey, 11 November 1816, Letters of Thomas Jefferson.

[18] Midwest Consulting Group, Personality Type Description INTJ, Adapted from Working Together by Olaf Isachsen & Linda V. Berens.

[19] "Survey Finds Most American Christians Are Actually Heretics" by G. Shane Morris OCTOBER 10, 2016, The Federalist.com https://thefederalist.com/2016/10/10/survey-finds-american-christians-actually-heretics/ accessed 12/19/2020.

[20] "Survey Finds Most American Christians Are Actually Heretics" by G. Shane Morris OCTOBER 10, 2016, The Federalist.com https://thefederalist.com/2016/10/10/survey-finds-american-christians-actually-heretics/ accessed 12/19/2020.

[21] "Survey Finds Most American Christians Are Actually Heretics" by G. Shane Morris OCTOBER 10, 2016, The Federalist.com https://thefederalist.com/2016/10/10/survey-finds-american-christians-actually-heretics/ accessed 12/19/2020.

[22] The State of Theology, An Outreach of Ligonier © 2018 http://thestateoftheology.com/ accessed 10/18/2018

[23] Five Key Findings on Religion in the U.S. by Frank Newport December 23, 2016. http://news.gallup.com/poll/200186/five-key-findings-religion.aspx

[24] Five Key Findings on Religion in the U.S. by Frank Newport December 23, 2016. http://news.gallup.com/poll/200186/five-key-findings-religion.aspx

[25] http://www.goodreads.com/author/quotes/40328.Billy_Graham?page=2 from Billy Graham, Unto the Hills: A Daily Devotional.

[26] Joe Carter, FactChecker: Are All Christian Denominations in Decline? The Gospel Coalition http://www.thegospelcoalition.org/article/factchecker-are-all-christian-denominations-in-decline/ accessed 5/20/18

[27] Joe Carter, FactChecker: Are All Christian Denominations in Decline? The Gospel Coalition http://www.thegospelcoalition.org/article/factchecker-are-all-christian-denominations-in-decline/ accessed 5/20/18

[28] "An Expanding Circle of Love and Justice" interview with Kateln Beaty. *Christian History*, Issue 124, pg 16.

[29] See Daniel B. Rundquist, Tears for Byzantium; The Entropic Course of American Exceptionalism, New Plymouth Press, LLC 2017

[30] Survey answers from Mr. J.G. 7/20/20

[31] This might have been the case up to the age of the modern background checks of the 21st century. Many churches now screen their people seeking to help with their youth programs.

[32] "Transgender people encouraged to become priests in Church of England diversity drive" By Olivia Rudgard, religious affairs correspondent The Telegraph, 26 MAY 2018

[33] The Psychology of Personal Constructs by George A. Kelly, Volume 2: Clinical Diagnosis and Psychotherapy, Quote Page 831, Published by W. W. Norton & Company, New York. 1955

[34] National Congregations Study, Faith Communities Today 2015, 2014 Religious Landscape Study 2014 by Pew Research.

[35] "Exploration of North America" http://www.history.com/topics/exploration/exploration-of-north-america accessed 9/16/2018

[36] http://en.wikipedia.org/wiki/Virtue_ethics accessed 12/13/17

[37] http://en.wikipedia.org/wiki/Virtue_ethics accessed 12/13/17

[38] http://en.wikipedia.org/wiki/Virtue_ethics accessed 12/13/17

[39] http://en.wikipedia.org/wiki/Virtue_ethics accessed 12/13/17

[40] Nicomachean Ethics, Book II

[41] Nicomachean Ethics Book VI

[42] MacIntyre, After Virtue, chp 16.

[43] Kelso, James L. An Archaeologist Looks at the Gospels, pg 63, Word Books 1975

[44] http://www.history.org/Almanack/life/manners/rules2.cfm accessed 1/6/2018

[45] http://www.mountvernon.org/digital-encyclopedia/article/george-washington-and-religion/ accessed 1/6/2018

[46] http://www.mountvernon.org/digital-encyclopedia/article/george-washington-and-religion/ accessed 1/6/2018

[47] Thomas Jefferson, The Anas, February 1, 1800, (written shortly after the death of first US president George Washington,) The Complete Anas of Thomas Jefferson

[48] Annals of the American Academy of Political and Social Science. Philadelphia: Published by A.L. Hummel for the American Academy of Political and Social Science, 1917. "Pax Americana", George W. Kihchwey. pp. 40+.

[49] See Charles L. Mee, The Marshall Plan: The launching of the pax americana , New York: Simon and Schuster, 1984.

[50] Lawrence Kaplan, "Western Europe in 'The American Century,'" Diplomatic History, 6/2/1982, p. 115.

[51] See Tears for Byzantium, the Entropic Course of American Exceptionalism by Daniel B. Rundquist. New Plymouth Pres, LLC 12/1/2017

[52] "Absolute Truth" By Lindy Keffer https://www.focusonthefamily.com/parenting/teens/absolute-truth accessed 8/19/18

[53] The Declaration of Independence

[54] Alexis de Tocqueville, Democracy in America

[55] St. Thomas Aquinas, Summa Theologiæ. From Summa Theologiae: A Concise Translation by St. Thomas Aquinas, Timothy McDermott, Christian Classics; December 1989, pg 152

[56] St. Thomas Aquinas, Summa Theologiæ. From Summa Theologiae: A Concise Translation by St. Thomas Aquinas, Timothy McDermott, Christian Classics; December 1989, pg 152-153

[57] In the 19th century, Austen Henry Layard, considered to be one of the first Archaeologists, uncovered the several different cities of Nineveh for the first time. Nineveh was the capitol city of Assyria, and through his discoveries he enlightened us with much of what we now understand about that culture. He writes, "A very superficial examination of the sculptures will prove the sacred character of the king…As in Egypt, he may have been regarded as the representative, on earth of the Deity, receiving his power directly from the gods, and being the organ of communication between them and his subjects. The intimate connection between the public and private life of the Assyrians and their religion is abundantly proved by the bas-reliefs…not only public and social duties appear to have been more or less influenced by religion, or to have been looked upon as typical, but all the acts of the king, whether in peace or war, were evidently connected with the national faith, and were believed to be under the special protection and superintendence of a Deity…the deeds of the king, and of the nation, are united with religious symbols, and with the statues of the gods." From Austen Henry Layard, Nineveh and Its Remains, (reprint) with Brian Fagan The Lyons Press 1st ed. 2001 Pg 371 -2

[58] http://en.wikipedia.org/wiki/List_of_Roman_birth_and_childhood_deities accessed 1/14/2018

[59] MacMullen, Ramsay, Christianizing the Roman Empire, pg. 4, 1984

[60] Kelso, James L. An Archaeologist Looks at the Gospels, pg 63, Word Books 1975

[61] Hilarion Alfeyev, Orthodox Christianity, Volume 4, pg 240 St. Vladimir's Seminary Press, 2016.

[62] "The Lives of the Pillars of Orthodoxy" Holy Apostles Convent and Dormitian Skete, 1990. Pg. 124.

[63] The Orthodox Church: An Introduction to Eastern Christianity by Timothy Ware Publisher: Penguin Books , Pg 40

[64] The Orthodox Church: An Introduction to Eastern Christianity by Timothy Ware Publisher: Penguin Books , Pg 40-41

[65] For further detail on this there are many sources today. John Julius Norwich's Byzantium series and History of the Byzantine State by George Ostrogorsky come to mind.

[66] "The Lives of the Pillars of Orthodoxy" Holy Apostles Convent and Dormitian Skete, 1990. Pg. 124-125

[67] Where have I seen this movie before? Oh yeah…Washington, DC.

[68] "Symbolism on Greek Coins" by Agnes Baldwin, Pg 1 -7, American Journal of Numismatics, 1915.

[69] "Symbolism on Greek Coins" by Agnes Baldwin, Pg 1 -7, American Journal of Numismatics, 1915.
[70] Signs and Symbols in Christian Art by George Ferguson. Pg 18. Oxford University Press, 1961
[71] Constantinople; Birth of an Empire by Harold Lamb, pg 295 (1957)
[72] Beckwith, John Early Christian and Byzantine Art. 2nd Edition, Pg 59 ,1979
[73] https://en.wikipedia.org/wiki/List_of_Byzantine_inventions accessed 3/3/2019
[74] Hilarion Alfeyev, Orthodox Christianity, Volume 4, pg 61 St. Vladimir's Seminary Press, 2016.
[75] "An Exclusive Creed" by Fr. Lawrence Farley, July 12, 2016 https://oca.org/reflections/fr.-lawrence-farley/an-exclusive-creed
[76] "St. Athanasius" New Advent http://www.newadvent.org/cathen/02035a.htm accessed 4/24/18
[77] http://en.wikipedia.org/wiki/John_Chrysostom accessed 4/21/2018
[78] http://en.wikipedia.org/wiki/John_Chrysostom accessed 4/21/2018
[79] Chrysostom, John. Hom. in Mt. 19,5: pp. 57, 280.
[80] Chrysostom, John. In Evangelium S. Matthaei, homily 50:3–4, pp 58, 508–509
[81] "St. John Chrysostom the Archbishop of Constantinople" http://oca.org/saints/lives/2018/11/13/103292-st-john-chrysostom-the-archbishop-of-constantinople accessed 4/24/18
[82] "St. John Chrysostom the Archbishop of Constantinople" http://oca.org/saints/lives/2018/11/13/103292-st-john-chrysostom-the-archbishop-of-constantinople accessed 4/24/18
[83] http://en.wikipedia.org/wiki/John_Chrysostom accessed 4/21/2018
[84] http://rusmania.com/history-of-russia/10th-century accessed 8/7/18
[85] Atlas of the Christian Church by Chadwick & Evans, Pg 129 – 130. Equinox, 1987.
[86] Hilarion Alfeyev, Orthodox Christianity, Volume 4, pg 128 St. Vladimir's Seminary Press, 2016.
[87] The Orthodox Church: An Introduction to Eastern Christianity by Timothy Ware Publisher: Penguin Books , Introduction Pg.8
[88] "Among Christians globally, Orthodox share falling, Catholic, Protestant shares increasing." November 8, 2017, The Pew Research Center. https://www.pewforum.org/2017/11/08/orthodox-christianity-in-the-21st-century/pf_11-08-17_orthodoxy-00-new-02/ accessed 6/2/2019.
[89] https://iocc.org/about/faqs accessed 2/29/20
[90] https://iocc.org/about/our-partners, accessed 2/28/20
[91] https://orderofsaintgeorge.org/questions-answers/ accessed 4/29/2020
[92] http://www.goodreads.com/quotes/search?commit=Search&page=12&q=religion&utf8=%E2%9C%93 accessed 1/29/18
[93] Menelaou, Iakovos. (2017). Byzantine Iconoclasm and the Defenders of Icons, John of Damascus and Theodore the Studite. Cairo Journal of Theology. 4. 49-65. https://www.researchgate.net/publication/320190812_Byzantine_Iconoclasm_and_the_Defenders_of_Icons_John_of_Damascus_and_Theodore_the_Studite accessed 6/2/2019
[94] "Roman Catholicism" Contributors: Francis Christopher Oakley, John L. McKenzie ET AL Encyclopædia Britannica, inc. January 09, 2019 URL: https://www.britannica.com/topic/Roman-Catholicism Access Date: June 02, 2019
[95] The Orthodox Church: An Introduction to Eastern Christianity by Timothy Ware Publisher: Penguin Books, Pg 48
[96] The Orthodox Church: An Introduction to Eastern Christianity by Timothy Ware Publisher: Penguin Books , Pg 43 -50
[97] "The Lives of the Pillars of Orthodoxy" Holy Apostles Convent and Dormitian Skete, 1990. Pg. 145.
[98] "The Lives of the Pillars of Orthodoxy" Holy Apostles Convent and Dormitian Skete, 1990. Pg. 148.

[99] "The Lives of the Pillars of Orthodoxy" Holy Apostles Convent and Dormitian Skete, 1990. Pg. 117.
[100] "The Lives of the Pillars of Orthodoxy" Holy Apostles Convent and Dormitian Skete, 1990. Pg. 152.
[101] "The Lives of the Pillars of Orthodoxy" Holy Apostles Convent and Dormitian Skete, 1990. Pg. 154.
[102] "The Lives of the Pillars of Orthodoxy" Holy Apostles Convent and Dormitian Skete, 1990. Pg. 149.
[103] "Pope meets Russian Orthodox leader 1,000 years after Christianity split" Published February 12, 2016 Associated Press
[104] Donald E. Queller, Thomas F. Madden, Fourth Crusade, the Conquest of Constantinople, 2nd Ed pg 37 1997
[105] Commentary by Mr. Nenad Nikolić is with Mr. Filip Djorić. February 9 at 7:06am, Roman and Byzantine History, Facebook study group.
[106] "The Lives of the Pillars of Orthodoxy" Holy Apostles Convent and Dormitian Skete, 1990. Pg. 163.
[107] John Julius Norwich, A Short History of Byzantium, Publisher: Knopf 1997, page 300
[108] John Julius Norwich, A Short History of Byzantium, Publisher: Knopf 1997, page 300
[109] John Julius Norwich, A Short History of Byzantium, Publisher: Knopf 1997, page 300
[110] John Julius Norwich, A Short History of Byzantium, Publisher: Knopf 1997, page 306
[111] "The Lives of the Pillars of Orthodoxy" Holy Apostles Convent and Dormitian Skete, 1990. Pg. 168.
[112] Thomsett, Michael C. (26 April 2010). The Inquisition: A History. McFarland. pp. 13–. ISBN 978-0-7864-4409-0.
[113] https://en.wikipedia.org/wiki/Albigensian_Crusade accessed 4/13/2020
[114] https://db0nus869y26v.cloudfront.net/en/Arnaud_Amalric#cite_note-4 accessed 4/13/2020
[115] "The Plot to Assassinate the Medici" Christian History Institute. (undated article) http://christianhistoryinstitute.org/it-happened-today/4/26 Accessed 4/29/18
[116] "The Plot to Assassinate the Medici" Christian History Institute. (undated article) http://christianhistoryinstitute.org/it-happened-today/4/26 Accessed 4/29/18
[117] "10 Torture devices used by the Catholic Church in the Inquisition" http://amredeemed.com/signs-of-the-end/10-torture-devices-used-by-the-catholic-church-in-the-inquisition/ accessed 2/5 2019
[118] "10 Torture devices used by the Catholic Church in the Inquisition" http://amredeemed.com/signs-of-the-end/10-torture-devices-used-by-the-catholic-church-in-the-inquisition/ accessed 2/5 2019
[119] "10 Torture devices used by the Catholic Church in the Inquisition" http://amredeemed.com/signs-of-the-end/10-torture-devices-used-by-the-catholic-church-in-the-inquisition/ accessed 2/5 2019
[120] "10 Torture devices used by the Catholic Church in the Inquisition" http://amredeemed.com/signs-of-the-end/10-torture-devices-used-by-the-catholic-church-in-the-inquisition/ accessed 2/5 2019
[121] "10 Torture devices used by the Catholic Church in the Inquisition" http://amredeemed.com/signs-of-the-end/10-torture-devices-used-by-the-catholic-church-in-the-inquisition/ accessed 2/5 2019
[122] "10 Torture devices used by the Catholic Church in the Inquisition" http://amredeemed.com/signs-of-the-end/10-torture-devices-used-by-the-catholic-church-in-the-inquisition/ accessed 2/5 2019
[123] "10 Torture devices used by the Catholic Church in the Inquisition" http://amredeemed.com/signs-of-the-end/10-torture-devices-used-by-the-catholic-church-in-the-inquisition/ accessed 2/5 2019
[124] Adapted from "Spanish Inquisition - Timeline" https://spanishinquisitionthetruestory.weebly.com/timeline.html accessed 9/1/18
[125] "Why Europe's wars of religion put 40,000 'witches' to a terrible death" by Jamie Doward

Published 6 Jan 2018, Last modified on Sat 13 Jan 2018 06.01 EST, The Guardian
https://www.theguardian.com/society/2018/jan/07/witchcraft-economics-reformation-catholic-protestant-market-share accessed 7/15/19

[126] An Open Letter on Translating, By Dr. Martin Luther, 1483-1546 Translated from: "Sendbrief von Dolmetschen" in _Dr. Martin Luthers Werke_, (Weimar: Hermann Boehlaus Nachfolger, 1909), Band 30, Teil II, pp. 632-646 by Gary Mann, Ph.D. Assistant Professor of Religion/Theology Augustana College Rock Island, Illinois.

[127] "John Knox and the Scottish Reformation", by Dan Graves. Christian History Institute http://christianhistoryinstitute.org/it-happened-today/5/2 accessed 5/2/2018

[128] "Why Europe's wars of religion put 40,000 'witches' to a terrible death" by Jamie Doward Published 6 Jan 2018, Last modified on Sat 13 Jan 2018 06.01 EST, The Guardian https://www.theguardian.com/society/2018/jan/07/witchcraft-economics-reformation-catholic-protestant-market-share accessed 7/15/19

[129] https://en.wikipedia.org/wiki/Peace_of_Westphalia accessed 7/15/19

[130] "By making a monetary contribution to the church, a penitent would receive a partial indulgence not to commit further sins, while at the same time, diminishing the time period that he/she was to suffer in PURGATORY for remission of his sins." From article, "Martin Luther, the Sale of Indulgences, and the Reformation" Hacienda Publishing https://www.haciendapublishing.com/randomnotes/martin-luther-sale-indulgences-and-reformation accessed 1/19/2019

[131] *Saeculum obscurum* (in Latin: the Dark Age) refers to the period of history of the Papacy during the first half of the 10th century, starting with Pope Sergius III in 904 and lasting for sixty years until the death of Pope John XII in 964. During this span, these Popes were influenced strongly by the Theophylacti family, and many of their relatives. The period was first identified and likely named by the Italian Cardinal and ecclesiastical historian Caesar Baronius in his *Annales Ecclesiastici*. Baronius' main resource for this history was the record of Liutprand of Cremona. Other terms are used to describe, such as the Pornocracy; German: Pornokratie, sourced from Greek pornokratiā, "prostitute rule." See also *Popes and Pornocrats: Rome in the early middle ages* by Lindsay Brook (2003). http://ia800208.us.archive.org/9/items/Papacy/1-lindsayBrook-PopesAndPornocrats.pdf

[132] In 1408 the third synod of Oxford, England, banned unauthorized English translations of the Bible and decreed that possession of English translations must be approved by the diocesan authorities. This Oxford Council declared:

"It is dangerous...to translate the text of Holy Scriptures out of one idiom into another, since it is not easy in translations to preserve exactly the same meaning in all things. We therefore command and ordain that henceforth no one translate the text of Holy Scripture into English or any other language as a book, booklet, or tract, of this kind lately made in the time of the said John Wyclif or since, or that hereafter may be made, either in part or wholly, either publicly or privately, under pain of excommunication, until such translation shall have been approved and allowed by the Provincial Council. He who shall act otherwise let him be punished as an abettor of heresy and error." Source: The Western Watchman, August 9, 1894, "The Word of God", The English Bible Before the Reformation, page 7.

[133] Tomasevich, Jozo (2001). War and Revolution in Yugoslavia, 1941–1945: Occupation and Collaboration. Stanford Univ: Stanford University Press. ISBN 978-0-8047-3615-2. Pg. 32.

[134] Tomasevich, Jozo (2001). War and Revolution in Yugoslavia, 1941–1945: Occupation and Collaboration. Stanford Univ: Stanford University Press. ISBN 978-0-8047-3615-2. Pg. 351 - 352.

[135] Ladislaus Hory und Martin Broszat. Der kroatische Ustascha-Staat, Deutsche Verlag-Anstalt, Stuttgart, 2. Auflage 1965, pp. 13–38, 75–80.

[136] Tomasevich, Jozo (2001). War and Revolution in Yugoslavia, 1941–1945: Occupation and Collaboration. Stanford Univ: Stanford University Press. ISBN 978-0-8047-3615-2. Pg. 30.

[137] Ladislaus Hory und Martin Broszat. Der kroatische Ustascha-Staat, Deutsche Verlag-Anstalt, Stuttgart, 2. Auflage 1965, pp. 13–38, 75–80.

[138] Tomasevich, Jozo (2001). War and Revolution in Yugoslavia, 1941–1945: Occupation and Collaboration. Stanford Univ: Stanford University Press. ISBN 978-0-8047-3615-2. Pg. 233 - 241.
[139] *Yugoslavia*, Holocaust Encyclopedia, United States Holocaust Memorial Museum website; accessed 1 July, 2019. https://encyclopedia.ushmm.org/content/en/article/axis-invasion-of-yugoslavia
[140] Watch, Helsinki (1993). War Crimes in Bosnia-Hercegovina. Human Rights Watch. ISBN 978-1-56432-083-4. Page 14. Retrieved 1 July 2019. https://books.google.com/books?id=nltdtAo38K0C&pg=PA14&hl=en#v=onepage&q&f=false
[141] Ramet, Sabrina P. (2006). The Three Yugoslavias: State-Building and Legitimation, 1918–2005. Bloomington, Indiana: Indiana University Press. ISBN 978-0-253-34656-8. Pg 119.
[142] Tomasevich, Jozo (2001). War and Revolution in Yugoslavia, 1941–1945: Occupation and Collaboration. Stanford Univ: Stanford University Press. ISBN 978-0-8047-3615-2. Pg. 529.
[143] Tomasevich, Jozo (2001). War and Revolution in Yugoslavia, 1941–1945: Occupation and Collaboration. Stanford Univ: Stanford University Press. ISBN 978-0-8047-3615-2. Pg. 529.
[144] Stanojević, Branimir. Alojzije Stepinac, zločinac ili svetac: dokumenti o izdaji i zločinu, Nova knjiga, 1986, p. 51
[145] Tomasevich, Jozo (2001). War and Revolution in Yugoslavia, 1941–1945: Occupation and Collaboration. Stanford Univ: Stanford University Press. ISBN 978-0-8047-3615-2. Pg. 555.
[146] Tomasevich, Jozo (2001). War and Revolution in Yugoslavia, 1941–1945: Occupation and Collaboration. Stanford Univ: Stanford University Press. ISBN 978-0-8047-3615-2. Pg. 381-384.
[147] Goldstein, Ivo; Goldstein, Slavko (2016). The Holocaust in Croatia. Pittsburgh: University of Pittsburgh Press. ISBN 9780822944515. Pg. 490.
[148] Jones, Adam & Nicholas A. Robins. (2009), Genocides by the oppressed: subaltern genocide in theory and practice, p. 106, Indiana University Press; ISBN 978-0-253-22077-6
[149] http://en.wikipedia.org/wiki/Ustashe#cite_ref-64 accessed 1 July 2019.
[150] "Holocaust Era in Croatia 1941-1945: Jasenovac" United States Holocaust Memorial Museum
[151] Ball, Howard (2010). Genocide: A Reference Handbook. ABC-CLIO. p. 124. ISBN 978-1-59884-488-7
[152] Goñi, Uki. The real Odessa: smuggling the Nazis to Perón's Argentina; Granta, 2002, p. 202. ISBN 9781862075818
[153] Phayer, Michael (2000). The Catholic Church and the Holocaust, 1930–1965. Bloomington, IN: Indiana University Press. p. 33.
[154] "Što je nama Stepinac?" by DRAGO PILSEL published 10/2/2014. https://www.autograf.hr/sto-je-nama-stepinac/ accessed 1 July, 2019.
[155] "Tied Up in the Rat Lines" by Yossi Melman, Jan 15, 2006. https://www.haaretz.com/1.5318382 accessed 1 July 2019.
[156] Pope Pius XII, *Meminisse Iuvat* http://catholic.net/op/articles/831/cat/1193/meminisse-iuvat.html accessed 8/6/20
[157] Pope Pius XII, *Meminisse Iuvat* http://catholic.net/op/articles/831/cat/1193/meminisse-iuvat.html accessed 8/6/20
[158] Pope Pius XII, *Meminisse Iuvat* http://catholic.net/op/articles/831/cat/1193/meminisse-iuvat.html accessed 8/6/20
[159] "Historical Events in 1958" http://www.onthisday.com/ accessed 8/6/20
[160] Huizing, Peter J. "The Second Vatican Council And Postconciliar Canon Law" Encyclopedia Brittanica http://www.britannica.com/topic/canon-law/The-Second-Vatican-Council-and-postconciliar-canon-law accessed 8/6/20
[161] Huizing, Peter J. "The Second Vatican Council And Postconciliar Canon Law" Encyclopedia Brittanica http://www.britannica.com/topic/canon-law/The-Second-Vatican-Council-and-postconciliar-canon-law accessed 8/6/20
[162] Huizing, Peter J. "The Second Vatican Council And Postconciliar Canon Law" Encyclopedia Brittanica http://www.britannica.com/topic/canon-law/The-Second-Vatican-Council-and-postconciliar-canon-law accessed 8/6/20

[163] http://en.wikipedia.org/wiki/Marie_Carr%C3%A9 accessed 3/15/2019
[164] http://en.wikipedia.org/wiki/Marie_Carr%C3%A9 accessed 3/15/2019
[165] AA-I025 The Memoirs of an Anti-Apostle by Marie Carre, Pgs. 7-8 TAN BOOKS AND PUBLISHERS, INC. 1991
[166] AA-I025 The Memoirs of an Anti-Apostle by Marie Carre, Pgs. 17-19 TAN BOOKS AND PUBLISHERS, INC. 1991
[167] AA-I025 The Memoirs of an Anti-Apostle by Marie Carre, Pgs. 12-13 TAN BOOKS AND PUBLISHERS, INC. 1991
[168] AA-I025 The Memoirs of an Anti-Apostle by Marie Carre, Pg. 14 TAN BOOKS AND PUBLISHERS, INC. 1991
[169] For more about this see The VATICAN. Its History. Its Treasures. by Ernesto – Editor Begni, 1914
[170] "Holocaust Era in Croatia 1941-1945: Jasenovac" United States Holocaust Memorial Museum
[171] https://en.wikipedia.org/wiki/Alperin_v._Vatican_Bank accessed 1 July 2019
[172] https://en.wikipedia.org/wiki/Alperin_v._Vatican_Bank accessed 1 July 2019
[173] Philip Pullella, "In move to transparency, Vatican bank issues first report" Reuters, October 1, 2013 http://www.yahoo.com/news/move-transparency-vatican-bank-issues-first-report-114416084.html accessed 2/11/18
[174] "Vatican Bank Opens Its Books For the First Time; The Vatican's Secretive Financial Institution Pulls Back the Curtain on Its Assets After Years of Secrecy" By Nate Rawlings Oct. 02, 2013 TIME online at http://world.time.com/2013/10/02/vatican-bank-opens-its-books-for-the-first-time/ accessed 2/11/2018
[175] Philip Pullella, "In move to transparency, Vatican bank issues first report" Reuters, October 1, 2013 http://www.yahoo.com/news/move-transparency-vatican-bank-issues-first-report-114416084.html accessed 2/11/18
[176] Philip Pullella, "In move to transparency, Vatican bank issues first report" Reuters, October 1, 2013 http://www.yahoo.com/news/move-transparency-vatican-bank-issues-first-report-114416084.html accessed 2/11/18
[177] Philip Pullella, "In move to transparency, Vatican bank issues first report" Reuters, October 1, 2013 http://www.yahoo.com/news/move-transparency-vatican-bank-issues-first-report-114416084.html accessed 2/11/18
[178] "Knights Templar heirs demand apology from Vatican" By Nick Squires, Rome 7:30AM BST 17 Jun 2011 The Telegraph. https://www.telegraph.co.uk/news/religion/8579801/Knights-Templar-heirs-demand-apology-from-Vatican.html accessed 11/29/2019
[179] "High-ranking priest caught in cocaine-fueled gay orgy in Vatican apartment" by Pete Baklinski, LifeSiteNews Jul 6, 2017 - 11:59 am EST
[180] 'Weaponization of faith': Examples from clergy abuse report" By MARK SCOLFORO Associated Press, 8/16/2016
[181] Weaponization of faith': Examples from clergy abuse report" By MARK SCOLFORO Associated Press, 8/16/2016
[182] "New York Catholic dioceses subpoenaed in sex abuse probe" by DAVID KLEPPER Sep. 07, 2018 Associated Press, https//apnews.com/5d03cfb0b1e9448cafe84704353c7f63
[183] http://www.usccb.org/issues-and-action/child-and-youth-protection/upload/Charter-for-the-Protection-of-Children-and-Young-People-revised-2011.pdf accessed 9/1/18
[184] "How the Saginaw Catholic Diocese sex abuse investigation unfolded" By Heather Jordan. 4/16/2018 MLIVE.COM http://www.mlive.com/expo/erry-2018/04/348f6e082c225/how_the_saginaw_catholic_dioce.html accessed 9/2/18
[185] "How the Saginaw Catholic Diocese sex abuse investigation unfolded" By Heather Jordan. 4/16/2018 MLIVE.COM http://www.mlive.com/expo/erry-2018/04/348f6e082c225/how_the_saginaw_catholic_dioce.html accessed 9/2/2018

[186] "The Pope declares homosexuals and anyone supporting 'gay culture' cannot become a Catholic priest" By GARETH DAVIES FOR MAILONLINE PUBLISHED: 05:58 EST, 8 December 2016, UPDATED: 13:20 EST, 8 December 2016, https://www.dailymail.co.uk/news/article-4013006/The-Pope-declares-homosexuals-supporting-gay-culture-Catholic-priest.html accessed 1/16/2019

[187] "Pope admits clerical abuse of nuns including sexual slavery" 6 February 2019. BBC. https://www.bbc.com/news/world-europe-47134033 accessed 2/6/2019

[188] "Among Christians globally, Orthodox share falling, Catholic, Protestant shares increasing." November 8, 2017, The Pew Research Center. https://www.pewforum.org/2017/11/08/orthodox-christianity-in-the-21st-century/pf_11-08-17_orthodoxy-00-new-02/ accessed 6/2/2019.

[189] Agnew, John (12 February 2010). "Deus Vult: The Geopolitics of Catholic Church". Geopolitics. 15 (1): 39–61. doi:10.1080/14650040903420388.

[190] "Catholic hospitals comprise one quarter of world's healthcare, council reports". Catholic News Agency. 10 February 2010. Retrieved 2/28/2020

[191] http://www.usccb.org/beliefs-and-teachings/how-we-teach/catholic-education/upload/2013-By-the-Numbers-Catholic-Education.pdf accessed 2/28/2020

[192] Gardner, Roy; Lawton, Denis; Cairns, Jo (2005), Faith Schools, Routledge, p. 148, ISBN 978-0-415-33526-3

[193] Zieglera, J. J. (12 May 2012). "Nuns Worldwide". Catholic World Report.

[194] "Vocations Online Internet Directory of Women's Religious Communities". Joliet Diocese Vocation Office. 2010

[195] "Press Release – The Nobel Peace Prize 1979". Nobelprize.org. 27 October 1979. Retrieved 2/28/2020

[196] "Press Release – Nobel Peace Prize 1996". Nobelprize.org. 11 October 1996. Retrieved 2/28/2020.

[197] "International Catholic Peacebuilding Organizations (directory)". Notre Dame, IN: Catholic Peacebuilding Network. 2015. Archived from the original on 3 April 2015. Retrieved 2/28/2020.

[198] https://www.kofc.org/un/en/todays-knights/what-we-do.html accessed 4/29/2020

[199] https://www.kofc.org/en/todays-knights/history/1882-1899.html 4/29/2020

[200] https://www.kofc.org/un/en/todays-knights/what-we-do.html accessed 4/29/2020

[201] Alexis de Tocqueville, *Democracy in America* V.2, Pt. 1, Ch. 1.

[202] G.K. Chesterton, Orthodoxy, http://www.goodreads.com/quotes/search?commit=Search&page=21&q=religion&utf8=%E2%9C%93 accessed 2/1/18

[203] Hilarion Alfeyev, Orthodox Christianity, Volume 4, pg 19 St. Vladimir's Seminary Press, 2016.

[204] http://www.crosspointearchitects.com/index, accessed 7/17/20.

[205] http://www.crosspointearchitects.com/the-signature-series accessed 7/17/20

[206] W. R. Lethaby and Harold Swainson, The Church of Sancta Sophia Constantinople a study of Byzantine building, 1894 Macmillan & Co. London & New York.

[207] Attributed to Fr. John Whiteford, Spring, TX

[208] ObamaCare architect: 'Stupidity' of voters helped bill pass BY ELISE VIEBECK - 11/10/14 05:13 PM EST The Hill online. Accessed 10/17/20

[209] Socialism vs. Capitalism: Which is the Moral System On Principle, v1n3 by C. Bradley Thompson, October 1993 http://ashbrook.org/publications/onprin-v1n3-thompson/ accessed 1/12/2019

[210] http://www.pewforum.org/religious-landscape-study/belief-in-absolute-standards-for-right-and-wrong/ accessed 1/7/2018

[211] http://www.pewforum.org/religious-landscape-study/belief-in-absolute-standards-for-right-and-wrong/ accessed 1/7/2018

[212] http://www.pewforum.org/religious-landscape-study/belief-in-absolute-standards-for-right-and-wrong/ accessed 1/7/2018

213 http://www.pewforum.org/religious-landscape-study/belief-in-absolute-standards-for-right-and-wrong/ accessed 1/7/2018
214 President Barack Obama's address at the National Prayer Breakfast on February 5, 2015.
215 See Daniel B. Rundquist, Tears for Byzantium; The Entropic Course of American Exceptionalism, New Plymouth Press, LLC 2017
216 "Wickard v. Filburn: The Supreme Court Case That Gave the Federal Government Nearly Unlimited Power" By Antony Davies and James R. Harrigan Foundation for Economic Education, Friday, February 7, 2020 accessed 2/12/2020. https://fee.org/articles/wickard-v-filburn-the-supreme-court-case-that-gave-the-federal-government-nearly-unlimited-power/
217 http://www.numberofabortions.com/ accessed on 12/5/2024
218 http://www.numberofabortions.com/ accessed on 12/5/2024
219 "Preventing unsafe abortion" 19 February 2018, Key facts, World Health Organization http://www.who.int/en/news-room/fact-sheets/detail/preventing-unsafe-abortion
220 http://www.numberofabortions.com/ accessed on 12/5/2024
221 The State of Theology, An Outreach of Ligonier © 2018 http://thestateoftheology.com/data-explorer/2018/27?AGE=30&MF=14&REGION=30&EDUCATION=62&INCOME=254&MARITAL=126&ETHNICITY=62&RELTRAD=62&ATTENDANCE=254 accessed 10/18/2018
222 http://www.pewforum.org/2013/01/16/religious-groups-official-positions-on-abortion/
223 "MEETING THE ORTHODOX Answers to commonly asked questions about Orthodox Christianity" Adapted from "Meeting the Orthodox" by Protopresbyter Thomas Hopko Dean of St. Vladamir's Orthodox Theological Seminary, Crestwood, New York, undated, page 8.
224 https://www.biography.com/artist/norman-rockwell accessed 5/9/2020
225 https://www.biography.com/artist/norman-rockwell accessed 5/9/2020
226 Specifically Ron Vogel's photography of models Carolyn Himmer, Betty Miller, Lorraine Mariott, Arroyana, Terry Bryan, Valli Fauver, Barbara Patrick, Sherly Trefton, Danielle Aubrey, Yvonne de Rosia, Sherry Wolfe, Angie McCrory, Jolene Johnson, Johanna Doherty, Chris Conway, Lenore Stewart, Sue Dover, Cynthia Ross, Barbara Evans, Didi Daniels, Brigitte Baum, Gretchen Gayle and many others.
227 http://glamourphotographers.yolasite.com/ten-photographers.php accessed 5/8/2020
228 http://glamourphotographers.yolasite.com/ten-photographers.php accessed 5/8/2020
229 "She Wrote Fake News for Cosmopolitan and Now Regrets Misleading Women on Feminism" By Kelsey Bolar The Daily Signal May 26, 2020, https://www.dailysignal.com/2020/05/26/she-wrote-fake-news-for-cosmopolitan-and-now-regrets-misleading-women-on-feminism/?utm_source=rss&utm_medium=rss&utm_campaign=she-wrote-fake-news-for-cosmopolitan-and-now-regrets-misleading-women-on-feminism?utm_source=TDS_Email&utm_medium=email&utm_campaign=MorningBell&mkt_tok=eyJpIjoiTVRnNU9UazNOams0WmpBeCIsInQiOiI2a2M2bmdpSW5cL0p6QWxlbzl0R1lpT2RGY0lGRDI3VlZXTmQ0amJ5OGxHR3hKUWl5bHRcL2lBWWtVVFNYdyb3Nqak90V04wdzk3dWpsUW8ycTNhTlhBRksxTamRMTXFld0Vmb3BhMUdjScjAwWnNcLzNpQVd3Q0RxNzdUcjZQVjNTQ0o5 accessed 5/26/2020
230 "She Wrote Fake News for Cosmopolitan and Now Regrets Misleading Women on Feminism" By Kelsey Bolar The Daily Signal May 26, 2020, https://www.dailysignal.com/2020/05/26/she-wrote-fake-news-for-cosmopolitan-and-now-regrets-misleading-women-on-feminism/?utm_source=rss&utm_medium=rss&utm_campaign=she-wrote-fake-news-for-cosmopolitan-and-now-regrets-misleading-women-on-feminism?utm_source=TDS_Email&utm_medium=email&utm_campaign=MorningBell&mkt_tok=eyJpIjoiTVRnNU9UazNOams0WmpBeCIsInQiOiI2a2M2bmdpSW5cL0p6QWxlbzl0R1lpT2RGY0lGRDI3VlZXTmQ0amJ5OGxHR3hKUWl5bHRcL2lBWWtVVFNYdyb3Nqak90V04wdzk3dWpsUW8ycTNhTlhBRksxTamRMTXFld0Vmb3BhMUdjScjAwWnNcLzNpQVd3Q0RxNzdUcjZQVjNTQ0o5 accessed 5/26/2020

[231] "She Wrote Fake News for Cosmopolitan and Now Regrets Misleading Women on Feminism" By Kelsey Bolar The Daily Signal May 26, 2020, https://www.dailysignal.com/2020/05/26/she-wrote-fake-news-for-cosmopolitan-and-now-regrets-misleading-women-on-feminism/?utm_source=rss&utm_medium=rss&utm_campaign=she-wrote-fake-news-for-cosmopolitan-and-now-regrets-misleading-women-on-feminism?utm_source=TDS_Email&utm_medium=email&utm_campaign=MorningBell&mkt_tok=eyJpIjoiTVRnNU9UazNOams0WmpBeCIsInQiOiI2a2M2bmdpSW5cL0p6QWxlbzl0R1lpT2RGY0lGRDI3VlZXTmQ0amJ5OGxHR3hKUWl5bHRcL2lBWWtVVFNYTXdyb3Nqak90V04wdzk3dWpsUW8ycTNhNXBRK0xTamRMTXFld0Vmb3BMUjdScjAwWnNcLzNpQVd3Q0RxNzdUcjZPVjNTSCJ9 accessed 5/26/2020

[232] "Northam, top state officials vow to protect women's reproductive rights" By Arianna Coghill and Emily Holter 1/18/2019 Capital News Service / The Virginia Gazette http://www.vagazette.com/news/va-vg-cns-reproductive-rights-0119-story.html accessed 2/7/2019

[233] "Northam, top state officials vow to protect women's reproductive rights" By Arianna Coghill and Emily Holter 1/18/2019 Capital News Service / The Virginia Gazette http://www.vagazette.com/news/va-vg-cns-reproductive-rights-0119-story.html accessed 2/7/2019

[234] http://www.goodreads.com/author/quotes/40328.Billy_Graham accessed 1/28/18

[235] http://www.umc.org/what-we-believe/our-social-creed accessed 1/7/2018

[236] http://www.umc.org/what-we-believe/economic-community Consumption Accessed 1/7/2018

[237] http://www.umc.org/what-we-believe/economic-community Trade and Investment Accessed 1/7/2018

[238] http://www.umc.org/what-we-believe/the-world-community War and Pease accessed 1/7/2018

[239] http://www.umc.org/what-we-believe/gun-violence accessed 1/7/2018

[240] "United Methodist Church Proposes New Position Statement Saying 'We Support Abortion'
REV. PAUL STALLWORTH AUG 28, 2018, Lifenews.com http://www.lifenews.com/2018/08/28/united-methodist-church-proposes-new-position-statement-saying-we-support-abortion/ accessed 2/7/2019

[241] "United Methodist Church Proposes New Position Statement Saying 'We Support Abortion'
REV. PAUL STALLWORTH AUG 28, 2018, Lifenews.com http://www.lifenews.com/2018/08/28/united-methodist-church-proposes-new-position-statement-saying-we-support-abortion/ accessed 2/7/2019

[242] "United Methodist Church Proposes New Position Statement Saying 'We Support Abortion'
REV. PAUL STALLWORTH AUG 28, 2018, Lifenews.com http://www.lifenews.com/2018/08/28/united-methodist-church-proposes-new-position-statement-saying-we-support-abortion/ accessed 2/7/2019

[243] "Struggling Minnesota church asks older members to go away" Associated Press Online accessed 1/20/20 https://apnews.com/9c9e0da7628a67e13c8a074725c4ef85

[244] "Struggling Minnesota church asks older members to go away" Associated Press Online accessed 1/20/20 https://apnews.com/9c9e0da7628a67e13c8a074725c4ef85

[245] "Racial Justice Ministries" http://www.elca.org/Our-Work/Publicly-Engaged-Church/Racial-Justice-Ministries accessed 3/24/2020

[246] "Justice for Women" https://www.elca.org/Our-Work/Publicly-Engaged-Church/Justice-for-Women accessed 3/24/2020

[247] http://download.elca.org/ELCA%20Resource%20Repository/Letter_MigrationPrinciples.pdf?_ga=2.248172615.1319193612.1515337550-802340544.1515337550 accessed 1/7/2018

[248] "ELCA Churchwide Assembly declares ELCA sanctuary church" posted 8/7/2019 https://www.elca.org/News-and-Events/8000 accessed 8/17/2019

[249] http://download.elca.org/ELCA%20Resource%20Repository/Environment_Climate_Change_101.pdf?_ga=2.245495108.1319193612.1515337550-802340544.1515337550 accessed 1/7/2018

[250] http://download.elca.org/ELCA%20Resource%20Repository/Circle_Of_Protection_Statement.pdf?_ga=2.39499491.1319193612.1515337550-802340544.1515337550 " A Statement on Why We Need to Protect Programs for the Poor" Accessed 1/7/2018

[251] http://download.elca.org/ELCA%20Resource%20Repository/For_Such_a_Time_Food.pdf?_ga=2.77239381.1319193612.1515337550-802340544.1515337550 PDF document "For Such a Time as This" Pray. Fast. Act. PROTECT SCHOOL MEALS AND SNAP FUNDING accessed 1/7/2018

[252] http://www.elca.org/Our-Work/Publicly-Engaged-Church/Peace-Not-Walls accessed 1/7/2018

[253] "Holy Conversations" Bishop Tim Smith, North Carolina Synod, ELCA. Undated booklet, page 8.

[254] http://www.sbc.net/bfm2000/bfm2000.asp accessed 1/7/2018

[255] http://www.goodreads.com/author/quotes/40328.Billy_Graham?page=2 accessed 1/28/18

[256] Frederick Douglass, Narrative of the Life of Frederick Douglass

[257] Gillan, Joanna, The White Slaves of Barbary 5/23/2019. https://www.ancient-origins.net/ancient-places-africa/white-slaves-barbary-002171 accessed 6/2/2019

[258] http://doctrineofdiscovery.org/dumdiversas.htm accessed 3/18/2018

[259] http://www.gilderlehrman.org/content/doctrine-discovery-1493 accessed 3/18/18

[260] http://www.gilderlehrman.org/content/doctrine-discovery-1493 accessed 3/18/18

[261] http://www.historynet.com/abolitionist-movement accessed 4/21/2018

[262] Backus, Isaac (1724-1806)." American Eras. . Encyclopedia.com. 13 Jan. 2019 <https://www.encyclopedia.com>.

[263] Backus, Isaac (1724 -1806) Isaac Backus on Religion and the State, February 4, 1788. The Debate on the Constitution : Federalist and Antifederalist Speeches, Articles, and Letters During the Struggle over Ratification : Part One, September 1787-February 1788, Various , Bernard Bailyn, page 931-932 Library of America, June 1, 1993

[264] Dinesh D'Souza, Twitter feed @DineshDSouza
"In 1860, on the eve of the Civil War, no Republicans owned slaves--all the slaves in America were owned by Democrats" 12:49 PM - 19 Aug 2016

[265] Dinesh D'Souza, "The secret history of the Democratic Party" Published July 22, 2016 Fox News

[266] http://en.wikipedia.org/wiki/Thomas_Jefferson_and_slavery#cite_note-6, Jim Powell (2008). Greatest Emancipations: How the West Abolished Slavery. St. Martin's Press. p. 250.

[267] http://www.historynet.com/abolitionist-movement accessed 4/21/18

[268] Catholicae Ecclesiae / On Slavery in the Missions, issued by Pope Leo XIII, Given in Rome, at St. Peter's, on November 20, 1890

[269] Seen at First United Methodist Churches

[270] Seen at a local United Church of Christ facility

[271] "The Secret Racist History of the Democratic Party" By Kimberly Bloom Jackson 5/3/2016 "By the mid-1860s, the Republican Party's alliance with blacks had caused a noticeable strain on the Democrats' struggle for electoral significance in the post-Civil War era. This prompted the Democratic Party in 1866 to develop a new pseudo-secret political action group whose sole purpose was to help gain control of the electorate. The new group was known simply by their initials, KKK (Ku Klux Klan). This political relationship was nationally solidified shortly thereafter during the 1868 Democratic National Convention when former Civil War General Nathan Bedford Forrest was honored as the KKK's first Grand Wizard. But don't bother checking the Democratic National Committee's website for proof. For many years, even up through the 2012 Presidential Election, the DNC had omitted all related history from 1848 to 1900 from their timeline -- half a century worth!"
https://www.americanthinker.com/articles/2016/05/the_secret_racist_history_of_the_democratic_party.html accessed 6/15/20
[272] https://en.wikipedia.org/wiki/List_of_LGBT_rights_organizations_in_the_United_States accessed 4/16/2020
[273] http://www.goodreads.com/author/quotes/40328.Billy_Graham?page=4 accessed 1/28/18 from Billy Graham in Quotes
[274] "No single gene associated with being gay" Published 29 August 2019, BBC News, https://www.bbc.com/news/health-49484490 accessed 9/1/2019
[275] "Tackling Discrimination against Lesbian, Gay, Bi, Trans, & Intersex People; STANDARDS OF CONDUCT FOR BUSINESS" Published by the United Nations Human Rights Office of the High Commissioner; SALIL TRIPATHI, CHARLES RADCLIFFE, FABRICE HOUDART. September, 2017, page 16.
[276] "Pastor Council sues Austin for the right to not hire LGBTQ people
Member churches oppose "homosexuality, transgender behavior" By: Alyssa Goard Posted: Oct 09, 2018 04:14 PM CDT / KXAN.com
[277] "Tackling Discrimination against Lesbian, Gay, Bi, Trans, & Intersex People; STANDARDS OF CONDUCT FOR BUSINESS" Published by the United Nations Human Rights Office of the High Commissioner; SALIL TRIPATHI, CHARLES RADCLIFFE, FABRICE HOUDART. September, 2017, page 9
[278] H.R.5 - Equality Act 116th Congress (2019-2020) CONGRESS.GOV https://www.congress.gov/bill/116th-congress/house-bill/5 accessed 5/11/2019
[279] http://www.awab.org/ accessed 8/17/2019
[280] "Texas Democrats Seek To Ban Christianity Using So-Called Anti-Discrimination Laws" by James Wesolek, January 28, 2019. The Federalist, http://thefederalist.com/2019/01/28/texas-democrats-seek-ban-christianity-using-called-anti-discrimination-laws/ accessed 2/6/2019.
[281] "Texas Democrats Seek To Ban Christianity Using So-Called Anti-Discrimination Laws" by James Wesolek, January 28, 2019. The Federalist, http://thefederalist.com/2019/01/28/texas-democrats-seek-ban-christianity-using-called-anti-discrimination-laws/ accessed 2/6/2019.
[282] California Legislative Information, https://leginfo.legislature.ca.gov/faces/billTextClient.xhtml?bill_id=201920200ACR99 accessed 9/23/2019.
[283] "Fifteen years in Iowa jail for burning pride flag" BBC 19 December 2019 https://www.bbc.com/news/world-us-canada-50861259 accessed 4/10/2020
[284] "US is behind push for independent Ukrainian church, ex-PM says" TASS, Russian News Agency published October 03, 17:47, http://tass.com/society/1024236 accessed 12/19/2018
[285] "Unholy row as Ukrainian church splits from Russian church
In the midst of a hybrid war, religious nationalism raises its head as Moscow warns it will defend religious interests in Ukraine." By GIOVANNI PIGNI DECEMBER 19, 2018 2:00 PM
[286] "US is behind push for independent Ukrainian church, ex-PM says" TASS, Russian News Agency published October 03, 17:47, http://tass.com/society/1024236 accessed 12/19/2018
[287] "Ukraine Raids Offices Of Russia-Aligned Priests Amid Push For New National Church" OAN Newsroom UPDATED 9:36 AM PT, Friday, Dec. 14, 2018
[288] https://www.foxnews.com/world/ukraine-orthodox-leaders-approve-break-with-russian-church

[289] "U.S. DEPT. OF STATE CONGRATULATES UKRAINE WITH CREATION OF NEW CHURCH," December 18, 2018. http://orthochristian.com/118010.html accessed 12/19/2018
[290] "U.S. EMBASSY CONGRATULATES UKRAINIANS WITH CREATION OF NEW CHURCH
Kiev," December 17, 2018, http://orthochristian.com/117972.html accessed 12/19/2018.
[291] Whose Money Stoked Religious Strife in Ukraine – and Who Tried to Steal It?" by JAMES GEORGE JATRAS 11/17/2018. Strategic Culture Foundation. http://www.strategic-culture.org/news/2018/11/17/whose-money-stoked-religious-strife-ukraine-who-tried-steal-it.html accessed 12/19/2018
[292] "RESOLUTION CALLING TO DECLARE WAR WITH RUSSIA IS INTRODUCED IN UKRAINIAN PARLIAMENT" Southfront 12/21/2018 http://southfront.org/ukrainian-mps-introduce-legislation-declaring-war-with-russia/ accessed 12/26/2018
[293] "WE HAVE TO SOFTEN ON LGBT TO NOT BE LIKE RUSSIAN CHURCH – HEAD OF NEW UKRAINIAN CHURCH" Orthodox Christianity, Kiev, December 25, 2018. http://orthochristian.com/118195.html accessed 12/26/2018
[294] "POROSHENKO 2.0: MONTENEGRIN PRESIDENT INTENDS TO SEEK AUTOCEPHALY FOR MONTENEGRIN CHURCH" Orthodox Christianity
Podgorica, Montenegro, December 25, 2018, http://orthochristian.com/118178.html accessed 12/26/2018
[295] "Not Gay or Homosexual, but Men and Women Created in the Image and Likeness of God" by Fr. Ioannes Apiarius 6/2/2019
https://www.orthodoxytoday.org/blog/2019/06/not-gay-or-homosexual-but-men-and-women-created-in-the-image-and-likeness-of-god/ accessed 8/17/2019
[296] "ThinkProgress is a news site dedicated to providing our readers with rigorous reporting and analysis from a progressive perspective. Founded in 2005, ThinkProgress is an editorially independent project of the Center for American Progress Action Fund. Over the past decade, the site has evolved from a small rapid response blog to a newsroom of reporters and editors covering the intersections of politics, policy, culture, and social justice." http://thinkprogress.org/about/ accessed 1/17/2019
[297] "The latest front in Russian infiltration: America's right-wing homeschooling movement This is the latest connection between Russia and the American religious right." By CASEY MICHEL, JAN 17, 2019, 11:03 AM, ThinkProgress http://thinkprogress.org/americas-biggest-right-wing-homeschooling-group-has-been-networking-with-sanctioned-russians-1f2b5b5ad031/ accessed 1/18/2019
[298] "The latest front in Russian infiltration: America's right-wing homeschooling movement This is the latest connection between Russia and the American religious right." By CASEY MICHEL, JAN 17, 2019, 11:03 AM, ThinkProgress http://thinkprogress.org/americas-biggest-right-wing-homeschooling-group-has-been-networking-with-sanctioned-russians-1f2b5b5ad031/ accessed 1/18/2019
[299] "Barack Obama microphone gaffe: 'I'll have more flexibility after election'" The Telegraph 2:42PM BST 26 Mar 2012,
http://www.telegraph.co.uk/news/worldnews/barackobama/9167332/Barack-Obama-microphone-gaffe-Ill-have-more-flexibility-after-election.html accessed 1/18/2019
Mr Obama says: "On all these issues, but particularly missile defence, this, this can be solved but it's important for him to give me space." Mr Medvedev replies: "Yeah, I understand. I understand your message about space. Space for you ..." Mr Obama retorts: "This is my last election. After my election I have more flexibility."
[300] http://www.goodreads.com/author/quotes/40328.Billy_Graham accessed 1/28/18
[301] "Top NASA Climate 'Data Fraudster' Named & Shamed" by John O'Sullivan 1/7/2017. Principia Scientific International https://principia-scientific.org/top-nasa-climate-data-fraudster-named-shamed/
[302] "The Historical Roots of Our Ecologic Crisis" by Lynn White, Jr. Source: Science, New Series, Vol. 155, No. 3767 (Mar. 10, 1967), pp. 1203-1207 Published by: American Association for the Advancement of Science, URL: http://www.jstor.org/stable/1720120 accessed 11/22/19

[303] "The Historical Roots of Our Ecologic Crisis" by Lynn White, Jr. Source: Science, New Series, Vol. 155, No. 3767 (Mar. 10, 1967), pp. 1203-1207 Published by: American Association for the Advancement of Science, URL: http://www.jstor.org/stable/1720120 accessed 11/22/19

[304] "Climate Worship Is Nothing More Than Rebranded Paganism" by Sumantra Maitra SEPTEMBER 26, 2019, The Federalist. http://thefederalist.com/2019/09/26/climate-worship-is-nothing-more-than-rebranded-paganism/ accessed 11/22/19

[305] Krauthammer, Dr. Charles; "Behold the New Socialism"; The Charlotte Observer, 12/12/09

[306] http://www.umc.org/what-we-believe/the-natural-world Energy Resources Utilization accessed 1/7/2018

[307] http://www.umc.org/what-we-believe/the-natural-world Animal Life accessed 1/7/2018

[308] NBC News, https://www.nbcnews.com/news/specials/climate-confessions-share-solutions-climate-change-n1054791 accessed 9/23/2019

[309] "Worship At Union" webpage dated September 18, 2019. https://utsnyc.edu/worship-at-union/ accessed 9/23/2019.

[310] "Worship At Union" webpage dated September 18, 2019. https://utsnyc.edu/worship-at-union/ accessed 9/23/2019.

[311] @UnionSeminary 10:35 AM - 18 Sep 2019

[312] "Pope Francis Wants to Add 'Ecological Sin' to Catechism" by THOMAS D. WILLIAMS, PH.D.18 Nov 2019 Breitbart https://www.breitbart.com/environment/2019/11/18/pope-francis-wants-to-add-ecological-sin-to-catechism/ accessed 11/19/19

[313] Letter to President Obama, Attorney General Lynch, and OSTP Director Holdren, September 1, 2015 http://www.iges.org/letter/LetterPresidentAG.pdf

[314] http://www.goodreads.com/quotes/search?commit=Search&page=7&q=religion&utf8=%E2%9C%93 accessed 1/28/18

[315] "NYC Mayor Threatens to Close Churches 'Permanently' for Meeting during Coronavirus" By Michael Foust ChristianHeadlines.com Monday, March 30, 2020 Accessed 4/23/2020

[316] "Online petition to recall Michigan governor receives more than 150,000 signatures" by Dominick Mastrangelo April 13, 2020 12:08 PM The Washington Examiner https://www.washingtonexaminer.com/news/online-petition-to-recall-michigan-governor-gains-more-than-150-000-signatures accessed 4/23/2020.

[317] "Protesters rally for NC to reopen. One woman arrested for violating governor's order." BY JOSH SHAFFER AND ASHAD HAJELA APRIL 14, 2020 12:05 PM, UPDATED APRIL 15, 2020 09:57 AM The News & Observer https://www.newsobserver.com/news/politics-government/article241999131.html accessed 4/23/2020.

[318] Dividing the number of unemployed by the total U.S. workforce. Figures from www.usdebtclock.org accessed 4/22/2020.

[319] "NY mosque remains open for daily prayers as churches all over America are hit with mandatory shutdowns" BY POLIZETTE STAFF APRIL 20, 2020 LifeZette https://www.lifezette.com/2020/04/ny-mosque-remains-open-for-daily-prayers-as-churches-all-over-america-are-hit-with-mandatory-shutdowns/?fbclid=IwAR2FE0GR2iSxLqJaWatkf1k5lZoMBgiOuH1wlbwV9hgnM_QMIOP5Ekf3qO0 accessed 4/23/2020.

[320] http://www.gordonconwell.edu/resources/documents/StatusOfGlobalMission.pdf The Center for the Study of Global Christianity at Gordon-Conwell Theological Seminary estimated 34,000 denominations in 2000, rising to an estimated 43,000 in 2012. These numbers have exploded from 1,600 in the year 1900. This figure, however, is disputed. Scott Eric Alt writing for the National Catholic Register reports, "There are not... 33,000 Protestant denominations. There are not anywhere close to it. It is a myth that has taken hold by force of repetition, and it gets cited and recited by reflex; but it is based on a source that, even Catholics will have to con-cede, relies on too loose a definition of the word 'denomination.'" His article can be found at http://m.ncregister.com/blog/scottericalt/we-need-to-stop-saying-that-there-are-33000-protestant-denominations. Accessed 2/9/2019

[321] Thomas Jefferson, Notes on the State of Virginia

[322] John Adams, The Letters of John and Abigail Adams, Letters to John Taylor, 1814, XVIII, p. 484
[323] Bertrand Russell, Why I Am Not a Christian, Watts & Co., for the Rationalist Press Association Limited, 1927 First published as a pamphlet and reissued many times, in many formats since.
[324] Mark Twain, Letters from the Earth: Uncensored Writings
[325] Thomas Jefferson, Letter to George Logan, 12 November 1816, Letters of Thomas Jefferson
[326] Thomas Jefferson, Letter to John Adams, April 11, 1823
[327] John Adams, letter to Thomas Jefferson, September 3, 1816
[328] John Adams, letter to FA Van der Kamp, December 27, 1816.
[329] Mark Bradshaw, That they May Be One, pg 99-100, 2017
[330] An Open Letter on Translating, By Dr. Martin Luther, 1483-1546 Translated from: "Sendbrief von Dolmetschen" in _Dr. Martin Luthers Werke_, (Weimar: Hermann Boehlaus Nachfolger, 1909), Band 30, Teil II, pp. 632-646 by Gary Mann, Ph.D. Assistant Professor of Religion/Theology Augustana College Rock Island, Illinois.
[331] Introduction and all ten points, http://orthodoxwiki.org/Hermeneutics, accessed 2/19/21. "Originally based on notes taken in Archpriest Michael Dahulich's Fall 2004 class on the Pentateuch at St. Tikhon's Orthodox Theological Seminary by User:ASDamick."
[332] http://www.catholic.com/encyclopedia/scripture, A. J. MAAS, accessed 2/19/21
[333] Mark Bradshaw, That they May Be One, pg 46-52 2017
[334] Archimandrite Meletios Webber, "The Mind, the Heart and the Way of Salvation" Divine Ascent, A Journal of Orthodox Faith; Number 9, 2004. Pgs 92-93.
[335] Protopresbyter Michael Pomazansky, "The Old Testament and Rationalistic Biblical Criticism" Selected Essays, Holy Trinity Monastery, pg 120.
[336] Protopresbyter Michael Pomazansky, "The Old Testament and Rationalistic Biblical Criticism" Selected Essays, Holy Trinity Monastery, pg 120.
[337] Bishop Kallistos Ware, The Orthodox Way, Revides Edition, St Vladimir's Seminary Press, 1979. Pages 58 – 59.
[338] Hilarion Alfeyev, Orthodox Christianity, Volume 4, pg 12 St. Vladimir's Seminary Press, 2016.
[339] The Creeds of Christendom, three volumes, Phillip Schaff, 1877.
[340] Mark Bradshaw, That they May Be One, pg 34-37 2017
[341] Mark Bradshaw, That they May Be One, pg 42-45 2017
[342] The State of Theology, An Outreach of Ligonier © 2018 http://thestateoftheology.com/data-explorer/2018/1?AGE=30&MF=14&REGION=30&EDUCATION=62&INCOME=254&MARITAL=126&ETHNICITY=62&RELTRAD=62&ATTENDANCE=254 accessed 10/18/2018
[343] Top 25 Countries In Car Accidents, http://www.worldatlas.com/articles/the-countries-with-the-most-car-accidents.html accessed 6/24/18
[344] Constantinople; Birth of an Empire by Harold Lamb, pg 289 (1957)
[345] See John Locke on the separation of Church and Magistrate (1689)
[346] John Adams, letter to Thomas Jefferson, January 23, 1825
[347] Benjamin Franklin, Articles of Belief and Acts of Religion, November 20, 1728.
[348] http://www.john-adams-heritage.com/quotes/ accessed 2/3/18
[349] http://www.john-adams-heritage.com/quotes/ accessed 2/3/18
[350] Thomas Jefferson, Letters of Thomas Jefferson
[351] James Madison, Letter objecting to the use of government land for churches, 1803
[352] See Daniel B. Rundquist, Tears for Byzantium; The Entropic Course of American Exceptionalism, New Plymouth Press, LLC 2016- 2017
[353] Federer, William J. America's God and Country; Encyclopedia of Quotations. Pg, 48 – 49. FAME publishing, Inc. 1994.
[354] Jefferson, President Thomas, extract from "A Summary View of the Rights of British America" July, 1774
[355] Jefferson, President Thomas, extract from his Argument in the Case of Howell vs. Netherland [ca. April 1770]. Monticello.org

356 Jefferson, President Thomas: Notes on Virginia Q.XVII, 1782.
357 The Holy Bible, Mark 15:2 Douay-Rheims
358 "New Documents Reveal IRS Headquarters in D.C. Buried Conservative Groups' Tax Applications" by Ali Meyer - AUGUST 3, 2016 4:58 AM The Washington Free Beacon
359 Mark Bradshaw, That they May Be One, pg 29, 2017
360 Dan Graves, "Damien Joins Hawaii's Leper Outcasts" Christian History Institute http://christianhistoryinstitute.org/it-happened-today/5/4 accessed 5/6/2018
361 Dan Graves, "Damien Joins Hawaii's Leper Outcasts" Christian History Institute http://christianhistoryinstitute.org/it-happened-today/5/4 accessed 5/6/2018
362 Peter Reid, "Texas church pays $10 million in medical debt for vets, local families" American Military News April 6, 2018
363 "Church pays off almost $8 million in medical debt for thousands of families" Fox8 KCRA POSTED 2:33 PM, OCTOBER 13, 2019, BY WEB STAFF, UPDATED AT 02:31PM, OCTOBER 13, 2019 https://myfox8.com/2019/10/13/church-pays-off-almost-8-million-in-medical-debt-for-thousands-of-families/ accessed 11/22/19
364 "Cincinnati church wipes out $46.5 million in medical debt for 45,000 families" By Caleb Parke, Fox News 2/27/2020. https://www.foxnews.com/us/cincinnati-church-wipes-out-46-5-million-in-medical-debt-largest-amount-for-nonprofit accessed 2/28/2020
365 The Orthodox Church: An Introduction to Eastern Christianity by Timothy Ware Publisher: Penguin Books , Pg 244
366 Socialism vs. Capitalism: Which is the Moral System On Principle, v1n3 by C. Bradley Thompson, October 1993 http://ashbrook.org/publications/onprin-v1n3-thompson/ accessed 1/12/2019
367 John Julius Norwich, A Short History of Byzantium, Publisher: Knopf 1997, page 247
368 John Julius Norwich, A Short History of Byzantium, Publisher: Knopf 1997, page 247
369 John Julius Norwich, A Short History of Byzantium, Publisher: Knopf 1997, page 263
370 "Our Social Principles, The Book of Discipline of The United Methodist Church - 2016" https://www.umc.org/en/content/our-social-principles accessed 8/24/2020.
371 https://www.elca.org/Faith/Faith-and-Society/Social-Statements accessed 8/24/2020
372 "Virtue Ethics and its Application within Lutheran Congregations" Jeff Mallinson, D. Phil., Issues in Christian Education online, https://issues.cune.edu/educating-in-lutheran-ethics/virtue-ethics-and-its-application-within-lutheran-congregations/ accessed 8/24/2020.
373 https://bfm.sbc.net/bfm2000/ accessed 8/24/2020.
374 http://www.vatican.va/archive/ccc_css/archive/catechism/p3s1c1a7.htm accessed 8/24/2020.
375 https://www.oca.org/orthodoxy/the-orthodox-faith/spirituality/the-virtues/the-virtues accessed 8/25/2020
376 https://www.oca.org/orthodoxy/the-orthodox-faith/spirituality/the-virtues accessed 8/24/2020.
377 St. Thomas Aquinas, Summa Theologiæ. From Summa Theologiae: A Concise Translation by St. Thomas Aquinas, Timothy McDermott, Christian Classics; December 1989, pg 237
378 St. Thomas Aquinas, Summa Theologiæ. From Summa Theologiae: A Concise Translation by St. Thomas Aquinas, Timothy McDermott, Christian Classics; December 1989, pg 237
379 St. Thomas Aquinas, Summa Theologiæ. From Summa Theologiae: A Concise Translation by St. Thomas Aquinas, Timothy McDermott, Christian Classics; December 1989, pg 201
380 St. Thomas Aquinas, Summa Theologiæ. From Summa Theologiae: A Concise Translation by St. Thomas Aquinas, Timothy McDermott, Christian Classics; December 1989, pg 203
381 St. Thomas Aquinas, Summa Theologiæ. From Summa Theologiae: A Concise Translation by St. Thomas Aquinas, Timothy McDermott, Christian Classics; December 1989, pg 203
382 St. Thomas Aquinas, Summa Theologiæ. From Summa Theologiae: A Concise Translation by St. Thomas Aquinas, Timothy McDermott, Christian Classics; December 1989, pg 54
383 St. Thomas Aquinas, Summa Theologiæ. From Summa Theologiae: A Concise Translation by St. Thomas Aquinas, Timothy McDermott, Christian Classics; December 1989, pg 54

384 Socialism vs. Capitalism: Which is the Moral System On Principle, v1n3 by C. Bradley Thompson, October 1993 http://ashbrook.org/publications/onprin-v1n3-thompson/ accessed 1/12/2019
385 St. Thomas Aquinas, Summa Theologiæ. From Summa Theologiae: A Concise Translation by St. Thomas Aquinas, Timothy McDermott, Christian Classics; December 1989, pg 238
386 St. Thomas Aquinas, Summa Theologiæ. From Summa Theologiae: A Concise Translation by St. Thomas Aquinas, Timothy McDermott, Christian Classics; December 1989, pg 396
387 http://en.wikipedia.org/wiki/Laissez-faire accessed 4/8/18
388 St. Thomas Aquinas, Summa Theologiæ. From Summa Theologiae: A Concise Translation by St. Thomas Aquinas, Timothy McDermott, Christian Classics; December 1989, pg 239
389 "The Big Bank Bailout" by Mike Collins Forbes online July 14, 2015, 04:22pm
390 Thomas Jefferson, Notes on the State of Virginia, Query XVII
391 Kyrill, Patriarch. "His Holiness Orthodox Patriarch of Moscow and All the Rus Cyril Has Condemned Communism and Social Justice Ideology. ." Facebook, Orthodox England Facebook Group, 29 Oct. 2021, www.facebook.com/profile/100064802735953/search/?q=patriarch%20cyrill. Unable to discover a Russian or other primary source of this quote
392 Plato's "Republic" Book VIII
393 Thomas Jefferson, letter to William Hamilton, April 22, 1800; http://www.loc.gov/resource/mtj1.022_0228_0229/?st=text accessed 7/11/18
394 "No Union Possible" Christian History Institute. http://christianhistoryinstitute.org/it-happened-today/5/15 accessed 5/15/2020.
395 "No Union Possible" Christian History Institute. http://christianhistoryinstitute.org/it-happened-today/5/15 accessed 5/15/2020.
396 President John F. Kennedy, Inaugural Address, January 20, 1961
397 ALIX LANGONE "This U.S. City Will Give Its Poorest People $500 a Month — No Strings Attached" Time.com / Updated: January 24, 2018 2:49 PM ET | Originally published: January 23, 2018
398 http://www.gordonconwell.edu/resources/documents/StatusOfGlobalMission.pdf, estimates that by 2014 there are 45,000 different Christian denominations. Accessed 3/23/2019
399 Adopted by the Holy Synod of Bishops of the Orthodox Church in America, 1990 http://oca.org/holy-synod/statements/his-beatitude-metropolitan-tikhon/of-what-life-do-we-speak-four-pillars-for-the-fulfillment-of-the-apostolic accessed 7/29/18
400 "What we believe" published by Corinth Reformed Church, Hickory, NC.
401 Mark Bradshaw, That they May Be One, pg 117, 2017
402 Ucc.org accessed 2/5/18
403 www.ucc.org "Equal Marriage Rights For All" Adopted at the twenty-fifth General Synod on July 4, 2005.
404 Backus, Isaac (1724 -1806) Isaac Backus on Religion and the State, February 4, 1788. The Debate on the Constitution : Federalist and Antifederalist Speeches, Articles, and Letters During the Struggle over Ratification : Part One, September 1787-February 1788, Various , Bernard Bailyn, page 931 Library of America, June 1, 1993
405 See Tears for Byzantium, the Entropic Course of American Exceptionalism by Daniel B. Rundquist. New Plymouth Pres, LLC, 12/1/2017
406 Way of the Ascetics By Tito Colliander, PDF edition. "On The Conquest of the World" pg. 9.
407 The words of Pontius Pilate, recorded in John 18:38
408 The Synaxarion, The Lives of the Saints of the Orthodox Church, Vol 1. 2nd ed. Pg 486. Indiktos, 2013.
409 http://www.goodreads.com/author/quotes/40328.Billy_Graham?page=4 accessed 1/28/2018 from Billy Graham in Quotes.
410 See "The Orthodox Way" by Kallistos Ware St. Vladimir's Seminary Press; New edition, May 28, 2002
411 Righteous John, Wonderworker of Kronstadt, My Life in Christ p.338

412 Lagat, Alex. "The Challenge of Denominational Proliferation: An Orthodox Critique of Protestantism." Facebook, Facebook, 4 Jan. 2024, www.facebook.com/alex.lagat.3551.
413 Adapted from
https://orthodoxwiki.org/Timeline_of_Church_History#Communist_era_.281917-1991.29 accessed 7/2/2019

www.ingramcontent.com/pod-product-compliance
Lightning Source LLC
Chambersburg PA
CBHW050100170426
43198CB00014B/2398